HONORÉ JAXON

HONORÉ JAXON

PRAIRIE VISIONARY

DONALD B. SMITH

Edited by Dallas Harrison.
Cover and book design by Duncan Campbell.
Cover photo: "Honoré Jaxon after his eviction, December 12, 1951, all his library and archives on a New York City Street." Hal Mathewson, New York Daily News, December 13, 1951. New York Daily News/N1421873.

Printed and bound in Canada at Gauvin Press.
This book is printed on 100% recycled paper.

Library and Archives Canada Cataloguing in Publication

Smith, Donald B., 1946—
Honoré Jaxon : Prairie visionary / Donald B. Smith.
Includes bibliographical references and index.
ISBN 978-1-55050-367-8
1. Jackson, William Henry, 1861-1952. 2. Riel, Louis, 1844-1885.
3. Riel Rebellion, 1885. 4. Labor leaders—Illinois—Chicago—Biography.
5. Real estate developers—New York (State)—New York—Biography.
I. Title.
FC3217.1.J33S54 2007 971.05'4092 C2007–904328–3

10 9 8 7 6 5 4 3 2

2517 Victoria Ave.
Regina, Saskatchewan
Canada S4P 0T2

AVAILABLE IN CANADA & THE US FROM
Fitzhenry & Whiteside
195 Allstate Parkway
Markham, ON, Canada, L3R 4T8

The publisher gratefully acknowledges the financial assistance of the Saskatchewan Arts Board, the Canada Council for the Arts, the Government of Canada through the Book Publishing Industry Development Program (BPIDP), Association for the Export of Canadian Books, and the City of Regina Arts Commission, for its publishing program.

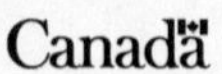

Dedicated to the memory of the late Cicely Plaxton (1895–1981), niece of Honoré Jaxon, who encouraged me to write this book.

CONTENTS

Honoré Jaxon wearing his military cap the day after the eviction, December 13, 1951.
Evelyn Straus, *New York Daily News/ N1421875.*

PROLOGUE

NEW YORK CITY, WINTER 1951–52

On December 13, 1951, the New York dailies carried short human-interest stories from the previous day about an extraordinary pack rat named Major Honoré Joseph Jaxon. "The Old Majah"[1] lived in midtown Manhattan, eight city blocks south of Grand Central Station and the United Nations Headquarters and four blocks east of the world's tallest skyscraper, the Empire State Building, the Eighth Wonder of the World.[2] Jaxon had just been evicted from his basement apartment at 159 East Thirty-fourth Street.

On page 1, the *Daily Mirror* ran a photo of the obviously shaken elderly man firmly clutching his cane, holding his chin high, sitting amid a small mountain of crated newspapers, magazines and books. The *Daily News,* "New York's Picture Newspaper," included a panoramic shot of the man in a black cowboy hat, draped in a blanket, seated on a pile of newspapers with his "library" behind him. He looked like someone who had just woken up, without knowing where he was. The *New York Times* captioned its photo the next day "Champion of Indians Dispossessed Here."

For five years, Honoré Jaxon rose at 5 a.m. to stoke the furnace of his fourteen-suite apartment building[3] – that is, until October 20, when landlord Walter Scott and Company discharged their aged custodian. As the *Herald-Tribune* quoted its spokesperson on December 13, "Because of repeated illness and several charges of building violations, it became necessary to end his employment with the company." In addition, Jaxon's tons of paper in the small cellar apartment constituted a Grade A fire hazard: "We feel very sorry for him, but we can't jeopardize the building and the health of our tenants."

A city official and a crew of three arrived around noon that cold mid-December day to remove his books, manuscripts, and personal belongings onto Thirty-fourth Street. The job, the *Daily News* reported, took more than three hours since the workers could reach the musty cellar apartment only by a sidewalk trap door and a twenty-foot ladder. Once stacked on the wide New York sidewalk, the paper-stuffed cartons and boxes comprised a pile six feet high, ten feet deep, and thirty-five feet long.

Even by august New York standards, Major Honoré Joseph Jaxon, covered with his blanket, wearing ancient clothes, running shoes, and his broad-brimmed black hat, was a character. Regally seated on an old orange crate, the white-bearded, fragile-looking man held court with representatives of the New York City press. The *Daily News* reported that he mentioned his birth in "the sweet grass hills of Montana." He "can't remember the date, but it was just before the South fired on Fort Sumter" to begin the American Civil War. Obviously well educated, he used a full and well-chosen vocabulary. Although he was just five feet, eight inches, in height,[4] his powerful voice gave the impression that he was much taller than he was.[5] The *New York Times* reporter learned from an acquaintance of "the Major" that "he was the son of an Indian maiden and an adventurous Virginian; that he spoke Latin and Greek, and was tried for treason by the Canadian Government."[6]

Shaken by his hasty eviction, Jaxon described the contents of his boxes as "the most valuable library in the US on the history of the American Indians."[7] For forty years, he had collected all this material. All day he sat on or stood protectively by his "library." Finally, when darkness fell, he made an agonizing decision. Harry Baronian, editor and publisher of the *Bowery News,*[8] offered refuge at his newspaper's office, but the paper could only temporarily store sixty boxes of his col-

Honoré Jaxon seated on his possessions in front of his former home, 157 East 34 Street, the day after his eviction, December 13, 1951. Arthur Brower/The *New York Times*/Redux.

lection. Without any other option, Jaxon sold the remaining two tons of newspapers, books, and magazines on the street as waste paper.[9]

The next day two truckmen carted the selected sixty boxes to the *Bowery News,* just two blocks away. The *New York World-Telegram and Sun* described how Jaxon's books and personal belongings had now been reduced to a pile six feet high but only four feet wide. The paper continued, "Mr. Jaxon dined this noon on hot milk and pea soup, and a mattress was spread out for him in the paper's kitchen, near the potbellied stove. Boxcar Betty, 'queen of the hoboes,' bathed his hands and face."

Baronian was a colourful individual in his own right. Then in his late thirties, he had come to New York over fifteen years earlier from his hometown of East St. Louis, Illinois, to seek his fortune. But his timing had been bad. Unable to find work during the Depression, the young Armenian American had spent a couple of years, in his words, "on the bum," living in flophouses, cadging drinks, and eating in soup kitchens of lower New York. Finally he got a job on the staff of the *Hobo News.* To stimulate interest in the paper, he advertised for a young society figure as a staff writer. He told an interviewer, "We're broadening the policy of our paper and taking in the other half."[10] In 1947, he began his own twelve-page tabloid on skid row and the hobo jungles, the *Bowery News.*

Often over the previous year, the Major had regularly dropped over to Harry's office and stayed for two or three hours, talking in his booming voice. As Baronian later recalled in his strong Manhattan accent, "The Old Majah was very sympathetic to labor. He was an idealist. He was always full of what Mistah Rooza-velt called 'social justice.' He was always talkin' about the Indians and the hoboes. He could see a real parallel in the way they were bein' handled by the Govament. He has some sort of idea of stagin' a one-man crusade for the two of 'em."[11]

The major resided at the three-room office of the *Bowery News* for the next two weeks. Three hoboes looked after him as best they could. Betty Link, or Boxcar Betty, the self-styled "Queen of the Hoboes," who used to be a hula dancer and snake charmer and who smoked cigars,[12] befriended him. As Harry recalled, "Box-Car Betty did the Major's shoppin' with what money he gave her from where he hid it, pinned to the inside of his shirt. She fed him lots of good hot soup and meat, and pretty soon the Major got back his strong old boomin' voice again." Walter Gregory, an ex-sailor, also volunteered. He washed the Old Majah every day and got him bedpans when he could not walk to the bathroom. A third helper, Bozo Clarke, the "Crown Prince of the Hoboes," had once studied for the ministry in New England. He kept the big pot-bellied stove filled with wood and roaring away at night.[13]

Baronian later recalled how his guest acted as "a real gent and always thanked everybody like a duke for any little favor you did for him."[14] But the Major constantly returned to his obsession: he must save his remaining sixty boxes, for he intended to build a library for the Indians on a tract of land that he owned in Saskatchewan, Canada. "The great passion of his life was to educate the Indians so that they'd get a better deal in this generation than they had in the past."[15]

Two weeks later Jaxon suffered a serious relapse. As Boxcar Betty told Harry, "He's a lot worse than he was when we took him in here first. I think he oughta go to the big hospital."[16] On December 27, after just over two weeks at the *Bowery News,* Jaxon was taken by police ambulance to the neighbouring Bellevue Hospital, one of the largest in the world, which stretched from Twenty-fifth to Thirtieth Streets on First Avenue. No one was ever turned away from Bellevue, which welcomed the city's poor and neglected.[17] Shortly after his admission, the authorities committed their new patient to a ward in the psychiatric section.[18] There the old warrior passed away two weeks later, on the morning of January 10.[19]

This story has haunted my imagination since the early 1970s, when I first heard of "Riel's secretary." For a third of a century, I gathered information on this extraordinary individual. Other projects intervened: three decades of teaching Canadian history at the University of Calgary, several biographies, a number of textbooks, and a history of Calgary. It also took the advent of the World Wide Web for me to locate necessary additional sources. Honoré did not escape me because, I think, his life makes an important point: *occasionally those on the fringe may see things more clearly than those in the mainstream.*

NOTE ON USAGE

A DISTINCTION WAS MADE IN THE NINETEENTH CENTURY between the Métis, or French Métis, of French and First Nations ancestry, and the Country-Born, or Metis of British and First Nations ancestry. For the purposes of this biography, I refer to both groups without the accent, except in direct quotations from printed and manuscript texts. Honoré Jaxon himself wrote the word in English as "Metis." In the Constitution Act, 1982, the Parliament of Canada used the term "Métis," in recognition of the Aboriginal status of people of mixed-blood ancestry, not included under the Federal Indian Act. But following the usage of Jaxon in English, I use the term "Metis" here. In the nineteenth century the term "half breed" was used in English to describe those of mixed-blood ancestry. The expression appears in this book only when used in a quotation from an original source.

Other matters of usage include the following. In their letters, both Honoré Jaxon and his wife Aimée Montfort Jaxon used *l'accent aigu* in writing their names. Newspapers and government record keepers did not; hence, I follow the exact forms in which their names were recorded.

Another point concerns the term "Baha'i." In a number of the older sources, the word is written simply as "Bahai." The spelling followed is that used in the citation.

For omissions in cited texts, I have used the form ... to indicate that the deletion is in the original; where I have made the deletion, I have used the form [...].

CHAPTER 1

YOUNG WILL 1861–77

WILLIAM HENRY JACKSON WAS BORN ON 3 MAY 1861, IN Toronto, to Thomas Gethyn Jackson and Elizabeth Eastwood Jackson, recent English immigrants, both children of Methodist ministers. To the south, the American Civil War, which would last four years, had just begun. Canada was still six years away from Confederation. In his boyhood in Ontario, Will acquired from his parents much of the personal self-confidence that shored him up on many occasions later in his life. His father in particular gave him an invaluable gift, the ability to think critically. While the Jackson family suffered great financial reverses in Canada, they made sacrifices for the education of their children, in the case of Will preparing him to enter the University of Toronto.

Thomas Jackson had attended an English boarding school. Shortly after the death of his father, Reverend Richard Jackson,[1] his mother, Elizabeth Gethyn Jackson, sent him to the Woodhouse Grove School in Yorkshire founded for the benefit of children of Wesleyan Methodist ministers. Thomas spent six years there.[2] At age eight, his first year at the school, he heard a lecture by Reverend James Evans, a Methodist missionary in the North-Western Territory of British North America.[3] The freedom and vastness of this territory were appealing to boys held in a world of constant supervision in classroom, dining hall, playground, and dormitory.[4]

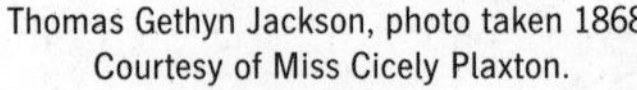

Thomas Gethyn Jackson, photo taken 1868.
Courtesy of Miss Cicely Plaxton.

Elizabeth Eastwood Jackson.
Courtesy of Joyce Arnold.

After leaving school, Thomas apprenticed with a dry goods merchant in Bridlington Quay, Yorkshire, on the North Sea. New vistas opened. He went to Canada in 1857, went back to England to marry in 1858, and returned with his bride.[5] Thomas, twenty-three, had married Elizabeth Eastwood, thirty, seven years older,[6] at the Wesleyan Methodist Centenary Chapel in her native city of York on September 3, 1858.[7] The Jackson and Eastwood families had been friends for years. Elizabeth's father, Reverend Thomas Eastwood, had served his church both as minister and as secretary to the Auxiliary Fund, a financial post. After many decades of service, he was superannuated at York, where he died in 1855.[8] In his will, he left land and investments to his widow, Anne Ogle Eastwood, and three daughters, Hannah (Mrs. Hannah Calder), Jane (Jennie), and Elizabeth (Lizzie), soon to be Mrs. Thomas Jackson.[9]

Physically Elizabeth and Thomas were quite different: she stood only five feet tall, while he was five feet, ten inches.[10] They also had quite different outlooks on life. In contrast to her husband, Elizabeth was definitely a realist, both of her feet firmly on the ground. As she wrote in one letter back to England, "I cannot look at things so brightly as Thomas does."[11] But they both shared the same intense Methodist faith, which strongly united them.

Elizabeth had a fine education, although she had never spent a day in school. Reverend Eastwood chose to educate his daughter at home. Her parents strongly encouraged her musical talent. On at least one occasion, the church officials allowed her, a great tribute to her ability, to play the organ in York's ancient St. Paul's Cathedral, also known as York Minster. Into her eighties, she continued to play the piano.[12]

A month after their wedding the Jacksons sailed to Canada.[13] Thomas, a storekeeper, had ambitions of making his fortune in the colony, then returning with his family to England to live comfortably there. The Jacksons originally planned to stay in Canada just five years.[14] Money from Elizabeth's side financed their relocation.[15]

In Canada, the newly married couple lived first on a farm near Weston, immediately west of Toronto.[16] Thomas looked for a country general store. At first, they considered starting up in Toronto itself, but as Elizabeth wrote to her sister Jennie back in York they discovered that "rents and taxes are enormous – a store in a good business street from 100 pounds to 400 pounds a year rent!"[17] Early in 1859, the Jacksons decided to buy an existing store in the hamlet of Stanley Mills, fifteen miles from Toronto, and just eight or so miles from Brampton to the west. It had three mills, a wagon shop, a blacksmith, a tailor, a seamstress, an inn, and a general store,[18] which the Jacksons now took over.

After living in the ancient city of York, Elizabeth found adjusting to a Canadian hamlet difficult. She wrote back to her sister Jennie a year after their arrival in Canada: "You don't know, and never can, half the good your letters do me. My being feels as though it had been cut into two. Half on this side the water half on that, your letters vivifying both. It is dangerous to transplant after the tree is grown, and it needs all the native soil that can be carried with it."[19]

Business-wise Thomas had difficulties obtaining credit for dry goods and hiring appropriate staff. Beginning a family added new responsibilities. Their first son, Eastwood, was born at Stanley Mills on June 6, 1859.[20] To help the family financially, Elizabeth ran the post office in their store, which, she explained to her sister, "is considered perfectly respectable here."[21] The 1861 census of Canada West, as Ontario was then known, records that "T.G. Jackson" had three employees, a frame house two storeys high, and four horses.[22] After only one year in Stanley Mills, he opened a second store at 279 Queen Street West in Toronto, which, with its attached living quarters, became their principal residence.[23] Here their second son was born on May 3, 1861.

With great emotion, Thomas Jackson wrote to his mother and sister in England on May 5 that Elizabeth had given birth to twins, "a fine boy at a quarter to six pm." Then, at a quarter past ten, "after suffering more than a martyrdom another boy was brought into the world dead." He added that "our living child is a fine healthy looking boy likely I trust to do well, he weighs 8 lbs in his clothes. We propose to call him William Henry in memory of my poor brother who was drowned."[24] Elizabeth, who had barely survived the ordeal, cherished William all her life, the twin who survived.[25]

Shortly after William Henry's birth, Thomas realized that his Toronto expansion was a mistake. The limited business transacted there led him to close it. From Stanley Mills, he travelled extensive distances to the north to sell manufactured goods, particularly cloth,[26] in return for farmers' produce. He had a hearty constitution for this demanding work, which involved travelling by sleigh in winter and by wagon in the other seasons.

Gradually the Jacksons began to feel a little more at home in their new community of Stanley Mills. They were good church people, puritanical in their interpretation of their Methodist faith: no dancing, no playing cards, and of course no drinking.[27] But they strongly encouraged music. Often the family, when the children were older, gathered around Elizabeth's piano to sing the grand old Methodist hymns as well as popular songs of the day.[28] The Jacksons actively participated in the Methodist community in Stanley Mills, helping in every respect with construction of a new brick chapel. Thomas ran the young men's Bible class.[29]

Born into a Methodist home, the Jackson children were the products of their parents' culture and values: the striving toward personal holiness, a belief in the value of hard work, the need to make a better world. The children also learned about the menace of the Roman Catholic Church. Like many other evangelical British Protestants, Methodists believed that Catholics had placed the human authority of the pope and his clergy over the divine authority of the Bible. They regarded Catholic practices, such as the sacrifice of the mass, the veneration of the saints and the performance of confession, as clearly idolatrous.[30] The *Thirty-Sixth Annual Report of the Missionary Society of the Wesleyan Methodist Church in Canada, from June 1860 to June 1861,* for example, announced the upcoming struggle for the Canadian church in its work in the North-Western Territory: "It is not Paganism, but Popery, which is the most hateful barrier of the Gospel on the Saskatchewan, as it is throughout the world: indeed, Popery is a spurious and foul Christianity in heathen trappings, and it is easier to persuade a cannibal to be saved than some dupes of Rome."[31]

On October 20, 1861, Reverend Enoch Wood, the superintendent of missions of the Wesleyan Methodist Church in Canada, came to Stanley Mills to dedicate the hamlet's new chapel. Elizabeth worked hard for the visit and welcomed the distinguished cleric to their home. Three hundred and fifty people attended the celebrations of the church's opening.[32] At the request of the Jacksons, the Methodist missionary superintendent baptized their five-month-old child "William Henry Jackson."[33]

After several years in Stanley Mills, the Jacksons' original goal to make and save enough money to return to live comfortably in England remained unfulfilled. Thomas became restless. By 1863, he believed that there must be greater opportunities elsewhere in the colony. Elizabeth preferred to return to England first and there reassess their options. She did not convince Thomas, as she explained to her mother: as "good as Thomas is to persuade in most things, I fail here, he has not succeeded as he hoped & will not return until his expectations have in some measure met with their fulfillment."[34]

At the time of the birth of the Jacksons' third surviving child, daughter Cicely, born on June 19, 1863 in Stanley Mills,[35] Thomas still wished to relocate but had not decided where. Reverend Enoch Wood had recommended Meaford on Georgian Bay to the north. But, in Elizabeth's words, "the enthusiastic descriptions of the Manitoulin island lately purchased from the Indians" led Thomas to suggest moving there, to the distant north shore of Lake Huron.[36] She voiced her opposition, as she wrote to her sister Jennie: "I would rather live on a crust of bread in England, than be self-condemned to such banishment."[37] Thomas next considered the town of Orillia, just north of Lake Simcoe.[38] Finally, after an extensive tour in early August of possible communities north and northwest of Toronto, he found what he regarded as the ideal location, a place called Wingham, inland from Goderich on Lake Huron. Elizabeth reported his joy: "He is very sanguine, thinks he has found the golden dollar."[39] She would have preferred to stay at Stanley Mills and grow up with the district.[40]

In late September, the family moved to Wingham, "Land of Promise,"[41] in Turnberry Township, North Huron County, about one-hundred miles north of Stanley Mills. The land, the southern portion of what was called the "Queen's Bush," had only been obtained, under great pressure, from the Ojibwa or Anishinaabeg (pronounced Ah-NISHAH-beg) (the plural form of Anishinaabe), about a quarter of a century earlier. The crown had secured this land at a council in 1836 held on Manitoulin Island. Reverend James Evans, the same Methodist missionary who spoke at Thomas Jackson's school in Yorkshire, was present. In essence, the lieutenant governor of Upper Canada had simply informed the First Nations that, in Evans' words, "he could not protect them in the possession of their land."[42] Under such pressure, the Anishinaabeg, few in numbers, withdrew.

The early settlers in North Huron County still harboured fears about the previous occupants. The Anishinaabeg now lived forty miles to the north at Saugeen on Lake Huron and even farther north at Cape Croker on the Bruce Peninsula.[43] Yet, on early farms in Turnberry Township, the local history recalls, "if the wife and children were left overnight when the husband was away, the door would be barricaded with furniture, in fear of Indians or wolves."[44] Years later Will's sister Cicely recalled "the stories of Indian raids" that she had heard in her childhood.[45]

The original village of Wingham was located at the junction of the north and south branches of the Maitland River. At this attractive spot, the government surveyors decided to make the town plot. Here

Upper Wingham, Josephine and Victoria Streets, 1860s. North Huron Museum, Wingham, Ontario.

the Jacksons built a large general store,[46] with their home in the same building, on Helena Street, next to the bridge over the Maitland. They included a prayer room over their kitchen in the new house,[47] for local Methodist services, until the community obtained their own church.[48] Elizabeth taught Sunday school and played the church organ.[49] The church history recalled that "The 'oldest inhabitants' tell us that Mrs. T. G. Jackson was a most estimable woman, faithful in all Christian activities, a woman having ability, zeal, tact and a great love for Christian service."[50] Regarding the town as ungodly, the Jacksons committed themselves to the fight to redeem those who had strayed. Wingham had only eighty families in 1865 yet supported six taverns.[51] In Canada, Elizabeth wrote, whisky was "as cheap as milk."[52]

In hindsight, the Jacksons made a terrible mistake in locating themselves on the government-surveyed "town plot." The more astute settlers chose their locations on a new townsite, "Upper Wingham," situated about half a mile to the east, across the river on higher ground. Thomas had bought and built in the middle of a flood plain.[53] It was not his fault as the government surveyors had placed the original townsite there. His mistake was to wait too long to relocate from Lower to Upper Wingham once he realized that the river flooded each spring. By the late 1870s, the locals called Lower Wingham the "frog pond."[54]

By 1866, Thomas had difficulty paying his creditors.[55] A serious fire in their rented quarters, only months after their arrival, had set him back.[56] But he faced an additional challenge. As his wife herself recognized, his heart was not in commerce. Elizabeth indirectly told her mother in England as much: "He is the greatest defender of Methodism you have met with, pity he wasn't a preacher is it not."[57]

"Pater," as Will called him in his later letters, loved politics and reading much more than business. He spent a great deal of time studying works such as Henry Hallam's two-volume *Constitutional History of England*.[58] Like Hallam, Thomas attacked the tyranny of English kings Charles I and James I and glorified the English Revolution of 1688. A great admirer of the Upper Canadian rebel William Lyon Mackenzie, Thomas believed, and taught his children, that every citizen had the God-given right to rise up in the face of tyranny. Locally, Thomas had the reputation of being "always a most rabid Grit," but, a Tory acquaintance added, "otherwise he was considered a very respectable man."[59] He ran for the Turnberry Township Council and was elected, serving a two-year term in 1866–67.[60]

Books were a crucial part of the Jacksons' lives. Elizabeth began to teach Will the alphabet when he was only three.[61] He loved learning. When the other boys went out to play, the bright child stayed at home to read. At age five, he read *Rollin's Ancient History*,[62] a child's history of ancient Greece and Rome. Elizabeth wrote to her sister Jennie when Will was six that "he is very fond of reading, will read in fact, all day long if permitted and you would be surprised what a straitforward account he can give of anything he has read."[63] But Thomas also gave Will a practical education, and Will became "quite handy in the use of carpenters tools."[64]

Our first glimpse of "Willie," a happy, well-adjusted child, is in 1869, from his first surviving letter, written at age eight, to his aunt Jennie Eastwood in England. After thanking her for her Christmas present, he added, "Please the next time you see Santa Claus in England, tell him that I am very much obliged for his present." In his stocking, he told his aunt, he found "a book, a popgun, a candy duck & candy mouse and some candies." He ended his short note warmly: "I send 8000 kisses to each of my relations and know that you will believe me to be your loving nephew. W.H. Jackson."[65]

Elizabeth was very protective of the children. As she explained to her sister Jennie in a letter written in 1865 or so, the two boys, "Eastie" and "Willie," were "excellent playmates, they might have plenty more, but I do not encourage them, Eastie is very sociable, would give anything away, give up the swing etc., but Willie is more tenacious as scarcely a lot in the place is fenced, it is a difficult matter to keep others away. There is no school in the place so that I am afraid there will be many rough unmanageable children in the town."[66] She set out to educate the boys herself until they reached age ten.[67]

Will's sister, Cicely, two years younger, was his frequent companion. All their lives they had a close relationship.[68] She remembered him as a child as "very truthful,"[69] someone who always kept his word. Bright, spirited, and a great lover of the outdoors, Cicely was a strong, independent individual. She was a good horsewoman.[70] During the troubles of 1885, she stayed alone with the Native workers at the family farm at the Forks, about twenty-five miles east of Prince Albert.[71]

Elizabeth sent Cicely to the Wingham Public School once it opened.[72] Like her mother, Cicely had a natural gift for writing. She later wrote an account of her childhood. All her life she remembered growing up by the Maitland River. "On summer nights the ripple and wash of the river lulled us to sleep. In winter the grist mill ran day and night except Sunday, and I remember that I used to waken at midnight on Saturday when the click, clack of the mill ceased." On the south side of the river opposite the house, "the forest primeval still grew to the water's edge."[73]

Not all of her memories were pleasant, certainly not the recollection of the spring floods. "When my father built his house by the river he was assured that it would never overflow its banks but altho the foundation of the house was built three feet above ground the water rose two or three inches on the lower floors on two occasions. Twice, in the summer, the dam broke in the night, and we were awakened by the sound of water running into the cellar windows, but the flood soon subsided."[74]

The Jackson children grew up in an overwhelmingly Protestant and British area.[75] The Protestants, generally speaking, distrusted the few

On April 25, 1870 the *Canadian Illustrated News* published this imaginative depiction of the execution of Thomas Scott on March 4, 1870. Glenbow Archives/ NA-1406–71a

Catholics in their midst. In the mid-1860s, the threat of a Fenian attack was perceived as a serious threat. The Fenians, an Irish American organization formed immediately after the American Civil War, included about ten thousand Civil War veterans in their ranks. They sought to end English rule in Ireland. Part of the Fenians' strategy was to "free Canada" from the British. In 1866, the Fenians actually launched an attack on the Niagara Peninsula. They won the skirmish at Ridgeway before withdrawing back across the Niagara River. That year all kinds of rumours circulated in North Huron County. Cicely later recalled being told (she was only three at the time) that "wild tales were spread by ignorant and mischievous persons that the Roman Catholics in Ontario were joining with the Fenians to massacre the Protestants on Xmas eve."[76]

The Red River Resistance of 1869–70 occurred at the very moment when Will's political consciousness was first awakening. Under the leadership of Louis Riel, then only twenty-five years old, the Metis, or French-speaking mixed-bloods in Red River, set up a provisional government to protest the Hudson's Bay Company's sale of their homeland to the Canadian government. While the Red River delegates discussed the terms of Red River's entry into the Dominion of Canada, then but three years old, Riel made a major mistake. He organized a court martial that recommended the execution of Thomas Scott, a loud-mouthed, aggressive Ontario Protestant who had taken up arms against the provisional government.

Scott's execution on March 4, 1870 ignited tempers in North Huron County. Shortly after Scott's death, an angry meeting took place at Blyth, fifteen miles south of Wingham. The fiery poster

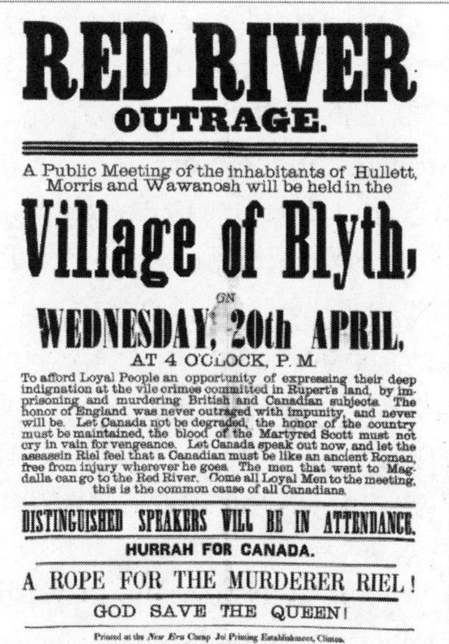

"Red River Outrage," the circular advertising the public forum held at Blyth, about fifteen miles south of Wingham, to protest the execution of Thomas Scott. Archives of Manitoba/N10307

advertising the meeting presented Scott as a martyr and demanded "A Rope for the Murderer Riel."[77] It compared the situation to that in Abyssinia (or Ethiopia). Two years earlier, in 1868, Britain dispatched an expedition under Robert Napier to confront Emperor Theodore. The Abyssinian leader had imprisoned British members of a diplomatic mission at Magdala. Napier, who was later created Baron Napier of Magdala for his exploit, rescued them and destroyed Magdala. The Blyth poster read, "Let Canada not be degraded, the honor of the country must be maintained. Let Canada speak out now, and let the assassin Riel feel that a Canadian must be like an ancient Roman, free from injury wherever he goes. The men that went to Magdalla can go to the Red River." Almost fifteen years later, Will recalled the hysterical hatred of Riel: "in my boyhood days," they portrayed him as a "Cutthroat, an outlaw, bold braggart, and indeed the embodiment of nearly all that is evil."[78]

The Red River entered the Dominion of Canada as the Province of Manitoba in July 1870. The dispatch of a Canadian military expedition to Red River prompted Riel, held to be responsible for the execution of Scott, to escape across the border into the United States.

Thomas took Will to his first political meeting at age eleven. His mother commented in a letter to her son Eastwood on August 15, 1872 how Willie had "caught the prevailing election fever having stood last Monday on rather a prominent position near to the candidates, nominators, seconders etc. and has been somewhat deranged in consequence! fortunate for you, that you escaped the contagion!"[79] Over sixty years later, his sister Cicely vividly recalled how her brother had returned, "greatly excited,"[80] from his first political meeting.

In the academic year 1872–73, the Jacksons made major financial sacrifices for their two sons. They sent them to the "City," as rural Ontarians called Toronto, to the provincial Model School. There the students of the Normal School, or what is now called a teachers' college, did their practice teaching. The school had high standards as well as a long waiting list to enter.[81] It was a credit to Elizabeth's fine teaching that they gained entrance and did well.

The boys came from a warm and caring family. Their parents supported them fully, always encouraging them to do their best. Elizabeth congratulated both of them on their first reports in the fall but cautioned them not to become complacent, for "your skiffs are not half way across the ocean of knowledge yet so do not rest on your oars until the Christmas holidays give you the very necessary breathing time."[82] Elizabeth, somewhat a micromanager, enclosed in her letter an incredible list of dos and don'ts. One example will suffice: "Be regular in all your habits – keep your feet dry – if stockings get wet change them at once if your boots require mending – take them to be mended – I hope you have all your winter clothes now – keep your coats & trowsers free from dust as the rainy days spoil clothes covered with the dust of summer."[83] She urged them to maintain "habits of Order, Cleanliness and above all a constant habit of prayer."[84]

One can understand, to an extent, Elizabeth's protectiveness. The boys were young, and many menaces existed in an unfriendly world. In letters to them in Toronto, Elizabeth mentioned Will's friend George Hutton, nine years old, the miller's son, who after an accident had to have his leg amputated.[85] Then George Matthewson lost his son George, also nine. He suddenly became ill and died of cerebrospinal meningitis within twenty-four hours.[86] But in this threatening world, she had no concerns about entrusting her two sons to the care of James Hughes, principal of the Model School, and, on the Sabbath, superintendent of a Methodist Sunday School.[87]

Hughes was a gifted teacher and administrator. At this point, he stood on the bottom steps of an extraordinary career that would see him rise to become Toronto's inspector of public schools. A tall, lean, athletic-looking man, he commanded respect by his very appearance. With complete self-assurance, he advanced his ideas about childhood education. He insisted on the importance of allowing the voice of a young person to be heard. He wanted children to be treated as individuals. "If a man," Hughes later wrote, "is to be free at maturity he must be free in the subordinate stages of childhood and youth."[88]

A story in the Toronto *World* on May 19, 1885, entitled "Riel's Youthful Secretary," provides an intimate view of Will as a young schoolboy in Toronto. The author of the article, published just a week after the fall of Batoche, spoke with both Reverend Elmore Harris, then the minister of the Yorkville Baptist Church, and lawyer Joseph McArthur.[89] Both men had stayed in the same boarding house as Will and Eastwood the year that they attended the Toronto Model School. Harris recalled how, in the early morning, before breakfast, Will sat himself down at his table. The university student rose early to keep ahead of his course material. At the table, the eleven-or-so-year-old Will pretended to study while all the time grinding his teeth. After Harris protested, his tormentor stopped, but the next morning, "instead of grinding his teeth, young Jackson would snap or champ them. On being besought to give this habit up he would begin another equally tormenting, such as scratching a pin on a book, cracking his heels etc." McArthur, too, recalled that Will loved practical jokes but added that "everyone liked the young mischief-maker."

In its article, the *World* included another story about Will during the year that he attended the Model School. Apparently he belonged to S.S. Martin's Bible Class at the newly built Sherbourne Street Methodist Church. Martin, a native of Lincolnshire, England, was a respected member of the Methodist community. He rose from employee to partner in the firm of Rice Lewis and Sons, wholesale hardware merchants.[90] One Sunday, out of the blue, Will abruptly asked the distinguished elder of the church about infant baptism. "What is your opinion of infant sprinkling? Do you believe in it?" With all of his inborn confidence, even at age eleven, Will had few inhibitions. His parents had encouraged him to ask questions.

Hughes had a high opinion of the boy's potential. Eastwood won first prize in mathematics while at the school,[91] but still Hughes ranked his younger brother higher academically. Will's thinking travelled along unconventional rather than in ready-made channels. In a letter to the

Photo of Eastwood on the left, aged 12, and Will, on the right, aged 10. Taken by W.O'Connor, Photographer, 63 King St. East, Toronto. Courtesy of Miss Cicely Plaxton.

boys' father at the end of the fall term, Hughes wrote, "I am most sincerely and heartily gratified with the boys, they are both good boys to begin with, and Willie especially is blessed with far more than ordinary ability."[92]

Shortly after his year at the Model School, Eastwood entered an apprentice program with Toronto's Lyman Brothers, wholesale druggists, to learn to become a pharmacist. His father was the first druggist in Wingham. With passage of the Ontario Pharmacy Act in 1871, all new pharmacists needed a licence, but those who had sold drugs before gained exception. Eastwood took courses at the newly established Ontario College of Pharmacy. In his final year, 1878, he obtained the top grade in chemistry in his class. At age nineteen, he received his licence from the college. The next year the young graduate left for Selkirk, Manitoba, to start a drug business.[93]

While most of Will's boyhood contemporaries quit after completing primary school, Will went on to high school in 1874 in Clinton, twenty-five miles to the south, not yet connected to Wingham by rail. To make sure he was ready for classics at Clinton High School, his parents paid for him and Eastwood to take private Latin lessons from James Young,[94] a Scottish schoolmaster who lived immediately to the west of Lower Wingham at a hamlet called Zetland.[95] He prepared Will well for his high school classics courses in Clinton. Latin was needed for matriculation, the right to enter the University of Toronto. In the first year at the University of Toronto, it remained a required course for all students.[96]

In Clinton, Will boarded with his aunt Mary Coates and her family. Thomas's sister and brother-in-law had moved to the village several years earlier. Edward Coates was a carpenter, and their son Charles was an apprentice cabinetmaker.[97] Will attended Clinton High School in the mid-1870s. Every Monday morning Elizabeth woke up early to get her son off to catch the 5 a.m. stage to Clinton.[98] He returned home on weekends.

Clinton High School enjoyed a good reputation. Students still paid fees for their instruction. In the mid-1870s, formal education remained a privilege for the few. The Ontario Education Act of 1871 made school attendance compulsory but just for children ages seven to twelve.[99] Only a small percentage of the high school age group attended secondary school, and a tiny percentage of this number went on to college.[100] Only one out of ten high school students aimed to matriculate – that is, gain the right to enter university.[101] Will intended to matriculate.

At Model School and now Clinton High School, Will was taught to revere Ontario's British connections. As Arthur Lower, the distinguished Canadian historian who attended elementary and high school and university in Ontario a century ago, later recalled, "We had history in the public school, we had history in the high school, and we had history in Varsity, and it was all English history."[102] In Will's case at least, this knowledge ultimately had some value. Later, in the North-West Territories, he benefited enormously from his firm grounding in English constitutional history.

Main Street Clinton about 1865. Courtesy of Kelvin Jervis.

The Clinton High School board had a visionary leader, Horatio Hale.[103] Clinton admitted girls as well as boys to its secondary school. Hale, an American-born lawyer, and an influential Clinton-area landowner and developer, won over the town to the idea.[104] Conscious of the need for the best school possible, the board employed in the 1870s an excellent headmaster, James Turnbull, MA (University of Toronto), "Scholar in Classics and Gold Medalist in Modern Languages."[105] His school won comments from school inspectors such as "remarkable for its general excellence"[106] and "an excellent high school. It has no superior in the Province."[107] Turnbull was singled out as a "very special teacher and manager."[108] In his Latin and Greek classes, he trained Will well for his university work to follow.

Hale, a very cultivated individual, so loved literature and learning that he named the streets in the tract of land that he and his wife developed after literary figures: Addison, Cowper, Milton, and Newton. Hale himself had attended university with one of America's greatest authors. The *Memorials of the Class of 1837 of Harvard University, Prepared for the Fiftieth Anniversary of Their Graduation,* confirms that he was a classmate of Henry David Thoreau.

In terms of his appreciation of North American Indian languages and history, Hale was extraordinary. He had a great love of indigenous peoples, dating back to his four years, immediately after Harvard, as the philologist with the United States Exploring Expedition to the Pacific under Captain Charles Wilkes. In Ontario, through a friendship with John Fraser, an Iroquois who later became a traditional chief of the Mohawk nation, Hale gained entry to the world of the Six Nations Confederacy, resident on the Grand River near Brantford, a short distance of about one hundred miles by rail to the southeast. While Will attended high school in Clinton, Hale completed his research work with a committee of chiefs on the history of the Six Nations Confederacy. His work later appeared as the *Iroquois Book of Rites* (1883). Hale was a close friend of George Johnson, his interpreter, and his English-born wife, Emily Howells. Their daughter Pauline Johnson later became one of the most celebrated poets in Canada at the turn of the century.

This champion of the North American Indian noted in the *Iroquois Book of Rites* that the "popular opinion of the Indian ... represents him

On the back of this photograph, Horatio Hale wrote, "This picture represents the chiefs of the Six Nations, on their reserve near Brantford in Canada, explaining their wampum belts (Sept. 14, 1871)." Pauline Johnson's grandfather John Smoke Johnson, Mohawk chief and speaker of the council, appears third from the right; her father, George H. M. Johnson, Mohawk chief and government interpreter, is shown second from the left. Library and Archives Canada/C-85137.

as a sanguinary, treacherous and vindictive being, somewhat cold in his affections, haughty and reserved toward his friends, merciless to his enemies, fond of strife, and averse to industry and the pursuits of peace." This, he added, is "wholly false." "The Indians," he wrote, "must be judged, like every other people, not by the traits which they display in the fury of a desperate warfare, but by their ordinary demeanor in time of peace, and especially by the character of their social and domestic life."[109]

When Will was a student in Clinton, his father became restless again. Thomas wrote to Reverend Enoch Wood, still the Methodist missionary superintendent, about the possibility of relocation to northwestern Ontario. The fact that Upper Wingham, incorporated as a village in 1874, had been chosen as the junction of the Toronto, Grey, and Bruce railway with the London, Huron, and Bruce line led to rapid development there at the expense of Lower Wingham. Thomas inquired about Port Arthur at the head of Lake Superior, then experiencing a mining boom. As Elizabeth commented, he saw Port

Arthur and Thunder Bay as "an El Dorado."[110] But Wood encouraged him to think of Winnipeg, close to the "Red River Country, Manitoba, and the Great Saskatchewan Valley."[111]

About this time, Elizabeth summarized the family's desperate financial state:

> Wingham itself is not to blame for our losses 1st we came to it too soon ere its course of traffic was fully determined and when the settlers had realized scarcely an existence from their quarter cleared farms of 100 acres, 2nd we were burnt out, 3rd we built too largely, 4th we gave too much credit this led to the 5th mistake, we took park lots in pay, with money, these must be cleared & farmed to make them pay interest – which also caused a divided attention to the main business – 6th we engaged a dishonest clerk.[112]

By 1877, things looked quite desperate for Thomas. He wrote to Eastwood in Toronto on September 6, 1877 about debt, "which is more to be dreaded than a wild beast." It is, he added, "the slow torture of the thumbscrew."[113]

With the good arable land now taken up in southern Ontario, many sons and daughters of Huron pioneers departed in the late 1870s for the American Midwest, the big American cities, and now, after the entry of the Red River or Manitoba into the Dominion of Canada, a growing number of Huron County migrants headed for the North-West Territories. Thomas and Elizabeth joined Eastwood, who had decided to move to Manitoba, in his migration westward. They left Cicely behind to complete her high school in Clinton and Will to finish his BA in classics at the University of Toronto.

CHAPTER 2

CALL TO GREATNESS

1878–84

THOMAS AND ELIZABETH SAVED ALL THEY COULD TO SEND their second-born son off to University College, University of Toronto, the only college and only major building on the campus in the late 1870s. Already they had helped to pay for Eastwood's courses at the Ontario College of Pharmacy. Eastwood apprenticed with Lyman Brothers and Company in Toronto, obtaining his certificate from the College of Pharmacy in 1878.[1] A few years later they sent Cicely to teachers' college in Winnipeg. They wanted all three of their children to obtain professional training. As Thomas told Eastwood when he was in Toronto studying pharmacy, "Keep out of Dream land, work & think, take care of your health and avoid all habits which help to destroy the brain, as you would serpents."[2]

Unfortunately for Will, his parents' finances hit rock bottom on the eve of his departure for university. As Eastwood wrote to his brother on February 28, 1878, "It is too bad Pa is nearly failing again we seem as if we were out of one trouble, only to be in another."[3] Without any firm guarantee that his parents could afford to send him to university in the fall of 1878, Will prepared for his matriculation exams. He passed thanks to his strong preparation at the Clinton High School and his dedication to his studies.[4] That winter he also appears to have mastered German from a German-language textbook. Apparently he taught himself. As he wrote to his sister, his German-

The university in 1876, as painted by Lucius R.O. O'Brien. University of Toronto Archives/B1965–0025/001P.

language book contained all the rules for pronunciation, and "all a learner has to do is to go steadily through *from the beginning without skipping the introductory part*."[5] He loved learning languages.

By fall, Will was at last in Toronto, sent off with as much cash for tuition and expenses as his parents could spare. To fortify him that fall, Elizabeth, after his first month, dispatched to him from Wingham a full trunk loaded with food.[6] Will loved his studies at University College. It was an attractive building, less than twenty years old. W.G. Hanna, a fellow student from Clinton High School, also matriculated and was in the same program.[7] William Hanna had the required black academic gown required to attend lectures.[8] Money was so tight for the Jacksons that Will arrived without one.[9] He had to obtain one.

The University of Toronto campus was beautiful. On the grounds, pines, cedars, and willows, among others, still stood in picturesque groves.[10] Two Russian cannon, now spiked, captured by Her Majesty's forces in the Crimean War, 1854–56, were placed on two stone pedestals in Queen's Park, on the eastern approach to University College. Queen Victoria herself in 1859 gave pairs of captured Russian cannon to principal cities throughout the British Empire.[11] Farther west, closer to the college, stood the monument, constructed in 1870, to the three undergraduates killed in action resisting the Fenian raids in the Niagara Peninsula a decade earlier.[12]

University College was very small in the 1870s, with only a few hundred students, all male, drawn primarily from the villages and towns of Ontario. Women gained entrance only in 1884. Will studied principally under Reverend John McCaul, professor of classical literature, logic and rhetoric and president of University College. He was the first professor appointed to King's College in 1842, as the university was originally known.[13] This cultivated gentleman came to Canada after a brilliant classical career at Trinity College, Dublin.[14] He had interests in music, writing, as well as his subject area of Greek and Latin studies. When the Civil War was raging in the United States, McCaul sympathized with the North and championed the emancipation of the slaves. But his liberal mindedness had definite limits. McCaul opposed the admission of women to University College.[15] Others in the professorate shared this opinion, including Daniel Wilson, McCaul's successor as president of University College in 1880. The professor of history and English literature believed in higher education for women but thought that men and women should not be mixed in their most excitable years. As Canadian historian Carl Berger writes, "He later admitted privately that lecturing on Shakespeare to young men in the presence of young women would be a trying ordeal because of the sexual allusions in some of the plays."[16]

Apparently Will did not take any courses from Professor Wilson, now recognized as Canada's first anthropologist.[17] The North American Indian interest of the Scottish-born-and-raised professor was unique in Canada in the 1870s. It would be another one hundred years, in fact, before the University of Toronto introduced Native history into the curriculum. As did his contemporaries, Wilson believed that the First Nations would diminish and melt away after contact with European civilization. What made his viewpoint more original was that he believed this development would strengthen the British population. He encouraged interbreeding and the slow absorption, and full incorporation, of the Aboriginal population into the non-Native society. The original peoples would be absorbed, in his words, "but not without leaving some traces on the predominant race, and perhaps helping it to adapt to its new home."[18]

At this stage in Will's life, no evidence exists to establish his own interest in Aboriginal people. Toronto, now overwhelmingly British (ninety-three percent),[19] had almost no Native residents. Speaking of his boyhood in the 1820s, the well-known Toronto artist Paul Kane noted in 1859 that "I had been accustomed to see hundreds of Indians about my native village, then Little York, muddy and dirty, just struggling into existence, now the City of Toronto, bursting forth in all its energy and commercial strength. But the face of the red man is now no longer seen."[20] Will's historical interest in the late 1870s was in ancient history, in the days of the Greeks and Romans. As was he, the Greeks were intense individualists.

Will liked McCaul. His colleague Wilson claimed that the president by the late 1870s was "now in that touchy irritable senility,"[21] yet his students still liked "Old Johnny."[22] Will wrote home that he was a "perfect encyclopedia of classical lore," who in his lectures "takes a pride in saying witty (?) things, which of course [are] loudly applauded." Will liked his studies. In that letter home on October 18, 1878, he reported that he now had the "hang of taking notes." "The other boys study 8 hours per day as far as I have heard, but I will lay out for 11 or 12, and thus get 10 on the average."[23] More good news for his parents, he mentioned that he had joined the Metropolitan Methodist Church's adult Bible class.[24]

His standing at the end of his first term, and over the course of his first two years, pleased Thomas and Elizabeth. During his first two years, Will stood in the top quarter of his class of over forty.[25] Apparently he was thinking of entering law after graduation.[26] The top student in the class, William Milner, was a Methodist clergyman's son who, on scholarship, had attended Upper Canada College, the elite private school in Toronto. Usually he took the top rank in classics, and he won the gold medal in his final year.[27] But Will derived great satisfaction from the results of the math exam that both he and Milner took in 1879. Jackson headed the list of those writing it. Milner stood at the opposite end of the scale, tied with four others for the second-lowest mark in the class of thirty-three.[28]

University College "football team," 1870. University of Toronto Archives/A73–0046/001.

Will took his studies seriously, but like his Grecian heroes, believers in the golden mean, he sought a balanced life. He wanted both a lively mind and a strong body. In his first term on campus, he joined the Association Foot-Ball Club, which followed English Rugby Union rules. Already he had played in his first month two good games of rugby, and he looked forward to practices, interspersed with regular games, on Mondays, Wednesdays, and Fridays.[29]

Much of Will's money that first term went for books, really basic reference works, such as a dictionary of Greek synonyms and one of Latin, Greek and Latin readers, and Greek and Roman history books. Will also had to pay for his room at his boarding house and for laundry, food, and firewood. The room itself was half carpeted, cheaply furnished, with one single bed and a few pieces of furniture. It was a thirty-five-minute walk from the university. Will certainly did not mind walking; in fact, it was regarded as both good for one's health and a prime form of recreation. The professors taught in the mornings, giving them the afternoons for other pursuits, including walking, while the mere lecturers and tutors taught in the afternoons.[30] But, to Will, over an hour just to get to and from the college seemed unnecessary. In contrast, his friend Hanna and three others had a place with richly carpeted and furnished bedrooms with a common front parlour with bay window and coal stove, and it was only a three-minute walk from the college. Will paid the same amount for his lodgings as did Hanna, four dollars a week. To save money, Will planned on saving fuel "by going early to college, and studying in the reading room, and coming back late." He also told his parents that he planned to find a better place as soon as possible.[31]

His horizons expanded in university. Will saw alternatives to the puritanical Methodist culture in which he had been raised. Professor McCaul instilled in Will a lifelong love of the classics. His study of the classical Hellenic civilization introduced him to modern political ideas when they were still fresh. In the North-West Territories, he took his Greek and Latin texts with him to Batoche and St. Laurent, the Metis communities in which he lived over the winter of 1884–85. Will had with him his copy of Plato's *Republic* and his edition of Horace's poems.[32] Over sixty years later, at the age of eighty-seven, Will, then known as Honoré, encouraged one of his great-nephews to continue studying Latin, and to begin Greek, to increase his "passion for freedom."[33]

The departure of his parents in late 1879 for the North-West Territories made it difficult for Will to pay for his studies and board. The Jacksons wrote to Will and Cicely from Winnipeg in early March 1880,[34] then from Portage la Prairie. At Portage, they opened up a store, and Thomas traded with First Nations people for furs.[35] Eastwood had settled first at Selkirk, Manitoba, but decided in 1880 to move farther west to Prince Albert in the Saskatchewan District. Thomas decided to relocate there. Elizabeth objected, but both Thomas and Eastwood held firm, "so I had to give in."[36] After a ten-week wagon trip, they reached the settlement on the banks of the North Saskatchewan. It proved a challenge for Elizabeth, "unused to animals and afraid of horses, and cattle," but she uncomplainingly joined her husband and older son on their trek north.[37]

Will passed his third year. Evidence exists that he remained in the program for his last year but did not, for whatever reason, write his final exams in the spring of 1881.[38] Then, in 1882, two years after his family's arrival in Prince Albert, he moved west from Wingham[39] to join them. The details of his last year in Ontario are not known. It appears that he remained in Wingham for a year after withdrawing from the university.

Big Bear's camp near Maple Creek, within present-day Saskatchewan, 1883. Library and Archives Canada/PA-50749.

In this period, family finances did not improve, which prevented him from returning to his studies. In 1882, he reached Winnipeg, then took the railway from there to what was then the end of the Canadian Pacific Railway at Troy, in the Qu'Appelle Valley. His sister Cicely later recalled that her hearty brother then walked alone with his possessions the nearly three hundred–mile distance from Qu'Appelle to Prince Albert.[40]

In 1882, the year of Will's arrival, Prince Albert, named in honour of Queen Victoria's late consort, celebrated its sixteenth birthday. Founded as a Presbyterian Indian Mission in 1866, a settlement had slowly grown up around the original mission station, on the banks of the North Saskatchewan. Cicely Jackson described what she found the following year: "It looked as if a giant had seized a handful of houses and scattered them over the river flat regardless of the point of the compass. ... The best defined street lay along the river bank. ... [T]he view would have been dreary but for the beautiful river that enclosed it from the north, at that time bordered by a forest of towering pines that from the water's edge stretched away into almost unknown northern regions."[41]

In Treaty Number Six (1876), the Cree, Assiniboine, and Chipewyan First Nations had dealt with the Canadian government over Canada's acquisition of a tract of land in what is now central Saskatchewan and Alberta, an area larger than all of England, Wales, Scotland, and Ireland combined. The First Nations welcomed the newcomers, receiving in return presents, a cash annuity, the promise of schools on their "reserves," a medicine chest in each of their communities, and most important of all, in the event of "any pestilence" or "general famine," the guarantee of government aid, "sufficient to relieve the Indians from the calamity that shall have befallen them."[42] The important Cree chief Mistawasis signed at Fort Carlton, seeing no alternative: "I for one think that the Great White Mother has offered us a way of life when the buffalo are no more. Gone they will be before many snows have come to cover our heads, or graves if such should be."[43] With the disappearance of the plains buffalo on the Canadian side of the border in 1879, the crisis for the First Nations began. By the early 1880s, the First Nations faced widespread starvation, dependent on stingy government rations. Canada's promises at Treaty Six of full support in times of "general famine" remained unfulfilled.

The settlers in the Prince Albert area, unlike the First Nations, did fairly well, at least up to the early 1880s. The population jumped from just over eight hundred in 1878 to roughly four times that number in 1881, and it rose to an estimated five thousand the following year. The Prince Albert district alone produced over half the wheat grown in the North-West Territories in 1881. Immigrant farmers continued to migrate to Prince Albert, one of the most fertile and settled regions west of Manitoba. By 1881, the town had become the commercial capital of the entire Saskatchewan Valley, the centre of a territory as large as southern Ontario itself. In contrast, Battleford remained a hamlet of wooden houses, Saskatoon an obscure village site, and Regina, just chosen as the new territorial capital, a scattered collection of tents and frame buildings.[44]

During this period of economic prosperity, little attention was paid to First Nations issues. In early 1882, surveyors began marking out the old Indian graveyard at the heart of Prince Albert into town lots.[45] Yet the Aboriginal population remained considerable, with several First Nation reserves around the town, Country-Born or English-speaking Métis communities to the southwest, and French-speaking Metis farther up the South Saskatchewan. Sioux refugees from the United States also lived in and near town but had no reserve as of yet. Known as hard workers, the Sioux women did washing and scrubbing, and the men sawed and split wood. The Sioux carried water in pails from the North Saskatchewan for those, like the Jacksons, who lived on River Street. Some years later the federal government placed the Sioux on a small reserve at Round Plain about ten miles northwest of town.[46]

Suddenly in 1882 the Prince Albert boom began to ebb. The federal government and the CPR made a decision that vitally altered the future development of Prince Albert and the northward-facing settlements of the Saskatchewan Valley, such as Battleford and Edmonton. The decision to change the CPR's route from the north to the south, announced in January 1882, diverted the course of settlement and investment. It directed attention to the empty farmlands and ranchlands of the south. The southern agricultural prairies now became the primary growth area, with the northern settlements definitely the land of second choice.[47] When Will arrived in the summer of 1882, the settlement, after the route change, had begun to lose its momentum. Still, many in the town optimistically believed that a spur line would soon be built to their well-settled district, linking it to the main line of the CPR.

When Will first arrived, he helped his father with his general store, in which he sold, among other products, farm implements.[48] Quickly he learned of the western farmers' deep hatred of the Canadian tariff. The high Canadian duties forced up the cost of machinery while at the same time leaving the price of wheat unprotected on a world market. The farmers thought that Ottawa paid little attention to their needs. Will knew about the federal government's harsh and unrealistic land regulations. His father lost his first homestead in 1882 when the federal land agent claimed that he had not fulfilled all the demanding terms of the Dominion Lands Act.[49]

Will looked for a homestead. He did a great deal of snowshoeing and, eight or so years later, could still tramp seventeen miles in five and a half hours.[50] From British traveller William Butler's stirring book of adventure, *The Wild North Land* (1873), he knew that the young British army officer had lived for several months in a log cabin at the forks of the North and South Saskatchewan rivers, thirty miles east of Prince Albert, "at the foot of the high ridge which marks the junction of the two Saskatchewans, deep in pines and poplars."[51] Butler had wintered there before setting out in February 1873 for the Peace River district on the great exploratory mission that he described in *The Wild North Land*. For Will, a halo of romance surrounded this district since Butler had once resided there.[52] Since Will saw several bears in this area in the spring and summer, he always went armed with his horse pistol and a hunting knife.[53] But his claim in the end proved too difficult to develop, and he lost interest in it.[54]

Within only half a year or so of residency in the Prince Albert district, Will became involved in politics. At university, he had studied the political theory of the ancient Greeks. He now became a participant in politics rather than an observer. Will had brought west with him a small printing press and had met a man in Prince Albert who could operate it. During the election campaign of March 1883 to elect a local representative to the territorial council in Regina, he published *The Voice of the People*, a two-page news sheet, both "plain-spoken and severe."[55] In his first issue of March 12, 1883, the young idealist wrote that

> The people of the North West are destined to undergo a fierce and prolonged struggle with the numerous monopolies which are fastening their relentless talons upon the vitals of their infant country, and it is essential that the members of our legislative council be men of integrity, firmness and energy, free from the slightest connection with oligarchical rings and cliques, or the least taint of self-interest and personal ambition, but imbued only with a lofty desire to serve their country's best interests.

Will brought out a second and final issue, on March 17, 1883.[56] The demise of *The Voice of the People* occasioned few tears by his mother. Elizabeth Jackson applauded his fight for justice for all, yet she added in a letter to daughter Cicely that "the role of political agitator is not what I would chose for Willie."[57]

In Prince Albert, Will continued to help his father with his farm-implement business. *The Voice of the People* might have been no more, but Will's political interests remained very much alive. The land boom had definitely ended by early 1883; by the end of the summer, all economic signs pointed downward.[58] He believed that he knew the cause, the imposition of a colonialist structure of executive rule from Ottawa.

Will reached Prince Albert to find it aflame with protest. At a mass meeting on October 16, 1883, about 150 residents, representing "the intelligence and bone and sinew of the settlement," formed a Settlers' Rights Association.[61] Much of the energy for the farmers' revolt came from Manitoba. The Manitoba and North West Farmers Union was founded in Winnipeg in mid-December 1883. The delegates, just as Louis Riel had done in 1870, drafted a "Bill of Rights." They demanded that Manitoba be granted its "provincial rights," including control of its public lands; that the national protective tariff be made a lower revenue tariff again; and that there be additional construction of branch railways.[62]

Having obtained a copy of their resolutions in January, Will spent the rest of the winter studying it.[63] He certainly wanted to be near the warm fire when he read it. Of that winter of 1883–84, Cicely later wrote that "Each day after my arrival was a little colder than the last until the cold became most intense in January and February. There were no mild spells – no thaws – just steady cold until I wakened on March 1 to hear water running down the pipes from the tin roof. What a blessed sound that was for it meant that we were nearing the end of the coldest winter that I had ever experienced."[64] Stoves proved inadequate to heat the recesses of rooms. The water supply froze in barrels standing by the fire.

Warm weather returned in the spring. By the time leaves sprouted again on the poplar trees, Thomas Jackson had lost his business.[65] The economy at Prince Albert was completely stagnant. While Eastwood's pharmacy continued on, his father's store disappeared. Thomas now spent much of his time developing their homestead about twenty-five miles to the east, on a beautiful horseshoe-shaped bend on the north side of the South Saskatchewan about three miles from the forks. Here the land sloped gradually from high land at the north to a pebbly beach. The tract was thickly wooded.[66]

That winter Will visited different settlements around Prince Albert in the hope of forming branches of a local farmers' union.[67] He thought that the federal administration of John A. Macdonald and the Conservative Party was responsible for much of the North-West Territories' hardship. All groups in the region, he argued, must work together for justice, to see it develop into a self-governing region, with an elected legislature, cabinet government, and territorial

James Isbister. Prince Albert Historical Society.

Andrew Spence. Glenbow Archives/NA-2172–31.

administration. Reformers must support the work of Frank Oliver, the *bête noir* of Lieutenant Governor Edgar Dewdney. Oliver fought in the Territorial Council in Regina for self-government.[68] Dewdney, who had concentrated as much power as he could in his own hands, opposed the council becoming a forum for opposition to the Conservative government, whose power he represented.[69]

The growing unrest in the area during the winter of 1883–84 led to meetings in the recently arrived Canadian and the well-established Country-Born settlements near Prince Albert, at St. Catherine's, Red Deer Hill, Halcro, and Colleston.[70] Will came to know a number of the leaders in the rural areas, men such as Tom Scott (no relation to the notorious Thomas of the Red River). Scott, born and raised in the Orkney Islands, had come to Canada to work for the Hudson's Bay Company and now had a large farm at the Ridge (Red Deer Hill) south of Prince Albert.[71] His father-in-law, James Isbister, a Country-Born, was the actual founder of Prince Albert in 1862, four years before Reverend James Nisbet established his Presbyterian mission on the site.[72] With great resentment, Isbister wanted to see in the North-West Territories "representative government, habeas corpus, and government officials responsible to the people, and not a gang of broken-down hacks from Ottawa, from which class our registrars, timber inspectors, and I may add police officials, appear to be selected."[73] A third individual, Andrew Spence, a Country-Born from neighbouring Red Deer Hill, chaired the farmers' committee, to become known as the Settlers Union.

Will's accent, pronunciation, and conversation marked him as an educated man. W.J. Carter, an early Ontario-born builder and contractor in Prince Albert,[74] later commented on the cleverness and ability of the young Will. He "was widely informed in all classes of literature and philosophy both ancient and modern. His memory of everything he had ever heard or read about was almost uncanny in its thoroughness."[75] The farmers badly needed him to help secure responsible government. Spence and others approached Will to become the secretary of their local farmers' union. The intense-looking young man with the big booming voice, but three or so years out of college, accepted his call to greatness. As secretary of the Prince Albert area farmers' union, he joined the growing movement to secure democracy in the North-West Territories.

CHAPTER 3
"RIEL'S SECRETARY," 1884–85

From his early boyhood, Will read voraciously: history, biography, and the great classical authors. He saw the struggle in the North-West Territories in much wider terms than did his English Canadian farm colleagues. Yes, the government in Ottawa impinged on their rights, but it threatened as well those of the original inhabitants. A young idealist, trained in the classics at the University of Toronto, brought up and encouraged by his parents to work for a better world, Will saw his moment emerging in 1884: he could act as a bridge between the Aboriginal peoples and the Canadian settlers in the northwest.

Early in 1884, Will learned of the Country-Born's plan to collaborate with the French Metis at the South Branch. At Lindsay School on May 6, three days after Will's twenty-third birthday, the Country-Born and the French Metis held a joint meeting. The Roman Catholic priests, the spiritual leaders of the French Metis, were not consulted. The participants decided to send secretly a delegation composed of three French Metis – Gabriel Dumont, Michel Dumas, and Moise Ouellette – joined by the Country-Born James Isbister to consult with Louis Riel in Montana.[1] A collection taken among the French Metis paid for the expenses of Dumont and Dumas. Ouellette travelled on his own, and the Country-Born and English Canadian settlers looked after Isbister.[2]

The initiative to bring Riel, the man who had forced the Canadian government to create the Province of Manitoba, back to Canada came from both Country-Born and French Metis. The English translation of the document the four delegates took to Riel best summarizes their grievances. It began, "We, the French and English natives, being convinced that the government of Canada has taken possession of the North-West Territories without the consent of the natives, [make several demands]." These demands included their "right of being represented in the North-West council, based on the native population living here." They called for title (patent) to the lands they possessed and occupied at the time, "without any prejudice to any more grants to which they are entitled for the extinction of their indian title to the lands of the North-West." They also requested government jobs connected with "the management of the Indians' affairs such as Indian agents, Instructorships or other offices for the benefit of the Indians in the North West Territories." Then came a salvo against the Hudson's Bay Company: "that the French and English natives of the North-West having never recognized any right to the lands of this North-West assumed by the Hudson's Bay Company or by the Dominion Government, claim an exclusive right to those lands along with the Indians."[3]

Louis Riel, about 1879. Photographer, A.J. Owen, Keesville, New York, Glenbow Archives/NA-504–3.

Much had happened in Riel's life since the Canadian military expedition reached the Red River in August 1870. The president of the provisional government, held responsible for the execution of Thomas Scott, had been forced to flee his homeland. In exile in the United States in the mid-1870s, Riel became convinced that the Holy Spirit had appointed him the "Prophet of the New World." Greatly upset, his relatives in Montreal had him committed to insane asylums in

Quebec. While under medical care for almost two years, Riel further evolved his ideas of the Metis as "the second Chosen People." His self-imposed task became to purify Catholicism.[4]

Eventually Riel realized that, by keeping silent on his religious revelations, the authorities believed he had recovered his sanity. He gained his release in early 1878, travelling later that year to the American Midwest, eventually relocating to Metis communities farther west. In Montana, he met and married Marguerite Monet, a young Metis woman, and began a family. In June 1884, the delegation from the Saskatchewan River Valley found him at St. Peter's Mission on the Sun River, where he worked as a teacher. Once he learned why they had come, Riel accepted their invitation to return with them to the South Branch with his wife and two small children. But at this stage he kept his religious ideas to himself. The delegation had come for the Riel of 1869–70, but unknowingly they brought back with them a totally transformed individual who believed that he was the "Prophet of the New World."

As soon as Riel arrived in the South Branch in early July, Will rode out to meet him. Charles Nolin and Maxime Lépine later recalled how the young man talked all night with Riel in Nolin's large house in St. Louis.[5] The Metis leader impressed Will as a skilled politician and a man of extraordinary religious faith and piety. As did Father Fourmond, one of the Metis' priests, Will saw how the Metis, many of them originally from the Red River, viewed Riel. They saw him, in the words of Father Fourmond, as their Joshua, their own prophet.[6]

Initially Riel emphasized a moderate constitutional approach, and he refrained from mentioning his new religion. On July 11, Riel, with several leading South Branch Metis, met the Country-Born and some English-speaking settlers at Lindsay School at Red Deer Hill. His statement to the jury at his trial on August 1, 1885 conveys well his initial impressions of his first days back in Canada:

> When I came into the North-West in July, the first of July 1884, I found the Indians suffering. I found the half-breeds eating the rotten pork of the Hudson Bay Company and getting sick and weak every day. Although a half-breed, and having no pretension

> to help the whites, I also paid attention to them. I saw they were deprived of responsible government, I saw that they were deprived of their public liberties. I remembered that half-breed meant white and Indian and while I paid attention to the suffering Indians and the half-breeds I remembered that the greatest part of my heart and blood was white and I have directed my attention to help the Indian, to help the half-breeds and to help the whites to the best of my ability.[7]

At Lindsay School, Riel proved much more calm and balanced than other speakers, such as Thomas Scott and Will Jackson himself.[8] Riel so pleased his audience of several hundred that a group of English Canadians requested him to speak next in Prince Albert. At first, he refused, but on receiving an invitation signed by over eighty individuals[9] Riel went and spoke on July 19 at Jimmy Treston's Hall, which he filled.[10] As he had at Lindsay School, Will acted as the secretary of the meeting.[11]

After the very successful gathering, Will invited Riel over to their place for tea. The family lived on River Street above Eastwood's pharmacy and store. Years later Cicely recalled their famous visitor as "fine looking, well built, broad shouldered, about five feet ten inches in height." His English, which he spoke with a slight French accent, was good. "He had not the appearance of a Metis," she added. Later Cicely saw him again, as "on three or four occasions Riel came to our place and the petition was written and re-written several times after my brother had visited different settlements to get the views of the people and their signatures."[12]

Will Jackson, the enthusiastic and energetic secretary of the Settlers Union, became Riel's link with the English-speaking settlers. On behalf of the allied Settlers Union and the French Metis, he drafted messages and letters and prepared a major petition to Ottawa. Will frequently went out to the French Metis settlements up the South Saskatchewan. In the words of Riel's biographer, George F.G. Stanley, "If not formally, at least unofficially, he became Louis Riel's secretary."[13] On July 28, Will summarized the aims of the Settlers Union alliance with the French Metis in a clearly written manifesto to the inhabitants of Prince Albert: "We are starting a movement in this settlement with a view to attaining Provincial Legislatures for the North West Territories, and, if possible, the control of our own resources, that we may build our interests rather than those of the Eastern Provinces. We are preparing a statement of our case to send to Ottawa."[14]

The Toronto *Daily Mail,* a conservative paper, later carried this reference to Will in the summer of 1884, one that rings true:

> Young Jackson used to travel about a great deal. If he saw a settler working in a field, he would climb the fence and sit down beside him for a while, till he sounded him. If he found that he was a Tory he generally gave it up; many Tories, in fact, chased him away from their premises. But if the settler was a Reformer, or if he was not much of anything, then Jackson preached to him of the frightful tyranny of the Government, and showed that agitation was the only recourse.[15]

Together Riel and his "secretary" prepared the drafts of their petitions in the South Branch. In their councils with discontented First Nations leaders, such as Chief Beardy and other chiefs near Duck Lake,[16] Will discovered additional injustices. Angry First Nations people told Riel that "The Government sent to us those [who] think themselves men. They bring everything crooked. They take our lands, they sell them and they buy themselves fine coats ... They have no honesty."[17] The speeches made a profound impression on Will. Later he wrote of Riel, "The oppression of the aboriginals has been the crying sin of the white race in America and they have at last found a voice."[18]

On August 18, Riel, his close associate Maxime Lépine, and Will met in Prince Albert with Chief Big Bear and two of his warriors at the Jackson apartment.[19] Contrary to his name, Cicely recalled that there was nothing physically big about the legendary Plains Cree chief. Big Bear refused to sign Treaty Number Six in 1876 for six years, until the starvation caused by the demise of the buffalo herds forced him to relent. Cicely recalled him as "a gaunt, rather small, old man of

Maxime Lépine. Archives of Manitoba/N10909.

Big Bear. Library and Archives Canada/C-1873.

about sixty with a deeply seamed face." Years later she remembered vividly the visit, even how the First Nations people ascended the stairs and their reaction on seeing the view from the second storey.

> The Indians came up very carefully, putting each foot sideways on the step. I opened the dining room door for them to enter. This room was about twelve feet square with two rather large windows overlooking the street and river. The door was in the corner of the side facing the windows and from it the river had the appearance of flowing immediately under them. The three Indians stopped short for a moment at the sight of the river and then, turning sharply along the side of the room, stood in the corner as far from the windows as possible. They were evidently not used to upper rooms. I offered them chairs but they preferred to stand.[20]

When Big Bear talked, Lépine translated his Cree into English and then Riel's English into Cree. Neither Big Bear nor the two warriors looked at Cicely, who remained in the room. She later recalled the gist of what she had heard. "The Chief said that he had heard that a petition was being sent to the Great Queen and the Indians had requests to make too. Buffalo were gone and they were starving. The Great White Mother had promised them provisions when game was scarce. They had asked the government at Ottawa for food but her people did not do as the queen told them."[21] Eastwood Jackson was also present with his sister and brother. He later stated that "Big Bear during the conversation complained that the conditions of the treaty had been violated by the Dominion government. He expressed his confidence that when the half breeds had secured their rights, they would assist the Indians to obtain theirs."[22]

Will immediately made his commitment to the First Nations known. On September 1, at a meeting at St. Laurent, he told those present that the North-West Territories really belonged to the First Nations and not to the Dominion of Canada. Both James Isbister and Thomas Scott attended. By identifying the land as belonging to the First Nations and not mentioning the Metis, Will unknowingly antagonized individuals such as Gabriel Dumont, for the French Metis, as well as the Plains Cree, presented themselves as the Aboriginal inhabitants. The legendary chief of the Metis plains hunters spoke six First Nations languages, as well as French, but only a few words of English.[23] This hardened warrior advised young Metis in battle, "Don't be afraid of the bullets, they won't hurt you."[24] Dumont was not fond of the Cree, having once clashed with Big Bear on a buffalo-hunting expedition and actually jabbed the chief in the stomach with the butt of his rifle, adding to the existing rift. To Big Bear, the Metis in the last days of the great buffalo herds were interlopers living off Cree buffalo.[25]

Will's support of Riel's attempt to extend the alliance of farmers and Metis to the First Nations proved unpopular with many settlers, who mistrusted them. The newly arrived settlers still remembered the "Minnesota Massacre" of 1862 in which five hundred non-Natives died at the hands of the Sioux. They also had even fresher memories of the "massacre" in 1876 of General George Armstrong Custer and 225 men at the Battle of Little Big Horn. They feared the encouragement of a Native uprising. The editor of the *Prince Albert Times,* who in May 1884 gave strong support to the campaign to secure western settlers' rights, switched by the early fall to a position of solid support for the government.[26] Money talks. Edgar Dewdney, lieutenant-governor

The North-West Council in 1885. Left to right, front row, Judge Hugh John Richardson (the judge in Will Jackson's trial, July 24, 1885), and immediately to the right Lieutenant-Governor Edgar Dewdney. Back row, second from right, Frank Oliver. Glenbow Archives/ NA-354–21.

of the North-West Territories, influenced the paper's about-face. He extended government patronage to the necessitous publisher.[27]

Frank Oliver, then a young Fort Edmonton politician, read the popular mood correctly. He had talked very tough in the beginning. In the territorial legislature at Regina, he battled for responsible government, so determinedly he later maintained that most people in the capital looked upon him as "a red-shirted and flame-breathing anarchist."[28] He wrote in his paper, the *Edmonton Bulletin,* on February 22, 1884, "If history is to be taken as a guide, what could be plainer than that without rebellion the people of the North-West need expect nothing, while with rebellion, successful or otherwise, they may reasonably expect to get their rights."[29]

Oliver's ardour for rebellion quickly cooled. By the fall, Oliver was aware that many settlers had expressed concern about a possible Native uprising and remained suspicious of the Metis leader. Oliver advised Will on October 22, 1884 to keep his distance: "A word privately about Riel, he may be a man of the greatest influence and the most high minded patriotism but he is political dynamite, or may be a political boomerang, in endorsing Riel you will be held up as endorsing his whole course and your enemies will have thus put in their hands the best possible weapon they can have against you."[30]

Will responded totally differently: instead of abandoning Riel, the young idealist bunkered in even deeper. He knew that the Mounted Police monitored his movements. On August 10, Sergeant Brooks, stationed opposite Batoche, wrote to Inspector Crozier that Will Jackson "seems to be a right hand man of Riel ... He has a great deal to say and I believe he does more harm than any Breed among them."[31] Will suspected that the NWMP even checked through his mail.[32] On September 29, Riel wrote to Eastwood Jackson, "rumors of pretty good source are getting afloat that the police are watching an opportunity to lay their hands on your brother ... If your brother finds himself unsafe, tell him that the french Halfbreeds invite him to come and remain this way amongst us. And if we are to be arrested, we will be together."[33] Will took up Riel's offer in the late fall.

Will relocated to what was known as the South Branch, thirty miles or so southwest of Prince Albert, to Batoche and neighbouring St. Laurent, situated along the picturesque banks of "la Fourche des Gros Ventres" (South Saskatchewan River).[34] "The Métis community of the South Branch," Diane Payment has written, "was in some ways an extension of the Red River Settlement and the early Manitoba experience."[35] The settlement straddled both the district's main road, the Carlton Trail, and the South Saskatchewan River, the main water route. In 1884, the French Metis recognized as their own territory all the land along the east side of the South Branch of the Saskatchewan River from Tourond's Coulee (Fish Creek) in the south to St. Louis in the north, a distance of about twenty-five miles.[36]

By mid-1884, the South Branch Metis population was estimated to be 1,300 people, over eighty percent of them originally from Manitoba. The remainder were born in what had become in 1870 the North-West Territories. The settlements included St. Laurent, Batoche, Fish Creek (Coulée des Tourond), Duck Lake, and the "Boucher settlement" (St. Louis). Until the demise of the buffalo herds on the Canadian side of the border in 1879, the people of the South Branch had been primarily buffalo hunters. Now most sought their living as hunters, gatherers, freighters, and farmers.[37]

Apparently South Branch Metis liked *l'anglais* ("the English man"), as their French Canadian relatives called all English-speaking Canadians, for they accepted Will among them. Louis Schmidt, Riel's secretary during the earlier Red River Resistance, but then living in Saskatchewan, has left a vivid word picture of Will among the French Metis: "Jackson was a young English Canadian from Prince Albert, very impassioned, but very well informed on many subjects. He took fire ('Il fut feu et flames') with Riel's arrival, and immediately followed him, going to all the meetings where he made long speeches. In the end he came to live amongst the Métis."[38] Michel Dumas, one of Riel's close associates, had been educated in French and English[39] and became Will's friend.

The French Metis welcomed English-speaking people who came among them without pretensions. Intermarriage had long before integrated families with the names of Ferguson, Fisher, and Ross into Metis society.[40] This individual from Prince Albert, English speaking and Protestant, impressed them. Philippe Garnot, a French Canadian who lived in the area, later reported, "As Jackson had acquired the reputation of being the best-educated man in the country, everyone greatly respected his opinion."[41]

The admiration was mutual. For Will, the French Metis world that he now entered was as remote as could be imagined. He was fresh and receptive to his new experiences. Apart from a large merchant such as François-Xavier Letendre *dit* Batoche, and the influential Metis politician and farmer Charles Nolin, both of whom had built large homes for themselves, the people at St. Laurent and Batoche attached little importance to accumulating goods and possessions. "Custom required that anyone who had a good hunt or good harvest shared it with his family and friends."[42] For most, sharing not profiting was the goal. The young romantic saw in the South Branch Metis the ancient freedom-loving Greeks whom he so admired, men and women willing to follow "a just and simple way of life."[43] Fur trader Alexander Ross wrote of the Red River Metis in *The Red River Settlement* (1856) that "They cherish freedom as they cherish life."[44]

But there was more to Will's attraction to the Metis than their intense individualism. The young man of twenty-three had a love interest at St. Laurent. Alexander Ross described young Red River Metis women as "slender, still more so than the men, but exceedingly well-featured and comely."[45] At the St. Laurent settlement, Will fell in love with Rose Ouellette, whose nickname was "La Rose,"[46] the sixteen-year-old daughter of Moise and Isabelle Dumont Ouellette, a sister of Gabriel Dumont. The Ouellettes had a family of eleven children.[47] Rose was born in Red River, at St. Norbert, in 1868, six years before her parents moved from Manitoba to the South Saskatchewan River Valley.[48] At sixteen, she was considered to be of a marriageable age, early marriages being the custom of the times in the North-West Territories.[49] Moise, then in his midforties, had been one of the three men who had travelled south with his brother-in-law to bring Riel back to Saskatchewan in June 1884.

The Ouellettes had a crowded household, for Moise's parents also lived with the family. After November 8, possibly in the same dwelling, resided as well the Riels: Louis, Marguerite, Jean (just two), and Marie Angélique, less than a year old.[50] The Riels remained with the Ouellettes until the outbreak of the rebellion.[51] This crowded home, or more likely a second home near the main farmhouse,[52] also housed Will while he was in the St. Laurent/Batoche area.[53] It was a warm dwelling in the late fall and winter; unlike the English Canadian settlers, the Metis knew how to build for their environment.

Rose's parents liked Will a great deal. Moise was a very good friend of Will's.[54] When Rose's sister married Joseph Bremner, on November 24, 1884, Moise asked Will to sign the registry as one of the two witnesses. The name "William Henri Jackson" appears in the registry book.[55] Times were tough for the South Branch Metis at this time, and the Bremner and Ouellette families could not sponsor a real Red River–style wedding, with eating, drinking, and dancing, with festivities going on with "unabated vigor and joyous hilarity for three days and three nights."[56] But the fiddling and dancing went on all night after the wedding.[57]

Moise and Isabelle's house guest, Louis Riel, also appreciated Will greatly. The Metis leader wrote in his journal this prayer: "We thank You, through Jesus, Mary and Joseph, for having watched over the following people until now, and we beg You through Jesus, Mary and Joseph to take care of them always, if You please: my friend William Henry Jackson, whom I have chosen as a special friend, and all his well-meaning followers."[58]

Rose's grandfather, José Ouellette, proved not so friendly. He disliked greatly *les anglais.* In fact, he believed that the Canadian government had stolen the land it owed him in Manitoba. He left there as a refugee from what had become a hostile land.[59] During the last day of the siege of Batoche, May 12, 1885, Dumont urged old Ouellette to fall back with the rest of the defenders to a more strategic defence point. He refused to move. Several times Dumont said to him, "Father, we must retreat." To which the nonagenarian replied, "Wait a minute! I want to kill another Englishman." Then José was hit and fatally injured.[60]

Gabriel Dumont in 1887. Coll Mallet, Union Saint-Jean Baptiste, Woonsocket, Rhode Island, US

Through the Ouellette family's kindness, Will entered into a different culture. The Protestant newcomer from Ontario discovered an original and vital people. The work of historian Diane Payment allows us to describe life in the South Branch in the late nineteenth and early twentieth centuries. In the late 1970s and early 1980s, she conducted extensive interviews with eighteen women elders born between 1886 and 1919. As she writes, "The testimonies of the women at Batoche suggest a predominance of French-Canadian tradition in their music and lifestyle, but a syncretism of Cree and Canadien is illustrated in their language, mentality, religious beliefs, and other cultural traditions."[61]

Allons, mon frére – allons manger! (Let's go, my brother, let's eat!). In terms of what they ate, the bicultural Metis took from both their French Canadian and Aboriginal backgrounds. The women made the Quebec specialties such as the savoury meat pie called *la tourtière,* a type of dumplings (*les glissantes*), and meatballs (*les boulettes*). They also prepared Native dishes such as the stew called *le rababou,* pemmican (*pemikan*), and bannock (*la galette*), unleavened bread.[62] Will loved bannock.[63]

Only with difficulty could he communicate with many South Branch Metis, as he only had Ontario school French, and the main language of the plains hunters was "Michif." Linguist Peter Bakker describes the Michif language as half Cree and half French. "It is a mixed language, drawing its verbs and associated grammar from Cree and its nouns and associated grammar from Michif-French. The Saulteaux language contributes some verbs, sounds and nouns to the mixture."[64] Since most children stayed in school only for a few years, they neither spoke nor wrote French or English fluently.[65] But Rose Ouellette probably spoke some French. It is known that her dad, one of the leading men in the South Branch,[66] greatly valued education; in fact, he and Pierre Landry had sent a petition to the Council of the North-West Territories in 1877 to request support for a school at St. Laurent.[67]

Will soon discovered that, appearances aside, the South Branch was not by any means an idyllic, peaceful world. Underneath the surface, a power struggle had begun between Riel and the men in black cassocks. Father Alexis André, a Breton, robust, thickset, and possessing muscles of steel, was the South Saskatchewan River Metis' Roman Catholic guide. Courageous and a good equestrian, he had accompanied the Metis on buffalo hunts. Firm in his manner, he knew how to impose obedience to religious observance, and every morning Holy Mass was offered and prayers said.[68] He had founded the mission of St. Laurent in 1871. Occasionally he had served as the spokesperson for the Metis in exchanges with the Canadian government, arguing for the registration of Metis lands in long strips with a narrow river frontage rather than into square townships.[69] By the end of 1884 Ottawa had still not responded to the petitions. In the mid-1880s, he continued as the superior of the district, with several priests – Father Fourmond at St. Laurent, Father Végreville at St. Louis, and Father Moulin, who served the new community of Batoche, founded in 1883, immediately east of St. Laurent.

At first, the priests believed Riel when he stated that he humbly accepted their religious authority. But soon they had contrary evidence. After the Bremner-Ouellette wedding, for example, Father Végreville stayed the night at the Ouellettes. The next morning Riel, also a house guest, vehemently began to attack the federal government, calling for a resistance against it as the only solution. He then implied that the priests and bishops loved money instead of imitating the apostles by living simply and supporting themselves. After additional attacks in early December, Father André laid down the law and told Riel that the Oblates now regarded him as an enemy. Only by bursting into tears, falling on his knees, and begging forgiveness did Riel escape being excluded from the sacraments. Végreville regarded him as *le pauvre fou* (the crazy person).[70]

Father André. Library and Archives Canada/C-28538.

This was the background against which Riel and his young Ontarian secretary, but four years or so removed from the University of Toronto, prepared the last draft of their petition to the governor general of Canada. As Louis stood and delivered his thoughts, Will jotted them down.[71] On December 16, Will, "Secretary, General Committee," sent the petition to Adolphe Chapleau, secretary of state for Canada. The document first emphasized the First Nations' condition, "so reduced that the settlers in many localities are compelled to furnish them with food, partly to prevent them from dying at their door, partly to preserve the peace of the Territory." The document then recalled the still unfulfilled promise to the Metis in the North-West Territories that they would receive 240 acres of land each, just like the Manitoba Metis had. Finally, the petition included requests on behalf of the 60,000 settlers in the North-West Territories: for provincial status, for representation in the federal Parliament and cabinet, and for complete control over the territories' natural resources.[72]

Encouraged by a perfunctory note from Ottawa a few weeks later acknowledging the petition's safe arrival,[73] Will immediately began preparing the additional documents, including a Bill of Rights. His brother Eastwood later provided the best summary of his activities as secretary of the Settlers Union in early 1885:

> As secretary he was enthusiastic in the work of drawing up petitions, etc. studying the subject deeply, in search of a constitutional basis, and in so doing deprived himself of necessary rest. About the 14th of last February he had finished the work, and having obtained the signatures of the Canadian and English Halfbreed members of the committee on the petitions in their final forms, started for the French settlement where Riel resided, to obtain the signatures of the French Halfbreed members.[74]

Poor Will was operating in a minefield, particularly with Louis Riel, an increasingly suspicious and unpredictable individual. The first breakdown in their relationship came in mid-January 1885. Riel visited Prince Albert on January 14 and 15.[75] The Jacksons invited him for dinner. Cicely later recalled that she served roast beef, but the cold was so intense inside their second-storey apartment that the salt and pepper on the outside did not melt. Riel immediately assumed that the Jacksons had tried to poison him. He rushed outside and made himself vomit.[76] From Charles Nolin, Louis Schmidt later learned Riel's version of the "poisoning." Schmidt added that hallucinations like this were becoming common with Riel, even at the Ouellettes. Riel sometimes imagined that there were people outside who wished to assassinate him.[77]

The second incident between Riel and his "secretary" occurred over Aboriginal rights. Will wrote to a correspondent on February 2, 1885:

> Let this be our aim. Let us sink all distinction of race and religion. Let the white man delight in seeing the Indian helped forward to fill his place as a producer of wealth, and let the Indian and Halfbreed scorn to charge a rent for the soil which God has given to man, upon the settler who comes in to help to build up the country and increase its public funds by his arts and machinery, and let us both unite in seeing that the fur country

be managed for the benefit of the Indians who live by hunting not for the good of a grasping company.[78]

Father Fourmond. Provincial Archives of Alberta/OB.2960.

Will believed in short that, although justice must be extended to the original peoples, at the same time Europeans had a right to come to North America. "Why," he added to his correspondent, "should God give a whole continent to 40,000 Indians and coop up 40,000,000 Englishmen in one little island?"[79]

Upon Will's return to the South Branch in mid-February, this issue led to heated discussion with Riel. All night, if we are to believe Eastwood, the Metis leader chastised him for his views on Aboriginal land rights. In a letter written on September 19, 1885, Will gave his account of what occurred. Riel believed, in his secretary's words, "that *every* nation is allotted its means of existence in the shape of a *land*." Will did not agree: "The main difficulty to my mind was that while the land of Canaan was specifically allotted to the Israelites the boundaries of other countries seemed to be determined simply by the ever-varying strength of the inhabitant peoples."[80] Riel refused to accept this view. According to Eastwood, the argument "became so fierce that Riel lost his self-control, revealing his true character and his determination to break out into rebellion in order to gratify his desire for revenge against the Canadian people for his supposed wrongs, and after divulging so much had my brother watched lest he should escape and reveal his designs to the authorities."[81]

He wanted to work for peace between the French Metis and non-Natives. At a public meeting at Batoche on February 24, 1885, he announced his complete withdrawal from all political activity in order – then came the bombshell – to study to become a Roman Catholic. Father Fourmond had talked so little with Will on spiritual topics

General view of Batoche, July 14, 1891. Photo by Steele and Wing, Archives of Manitoba, Victor Acker Collection, 15.

that he incorrectly believed that the young English Canadian was a *zélé Anglican* (a zealous Anglican). He did not even know that he was Methodist.[82] That made no difference now, for after Will converted the priest embraced him, as "le jeune homme le plus instruit, le plus distingué de P-A."[83] ("The best educated, the most distinguished young man in Prince Albert").

A week later, at the English-speaking settlement of Halcro, immediately south of Prince Albert, Will repeated his announcement.[84] Two days later, on March 5, his father rushed to the South Branch to plead with him not to enter "the Romish Church."[85] Thomas Jackson's secret dream, in fact, was that the Methodist Church would send a missionary to convert the South Branch Metis to Protestantism,[86] not that his son adopt the Catholic faith. Thomas said directly to his son that his mother would die of grief if he did not return with him.[87] Eastwood wrote to Riel himself urging him to allow his brother to go immediately to Prince Albert with their father.[88] But Will refused to leave, even after his mother herself went to Batoche on March 17 to plead with him not to join the Catholic Church. She stayed up all night with him the eve before his baptism.[89]

The former Methodist was baptized "Joseph" on March 18, 1885. But he remained a Catholic only temporarily: a few days later he chose to adhere to Riel's new religion. Openly breaking with the priests, the

Metis leader now shared his revelations.[90] From what Will told George Orton, a doctor with the Canadian military expedition, immediately after his capture, he might have seen Riel's new doctrine as a sort of reformed Catholicism, similar in some respects to the Protestant faiths. When Orton asked him about Riel's religious ideas, Will replied, "He said that they were not in accordance with the Roman Catholic religion. He did not believe in many of their views, and thought that a good deal of idolatry had crept into the Church, and that he (Riel) had been commissioned by God to purify that Church."[91] The South Branch priests, seeing their model convert accept Riel's Faith, believed he had gone crazy.[92]

On the eve of the outbreak of the resistance, Will remained with the Metis, hoping to bring about a peaceful understanding between them and the settlers. He felt torn within, for "to one side I was allied by blood, to the other by ties of religion, friendship and concurrence in certain political views."[93] Unfortunately, like neutrals in most armed conflicts, he became the enemy of both sides. After the first clash at Duck Lake March 26, the Metis, doubting his loyalty in a fight against his own people, imprisoned him. After the fall of Batoche six weeks later, the Canadians in turn seized and held him prisoner. Will was taken by the Canadian troops to Prince Albert and placed in the small jail that contained thirty other prisoners. He was thrown into an eight-foot by ten-foot cell with five Metis; the cell had no chairs, tables, or beds, and the men slept on the vermin-infested floor with only a blanket.[94]

The stress of the following days, as well as that of the weeks that preceded his imprisonment, led to a mental breakdown. Cyril Greenland, a professor in the School of Social Work, Department of Psychiatry, McMaster University, and Dr. John Griffin, formerly the general director of the Canadian Mental Health Association, speculated in a 1978 article that "he probably suffered from some transient form of hysteria precipitated by physical exhaustion and intense religious and political excitement." Interestingly, they added, Riel's behaviour was equally erratic and violent. "Contemporary accounts," they noted, "leave no doubt that he was also in a state of acute emotional excitement combining fear, anger and exaltation."[95]

As Will left Batoche, he saw around him the farms laid to waste and the village in ruins. The sisters, the Faithful Companions of Jesus, who had run a school at St. Laurent, commented on the land around Batoche, one week after the troubles ended: "We crossed smiling prairies dotted with thousands of flowers but covered with the remains of horses and cows that had been killed by the cannon. The numerous houses that formerly bordered the road had disappeared. All that remained of them was a pile of ashes and burned scrap-iron."[96] Will perhaps already knew that Rose's grandfather had died on the last day of the battle, and the Canadians held her father as a prisoner.

The trip to Regina as a prisoner was rough. Will went shackled to an old First Nations man in a heavy wagon without springs. One night the soldiers staked him out on the ground on his back, his arms so tied that he could not touch his face, preventing him from protecting himself from the swarms of mosquitoes hovering over him. They told him that he was going to be hanged in Regina.[97] What sustained Will? The idea that he would have a state trial, a chance to defend his and Riel's actions, an opportunity to expose the total incompetence and maliciousness of John A. Macdonald's administration in the North-West Territories.

CHAPTER 4

THE TRIAL, THE LUNATIC ASYLUM, AND EXILE 1885–86

In the early afternoon of 24 July 1885, the North West Mounted Police escorted prisoner Will Jackson by wagon from his prison cell at the NWMP barracks to the courthouse. The two-mile-long journey over the open prairie underlined yet again in Will's mind the endless corruption of Prime Minister John A. Macdonald's political system. Will had no use for those who pillaged under the mask of politics. Three years earlier Lieutenant-Governor Edgar Dewdney had selected Pile o' Bones as the new capital of the North-West Territories. He and several friends shared a vested interest in the site. They held, in fact, a tract of 480 acres just west of Pile o' Bones, now renamed Regina in honour of Queen Victoria.[1] Dewdney sought to profit from the selection of this site.[2] Seizing the opportunity to enhance the value of his land, he located the lieutenant-governor's residence, the North-West Territorial Building, and the NWMP barracks close to his property.

The wagon carrying the accused with red-coated guards on each side moved along one of the infant community's main east-west roads, named Dewdney Avenue. Will saw no trees, and the grass was short and turning brown.[3] There were few people in sight until the party reached the district around the CPR station, which, despite Dewdney's best efforts to bring the centre closer to his land, remained the town's magnet, its commercial and residential centre. Probably fewer than

Arrival at the Court House, Regina, 1885. Library and Archives Canada/C-18091.

one thousand people lived in Regina in the summer of 1885.[4] Finally they pulled up before the two-storey courthouse, at the southeast corner of Victoria Square, directly south of the CPR station. In a public trial, Will wanted to reveal the "neglect, mismanagement, and betrayal of Northwest interests." Without mercy he would disclose, "the condition and prospects of the people of the Northwest after fifteen years of Ottawa misrule."[5] The man known as Riel's secretary saw himself not as a rebel but as a "peacemaker between the aboriginal & immigrant population of the North West."[6]

Viceregal representative Dewdney was a tall, good-looking man with bushy, mutton chop whiskers.[7] The well-bred Englishman, just months away from reaching half a century, had done well in British North America. Brian Titley, his biographer, regards him as "a representative of that class of adventurer who saw in the western frontier an unprecedented opportunity for self-aggrandizement."[8] Canada's most senior official in the North-West Territories,[9] had an "abiding passion for making money."[10]

After training as a civil engineer, Dewdney went to British Columbia from Britain. Finding work as a surveyor and road builder, he built the Dewdney Trail, the wagon road that ran from Hope to the Kootenay goldfields. After his successful election to the House of Commons in 1873, he allied himself with Macdonald. They became lifelong friends.[11] In 1879, the prime minister selected Dewdney as the

Indian commissioner for the North-West Territories, responsible for overseeing implementation of the treaties with the First Nations. Two years later Macdonald topped this by appointing his confidant lieutenant-governor as well. The dual appointment made Dewdney, "a virtual autocrat in the North-West."[12]

The *Manitoba Free Press,* the great Liberal Party paper of the west, had little respect for Edgar Dewdney. Just four months before his dual appointment, it wrote, "He has lost no opportunity of making money at the country's expense. His friends have got fat contracts, and he has profited accordingly. He has used the public money to enhance the value of his private property."[13] Frank Oliver, the Liberal member from Edmonton in the North-West Territorial Assembly, bluntly termed the decision to appoint Dewdney to these posts "a huge and costly mistake."[14] (Not that the Liberals could claim any greater virtue. Clifford Sifton, the most powerful western Canadian Liberal in the late 1890s, stated but ten years later, "I have lived among western people nearly all my life, and know their way of looking at things; and one of the principal ideas western men have is that it is right to take anything in sight provided nobody else is ahead of them."[15])

In late June 1885, the governor, or "Your Honour" as he was now addressed,[16] received a letter at Government House from Will Jackson, writing from a sparsely furnished cell in the neighbouring NWMP barracks. On June 27, Ottawa's viceregal representative passed a copy on to the prime minister: "My dear Sir John I enclose a copy of a letter received from Jackson who is one of the Rebels in gaol here – I think he is crazy."[17] Jackson proposed a meeting between Louis Riel, "assisted perhaps by Messrs. Ouellette, Nolin, Lepine & Champagne, with yourself and such other members of the council as may be appointed for that purpose – myself continuing to act as Mr. Riel's private secretary, or in whatever capacity might best further the interests of our combined movement." To allow them to do their work, Will sportingly added to his request that "Mr. Riel and myself be allowed a separate apartment for a few days and amply provided with writing materials and rations of eggs, milk and fruit while the others be dismissed peaceably to their respective homes. If the materials are provided I can myself attend to whatever services we may require in the

Edgar Dewdney, Lieutenant Governor of the North-West Territories. Glenbow Library and Archives/NA-4035–143.

way of cooking or washing." Then Will introduced the key proposal: "We would be open to receive visits from any of the authorities or members who might wish to discuss matters preliminary and in a very short time a general conference might be opened at which everything could be settled in detail so far as the North West is concerned."[18] Fresh, spontaneous, and imaginative, this letter represented the young Will Jackson at his best.

Dewdney had no intention of organizing a "general conference" on the federal government's conduct before and during the troubles of 1885. "Your Honour" had a road builder's mind, straight lines only. His job was to uphold the Conservative Party and its leader, which meant no consultation with "rebels." The lieutenant-governor already knew the approach to take with Jackson. Well before his trial began, he pronounced him "crazy."

Riel's trial began on July 20. It opened at 11 a.m. The lawyers in their black gowns and white ties sat at the barristers' table facing trial magistrate Hugh Richardson. The small brick building almost burst at its seams. In the confined quarters, the people mixed together in a blaze of colour: onlookers in dark coats, vests, and ties; NWMP officers in brilliant scarlet tunics; a scattering of their wives in their summer finery in the visitors' gallery. All suffered silently in the oppressive mid-July heat.[19]

After the preliminary procedures of the first day, the court met again at 10 a.m. the following day. Immediately the defence lawyers requested a month's adjournment to allow them to secure the presence of a lengthy list of witnesses. Judge Richardson summarily allowed them just one week. The court adjourned at 11:45 a.m., till July 28.

Profiting from this adjournment, the presiding magistrate now scheduled for July 24 he trial of "Riel's secretary," still isolated and held in solitary confinement[20] at the NWMP barracks.

Will's trial was scheduled to begin at 3 p.m.[21] that day. Will again wanted a state trial, one that would allow him to expose Ottawa's neglect of the settlers, the Metis, and First Nations. He would defend Riel and his followers. They were not, to use early-twenty-first-century parlance, "terrorists." They had serious grievances. Ottawa was responsible for the tragedy of Batoche.

For weeks, the accused man had mulled over what he would say. Perhaps he would call as a character witness someone like the well-respected Dr. A.E. Porter, the first medical doctor in Prince Albert. He had supported the petition of December 16, 1884. Years later Porter wrote of Will that he had "set forth the situation in a spirit of fairness and tempered sense. But the forces of ignorance of a local situation were too strong for the forces of reason that were behind the first settlers' petition."[22]

Down Will stepped from the wagon. Two guards escorted him into the courtroom. He defiantly kept his hat on his head.[23] At this point, he had no idea of the Crown's strategy for his trial, how it would proceed against him.[24]

The charge of "treason-felony" stood but one degree below that of "treason," which carried the death penalty. Judge Richardson gravely read the indictment, in all its solemn and imposing terminology, "That William Henry Jackson ... feloniously and wickedly did compass, imagine, and intend to deprive and depose our said Lady the Queen from the style, honor and royal name of the Imperial Crown of this realm."[25]

On the cusp of turning sixty, Richardson had come west nearly ten years earlier from Ottawa, where he had served as chief clerk of the Department of Justice. His appointment as one of the stipendiary magistrates for the North-West Territories brought him first to Battleford, then Regina, after its selection as the new territorial capital. Besides holding trials throughout the territories, he acted as legal adviser to Lieutenant-Governor Dewdney.[26] Richardson knew little about Aboriginal issues. In his sentencing of Big Bear, on September

25, 1885, for example, when the Plains Cree leader frequently said "when we owned the country," Richardson informed him that he was mistaken, that Queen Victoria and not the Indians had owned the land. Her Majesty, in fact, had allowed them to make use of it, permitting them to take for their reserves the "choicest portions of the country."[27]

The prisoner rose. In his big, booming, powerful voice, Will replied to the charge: "As far as responsibility of mine about what you call rebellion, I have always declared myself perfectly responsible, that is, to say, as Riel's secretary, and I wish to share his fate whatever that may be."[28] The rebellion was over. Batoche had fallen on May 12. Riel had surrendered on May 15. Poundmaker had turned himself over to the Canadians on May 26. Big Bear had given himself up on July 2. Yet Will Jackson refused to give way. He wanted a real trial, one in which he would expose the "incompetent, partial and unjust administration," which had placed immigrants under officials "unacquainted with their requirements," which had deprived Frenchmen of "the civil and political privileges guaranteed to their ancestors and themselves by the Treaty of Paris," which had "robbed" the Indians "of the rights of self-government appertaining to them from time immemorial."[29] Will also anticipated in subsequent trials serving as a witness in favour of other prisoners.[30] He still had no idea what had transpired between his distraught family and a government most reluctant to undergo any thorough examination of its administration of the North-West Territories.

Well before Will stepped into the courtroom, unknown to him, an understanding had emerged between the Crown and the defence. Both sides – his family, his defence counsel, the two doctors who had examined him, the prosecuting attorneys, and the officials of the Department of Justice – had agreed on the action to be taken. Will Jackson would not have his showcase trial, one in which he would reveal the real economic and political reasons for what the crown called the "North West Rebellion." Why? Because both the defence and the prosecution accepted that the prisoner, "Riel's secretary," was insane.

The Jackson family had called in Joseph McArthur from Winnipeg, where he now practised, to defend Will.[31] Fifteen years earlier, when Will and Eastwood had attended the Toronto Model School, they had

Leading South Branch Metis, in irons in Regina. Saskatchewan Archives Board/R-B714.

boarded with McArthur and Elmore Harris in the same rooming house. Immediately after Will spoke, McArthur stood and simply said eleven words: "I propose to answer, 'not guilty,' on the ground of insanity." Will's blood froze. That one word, "insanity," would prevent him from defending his actions and from serving as a witness in the trials of his friends. Then came the Crown's representative, B.B. Osler. The prosecuting attorney repeated the same detested word.[32] The final unexpected blow came with the appearance of the first witness.

The Crown called Eastwood Jackson forward to identify the handwriting of a note signed on March 23, 1885 by Riel, "per William Joseph Jackson private secretary." The short message sent to Metis relatives of Riel included this line: "Justice commands to take up arms, to the end that we may attain our common salvation." Eastwood identified the note as having been written by Will. Then Osler asked a second question: how did his brother William gain the name Joseph? Eastwood replied, "From the time he was christened in the Roman Catholic church he has been insane."[33]

NWMP Chief Surgeon Dr. Augustus Jukes and Dr. Robert Cotton, the local Regina doctor, who had also examined Will in Regina, both testified. Neither had any expertise in insanity. Neither spoke of Jackson's state of mind during the troubles at Batoche. As lawyer George R.D. Goulet has written, "An acquittal based on an insanity plea required proof that an accused was insane when the offence was committed, not at a later date."[34] Yet no detailed cross-examination of the witnesses about Will's state of mind in March 1885 followed.

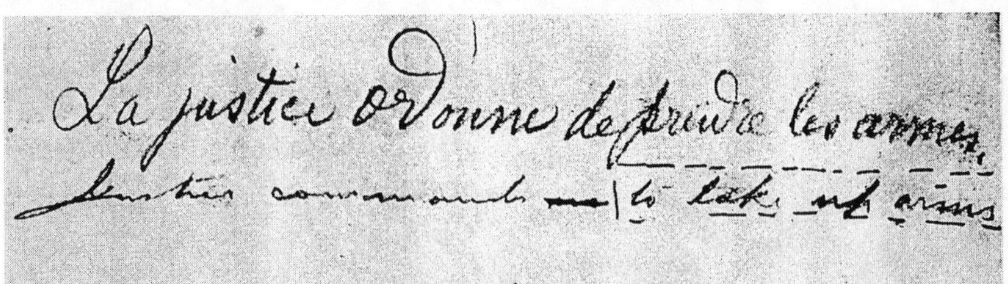

La justice ordonne de prendre les armes

Justice commands to take up arms

This manuscript reveals the degree of collaboration between Will Jackson and Louis Riel at the onset of the troubles of 1885. Riel composed the original French sentence, the translation of which is in Jackson's hand. Library and Archives Canada, RG 13 B2, vol. 814, p. 2327; reproduced in The Collected Writings of Louis Riel, 5 vols., ed. George F.G. Stanley (Edmonton: University of Alberta Press, 1985), 3, frontispiece.

Jukes mentioned in his testimony that Will's religious journey had not ended with Catholicism. In fact, Will had later accepted Riel's new religion, which "he thinks it is his duty to sustain."[35] This information confirmed the general opinion in the courtroom that Will Jackson had completely lost his mental equilibrium. Both Protestants and Catholics agreed on this issue. Protestants accepted that Will's espousal of Romanism, then his adherence to Rielism, provided conclusive evidence of his mental instability. Although Roman Catholics saw wisdom in his conversion to their faith, his later acceptance of Riel's heresy confirmed his insanity.

After hearing both the defence and the prosecution, Judge Richardson addressed the jury: "Are you satisfied he was insane at the time he committed the offence charged? Are you all agreed?"[36] Immediately the six-man jury announced its verdict: not guilty by reason of insanity. The trial in Regina of "Riel's secretary" lasted, from start to finish, just one hour. As the *Regina Leader* on July 25 tersely summarized, "Wm. Henry Jackson, charged with treason felony, tried to-day [actually it was the day before], was proved insane and sentenced to be kept in the guard room, Regina, during the pleasure of the Lieutenant-Governor."[37]

Eastwood visited Will immediately after the trial. He found him in a terrible state of mind. On account of his conversion to Catholicism, then his acceptance of Rielism, Eastwood was totally convinced of his brother's mental imbalance. Will's behaviour during this visit indicated that his serious mental illness continued.

How did Will regard the visit? He bore considerable resentment, even rage, against Eastwood. His brother's damaging testimony had eliminated the possibility of a public trial and the chance of testifying in the trials of his Metis friends. It took a week for Will to begin to calm down. When Eastwood returned on August 2, his brother finally seemed more composed. Eastwood wrote back to his parents and sister Cicely: "I saw Willie to-day and though his ideas are still unsound he is greatly improved. ..." He added, "he spoke more freely and looked better than I have seen him yet." Will even mentioned that "Riel attacked him and accused him of being his mortal enemy and of having tried to poison him (as he did me)." He also explained that at Batoche "he had opposed Riel's ideas amongst the Canadians and English halfbreeds but had not opposed Riel himself."[38]

A week later Will, in handcuffs, left the guardhouse at the NWMP barracks in Regina, dispatched by the lieutenant governor to his new home, the lunatic asylum at Lower Fort Garry north of Winnipeg.[39] The wagon sped past Dewdney's tract, along the west-east avenue that bore his name, past Dewdney's house and the council house where Dewdney presided over council meetings, to the CPR station. Under the lieutenant-governor's warrant, dated August 8, 1885, the authorities whisked Will away, under the category of "dangerous lunatic," to Selkirk, Manitoba.[40] Opened in 1884, the asylum in the "Old Stone Fort," as Lower Fort Garry was known, housed approximately thirty-five patients. The women resided in a building near the fort's west gate.

Witnesses in the trial of Louis Riel. Will's brother Eastwood appears standing at the far right. Glenbow Archives/NA-3205–10.

One of the most famous photos in Canadian history: Louis Riel addresses the jury in the Regina courtroom, late July 1885. Glenbow Archives/NA-1081–3.

The men lived in the fort's old three-storey warehouse.[41] The authorities placed Will in Ward 2, room P 92.[42]

The condition of the patients varied from mild disorders to the furiously disturbed and violent cases. Dr. David Young served as medical superintendent. He followed a humane policy, controlling any violent behaviour through persuasion and patience. Discipline was relatively relaxed. A delightful story throws a great deal of light on his administration of the institution. Young made this entry in his journal on May 25, 1885, two and a half months before Will arrived. He reported on the party held the previous day to celebrate Queen Victoria's birthday: "We had various games and dances with music during the day. In the evening those who wished went over to the female ward and danced from 7 p.m. to 9 p.m. Mr. C. made an oration, Mr. C. and W.R.J. sang songs. Ice cream, cake and lemonade being handed around they all retired after singing 'God Save the Queen' having enjoyed the evening very much."

A high wooden fence enclosed the grounds around the buildings, with the gates often left open. If a patient disappeared, Young contacted the Winnipeg police and sent out available staff to search.

Before Will's arrival, the institution had always found and brought back all who had left it.

Will made a good transition, as Young's diary indicates:

> August 29: improving but developing a good deal of stubbornness and disinclination to submit to rules.
> September 16: Refuses meals, says he is fasting on account of the position of Louis Riel.
> September 19: ... broke his fast this evening having eaten nothing since dinner on the 15th. Lost nine pounds in this time.[43]

The day Will ended his four-day fast, September 19, he wrote a long letter to his parents. His outlook appeared to be positive: "Mother must not trouble herself anymore about my lacking sleep – for I can both sleep soundly and eat heartily – both requirements being exceedingly well catered to in this establishment." Believing that the asylum authorities would keep him until the following spring, Will hoped "to make the most of the interval in improving myself in such directions as may be practicable." He asked his parents to send books and newspapers as well as his guitar, writing materials, and stamps. The books he requested included the Bible, Horace's poems, Plato's *Republic,* and the American economist Henry George's *Progress and Poverty.* The books were absolute necessities, "for the monotony of this place is enough to drive a man crazy of itself." He also requested a football "for leg exercises." The patient included other requests. He asked his parents to send ten-pound cases of white clover honey to Poundmaker, Big Bear, Moise Ouellette, and Maxime Lépine, all at Stony Mountain Penitentiary in Manitoba, and to Louis Riel, in the NWMP barracks at Regina. Then he added, "Whatever you do please look after Mrs. Riel & the children."[44]

In his letter, Will took great pains to explain why he had become a Catholic and then a follower of Riel's religion: "As you are aware from my letters and conversations of last March I had satisfied myself that the Roman Catholic rule of life was most accordant with the Sermon on the mount – that is church discipline and government were most conclusive to the restraint of believers to the path of duty indicated by

Will Jackson's bust of Riel. Parks Canada, Lower Fort Garry National Historic Park/ photo 3833.

that rule – that the invocation of the prayers of the Virgin Mary and of the saints was not idolatrous." After his conversion, he believed "that the besetting and inherited sin of Protestantism was dis-obedience and that the Pope and through him the priests must be obeyed at all costs as diversely gifted spiritual directors." Will also informed his family that, just prior to the battle at Duck Lake on March 26, he had accepted Riel as his "director of conscience," having received proof of his "supernatural power." On account of his acceptance of Catholicism, and then his selection of Riel as his spiritual director, he knew exactly where he stood: "My joining the Roman Catholic church has cut me off from the assistance of the Protestants while my adoption of Mr. Riel has lost me the countenance of the majority of Roman Catholics."[45]

In his letter of September 19, Will explained to his family that he liked Dr. Young and was not fasting on account of his or the attendants' behaviour toward him. He fasted because he feared that Riel might be executed. Regarding his continued incarceration in the asylum, he added, "I believe that the Doctor and most if not all the attendants would like to see me get away – but their position, as you are probably aware, is a somewhat peculiar one – it being a moot question not less among them than at Government headquarters as to whether whatever public advantage might be derived from my liberation would not be more than counter balanced by private disadvantages to themselves."[46]

His enforced sojourn in the mental hospital allowed Will to catch up on his reading and hobbies. While in the institution, he carved a

Cicely Jackson, Will's devoted sister. Courtesy of Miss Cicely Plaxton.

bust of Riel, which he presented to Young on October 17. He also practised playing the guitar. In light of his improved condition, the authorities allowed him to come and go as he pleased at Lower Fort Garry. On occasion, Will took long walks and stayed out late. The staff would impose a mild punishment, temporarily withdrawing his grounds privileges but always restoring them. The authorities believed his mental breakdown over.

Cicely Jackson, then studying in Winnipeg to become a teacher, visited Will in the early fall. She learned that in his walks away from the asylum "he had evidently been talking with the half breeds around and was well posted in every thing concerning Riel."[47] Increasingly Will felt that he must leave the institution to warn the settlers that they "were sleeping on a volcano. ... [S]ecurity can never come back to the Northwest again for if Mr. Riel is hung and the prisoners kept at Stony Mountain a bloody cruel war will result."[48] Two weeks before Riel's announced day of execution on November 16, Will decided to escape. On November 2, in the early afternoon, he walked away. Because he frequently left his room, his departure was not immediately reported to Young.

When the search for the absent inmate began, Will already had a considerable head start. They could not locate him. Young was not concerned; as he later explained,

> It may be as well to state here, since so much interest was taken in this case, that he was exactly on the same footing as any other patient in this Asylum. He was neither allowed more or fewer privileges than were granted to others who had shown by their conduct and mental improvement that they might be trusted

> outside the walls without an attendant. His escape was entirely due to the fact that more confidence was placed in his word than after events justified. As he was harmless and quite able to earn his own living no one had any interest in keeping him here except his friends, and they only that he might secure that treatment which they hoped would eventually lead to his complete restoration to health.[49]

Southward to the American border Will sped, toward Minnesota and Dakota Territories. For five days, he ate only some nuts and berries and a little flour. At night, he slept in the intense cold, without any overcoat, under railway crossings.[50] He entered the United States at St. Vincent, Minnesota, from where he sent a postal card stamped Monday, November 9, to his sister Cicely in Winnipeg. The note simply stated that "he had no money" and that "his feet were in a bad way." All he had for footgear were moccasins, now in tatters after his long journey.[51] From St. Vincent, he moved farther south. Another letter to Cicely dated about November 15 followed from Crookston, Minnesota. There Father de Carufel, a Roman Catholic priest, took him in "and tended his feet, gave him boots and fed him till he was able to travel."[52]

Riel's impending execution approached: November 16. Will wrote lawyer Joseph McArthur in Winnipeg on November 13 to say that he still firmly believed "in the divine mission of Louis Riel." Then he explained his intention "to go south and work for the cause of Riel & the Metis." At some point, he wanted to write an account "giving the inner history of the recent troubles." Then Will added an ominous note that "If Riel is finally executed I advise you to fast for a day before & three days after."[53] The same day he sent a telegram to John A. Macdonald warning him not to proceed with the execution of the condemned Indians scheduled to die at Battleford on November 27. As he pointed out, the First Nations did not regard the recent conflict as a rebellion;

> On the contrary they consider that the advantage in that respect lies with them as the aboriginal occupants of the soil – thence

> they regard Wandering Spirit & his companions, no less than Mr. Riel, as virtual prisoners of war – and their execution will consequently be remembered and avenged even more bitterly than would have been the execution of the prisoners held by the Indians & Metis prior to the battle of Batoche but whose lives were spared out of deference to a rule of civilized war which they feel ought now to be allowed to operate in their own favor.[54]

On November 14, Will again telegraphed Macdonald from Crookston, this time in French, to warn that Riel's death would only provoke a more dangerous and atrocious outbreak.[55] Another telegram to Macdonald followed, also in French, on November 15: "Commute all the sentences of the condemned to two years, and I will serve."[56]

The Canadians hung Riel in Regina the next day. (On November 27, 1885, Indian families from the surrounding reserves were brought to the Battleford barracks to witness the mass execution of the eight condemned warriors.[57])

On November 20, the *Crookston Herald* interviewed the fugitive. The *Herald* reporter described him as "a short, although well built man, who looked as if he had seen considerable rough usage." But despite his dishevelled appearance, he found Will "a man of intelligence," an individual "posted on all the important questions of the day."[58] Will's speech in the Crookston Opera House on November 25 on "Riel and the North West"[59] won the support of the *Herald,* which noted, "He was not eloquent but told his story with an earnestness that brought conviction."[60] One of the paper's readers went much further, noting, "They found the lecturer to be a scholar, a profound thinker and thoroughly versed in his subject."[61] At the meeting, the audience passed a resolution that Riel's execution was "the legal murder of a patriot and statesman."[62]

Will's reception in Crookston buoyed his spirits. Will thought again of Rose Ouellette. From Fargo, Dakota Territory, he wrote to a friend from the office of the *Argus* newspaper and mentioned "ma demoiselle La Rose Ouellette." He knew the burden that she carried:

her grandfather José had died defending Batoche, and her father had received a three-year sentence to Stony Mountain Penitentiary. Will had a proposal that he mentioned to his friend: "If I can make enough money I would like to pay her way at some good convent on this side of the line for a couple of years by which time I would be in a position to quit single life. In regard to my sister, I would like to pay her way also at some convent – preferably the same one, as I would like the two girls to learn to love one another."[63]

Will travelled next to neighbouring Fargo, Dakota Territory. Alas, there he did not receive as good a reception as he had in Crookston, the explanation offered for the poor turnout being that "It seems to be the general opinion here that a white man who is making an Indian of himself is unworthy of attention."[64] Generally his audiences at lectures remained small. The *Fergus Falls Journal* liked his talk, stating that his facts and arguments "made a deep impression on the auditors, and proved that Mr. Jackson knew what he was talking about."[65] Other talks followed in St. Paul and Minneapolis and in Chippewa Falls and Eau Claire, Wisconsin.[66] In Chippewa Falls, the *Times* praised "his ease, his eloquence and the thoroughness with which he explained the entire history of the Northwest."[67] In Eau Claire, the lumber magnates of that city refused to allow Will use of the YMCA hall. He termed them "pious frauds" and gave the address elsewhere. At the meeting, he made a very useful contact, Charlie James, who, impressed by his talk, gave him an introductory letter to Albert Parsons and other anarchist comrades in Chicago.[68]

In his lectures, Will stressed the constitutional side of the story. Riel, he argued, had "made the fight because it had to be made."[69] Had he been insane? Absolutely not, Will replied: "What was termed 'insanity' with him and Riel was their admiration of the Indian mode of living, that it was free from selfishness, and from the grasping for property and riches as among the whites."[70] Before his audiences in Dakota, Minnesota, Wisconsin, and Illinois, the visitor, in a tattered grey tweed suit with patches on the knees of his pants and moccasins on his feet,[71] defended Riel and called for the independence of the North-West Territories. But his lectures made him little money, and Will could not keep up his tour. In a letter home from Chicago on

January 24, he admitted his lack of financial success: "I find the expenses have eaten up the receipts so far."[72]

Will wrote to his parents using the stationery of "Peck Bros. & Co. Manufacturers of Fine Brass Goods for Water, Gas and Steam." He gave them the firm's mailing address as his contact point in Chicago. Oliver Peck, secretary of his company's Chicago office, had met him, possibly at one of his talks. What impressed the business leader the most about Will was his "absolute honesty of purpose."[73] He welcomed the political refugee from Canada as a house guest. Although obliged to leave on a business trip to Texas, he told Will that he could stay on at the house, if he wished, as Mrs. Peck and the servants would still be there.

Unfortunately, after Mr. Peck left, a serious problem developed, one that hints at the intense mental strain under which Will suffered as a result of his treatment as a prisoner at Batoche, his imprisonment by the Canadians, his trial, the lunatic asylum, his escape, his wanderings in Dakota, Minnesota, Wisconsin, and now his new arrival in the huge city of Chicago. As Oliver Peck later explained to Elizabeth Jackson, Will's mother, "It seems your son had a habit of walking up and down at night keeping up a rambling talk with himself and it so worked upon Mrs. Peck's nerves that she became frightened and wrote him a note politely asking him if he would not get quarters elsewhere." Will took great offence at this request and left in a huff. Two and a half months later the Pecks had not heard a word from him. Oliver explained all of this to Elizabeth, who contacted him in mid-March asking for the current address of her son.[74]

On March 16, 1886 came what should have been the grand moment of Will's American lecture tour. At Eau Claire, a Knights of Labor Assembly presented him with a travelling card, which allowed entry to Knights meetings.[75] The unionists welcomed to their city a close associate of Louis Riel. The Chicago labour movement knew of him and the resistance. Before the Metis leader's execution on November 16, 1885, eight hundred Chicagoans signed a petition appealing for remission of his death sentence.[76] *The Alarm,* the anarchist newspaper in Chicago, edited by Parsons, noted the Chicago memorial service to Riel in its issue of November 28, 1885. At the well-attended meeting,

August Spies, the editor of Chicago's *Arbeiter-Zeitung,* the leading German-language anarchist paper, directly referred to his "legal murder" and then added, "Louis Riel was strangled by the British government." In its report of Spies' talk, *The Alarm* cited his concluding remark: "He was not hanged because blood had been shed, but because he was a rebel against the existing order."[77]

The Knights of Labor put up nearly $200 to rent Chicago's huge Central Music Hall the evening of March 16, 1886. Situated in the business district on the southeast corner of Randolph and State streets, the Central Music Hall was Chicago's finest theatre.[78] The Knights advertised the talk as the "Anniversary Celebration of the Recent Northwestern Declaration of Independence. *Why We Fought; How We Fought; Why We Shall Fight Again.*" They introduced their speaker as "William H. Jackson, Private Sec'y of Louis David Riel and the Provisional Government of the Northwest."[79] The Knights had great expectations of an evening of tremendous labour solidarity for the executed Riel and the Metis people of the North-West Territories. Unfortunately they lost heavily on the evening. Few of the working poor could pay the admission charge of twenty-five cents at a time when the daily wage of an unskilled labourer came to only about a dollar.[80] Also, the inexperienced speaker proved disappointing. Carried away completely with his subject, Will addressed his small audience for nearly six hours.[81] All the points that he had originally planned to include in his Regina trial that never was must have been brought forward. But it was too much.

The *Chicago Inter-Ocean* noted its disappointment: "The lecture was a very full statement of the trouble between Canada and the half-breeds of the Northwest, but for a popular lecture it was at least four times too long."[82] The *Chicago Tribune* proved a tad more generous: "He is a man of medium stature, not graceful in appearance, nor very fluent in speech, but he says what he has to say in a natural and impressive style that chains the attention." The *Tribune* then added, "His dark complexion and high cheekbones would indicate his origin even to a stranger."[83] It thought that he was Metis.

CHAPTER 5

JACKSON BECOMES JAXON
1886–89

IN DAKOTA TERRITORY, MINNESOTA, WISCONSIN, AND THEN Illinois, Will experienced his first sense of distance from his past, not just physically but also mentally. Where no one knew him, he could reinvent himself and live a totally different life than the one he had lived in Canada. When people took him for "Indian," he accepted it. Gradually he realized that his relocation south of the forty-ninth parallel created an opportunity. He could shed his past and create a new identity, one that he could use to attract attention to his ideas for social justice. In the late 1880s in Chicago, Will dropped his English name for a French-sounding "Metis" replacement. He worked through several variations of his new title. William Henry Jackson first became William H.J. Jaxon or William H. Joseph Jaxon, then H. Joseph Jaxon, and finally Honoré Joseph Jaxon.

The Canadian in exile walked Chicago's long flat streets endlessly in January and February in the cold, inclement weather. Blasts of wind off the plains carried snowstorm after snowstorm.[1] The parks had no groves of trees like Queen's Park in Toronto. On account of the devastating fire of 1871, the city had a dearth of mature trees.[2] Apart from the Pecks, from whose home he had just hastily decamped, he knew no one and had almost no money in a bustling city dedicated to the god mammon. An English contemporary described it in this fashion: "An overhanging pall of smoke; streets filled with busy, quick-moving people; a vast aggregation of railways, vessels, and traffic of all kinds; and a paramount devotion to the Almighty Dollar are the prominent characteristics of Chicago."[3]

America's fastest-growing city had become the rail centre of the nation. In 1890, the metropolis stretched for miles and miles over the flat prairies spreading westward from Lake Michigan. Half a century earlier only one hundred people had lived here, in the middle of a stinking wild onion swamp at the foot of Lake Michigan. Now railways and steamships linked the industrializing northeast and the farm-frontier west, with Chicago at the centre. The city's population grew to 300,000 in 1871, to 500,000 in 1881, and to over one million ten years later. During the 1880s, Chicago's total population increased at a rate five times faster than that of New York City.[4] Almost everyone in the city was a newcomer. In 1890, nearly eighty percent of Chicagoans had been born abroad, most of them in Europe.[5]

No egalitarian paradise here: the economic inequality in Chicago as in other large North American cities in the Gilded Age – the phrase that Mark Twain and others used to term this age of excess[6] – was extreme. While the big meat packers such as Armour and Swift and merchants such as Marshall Field and Montgomery Ward made vast fortunes, working men toiled from dawn to dusk for a dollar, and women earned half as much, five cents an hour. The rich lived in mansions, the working poor in wretched and disease-ridden slums that lay just beyond the central business district. The immense influx of migrants greatly increased the congestion. Often, with the wrong winds, even on the Gold Coast on the lake, refuge of the wealthy and the powerful, the air smelled of the sweet, nauseating odour of death from the slaughterhouses.[7]

At first, Will lived on a dollar a week,[8] but by February his fortunes improved. He met local carpenters affiliated with the Knights of Labor who, with other Chicago unions, had just begun to organize their campaign for an eight-hour workday and an hourly wage of thirty cents. Chicago labour leaders formed the Eight Hour League in the fall of 1885. Labour held the ten-hour day responsible for the continual physical and emotional exhaustion of wage earners. By reducing hours by one-fifth, they could redirect energy to improving themselves and their social class.[9] On March 15, the very day before Will's big lecture in the Central Music Hall, labour leader R.C. Owens and others spoke at Turner Hall on West Twelfth Street about making eight hours a day's labour.[10]

The formation of a common labour front was difficult. A major line of demarcation existed between German-speaking immigrants from Central Europe (including Polish, Hungarian, and Czech artisans) and English speakers of immigrant background, such as the British and the Irish, who shared a common language with the native-born. Religious divisions between Protestant and Catholic added to the disunity.[11] By the end of the 1870s, two groups had emerged among trade unionists in Chicago. The first, the Knights of Labor, a workers' organization, with economic objectives, sought to unite skilled and unskilled, men and women, black and white. The second, more politically focused in their objectives, were the socialists in the Socialist Labor Party.[12] Yet both groups were not entirely separate, as some individuals had dual membership.[13] In 1884, a new group emerged, the International Working People's Association, a militant body dedicated to "agitation for the purpose of organization [and] organization for the purpose of rebellion."[14] The revolutionary socialists, or anarchists as they came to be known, made real inroads in the German-speaking community.[15] The anarchists had given up hope of finding a peaceful path to socialism through elections and legislative changes. They sought to liberate society from all state control, whether capitalist or socialist.[16] Some anarchists, such as August Spies and Albert and Lucy Parsons, indulged in "bomb talking" to frighten the authorities, but this was pure rhetoric since they never made and used explosives.[17] The anarchists became the new dynamic in working-class Chicago, the centre of the labour left in the United States in the late nineteenth century.

Almost two decades after his arrival in Chicago, Honoré Jaxon, as he was then known, recalled his first contact with the local labour movement. In a 1905 interview with the *Chicago Record-Herald,* he explained that he had come with the intention "to enlist sympathy for my people in the Northwest." But, he continued, "I found as soon as I arrived here that the people of the United States had troubles of their own – labor troubles which involved some of the same principles for which we had been fighting." Subsequently he had joined and become involved in the carpenters' union. Within three weeks, he added, they had appointed him secretary of their central council, with responsibility for carpenters' participation in the fight for the eight-hour day.[18]

Other sources collaborate much of Honoré's testimony given in this 1905 interview, but the date of his joining the carpenters' union was after the Haymarket incident of May 4, 1886, not before. A *Chicago Tribune* article of October 1, 1886 reported his involvement in the union: "He joined the Carpenters' Union, was soon elected to an office, and among the ignorant class he gathered about him he has become little less than a demi-god."[19] Will's letter of September 6, 1886, to Michel Dumas, a Metis friend from South Branch days, but then in exile in the western United States, confirms other essential details. But the Dumas letter places the timing of his appointment to head the carpenters' agitation a little later than what is implied in the 1905 interview, to June or so, not April. In short, Will became fully involved in the eight-hour-day struggle after the Haymarket tragedy of May4, 1886. Here is what he told Dumas on September 6:

> Ten or twelve weeks ago I was walking the streets of Chicago with only five cents in my pocket, dead broke, not knowing which way to turn, I entered a hall where a society of carpenters were discussing the eight hour agitation – they had a regularly organized central committee representing all the carpenters in the city but their ideas were confused & conflicting – I listened in silence; in the third meeting I began to speak, & in three weeks I was placed in full control of all the executive machinery.[20]

On May 1, or "Emancipation Day," one-third of a million labourers across the United States participated in a coordinated general strike for the eight-hour day.[21] In Chicago, the epicentre of the movement, anarchist August Spies led a parade of eighty thousand up Chicago's Michigan Avenue. Eighty-five thousand Chicago workers laid down their tools, part of a national strike of some three hundred thousand labourers. From rooftops, militia and Pinkerton agents watched the anarchist-led parade, with troops armed with Gatling guns, just in case.[22]

Many anticipated major labour unrest in Chicago after the day of protest. Armed conflict occurred two days later in a battle between police and workers at the McCormick Harvester plant. Police attacked and killed two strikers. On the evening of May 4, outraged workers demonstrated in downtown Chicago to protest police brutality at the McCormick plant. About 2,500 people gathered at Haymarket Square. All remained peaceful until the police tried to disperse the meeting, whose numbers had already begun to dwindle. Suddenly someone – no one knows who – threw a bomb into the ranks of the police. During the rioting that followed, seven police and four workers died, most of the deaths occurring when the police panicked and opened fire on the crowd, killing in the darkness several police constables as well as workers.[23]

The bomb blast triggered an avalanche of events. The next day Chicago's ultraconservative press called for revenge. Fear now enveloped the city. Chicago's press, business, and political leadership used Haymarket to discredit the labour movement. Police raided working-class neighbourhoods. In the panic that followed, the police arrested two hundred labour and socialist leaders. Without any proof, the authorities ruled that the bomb had been the work of anarchists, socialists, and communists.[24] Eight anarchists were subsequently held for trial, without any concrete evidence to prove that they had made or thrown the bomb – only three of the eight had attended the meeting.

One week after the Haymarket affair, the Carpenters Contractors Council reneged on its earlier acceptance of the eight-hour day. It declared its intention to return to ten hours per day.[25] At this inauspicious moment for Chicago labour, one of its darkest hours, Will Jackson provided hope. The newcomer from the North-West Territories organized a successful strike of carpenters for the eight-hour day. As he explained in the 1905 interview, once appointed to the task, which would have been after the Haymarket tragedy, he had sent volunteers to each ten-hour job site to learn who among the non-union ten-hour carpenters would support them and who would not. Having identified the obstructionists, he had advanced to the next stage.[26] He had organized two mass meetings, one for the English-speaking carpenters, the other for those speaking other languages. Well aware that detectives had planted themselves in the assembly halls, Will had given out false information of what would follow. Secretly his committee, in separate communication with each squad, had dispatched unarmed union carpenters to work sites across the city, always making sure to send them to locations distant from where they normally worked. To encourage the most persistent obstructionists to vacate the work sites, some squad members had used their fists, others had fired slingshots, with the projectiles "being aimed at those parts of a non-unionist's anatomy where no serious harm could result."[27]

The job action continued for six weeks. No non-unionist suffered injury worse than a few scratches.[28] As the incidents occurred simultaneously at different locations, the police could not act quickly enough to interfere.[29] Finally the smaller city contractors conceded the eight-hour day for carpenters. While the larger millmen-contractors still held out, at least a partial victory had been won.[30] Later, at a public meeting in 1893, Will, or Honoré as he was then known, proudly recalled that seven years earlier he had "headed up a gang of 800 strong men who knocked out the ten-hour 'scabs' in favor of an eight-hour movement."[31]

With his customary enthusiasm for a cause in which he believed, Will joined the struggle to save the eight Haymarket prisoners. The court convicted them in late August 1886 of inciting violence. It imposed a sentence of death by hanging for seven of the defendants, including Albert Parsons and August Spies, and a fifteen-year prison term for the eighth, Oscar Neebe. They had been tried for their ideas, not for any deeds. American historian Donald L. Miller has written, "It was perhaps the most dramatic trial in the history of American jurisprudence and easily one of the most unjust. In a sense, it was not a trial at all but a panicky prelude to a community lynching presided over by a judge, Joseph E. Gary, who allowed men on the jury, including the jury foreman – a salesman for Marshall Field – who were convinced the defendants were guilty."[32]

Supporters of the condemned arose even from among Chicago's business community. Lyman Gage, for instance, executive officer of the First National Bank of Chicago and future secretary of the treasury under President William McKinley, stepped forward with others to urge executive clemency for the condemned men.[33] The defenders of the condemned had no success whatsoever. Will himself was strongly convinced that they were innocent: "To that meeting Mrs. Parsons had her two little children – I know that no conspiracy was ever entered into on that occasion."[34]

Lucy Parsons. Labadie Collection, University of Michigan.

Lucy Parsons, the part African American, part Hispanic wife of Albert Parsons, began the fight to have the convictions overturned the very day the verdict was read. Will became the secretary of a new defence committee and signed, as secretary of the group, the appeal for funds for a new trial.[35] On October 21, 1886, he drew up the Anarchist Publishing Association articles of agreement and obtained the signatures of all eight of the prisoners to the agreement, the intention being to publish their speeches delivered "at the Haymarket and in the courtroom as revised and corrected by them."[36] Each of the convicted men had been called upon to speak in court in early October before sentence was pronounced. Their speeches lasted three days.[37]

Will visited the Haymarket defendants in jail; in fact, he had an opportunity to urge Albert Parsons to appeal for clemency to try to save his life. Two years later Jackson recounted what had happened. "Our late comrade reminded me that every reform had its martyrs. He felt as if he would rather die fighting for freedom than die a slave." "But," Will replied, "it is better to live and continue to fight for freedom than it is to die before you are free. Dead fighters could not fight. A dead martyr was not worth a —— as a warrior."[38]

Already before Haymarket, Parsons had suffered greatly for his political views, as Haymarket historian Paul Avrich writes: "He was cursed, hounded, pushed down stairs, and threatened with lynching. He saw innocent people clubbed and fired upon by the police, while the newspapers advocated the use of grenades and Gatling guns against those who agitated for better conditions."[39] Unlike the other seven, Parsons was native-born, a member of an old American family; the others had been born in Europe, six in Germany and one in England. Two prisoners, Samuel Fielden and Michael Schwab, eventually asked for mercy, and the governor of Illinois on November 10, the day before their scheduled executions, commuted their sentences to life imprisonment. But neither Albert Parsons, nor August Spies, nor George Engel, nor Adolph Fischer, nor Louis Lingg would ask for mercy. The twenty-one-year-old German American Lingg spoke little English, having arrived in the United States only in 1884.[40] In his address before his sentencing, Lingg made this defiant statement to the court: "I despise you. I despise your order; your laws, your force-propped authority. Hang me for it."[41]

On November 11, 1887, four of the condemned were hanged in the Cook County jail; the fifth, Lingg, had cheated the executioner the day before by biting down on a dynamite cap.

Will's relationship with the condemned and the radical anarchists in general was not entirely harmonious. Will had no tolerance for the violent, distorted form of anarchism, the promotion of senseless violence, the love of dynamite that an element of the movement promoted. The appeal of anarchism for Will came from its idealistic philosophy. He believed that society could exist without the state, capitalist or socialist, coercively enforcing rules of conduct. Wherever authority is asserted and self-expression limited, the anarchist reacts.[42] Will might best be called a philosophical anarchist.[43] He believed that the state, or any organization that he belonged to, had no right to tell him or anyone else how to behave. The anarchist ideals of mutual cooperation and anti-authoritarianism attracted him.

Very early in his Chicago years, the young idealist learned that the virtuous did not necessarily all stand on the same side. The German anarchists who initially supported his publication of the condemneds' speeches to the court after sentencing cheated him. In early December 1886, four individuals connected with Chicago's Central Labor Union wrote a letter to *The Knights of Labor* announcing that the Central Labor Union had revoked its approval of Will's participation in the publication of the speeches by the condemned anarchists.[44] A year later Will shared his bitter disappointment in a letter to his father on November 14, 1887; he wrote the letter shortly after the executions. Will explained that he had translated Louis Lingg's final statement to the court on October 8, 1886: "It is my translation of his speech in German at the time of passing sentence upon him which appears in the book containing their speeches. I myself prepared the greater part of the plates used in the book but the gang in control of the German element here swindled me out of the money & time I invested therein for the most part."[45]

Will had learned more about the treacherous waters of Chicago labour politics when the United Labor Party, an independent workers' party, was formed in late 1886, after the Haymarket tragedy. Strongly supported by German American workers, the socialists, with the Knights of Labor no longer in the ascendant, and the anarchists very much on the decline, took over the United Labor Party.[46] The Chicago Carpenters' Assembly of the Knights of Labor had sent Will as one of their delegates to an organizational conference in early January 1887. Although the American and the French groups in the conference supported him, the Germans did not.[47] Immediately the Carpenters' Assembly of the Knights of Labor protested against his rejection: "We have received your communication concerning our delegate to the United Labor conference, W.H. Jackson, and we are at a loss whether most to admire the audacity with which you have presumed to attempt the rejection of a man who we had distinctly informed you was the unanimous choice of our assembly, or to despise the petty prejudice and contracted understanding by which your audacity would appear to have been inspired."[48] Will was not admitted. Disenchanted, he cut back on his involvement in Chicago labour politics.

Information flowed on an irregular basis between Will and his parents. In early 1886, his father feared that Will was being persuaded to enter the Roman Catholic priesthood.[49] That concern was soon superseded by his mother's alarm about her son's idea of edifying literature. After Elizabeth learned the titles of the books "Willie" had suggested his sister Cicely read, she was horrified. She wrote to her daughter on December 30, 1886 that "the authors W recommended to you are atheistical and communist, they would need to be read with great caution." She continued: "Unless he keeps up a continual and prayerful reading of the Bible the books and men with whom he is associating cannot fail to do him harm if he has not got on the wrong track he is certainly walking very near to it."[50] Will added to his mother's concerns when he wrote on May 25, 1887 that he had not been "inside a church" for a long time.[51]

Economically Will's first years in Chicago proved very difficult. At one point in the summer of 1887, Will told Cicely that he "had to live [a] large part of the time on a 5 cent loaf per day and sleep out at nights."[52] He described this lifestyle in a letter to his father as living "like a coyote – bread and water and sleeping outdoors."[53]

Unfortunately Will's business ventures were marked by naiveté and ineptitude. In terms of business acumen, Will truly was his father's son. From conversations with her mother, Cicely Plaxton later learned about her grandfather as a merchant. Basically, whenever "someone came along with a sad story, he always gave them a handout – he couldn't say no. The only thing he didn't learn to do was make money."[54] Will also was too trusting. First several German American anarchists had cheated him (he claimed)[55] over the preparation of the Haymarket defendants' speeches. Then, toward the end of his first year in Chicago, an associate swindled him out of his "printing outfit."[56] And, during his third year in Chicago, his trusted office partner ran off before he had paid his share of the office rent.[57]

Very clever in a number of areas, Will had major deficits in other sectors. He had, for instance, considerable difficulty in focusing on one topic for a lengthy period. One of his ambitions was to write a history of Riel and the troubles in the North-West Territories. He told Michel Dumas as much in his letter of September 6, 1886: "I am intending to publish a book on the situation for the benefit of those whom I cannot address personally, and would be well to have our present-position *authoritatively set down and declared.*"[58] Brave words, but the book failed to come forward, over the next ten years, over the next half century.

In fairness, in regard to his history of 1885, probably Will realized that no market existed in the late 1880s for his book. The working class was interested, but would they purchase it? Could they read it? Child labour was still rampant in the United States. As August Spies said, "In this enlightened country the children of the wage-workers do not attend school in the average more than two years; they learn just enough to serve as a piece of organic machinery, and as such they are 'let out' to benevolent and Christian employers in their tenderest years."[59] And what interest was there among the ruling classes, who had the education and the leisure to read it? Oliver Peck, for instance, wrote to Will's mother in the spring of 1886: "We all think however he is wasting his time and undoubted talent upon this Reil [Riel] subject and is in fact a monomaniac upon the subject[.] Americans generally regard (whether rightly or not) Reil [Riel] as a troublesome pretender and fanatic and I dont think they are suficiently [sic] interested in the No. West troubles to furnish your boy with much financial success on that subject."[60]

Will spent an enormous amount of time on projects that interested him. Most were not connected with making money. Fortunately one of his projects did work out well for him, his membership in the Chicago committee of Credit Foncier, an American colonization company sponsoring a model communal settlement at Topolobampo Bay, Sinaloa, on the west coast of Mexico. For some time, Will discussed with Albert Kimsey Owen, the colony's leader at Topo, the possibility of his Metis compatriots settling there.[61] He liked the idea of a Metis relocation to Mexico, "as the Mexican Republic was in point of fact a kind of Half-breed Nation itself and similar to us in many things."[62]

Will's correspondence with Owen has survived. It provides a fascinating glimpse into his state of mind in the late 1880s. Being removed from all who once knew Will in western Canada, not always eating properly, having an incredibly vivid imagination, and being submerged in the hotbed of Chicago labour politics – all contributed to some rather incredible thinking. His belief that he was Metis took on a life of its own. In his introductory letter of April 4, 1888, Will reviewed the history of "my comrades in the North." No ambiguity at all about his own racial background: "A mixed race of the Aborigines and venturesome spirits from various European nations we have long held the *core* of the North American continent." His brief historical summary of the Canadian government's intrusions into their territory contained the plausible and the outrageous. His reference to William McDougall, the Canadian governor dispatched to the Red River in late 1869, belongs in the outrageous category. Correctly Jackson pointed out that McDougall was denied entry to the Metis homeland, but then he added, "We drove him out of our sight – and in his camp we found sketches of a plan to bring in the Chinese, mix them with our people and so form a Helot population to till the estates of Canadian absentee[s] carved out of our free country."[63] This reference to the Chinese, feared by Chicago trade unionists as cheap labour,[64] shows that limits existed to Will's universalism. The labour leaders of the day, while accepting the integration of virtually all other groups into the labour movement drew the line at the Chinese. They feared that vast numbers of Chinese immigrants would be a major impediment to organizing unions, and maintaining an American standard of living.[65]

This introductory letter of April 4, 1888 also contains undoubtedly factual material, in particular this reference to Batoche: "My own property was destroyed including a very valuable library of Greek and Latin classics which I had purchased from Cambridge while a student at Toronto University." But Will could not end there, instead concluding the sentence, after mentioning "Toronto University," "to which my father (a fur trader) had sent me in my youth."[66] While his father might have done a little trading for furs while in Wingham, the general store owner was not a full-time fur trader. Later, in Portage la Prairie around 1880, he had been engaged more directly in the fur trade, but at that point Will had left University College.

Will explained to Owen that he earned a living in construction. At the present time, he wrote, he worked "with my own hands building sidewalks and curb walls on contract (It would kill me to work for wages)."[67] He had bigger dreams, he added: "I am devoting my time mainly to architecture and Engineering having a tendency toward construction and a tolerable start in Mathematics."[68]

Owen, a utopian reformer, the visionary behind the cooperative community in Topolobampo, kept up his correspondence with his new "Metis" pen pal for about two years. The civil engineer dreamed of founding the perfect agricultural colony, based on cooperative principles. It was to be supplied by a railway from the United States, with entry at El Paso, across the Sierra Madres, to Topolobampo Bay. He envisioned that his perfect city, Topolobampo, would become a centre for Pacific trade, with the shortest rail link to the great American industrial cities.[69]

Will never went to Topolobampo, but he did benefit from his association with the group organizing the venture. The president of the Chicago committee of the scheme, a machinist, allowed him to use his office. With new business cards advertising his sidewalk and curb contracting, Will obtained work. He "got 50 cents worth of Business cards printed on credit – borrowed a square[,] saw[,] hammer[,] chalk line[,] level, crowbar and spade – and began placing bids as a 'Builder and contractor.'"[70]

In late 1888, Will decided upon a new career, and it was not architecture or engineering but something completely different, medicine. The first reference to a medical topic appears in his surviving correspondence in 1887. Will told Cicely in a letter on December 18, 1887 about the Hahnemann Medical College: "I have several lady friends attending there and they will all make big incomes when they come out."[71] He held back nothing in his notes home. His poor mother already struggled to keep up with all his activities in Chicago. Now Will reported on September 24, 1888 that he had just invested $85 of his $100 surplus into tuition and textbooks for the twenty-one-week courses at the homeopathic college. With his customary enthusiasm, he added, "The college has the reputation of being the best in the West – and I shall pay particular attention to surgery."[72]

Leaving his foreman in charge of the construction work of his curbs and sidewalks,[73] Will attended the full course, actually enjoying it. Chicago at the time was the centre for homeopathic medical

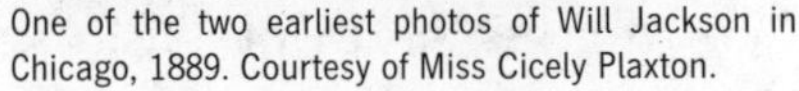

One of the two earliest photos of Will Jackson in Chicago, 1889. Courtesy of Miss Cicely Plaxton.

The second of the two earliest photos of Will Jackson in Chicago, 1889. Special Collections, University of Saskatchewan.

education in the United States. The school, founded in 1860, had become coeducational in 1871. Apart from its emphasis on homeopathic therapeutics, instruction at the college resembled that of Chicago's "regular" medical schools.[74] At first, surgery upset Will, but he soon left his squeamishness behind: "Believe me, the dissection-room ordeal is a mere bagatelle. After the first cut is made on a human body, all sensitiveness departs and the place simply becomes an ordinary butcher shop with the usual accompaniments of denuded joints and scraps of meat."[75] He hoped to receive his MD in the spring of 1890, the final session to begin on September 17, 1889.[76]

But Will did not finish his medical studies; new competition in the sidewalk contracting business cut into his revenues. In the fall of 1889, he wrote to his mother again to say that he still hoped to stay in the medical area but was not returning to the college that fall. He added this information in his letter of September 29, 1889: "Meantime I am located as a student in the house of a very clever lady physician with whom I have exceptional opportunities of studying gynecology clinically, and I am therefore making good head way with my studies." Life with Will was like trying to hold on to the tail of a kite in a full wind. As there are no further references to medical training in his surviving correspondence, it probably ended shortly after this.

Will did not tell his family his really big story, that he had changed his name and his race. He signed his letter addressed to his father, mother, Eastwood, and Cicely "Your loving son and brother." He did not inform them that in Chicago he was now William H. Joseph Jaxon. After the Chicago newspapers, in a case of mistaken identity, reported a William Jackson, a "half-breed" loafer, just expelled by the Knights of Labor in Chicago,[77] Will issued a clarification. The *Chicago Tribune* on April 10, 1889 published his letter, under the signature of "William H. Joseph Jaxon": "It being my lot to be a half-breed Indian and to fill the position of Secretary of the Metis Council, my surname is also being pronounced similarly to that of the alleged speaker, I am lead [sic] to believe that it was the intention of the paragrapher to identify me with him, to the disparagement of myself in particular and of my race in general."[78]

In many ways, his adoption of a new name in 1889, on top of his new race, proceeded logically from his arrival in Chicago in January 1886. While in the Prince Albert jail, Will wore a Metis headband in his cell.[79] In Chicago, he completed the physical transformation. He decorated his rented room as a Metis hunter's shack. At home, he began baking his own bannock.[80] When asked about his identity, he said Metis. Finally, in May 1889, he took the final step in his reinvention and called himself William H. Joseph Jaxon, which shortly afterward he shortened to H. Joseph Jaxon.[81] By 1891, he refined things a little more, signing his name Honoré Joseph Jaxon, the designation that he retained for the rest of his life. At this point, Will informed his family in Saskatchewan that he had a new name.[82] Apparently he did not tell his parents that he now presented himself as a Metis.

After the troubles of 1885, many Metis in western Canada, with similar physical features to French Canadians, crossed the colour line and became non-Native.[83] Others changed their names because of fear.[84] Very eloquently one mixed-blood descendant expressed his father's dilemma this way: "Racism followed him in later years like an ever-pursing, venomous snake that might strike at any moment. Dad dreaded that wherever he went he might hear, 'Mind yourself, he has Indian blood.'"[85] Exactly at the moment that many fair-skinned Metis crossed over into the dominant society, Will Jackson, now Honoré Jaxon, travelled in the opposite direction, from white to self-identified Metis.

Why Jaxon? Why Honoré? His niece, Mary Plaxton Grant, later recalled why he had chosen Jaxon as his new last name. "The Jaxon," she wrote to researcher Cyril Greenland, "was because he said the 'cks' of Jackson should be an 'x' (Greek idea)."[86] She added that, since he had never liked his first name, Willie, with pleasure he had dropped it.[87] For a few months in early 1889, he called himself W.H. Joseph Jaxon.[88] The Joseph had arrived with his baptism at Batoche into the Roman Catholic Church on March 18, 1885. Yet this still was not perfect since, by 1889, his devout Catholic phase had long ended. This led him, a few months later, to tweak his new designation a little more. He kept Joseph as his new middle name and moved forward Henry, his old middle name, in a slightly altered form. At Batoche, the Metis had not called him William, too difficult to pronounce, the French equivalent, Guillaume, being so different in sound. Non-English speakers apparently used his middle name Henry, or Henri, to refer to him; at the time of his baptism into the Roman Catholic Church, Father Fourmond recorded his name as "Henry Jackson."[89] Metis Louis Schmidt also referred to him in his journal as "Henry Jackson."[90] When Donatien Frémont wrote his sketch of Riel's second "secretary," he believed that his first name was "Henry."[91] The French pronunciation rendered Henry, or Henri, as almost Honoré. Gabriel Dumont apparently referred to his nephew, Henri Smith, as both Henri Smith and Honoré Smith.[92] Since there was no major difference in sound, the Canadian exile in Chicago, in full identity transfer, chose Honoré as his new first name. It sounded French. Honoré Joseph Jaxon was born.

CHAPTER 6

"CHICAGO'S LONG-HAIRED CHILD OF DESTINY," 1889–96

In the early 1890s, Honoré became a public personality in America's second largest city, but he was not beloved by all. The *Chicago Times* on June 19, 1894 sarcastically termed him "Chicago's long-haired child of destiny." No fan of his, the paper added, "He is Indian for revenue, and he maps out revolutions and plots for the advertising he may obtain."[1] The *Times* had good reason to attack him, as less than a year earlier Honoré had made the newspaper a laughing-stock in the city. He had organized a World Conference of Anarchists within the Chicago daily's own office building, on the floor directly below the paper's editorial rooms.[2]

To support himself in the late 1880s and early 1890s, Jaxon built sidewalks and curb walls on contract. He initially did well at it, even hiring his own crew.[3] After work, he put his university training to use, tutoring in Greek and science as well as Hebrew, which he apparently learned on his own.[4] With his fellow construction workers, he also perfected his spoken German.[5] Construction provided his livelihood, but making people think remained his constant preoccupation.

In at least one respect, the *Times* was correct: Honoré loved to see his name in print.[6] He realized the interest that he could attract as a North American Indian. Few Native Americans skilled and articulate in English lived in late-nineteenth-century Chicago.[7] Conventional wisdom held that the Native peoples were "a vanishing race." In the words of Carter Harrison, five-time mayor of Chicago (1879–87, 1893) and editor of the *Chicago Times,* the Indians were "relics of former ages, who are now living upon the bounty of the conquering whites." "They had to go," he added in his book *A Race with the Sun* (1889), "for civilization's sake."[8]

Jaxon's straight, raven-black hair, worn quite long, confirmed to many that he had First Nations ancestry.[9] The amount of Aboriginal background varied. The *Chicago Times* believed that Jaxon was "probably an eighth blood aboriginal American,"[10] the *Chicago Tribune* "one-fourth Indian."[11] James Aldrich, commissioner of public works for Chicago (1891–93), assumed that he was a "half-Indian."[12]

His "identity" as a "Metis" opened doors for Jaxon. At the founding convention of the new third party, the People's Party of America, in Omaha, Nebraska, on July 4, 1892, he convinced the organizers to allow him to address the 8,000 delegates. The party that, theoretically at least, recognized no difference of race, colour, or sex,[13] appealed to his sense of values. Speaking as "a half breed Indian of the Metis tribe," he reviewed for half an hour "the Indian's views upon the land question."[14] In his remarks, he stressed his own public policy agenda to advance the cause of the labouring classes, including the need for public ownership of railways. As a Metis spokesperson, Honoré had more freedom than a college professor. As American historian Carlos Schwantes has written, in the late nineteenth century "the ivy-covered bastions of conservatism and elitism would likely terminate a professor for advocating such heresy as the government ownership of railroads."[15]

Mary Elizabeth Lease, the great Kansas female orator, befriended Jaxon, an indication of the power of his ideas and presentation.[16] This extraordinary woman had once done washing for fifty cents a day, raised four children, and then become a successful lawyer. Historian Carleton Beals provides this vivid description of her: "As a platform speaker, with her splendid voice, her tall, slim, taut body, her imperious queenly carriage, her quick extemporaneous oratory, her swift cutting wit, she was unequaled."[17] Earlier this Kansas cyclone had gained lasting fame by advising the farmers to "raise less corn and more hell."[18] Seeing in Honoré a kindred spirit, she endorsed his work.[19]

Michel Dumas. State Historical Society of Montana, Helena/942–020.

Through his continued contact with Michel Dumas, Honoré maintained a link with the South Branch Metis. He had tried to keep in touch with Gabriel Dumont,[20] but the Metis military leader could not write in French or English, hence his link with Michel Dumas, one of Dumont's officers.[21] After the amnesty of 1887,[22] Dumas had moved to Manitoba.[23] For a while, the two men had lost touch with each other, but they became reconnected.[24] Dumas spent three weeks in Chicago with Will, now Honoré, in the summer of 1889. This house guest must have been challenging for Jaxon, as Michel had a real substance abuse problem; in fact, he had just been let go from Buffalo Bill's Wild West Show, which he had briefly joined in the spring of 1889,[25] due to his persistent drunkenness.[26] The two men apparently met again on Jaxon's trip to northwestern Ontario and Manitoba in early 1891. Some mining interests hired and sent Honoré to check out some possible properties in the area. The intensity of his feelings about Metis rights is apparent from a letter sent to his family in February 1891, from Savanne on the CPR, about sixty or so miles west of Port Arthur: "That Canada legally or rightly holds the North West is a lie; that she keeps armed men in it is an invasion; that she grants title to its resources is a robbery; and the curse of God will never be lifted from Canada's people as long as this outrage is persisted in."[27]

Honoré returned to Chicago in early summer 1891 to find the city's plans for the commemoration of the four hundredth anniversary of the arrival of Columbus well under way.[28] Before he had left for Canada, he had proposed that the Metis Council become involved in a North American Indian exhibit, a suggestion that gained the support of the States Association of Chicago. The proposal had mentioned the possible Metis organizers: "Gen. Gabriel Dumont, the Hon. H. Joseph Jaxon, and Gen. Michel Dumas."[29] At a June 1890 meeting, Jaxon, the only one of the three present, had explained who the "Metis" were, as in the United States the racial category did not exist. Playfully he had told those assembled that "the name metis means mixture, but in their case they believed the mixture to be better than either of the components."[30] Honoré had become the States Association's contact person for the Metis Council.[31]

In early 1890, Congress selected Chicago as the site of the World's Columbian Exposition to commemorate the four hundredth anniversary of Columbus' landfall in the Americas. Chicago won out over larger New York City thanks to Chicago banker Lyman Gage. His ability to raise several million additional dollars in a twenty-four-hour period allowed Chicago to beat New York's final offer.[32] Congress then established Dedication Day for mid-October 1892 to honour the moment four centuries earlier when Columbus had first sighted land in the Americas. The formal opening would occur on May 1, 1893, to allow Chicago one more year to prepare. Gage was named the first president of the Chicago board of directors of the World's Columbian Exposition.[33]

Plans advanced for the construction of the "White City" at Jackson Park at the southern end of Chicago. The site would contain a multitude of neoclassical palatial exhibition buildings lathered with plaster of Paris and painted a chalky white. The Midway Plaisance, a mile-long avenue that ran at a right angle to the White City, would include exhibits and concessions. Harvard University's Frederic Ward Putnam, the organizer of the anthropology building at the exposition, became the nominal director of the midway's ethnological villages. The Harvard professor of ethnology conceived of the midway as a living outdoor museum of "primitive" human life, an exhibit to measure the progress of human beings in contrast with the White City's ideal of civilization.[34] The organizers selected "progress" as the 1893 World's Columbian Exposition's theme.[35]

On October 19, 1891, the *Chicago Tribune* took note of Jaxon and his work, "arranging on behalf of the Metis National Council for an encampment of several thousand Metis and Indians during the exposition." Lyman Gage, a tolerant and socially conscious individual,[36] knew Honoré[37] and endorsed him and his Metis National Council. His strong letter to George Davis, the fair's director general, read, "This will present Mr. H.J. Jaxon very well known to me. He wants to talk with you about an Indian Camp for the Metis Tribe to which he is by blood related. He has no motives except good ones & I hope you will give him a little of your valuable time."[38] James Nye, an influential Chicago hardware merchant and political leader,[39] backed up Gage's letter to Davis with a strong one of his own: "Permit me to introduce to you Mr. H.J. Jaxon as a native of the Metis Indian Nation, a man who is thoroughly acquainted with the Indian character – of the highest personal character himself and who is actuated by the purest patriotism in his plans for the Indian Exhibit at the World[']s Fair. He has the courage and physical strength to carry out any undertaking and I commend him to your favorable opinion."[40]

Honoré believed in the need to educate non-Aboriginal people about the Native population. In ignorance, many North Americans of a European background categorized themselves as the "civilized" and the Indians as the "savage." They knew nothing of the North American Indians' history or culture. His powerful friend Gage, for instance, described the early Native inhabitants of the Chicago area in this manner: "In the early part of the present century this region of country was occupied by a race of people, warlike, cruel, revengeful. Broken up into tribes mutually hostile, and frequently at war with each other, they became the easy victims of a superior race."[41] To Jaxon, if there was a superior race, it was the North American Indian, not the European settlers and their descendants. In a letter back to his family in Saskatchewan, he wrote on November 1, 1891 that "The Indian character is more generous, more willing to share God's blessing, less inclined to derive a satisfaction from the contrast between one's own prosperity and another's poverty. Therefore let the Indian acquire the whole man's science & let the white man copy the Indian's character."[42]

Jaxon's friend Henry Standing Bear, a Sioux (Lakota) graduate of the Carlisle Indian School, the most famous of the American Indian residential schools, gave Honoré up-to-date information on contemporary Aboriginal life. Standing Bear endorsed his project in a letter dated 15

January 1892 to Indian Commissioner T.J. Morgan. In his note, he mentioned favourably "Mr. Jaxon who perhaps had talked with you on his plan of making arrangements for Indians coming to the fair, where they may be received and care[d] for."[43] On February 15, 1892, he signed with Honoré, as secretary of the Metis National Council, and a Manuel S. Molano, a South American representative ("South American Secretary to the Indian RE. Com."), a joint letter to Professor Putnam praising him for discouraging "the perpetration of any Wild West show at the expense of the dignity and interest of the Indian Nations."[44]

In 1892, Henry Standing Bear, born about 1869,[45] was in his early twenties. The Carlisle graduate had just spent eight years at the Indian school, where he had acquired a good command of English. Unfortunately not much personal information is available on him, but a great deal exists on his family thanks to his older brother Luther Standing Bear, also a Carlisle graduate, who wrote four books. The Standing Bears came from a traditional Lakota family, the name of the western bands of plains people now known as Sioux, the eastern bands calling themselves Dakota. Their homeland covered part of North Dakota, all of South Dakota, and part of Nebraska and Wyoming.[46] In the first years of the two brothers' lives, the American government had succeeded in forcing the Lakota onto reservations. Their father had fought in 1876 against Custer at the Battle of Little Big Horn. In 1879, Luther had travelled east to Carlisle, the Indian residential school in distant Pennsylvania, followed four years or so later by Henry.

In the North-West Territories, Honoré had met Big Bear and other First Nations people, Sioux refugees had done occasional work for his family in Prince Albert, and in June 1885 he had been chained to an Indian on the journey from the Prince Albert jail to the NWMP barracks in Regina. Yet he knew few bicultural First Nations people as skilful as Henry in English. He could explain Native culture so fully in English. The Lakota's natural egalitarianism attracted Honoré. As Henry's brother Luther wrote in his book *Land of the Spotted Eagle* (1933), "Possessions were given away until the giver was poor in this world's goods and had nothing left but the delight and joy of pure strength. It was a bounden duty to give to the needy and helpless."[47] In contrast,

Honoré believed that the average capitalist "wishes to tie a man to his chariot wheels."[48]

The Wounded Knee disaster had occurred only a year before Henry met Honoré in Chicago. On a frigid morning in late December 1890, an encounter between the US Army and several hundred Lakota had led to the killing of thirty-nine American soldiers and over 150 Lakota men, women, and children. The disaster had been sparked by panic on both sides.[49] One year after this horrific tragedy, Henry Standing Bear of the Pine Ridge Agency in South Dakota, using stationery with the heading "Indian Reception and Arrangements Committee for the World's Columbian Exposition, H.J. Jaxon, Chairman. Suite 12, 170 E. Washington St., Chicago," wrote to Indian Commissioner T.J. Morgan. Standing Bear voiced concerns about the individuals entrusted with bringing First Nations people to the fair. The Lakota wanted "to come as men and not like cattles [sic] driving to a show. Before the public they want to bring some impression that they are men and respectable."[50]

The *Chicago Tribune* on October 19, 1891 took note of Jaxon's work, "arranging on behalf of the Metis National Council for an encampment of several thousand Metis and Indians during the exposition. There was just one complication in all of this, a woman named Emma Sickels. Initially hired to help Professor Putnam, she resented his indifference to her suggestions about how best to involve the First Nations in the exposition. Her bitterness reached new heights when Putnam informed her on December 30, 1891 of the plans of the Metis National Council. He wrote that it "proposes to send delegates amounting to about one thousand from various tribes. These delegates are coming at their own expense and will live at their own expense on grounds which they have hired south of the Exposition. These various representatives of Indian tribes from Canada to the Indian Territory are coming for the purpose of learning all they can from the great Exposition." Then Putnam added, "I regard this movement of the greatest importance to the welfare of the Indian and one which will do more to help him in his advance to civilization than any one thing that could be done for him. I have therefore encouraged it in every way I can and have assured the Secretary of the Metis

Council, Mr. Jaxon, of my hearty cooperation and support."[51] In short, he was telling Sickels that he no longer needed her.

Suspecting that Jaxon might not be all that he claimed to be, Emma set to work and checked out his credentials. She wrote to Lawrence Herchmer, commissioner of the North West Mounted Police in Regina. He replied on April 19, 1892 with some startling news, that "a White man named William Jackson was Private Secretary to the late Louis Riel in 1885. His present residence is not known here."[52] Could William Jackson and Honoré Jaxon be one and the same? Sickels contacted the Canadian minister of the interior in Ottawa, the individual now known by many as "the man who hanged Riel."[53] In 1888, John A. Macdonald had repaid party loyalty. He had elevated Edgar Dewdney from the post of lieutenant governor of the North-West Territories to the federal cabinet as minister of the interior. From Ottawa, Dewdney fired back to Miss Sickels this note: "In reply to your enquiries respecting Mr. Honore J. Jaxon, I may say that he is a man in whom no reliance whatever should be placed. He is a worthless character, and has on several occasions, while in this country, acted like a man whose mind was deranged."[54]

Emma Sickels still lost her job, but she at least had the satisfaction to see Jaxon, her rival, released as well from involvement with the Native participation in the World's Fair. She raised a ruckus, even obtaining an interview in the *New York Recorder.* The paper reported on June 2, 1893 her comment that Jackson was "an escaped lunatic."[55] Despite this information, Professor Putnam held on to Honoré a little longer. The exposition buildings were officially dedicated on October 21, 1892, exactly four hundred years, by the revised calendar, following Columbus's sighting of the West Indies. Professor Putnam in a letter on November 24, 1892, to Director General Davis, commented that he found Jaxon "a man of intelligence and education." He added that he was present "on the stage at the Dedicatory Ceremonies, and, I think he took part in the Congress Auxiliary ceremonies in the evening (but I was not present)."[56] Apparently Jaxon went to the opening event as the representative of the "Metis Indian nation of Canada." The attendants seated him with the foreign diplomats.[57] Honoré sent his sister "newspaper clippings describing my adventures Dedication Day at the Fair."[58] All correspondence between Putnam and Jaxon ceased after the opening ceremonies.

Less than seven years after his arrival in Chicago, Honoré Joseph Jaxon had become a minor local celebrity. With his customary surplus of energy, he successfully assisted other city reformers to expose a graft ring at City Hall.[59] He also worked, with his friend James Nye, in March 1893 to try to convince Lyman Gage to run against ex-mayor Carter Harrison, then editor of the *Chicago Times,* in the race for mayor that April.[60] In the end, Gage decided not to enter the election. Harrison won. Three years later the highly regarded Chicago banker became President William McKinley's secretary of the treasury.

In Chicago, Jaxon made a number of good journalist friends, especially among the members of the Whitechapel Club, organized for "no other purpose than the promotion of good fellowship, with good liquor on the table and a good song ringing clear."[61] A group of junior reporters and cartoonists, "young and madcap," together with a few congenial spirits in other occupations, founded the club. According to one member, humourist Opie Read, they welcomed into their membership individuals with some sort of peculiarity or perilous adventure: "One man was admitted because he had never been known to pay a debt. Another man because he had never been known to smile. I was taken in for the ability to walk without crutches after having edited a newspaper in the hills of Kentucky."[62]

Club members met in the back room of Kosters', a saloon close to the offices of the *Times,* the *Herald,* and the *Examiner,* all Chicago dailies. On the main floor, the dim light came from gas jets hidden behind skulls mounted on the walls. A member who was the superintendent of a hospital for the insane donated his collection of skulls. He had made a study of skulls to try to determine whether differences existed between skulls of normal persons and those suffering from mental illness.[63] The Chicago police donated weapons from actual homicides that were displayed on the walls. Upstairs a series of photos showed Chinese pirates before and after beheading. The organizers named their club after the London slum where Jack the Ripper had done his killings. Together the young men talked the radical politics that their own newspapers refused to print.[64]

Honoré loved English poetry, Dante Gabriel Rosetti being a favourite.[65] No doubt he knew the English poets of the early nineteenth century as well and was aware of Shelley's burial ceremony. After his death, Byron and other of his friends had favoured a "revival of an ancient practice once sacred in Italy and Greece,"[66] namely cremation. Honoré also knew of the ancient practice from his classical studies. After a Chicago friend of his took his own life, Jaxon wanted to fulfill his last request, a difficult one in late-nineteenth-century North America: his friend had wanted to have his body cremated. Honoré was willing to go ahead with it, but who would help him? Naturally he approached his bohemian friends at the Whitechapel Club. As Willis Abbot of the *Chicago Times* later wrote, "Jaxon, always given to romanticism, saw himself pronouncing a funeral oration over his dead friend in true Greek style."[67] The Whitechapel Club enthusiastically agreed to participate. On the Indiana dunes on Lake Michigan, about fifty miles southeast from Chicago, they erected a huge pyre. Honoré conducted the ceremony. The *Chicago Inter-Ocean*, for one, was horrified: "The whole affair was revolting to the average men and women who have imbibed the spirit of the nineteenth century of Christian civilization."[68]

Both his political life and his social activism seriously hurt Jaxon's business. Initially, Honoré had prospered at contracting and even once won a $50,000 contract. But his unpaid off-work activities caused him to so neglect his major contract that he eventually had to let his employees go. Subsequently a rival contractor completed his sidewalks.[69]

Many Canadians visited Chicago the year of the World's Fair. Honoré's old Model School principal, James Hughes, for instance, attended the World's Educational Convention in July, at which he was elected president of its Elementary Department.[70] Hughes, now the inspector of Toronto public schools, had made the establishment of kindergartens his most important objective. The educator firmly believed that each child was an individual in his or her own right. The former principal of the Toronto Model School wanted each student to have the freedom to become as creative as possible. Strongly he opposed regimentation, making schools into army boot camps. In his annual report for 1893, Hughes insisted that "coercive and autocratic discipline necessarily dwarfs character; that obedience should not involve subserviency; and that all discipline is evil that checks spontaneity."[71] What fun if he had met Honoré and learned of his life since his move to western Canada and his subsequent relocation to Chicago. But of course Hughes would not have known that his former student at the Model School was now Honoré Jaxon.

In a delightful example of happenstance, Honoré almost met up with a distant connection from his high school days in Clinton, Ontario. Horatio Hale attended the Congress of Anthropology in August and September.[72] He presented a paper, in fact, on "The Fall of Hochelaga," the St. Lawrence Iroquoian settlement at the site of what is today Montreal. In his text, Hale discussed the various reasons for the disappearance of the Iroquoian people from Cartier's time in the mid-1530s to that of Champlain, who founded Quebec in 1608. Interestingly he called for consultation with modern-day descendants of the Huron and the Iroquois, both Iroquoian-speaking peoples. In a visionary statement, he wrote, "Our students of history have been too generally a book-worshipping race, unwilling to accept any testimony with regard to ancient events which is not found in some contemporary page, either written or printed."[73] At the end of his address, Hale again called for consultation with Native peoples across the continent about their past.[74] The former chair of the Clinton High School Board was unaware that a former student of the school had stood on the podium of the stage of the opening ceremonies of the World's Fair as a representative of the Metis Nation. Already Hale had urged the sponsoring of research among Aboriginal peoples to avert violent and costly conflicts: "It is easy to see how, when these native laws and usages are not understood, collisions might at any time arise in which each party would naturally claim to be in the right."[75] How ironic that he did not know that a Clinton High School graduate had met Big Bear and Gabriel Dumont and had served as Louis Riel's secretary.

Honoré would likely have missed sessions of the Congress of Anthropology since he had his hands full with another world congress, one devoted to anarchism. Mayor Carter Harrison had refused to permit any such convention in the city unless the police attended all proceedings.[76] Honoré went ahead without permission. Chicago's leading "Indian" activist had rented a room in the *Chicago Times* building right next to the office of the paper's owner, Harrison himself, who had just won re-election in April as mayor of Chicago. Thirty anarchists from across the United States and a few from Europe met in Jaxon's office in late September. Honoré had fixed it up to resemble a teepee. As Willis Abbot of the *Chicago Times* described it, "A tent, the apex fastened to the ceiling, filled the whole space, so that nothing could be seen of walls or windows. Buffalo robes and Indian blankets covered the floor and the benches, while pipes, guns, tomahawks, feathered headdresses and all the appurtenances of aboriginal life lay round about. An aboriginal odor also characterized the spot, since it was virtually devoid of any method of ventilation."[77]

In attendance at the congress, among others, were Lucy Parsons, the widow of the Haymarket martyr; the Chicago anarchist Voltairine de Cleyre; Van Ornum, author of "Why Government at All?"; and the well-known anarchist from Eau Claire, Charlie James.[78] De Cleyre, one of the finest American anarchist writers of her generation,[79] later recorded her impressions of Honoré's living quarters, "that quaint, obscure room, with its Indian tepee put up within the walls, and with a bench-seat running round within its octagonal outline, after the manner of an Indian council."[80]

Once the *Times'* rival, the *Chicago Inter-Ocean,* learned about the conference from a source in New York, it ran the story on October 20. The "special telegram" quoted an "informant" who described "Mr. Jaxson" "as a brilliant but erratic man of Indian blood, and he, with a grim sense of humor, arranged to have the meeting held in the Times building, under the nose of the mayor of the city. Their meetings were held three times a day for ten days, and the whole ground of anarchistic agitation was gone over."[81] Once it obtained the manifesto of the Congress in early November, the *Chicago Tribune* published it, including the key paragraph, that no human or class of humans can be trusted with the government of other humans. "That government always means the slavery of the governed, and that relief from the evils of government must be sought in lessening its powers and functions – that is abolishing it."[82] Thousands of dollars could not have purchased greater publicity for the anarchists' cause.

Honoré Jaxon in the late 1890s, on the extreme left. Way and Williams Collection, Special Collections and Rare Books, Walter Clinton Jackson Library, The University of North Carolina at Greensboro.

Not wishing to return to sidewalk contracting, loving the excitement and attention that came from political activism, Jaxon next joined America's first national crusade against unemployment, a march to Washington in late March 1894. Led by Jacob Coxey, the petitioners hoped to persuade Congress and President Grover Cleveland to create public works jobs and increase the money supply to lift America out of its two-year-long depression.

Honoré approached the *Chicago Times* with a suggestion. Willis Abbot, then a member of the paper's editorial board, remembered Jaxon well and included a reference to him in Coxey's army in his memoirs: "Proud of his Indian blood, he used often to come into my editorial office in the midnight hours to discuss the wrongs of his race and the still greater wrongs of the Chicago poor." He asked nothing for himself, except once: "The only thing he ever asked of us was a commission to lead the march of the Coxey army to Washington, on foot, with but a few pounds of oatmeal and tea for provender, in order to demonstrate the superiority of the noble red man as a marcher on short rations." He received the assignment.[83]

With the well-known Chicago Metis in its vanguard, the small army of over one hundred unemployed people left Massillon, Ohio (near Cleveland), for Washington in a sharp, frigid wind, in snow and sleet.[84] A brawny African American from West Virginia, Jasper Johnson, served as the army's standard-bearer.[85] The free-spirited Jaxon, claiming to represent Native Americans, travelled dressed in the costume of the Metis and carried only a blanket, a hatchet, and a few cooking utensils.[86] The *Pittsburgh Post* interviewed him en route. It wrote on March 31 that the "half-breed Indian" was "a man of keen wit and is consumed with a love of his people."[87]

Marching on ahead of the others, Honoré made it from Massillon to Washington on foot in eleven days.[88] Unfortunately his newspaper feature for the *Chicago Times* proved a dud,[89] but Honoré never let a failure get him down. He stayed some weeks in Washington, where he found a new audience for his wild, radical talk. On June 18, the *Washington Post* disclosed an anarchists' plot to bomb the White House, the treasury building, and the war and navy building. Papers across the United States picked up the extraordinary story of the plot. Their source was "a half-breed of unknown tribal origin. He is about forty-five years old, five feet eight inches tall, and has the high cheek bones and coppery complexion of the red men. His hair is raven black and very straight. He wears it long, and at the back it is chopped off, down on his neck as if done with an ax."[90] Back in Chicago, the *Time*s roared with laughter at the eastern press, so easily taken in by the harmless Honoré Jaxon:

> The proposition in itself is a mild one for Jaxon to make and to that extent discredits him. His long march with Coxey seems to have impaired his powers. If he had been in this usual cheerful frame of mind his plan would not have halted at dynamiting the treasury building; it would have comprehended burning some hundred federal officeholders at the stake and holding the house, senate, and foreign embassies to ransom. Such a villainous everyday scheme as that imputed to Jaxon is one that a man with a common school education might formulate and get no headache. At home in Chicago Jaxon would reel off while you wait specifications for an uprising which in theory would terminate in the hold-

> ing of a sun dance in the county building and the lighting of a Metis council fire in the Criminal Court building. It was his practice, when he had his daily plot for revolution well in hand, to seek some yearling reporter and impart the plan in strict confidence.[91]

After the excitement of the Columbian Exposition, the Coxey march, and his Washington "plot," Jaxon, now thirty-three years old, not forty-five as the *Washington Post* described him, took a break from political activism. But before he did, he reported on his recent activities to his family in Saskatchewan: "Dear Folks, Don't be disturbed about these rumors of war & explosions in connection with my name. They simply mean that I have been hitting the editors hard and that they want to down me. Only they won't succeed."[92]

Honoré returned to Chicago in October[93] and took a sabbatical from political activity. He returned first to his sidewalk construction; then, always ready to try something new, he studied law for some months in the office of Luther Laflin Mills, a distinguished Chicago criminal lawyer and member of the Whitechapel Club before it disbanded in the mid-1890s.[94] He described his employer in a letter home that summer as "the first ornament of the Chicago Bar."[95] On 10 January 1896, Honoré wrote to his mother about his first courtroom appearance, "in defense of a young man who had killed one of two 'toughs' who were attacking his wife."[96] He used his own letterhead in the next letter of May 3, 1896, with his address the same as Luther Laflin Mills but clearly printed at the top "Honoré J. Jaxon Advocate." At the time of writing, he added, he was "in the midst of a burglary case."[97]

On November 7, 1895, Honoré marked his tenth year "over the 49th line."[98] He had not forgotten his three years in the North-West Territories; in fact, he returned to fasting in commemoration of a rite recommended by Louis Riel. On one of his retreats, Honoré blazed a tree in the sand hills of Lake Michigan, just over the Indiana state line, with this Latin inscription:

> Hic, per tres dies, ob. L.D. Riel
> exsequiis, dietis, vigilia feci.
> [Freely translated, this reads,

Here, for three days, in memory of L.D. Riel
have I held vigil, fasting, according to the rite.]

A hunter found the blaze with this inscription in this wild, wooded area, with the wastes of sand piled by wind and water into steep hills. The blazed tree was within sight of the spot where, three years earlier, the Whitechapel Club had erected the funeral pyre for the cremation of Morris. Several months later his identity came out in a feature article in the *Chicago Tribune,* on April 26, 1896, "A Mysterious Vigil: Romantic Tale of the Sand Hills."[99]

Four months before the story of the blazed tree appeared, in early January 1896, Honoré wrote to his mother back in Saskatchewan: "Study the Indian and his ways if you would find the light which alone can save the white man's civilization."[100] He seems to have been redirecting his search for spiritual truth to the Aboriginal peoples. Little did he know that within three years both his brother Eastwood and his mother would live on a Saskatchewan Indian reservation.

CHAPTER 7

HONORÉ IN LOVE

1897–1907

IN MID-1896, THE TIDE APPEARED TO TURN FOR THE JACKSON family. The election of the Liberals under Wilfrid Laurier on June 23 provided the break that the family needed; few had stronger Liberal credentials in the Saskatchewan River Valley. Eastwood's health had declined in the late 1880s, and he had sold his drugstore in Prince Albert in 1887 due to illness.[1] He had begun farming about a mile west of his parents near the Forks.[2] Now, with the Liberal victory, he at last might have a chance to obtain a government job.

From Chicago, Honoré wrote enthusiastically to the new Canadian prime minister on June 24, 1896. It was the very day after the election, and coincidentally St. Jean Baptiste Day, the national holiday of Quebec. He wrote, "As one of the men whose cause you so nobly championed in 1885, I send you my sincerest congratulations."[3] Laurier had defended the Metis after the troubles of 1885. "If I had been born on the banks of the Saskatchewan," he said, "I would myself have shouldered a musket to fight against the neglect of governments and the shameless greed of speculators."[4]

But all of this was tricky for Honoré. He could take no chances, in his letter to the prime minister, of inadvertently providing information that might reveal his true identity. A decade earlier Laurier had mentioned Will Jackson on March 16, 1886 in the House of Commons: "We have it now as a fact of history that while Riel was inducing that rebellion, he chose as his chief adviser and secretary, a man notoriously insane, William Joseph Jackson, who signed his letters and Orders in Council. Will it be pretended by any man that if Riel had been in his senses, if he had a sane and discerning mind, he would have accepted an insane man as his chief adviser?"[5] If Laurier realized that Jaxon had been judged "notoriously insane" in 1885, then what credibility would he have in 1896?

Carefully Honoré implied that he had fought in 1885, but he gave no indication that he had been, in a previous life, "William Henry Jackson, Riel's secretary." Toward the end of the letter, he wrote, "I feel that it is equally certain that no less now than in 1885 will you be a true friend to my Metis and Indian compatriots in their endeavor to preserve the loving simplicity and beauty of the free life of the prairie despite the encroachments and invasions of a corrupting and ideal-wrecking civilization." He concluded with a line in French, "Sur ce je vous serre cordialement la main" ("In concluding I cordially shake your hand"), and signed the letter Honoré Joseph Jaxon.[6]

In time, the Liberals delivered their reward for faithful service to the Jackson family, the power of federal civil service appointments now being in their hands for the first time in nearly twenty years. In due course, in 1898, Eastwood received a posting as clerk for the Carlton Indian Agency. It encompassed seven reserves west of Prince Albert, with headquarters at the Mistawasis reserve, named after the famous Plains Cree signatory of Treaty Number Six.[7] Thomas Jackson's death in Prince Albert in 1899[8] led Elizabeth to join her son there.

In 1897, Honoré, now thirty-six years old, also turned a corner. He fell in love, first with the Baha'i faith. The believers followed the teaching of the founder, Baha'u'llah (1817–92). The Baha'i faith began in Persia [Iran] with the announcement of the new age by Baha'u'llah's forerunner, known as The Bab (The Door). Followers of the faith stress the simplicity of living and service to suffering human beings. They regard humankind as belonging to one race. In essence, they regard the great religions, including Islam, Christianity, Hinduism, and Buddhism, as one. Unreservedly they accept the validity of the other great faiths.[9] They believe in the equality of men and women. They see a harmony between science and religion. The Baha'i faith has no clergy. The son of Baha'u'llah, Abdu'l-Baha (1844–1921), became the appointed interpreter of his writings after his father's death.

Although in the beginning Honoré had only partial knowledge of the faith, he was attracted to it. The fact that the majority of adherents were neither Western nor Christian appealed to him. He joined the community in 1897[10] and remained within its orbit for the next two decades. In his own words, he embraced the "Bahai Revelation" since it "seeks simply the renewing of that Truth in all religions which constitutes the bond that ties religious people together."[11] He also liked a great deal the faith's emphasis on the need to abolish the extremes of wealth and poverty.

Within the Baha'i movement, Honoré found spiritual fulfillment, and finally he found something more: through the faith, he met a kindred soul, his future wife, Aimée Montfort, a woman who appreciated him, who tolerated his eccentricities, who loved him. Honoré joined the Baha'i faith, or was already a member, by June 18, 1897.

At the time, the Chicago Baha'i community numbered about one hundred people.[12] Mrs. Minerva Montfort and her two daughters Aimée and Blanche became members later that year.[13] According to the Chicago City Directory for 1897, Aimée was a teacher who lived with her mother, sister, and brother in Chicago's Near West Side on South Homan Avenue. Census information indicates that Aimée had been born in Ohio in 1867.[14] In 1897, she was thirty years old, six years Honoré's junior. A devoted member of the Baha'i faith, she became active in the Chicago community's Women's Assembly of Teaching, first as a board member and later, in 1906, as its president.[15]

Honoré voiced only one complaint about Aimée's public speaking on Baha'i subjects to wealthy people. He noted in a letter to his mother, brother, and sister in Saskatchewan that she was "much beloved by all and especially by aristocratic dames attracted to the cause." In fun, he added, "Personally I warn her against the snare of vanity which underlies the habit of preaching. Am I not a truly brave man?"[16]

Very little is known about Honoré's previous romantic interests. His first known girlfriend was Rose Ouellette, Moise's daughter, at Batoche. Half a year or so after Honoré reached Chicago, he asked

Aimée Montfort Jaxon. Courtesy of Mrs. Teddy Paul.

Michel Dumas about her.[17] He enquired of Eastwood, in a poignant note in the spring of 1887, "Is La Rose Ouellette married yet?"[18] Actually she was. She had married Saloman Boucher of neighbouring St. Louis on September 20, 1886.[19] In his second year in Chicago, 1887, Honoré did have a serious girlfriend, but, in his own words, "when I got broke the lady's affections seemed to peter out."[20]

Information on Aimée's background is limited, apart from census information, which confirms that her father died when Aimée was quite young. From her surviving letters, it is clear that she did not enjoy good health. Probably it was on account of her several health challenges that she left teaching and switched to office work, usually in the business correspondence area, in which she excelled.[21]

Aimée's intelligence attracted Honoré. Aimée loved literature, and she could talk in depth about it. Shakespeare was a particular interest. She took a course on his plays at the University of Chicago. As an older woman, she wrote of the inner wisdom that his work provided. He gave the young "a philosophy on which to build a life standard that would guide them in practical affairs and protect them from making decisions and taking actions that are inimical to common sense and result in consequences that are often dire." A reading of Shakespeare's classics enriched life "in a real way, to prepare one for meeting and understanding crises that do come into everyone's life."[22]

A former teacher, Aimée related well to people[23] since she responded well to new ideas and kept abreast of contemporary issues. A friend once called her a "strenuous intellectual," and indeed she was. In a letter, she once explained, "I read voraciously on all subjects from all points of view, for & against. I dissect, analyse, reconstruct & follow diligently all suggested & parallel trails of thought. And I think intimately all the time. And I refuse to remember what others think & say holus-bolus. I use it only as seed. The fruit must be [of] my own cultivation."[24]

In a letter written some years later about H.G. Wells' *Outline of History,* Aimée revealed her impressive intellectual range:

> His book fills a long, long need, one I have been searching for years – the presentation of the movement of the whole human race from away back in dim ages on and up to and through the present time with a logical forecast of what is before the race just ahead and beyond. He has interpreted the historical movement of the race – shows what has come out of the activities of us folks en masse, and what is likely to follow. It presents the whole field of history, broadly, logically, fully, and in most fascinating style. It offers the most magnificent survey of civilization in the making and is an education in history finer and larger than that to be obtained from any other source.[25]

In turn, Aimée liked her husband's mind. His ideas about the equal position of women in society were progressive and enlightened. He supported her opinions, such as her belief that a woman should "study and do interesting things until she is 30 at least and then marry somebody that can give her the setting her mind and person need to give the highest expression to her talents and abilities."[26] But Aimée loved Honoré most of all on account of his honour. As she wrote to her new mother-in-law early in 1900, "Among men his honor and integrity are without blemish; he is all any mother should desire in her son and my hero. If he has not material wealth it is due to a most sensitive conscience and principles that will not permit his deviation from the fine line of rectitude."[27]

Aimée realized that Honoré had some eccentricities, but she accepted them. This intelligent and perceptive woman quickly identified the turning point in her new friend's life, the events of 1885. She later wrote, "That period made a changed man of him and accounts for much in him that is odd but which I have accepted because I understood the reasons and causes back of all."[28]

When she first met Honoré, Aimée realized his impoverishment. He told his family back in Saskatchewan, and no doubt mentioned to her, that in "the month of November 1896 my food bill was 43 cents, and from June 1/96 to Feb 1/97 I lived on about $17 – sleeping in a factory and cooking my own food – mainly corn meal & Graham flour – and meanwhile keeping up a smiling front and comparatively clean linen before the outside world. These experiences are at once the reward and penalty of maintaining our individuality – of refusing to be any man's slave."[29]

This fierce independence continued. Aimée is undoubtedly the individual mentioned in Honoré's letter to his mother and brother and sister on February 24, 1899. Honoré explained his financial situation: "I am struggling through to the spring time but I would have suffered for food had not a good friend smuggled bread and meat to me, having first surreptitiously abstracted it from the larder of the well supplied family of which *she* is a member."[30] Aimée's mother and sister so objected to his abject poverty that they tried to discourage the match.[31]

Honoré and Aimée actually married on February 12, 1898,[32] but they kept their union secret for two years, living separately. Aimée continued on at her mother's with her sister, while Honoré continued to move, like a nomad, from residence to residence. But in 1900 their economic situation improved and allowed them to announce their marriage and live together. They rented a little three-room back flat, on the upper floor of a nice frame house in West Chicago, in the area immediately adjacent to the downtown, now called the Near West Side. It was a very multicultural district.[33] The home belonged to an older couple. They kept a cow and sold the Jaxons fresh milk for six cents a quart.[34] Honoré added in a letter a month or so later that his wife was "an ideal homemaker being very loving and very domestic and very very tidy."[35] Thanks to Chicago's elevated electric railway system, they were closely tied to the central business district, which pleased Aimée. From their home, they would hear the deep rolling thunder from the passing trains. The West Side had three elevated lines with stations placed on average less than a third of a mile apart.[36]

The Jaxons moved a year or so later but stayed in the West End.

Honoré Jaxon as a contractor, wearing the top hat. Courtesy of Lorne Grant.

Honoré described their new home in a letter to his mother on December 12, 1902: "The present tepee is on a 'mean street' and on the border between the slum district and the Boulevard region – the front door being in the former and our windows opening within view of the latter."[37] He loved the humour of the situation. In his words, "so far as Aimée's society friends are concerned we are of course in the deep dark woods." Yet "while our circumstances of purse condemn us to live in the slums yet we are entertained at the table of the denizens of the Lake Shore Drive region."[38]

The new bride worked very hard to make her husband focus more on his contracting business and give it a firm economic base. Honoré tried to turn over a new leaf. He had already dropped plans to become involved in the Yukon and Alaska Gold Rush through the Yukon River Trading Company.[39] He had also abandoned his participation in a project in Chicago to make gold out of the base metals.[40] To please Aimée, he tried to become a little more conventional. He knew what a treasure she was and wanted very much to please her. As he wrote to his mother on 18 January 1900, "Aimée is indeed one in a million." "I do not believe that any other girl would tolerate my set ways and accommodate herself to them as she does."[41]

The man who regularly evaded the federal census taker[42] now boldly listed his name in the city directories from 1898 to 1902 as

State Street looking north from Madison Street, downtown Chicago, around 1905. Photographer Barnes-Crosby. Chicago History Museum/ICHi-19294.

"capitalist." In the first years of their marriage, Honoré did try to become economically successful. He returned to his sidewalk construction business and obtained office space, or more likely "a place to hang his hat," in one of Chicago's most prestigious office buildings, the Home Life Insurance Building. His good friend James Nye, a partner in the firm of the Ducat and Lyon General Insurance Agency, appears to have arranged this, allotting him some space in their office.[43]

Chicago's business district went through great change in the late 1880s and 1890s. The invention of the passenger elevator and of structural steel made tall buildings possible. Steel had formerly been used almost exclusively for bridges, but now came an opportunity to adapt it to architecture. The Home Life Insurance Building at the corner of LaSalle and Adams Streets had a fireproof metal frame and became Chicago's first steel-framed skyscraper in 1885.[44] Other tall buildings that represented the Chicago school of architecture followed. The booming economy of the 1880s created the pressure for going upward since Chicago's business district had an area of only about half a square mile. There was nowhere to go but up.[45]

But it proved to be a very tough assignment to transform Honoré into a successful business person. The major stumbling block remained the basic one of collecting on his contracting accounts, as he wrote in a letter to his mother, brother, and sister on July 21, 1901: "in some cases collections are proving tedious."[46] He also had too many other interests and could not say no. When asked, for instance, by Chicago's Behais Supply and Publishing Board to translate a French-language text on the Baha'i faith, he accepted. The publication, a twenty-six-page booklet entitled *An Investigation of Bahaism: An Address Concerning the Bahais Religion, Delivered at the Paris Exposition of 1900, before an Assembly of Learned and Prominent Men,* by Gabriel Sassi, was published in December 1901. The cover included the credit line "Translated from the original French manuscript by Honoré J. Jaxon of Toronto University."[47]

Home Insurance Building, Chicago, around 1905. Chicago History Museum/ICHi-19291.

As an "Indian" in Chicago, Honoré also had responsibilities. Jessie W. Cook included him in her article "The Representative Indian" in the May 5, 1900 issue of *The Outlook.* She described him as "a lawyer of Chicago" and included a photo of him.[48] In late January 1901, he spoke to the Society of Anthropology in Chicago on the American Indians.[49] As he'd had little contact with Aboriginal people since 1885, one wonders what he actually said. But Honoré did keep in touch with Henry Standing Bear, his Lakota Sioux friend of the early 1890s.[50] He tried to help where he could. In 1904, three Lakota Sioux on a Wild West Show train were killed and sixteen hospitalized in a major rail accident near Chicago. Dr. Carlos Montezuma, an Apache practising medicine in the city, stepped forward to obtain a proper financial settlement from the railway for them.[51] Honoré joined him. His friend Henry Standing Bear's brother, Luther, was one of the individuals severely injured.[52] Luther later recalled the disaster in his book *Land of the Spotted Eagle* (1933): "Our train, while stopped for a few moments, was crashed into by a swift-traveling one, and a passenger car filled with Lakota braves was torn to splinters, and human bodies crushed in among the wrecked steel and timbers."[53]

In terms of the North American Indians' future, Honoré, in a rare acceptance of conventional wisdom, believed that they were a vanishing people. With the populations of many First Nations groups declining, most authorities accepted this view. John Maclean, the author of *Canadian Savage Folk: The Native Tribes of Canada* (1896), included a section of about fifteen pages in his book on this topic, entitling it "The Doomed Race."[54] The best academic opinion in Canada confirmed that the First Nations would disappear. As Principal George Grant of Queen's University in Kingston, Ontario, bluntly stated, "It must be said that, do what we like, the Indians, as a race, must eventually die out."[55] Honoré accepted this opinion. In a comment to the *Chicago Inter-Ocean* on May 15, 1907,[56] he referred to the "race that is going and has gone." Certainly anyone looking at the article, "The Representative Indian," in the May 5, 1900 issue of *The Outlook* could see how minuscule in numbers the Native Americans had become: 250,000 Native Americans compared with seventy million non-Natives.[57]

Over a century later, all of this has, of course, been proven completely false. The Aboriginal populations are rapidly increasing due to the medical advances of the twentieth century, in particular improved nutrition, hygiene, and progress in the prevention and treatment of infectious diseases.[58] But Honoré belonged to his own time and place and could not predict this turnaround.

By 1903, he became involved again in union issues[59] with an entertaining Irish American friend, Timothy P. Quinn. While his comradeship with Quinn did little to alleviate his hand-to-mouth existence, it did lead to a great deal of fun.[60] Like Honoré, Tim involved himself in radical political issues, most recently in organizing mass meetings in the interest of John Turner, the English anarchist and labour leader who had been detained on Ellis Island, New York.[61]

The friends wished to be recognized as delegates to the Chicago Federation of Labor, but they had to be sent by a union. Tim Quinn decided to form the Solicitors and Canvassers' Union, open to anyone who simply offered anything for sale, from shoestrings to stocks and bonds.[62] Originally the new union had three members, but after the president, who had elected himself, quit only two members remained: Jaxon and Quinn. The *Chicago Tribune* later provided an entertaining history of the two-man labour combination:

> There was a meeting of the union once a month for a time. The only matters discussed were anarchistic theories, all the members of the union being anarchists, but divided into two species, philosophic and constructive, words which conveyed some meaning to their minds. Jaxon, master of polysyllables, prepared long treatises which he endeavored to read to Quin[n], who retorted with the text of florid and impassioned appeals which he dispatched periodically to the various crowned heads of Europe.[63]

The Chicago Federation of Labor needed them both and accepted this "union" as legitimate. The federation's paper, the *Union Labor Advocate,* immediately approached Honoré to join the editorial board. He accepted. Greatly impressed by his work, George Hodge, the publisher, on June 29, 1906 gave this sterling endorsement of Honoré's assistance:

> Mr. Jaxon himself is a man who has donated to the advancement of the labor cause in this country a great deal of time and effort that he could ill spare from his business and professional work in construction lines, and is well thought of in the labor movement. He has to his record the drafting of some of our most important official documents. Some of these have given him a national reputation in labor circles, and anything written by him is given unusual attention.[64]

In 1905, Jaxon worked with other community members to convince Chicago's city fathers to build a Grecian peristyle,[65] or a row of columns surrounding an open court, by the lakefront. It could become a speaker's corner, Chicago's equivalent of London's Hyde Park. He joined with a group of Chicago residents, several doctors, lawyers, and business people, to organize a petition to the Parks Board of Chicago, urging it to take "steps to erect in one of our public parks a Peristyle for purposes of public concourse and assembly; and to the further suggestion that to this end you acquire possession of the polished granite columns (including their bases and capitals) now about

The Grecian Peristyle. Courtesy of Lorne Grant.

to be removed from the old Cook County Court House."[66] The *Chicago Tribune* carried a story on the proposal, "Plans Kiosk, Using Columns of the Old County Building," on September 3, 1905.

In the early years of the twentieth century, Honoré also devoted a great deal of time and energy to the Spirit Fruit Society,[67] a small utopian sect, which relocated from Lisbon, Ohio, to Chicago and then from Chicago to Ingleside, about fifty miles northwest of the city. With his knowledge of construction, Jaxon helped to design the Spirit Fruit Temple, their large communal house in Ingleside.[68] The Spirit Fruiters sought equality of the sexes and pursued an anarchist-like lifestyle of unrestricted freedom. Elbert Hubbard, one of America's foremost disciples of John Ruskin, the celebrated English art critic, and William Morris, the English poet, decorator, and artisan, came to know Jacob Beilhart, the founder of the Spirit Fruit Society, very well. In 1905, Hubbard described him in this manner: "Jacob does not want you to do what he does, nor believe what he does. He only asks you to live your own life – express yourself according to the laws of your own nature."[69] But Jaxon broke with the Spirit Fruit Society immediately after Beilhart announced that buildings should be constructed without plans, a statement that seemed so foolish to Honoré that he left the community.[70]

In his spare hours, he designed a new tunnelling machine that he claimed would cut the cost of excavating tunnels.[71] He also drew up plans, which he patented, for building structures complete with a device for preventing or decreasing the effects of earthquakes.[72] On account of his promotion of concrete in building construction, he became secretary of the Art and Architecture section of the National Cement Users Association, but this volunteer job, as usual, came without a salary.[73] Jaxon was busy. As he wrote to his mother and Eastwood on August 30, 1905, "Lord if you knew how many irons I keep ever lastingly in the fire you would forgive the long intervals in my letters."[74]

Honoré believed that the real obstacle to his economic success came from his lack of capital. As he once wrote to Eastwood, "Life is as helpless without capital as a carpenter is without his kit of tools."[75] But Aimée had a clearer vision. She saw her husband's real problem as his unlimited compassion for the unfortunate. In his own words, Honoré had spent his two decades in Chicago "trying to make the world better"[76] without pay.[77] She lamented years later that he should have made his fortune first, then used his money to help others: "If H[onoré] had not got mentally switched for some reason against possessing any property at all, of any nature, he could have made a million long before he was 30 and then could have accomplished so much more, I believe, than with the exhausting struggle against want that has always been his lot."[78]

Honoré's name again appeared in newspapers across the United States in early spring 1907 – thirteen years after his massive coverage in 1894 as a member, and ex-member, of Coxey's Army. President Theodore Roosevelt had recently denounced the leaders of the radical Western Federation of Miners (WFM). Two of the federation's leaders and one of their close associates had been charged with complicity in the assassination in 1905 of the union-bashing former Idaho governor Frank Steunenberg. Roosevelt had called WFM president Charles Moyer, national secretary-treasurer Big Bill Haywood, and their friend George Pettibone "undesirable citizens." Immediately Jaxon protested against the president's use of such language, "designed to influence the course of justice in the case of the trial for murder of Messrs. Moyer and Haywood."[79] From the hundreds of protest notes that Roosevelt received, he selected just one for his reply, Honoré Joseph Jaxon's, the one written under the heading "Cook County Moyer-Haywood-Pettibone Conference. *Death* – can not – will not – and shall not claim our brothers!"[80]

Honore Jaxon, Chicago 1907. *Chicago Daily News.* Chicago History Museum/DN-0004855.

For more than a decade, his years of a great public profile in Chicago seemed to be well behind him, but now Honoré was back. He loved the attention. Of the celebrated Metis, the *Saturday Evening Post* wrote, "He looks like an Indian, talks like a graduate of Oxford and writes like a professor of rhetoric." The *Post*'s fact-checking was minimal. The magazine stated that it interviewed him at his place in West Chicago, "two cluttered rooms at the back of a vinegar factory." Actually it was Shaw's Pickles, a pickle, not a vinegar, factory.[81] His lodgings, the *Post* continued, were "full of books, and scientific apparatus, and firewood, and chemicals, and pictures, and old clothes and various other things, and on the walls hang diplomas from the University of Toronto and parchments telling of honors won in Greek and Latin."[82] As he never graduated from the University of Toronto, the *Post* reporter got that detail wrong as well. No evidence survives that he won any prizes in his classical studies.

The Chicago press knew a great deal about Honoré's amazing life, thanks to information that he himself supplied. Henry Barrett Chamberlin, for example, noted in a 1907 feature article in the *Chicago Record-Herald*, "he has touched the edges of law, architecture and medicine; has lectured, organized trade unions, solicited insurance, sold stocks and bonds and hunted buffalo for a living."[83] All of this was more or less true, with the exception of the buffalo hunting. In supplying the details to eager reporters, Honoré emphasized that he had been imprisoned at Lower Fort Garry, from which he had escaped. He wanted them to know that he had been "Riel's secretary." He did not want anyone to know that he had not been convicted at his trial but rather judged insane and committed to a lunatic asylum.[84]

Others were not impressed. Resentful that Jaxon had written his letter as a member of the Moyer-Haywood-Pettibone Defense Conference instead of the Chicago Federation of Labor, jealous of the publicity angle lost, the federation expelled him.[85] This pushed Honoré in another direction. He had long planned on making an extended trip with Aimée to Saskatchewan to see his mother, brother, and sister (his father had died in 1899).[86] Honoré had even constructed a large teepee for them to sleep in on their travels over prairie trails.[87] He began in the winter of 1906–07 to make arrangements to store his "three to four tons of accumulated treasures."[88] During the waiting period, he continued working as the secretary for J.H. Zedricks and Company,[89] a general mail-order house in Chicago but an extraordinary one. Zedricks was an African American business person, a rarity in Chicago at this time.[90]

Extremely grateful for his timely support, the Western Federation of Miners dispatched their Metis champion to St. Louis, Missouri, to raise awareness about the Idaho court case.[91] Honoré spoke effectively before the Central Trades and Labor Union of St. Louis: "Jaxon's speech sparkled with epigrams and humorous remarks, and he made repeated references to the 'Great Spirit,' disclosing his Indian birth and training, which he said he was proud of."[92] The Western Federation of Miners next sent him to Winnipeg as their emissary to the annual convention of the Trades and Labour Congress of Canada. Aimée accompanied him.[93] In Winnipeg, their western Canadian adventure began.

CHAPTER 8

RETURN OF THE "NATIVE" SON

1907–09

LIKE A MODERN-DAY RIP VAN WINKLE AWAKENING AFTER A long sleep, Honoré found the northwest transformed. He had left twenty-two years earlier.[1] The open grassland was now fenced in and farmed. A human tide of settlement was sweeping the west, particularly Alberta and Saskatchewan, the "new provinces" created out of the old North-West Territories in 1905. Now in their eleventh year in office, the Liberals ruled in Ottawa. The Conservatives, the dominant party in Honoré's youth, were out. The most prominent westerner in Wilfrid Laurier's current cabinet was Honoré's old acquaintance Frank Oliver. In 1885, he had opposed the tyranny of Ottawa's viceregal representative Edgar Dewdney; now, in 1907, he was the federal minister of the interior.[2]

Once in the west, Honoré discovered that fellow University of Toronto classics student Fred Haultain[3] had served as premier of the North-West Territories immediately before the creation of the "new" provinces. Haultain had led the fight in the early 1890s to eliminate French-language rights in the North-West Territories.[4] Hugh St. Quentin Cayley, his old classmate in first-year classics at University College, the member in the territorial assembly for Calgary in 1889, had raised the "dual language question" in the Legislative Assembly. Subsequently the assembly had voted to end French-language rights in the North-West Territories.[5]

When Honoré had lived in the North-West Territories from 1882 to 1885, it had been truly an Aboriginal, French- and English-speaking country. Not so now, as both Alberta and Saskatchewan presented themselves as homogeneous English-speaking settler provinces. Gone was the old official bilingualism. Gone as well was any approximation of numerical equality between Aboriginal and non-Aboriginal people. As late as 1885, Aboriginal people had still constituted the majority in two of the three provisional districts of the North-West Territories. In 1885, Aboriginal people around the major settlements of Prince Albert, Battleford, Calgary, and Edmonton had outnumbered Euro-Canadians.[6] But by 1907 Aboriginal people were a small minority in the "new" provinces.

The more tolerant racial attitudes of the pre-1885 days had vanished. Western Canadian historian Sarah Carter emphasizes the division of the post-1885 world: "If there was a shred of tolerance before, or the possibility of working towards a progressive partnership, it was shattered in 1885, as thereafter Aboriginal people were viewed as a threat to the property and safety of the white settlers."[7]

The new dominant society believed in a racial hierarchy. The 1901 Canadian census clearly specified how federal enumerators had to record racial background. Skin colour determined it. The "Instructions to Officers" noted that "The races of men will be designated by the use of 'w' for white, 'r' for red, 'b' for black, and 'y' for yellow." The instructions expanded upon this point: "The whites are, of course, the Caucasian race, the reds are the American Indian, the blacks are the African or Negro, and the yellows are the Mongolian (Japanese and Chinese). But only pure whites will be classed as whites; the children begotten of marriages between whites and any one of the other races will be classed as red, black, or yellow, as the case may be, irrespective of the degree of colour."[8] No doubt here about who occupied the highest rank in the white, red, black, and yellow colour scheme. The adjective "pure" described only the "white race."

Honoré had changed as much as the North-West Territories. As usual, compared with the rest of the crowd, he travelled in the opposite direction. In 1907, "white" Will Jackson of 1885 was no more, replaced by "red" Honoré Jaxon. By identifying himself with a people who faced widespread discrimination, he risked the whiplash of prejudice himself. Native writer Joe Dion recalled the atmosphere for Metis, the children of white fathers and Indian mothers, in this era: "Those who show their Indian heritage to a greater extent have a tougher time; unlike their fairer skinned brothers they are not so readily accepted by their white fathers. Their inclination therefore, is to their mother's people, but there was a law which said they could not mix with Indians; in fact they have been arrested for trespassing on Indian reserves."[9]

Non-Native commentators confirm Dion's presentation of prairie Canada as an anti-Aboriginal environment. A.E. Smith, a Methodist minister in the 1890s in Prince Albert, commented on racial relations in his city: "Prince Albert had a population of about 3,000. Fifty per cent were of French-Indian origin. They were disrespectfully called 'half breed' and were discriminated against as 'inferiors.'"[10] In 1908, Archibald Blain, acting deputy attorney general of Alberta,[11] spoke with members of Alberta's Legislative Assembly from constituencies near Indian reserves and with several others "who are supposed to know something on the subject." Writing to the respected Toronto lawyer S.H. Blake, he commented, "I might say that most of those with whom I have spoken are not, I would gather, very much in sympathy with the Indian, nor with the efforts to better his condition. They look upon him as a sort of a pest which should be exterminated."[12] The dominant society in western Canada passed these negative attitudes on to the next generation. Canadian playwright and author Leonard Peterson, for example, raised in Regina in the 1920s, recalled little positive that was said about Native people in his childhood, the attitude being that their world was "primitive, backward, a nuisance, something to be swept aside."[13]

Yet Honoré escaped prejudice for two reasons. First, this "Metis" was obviously superior in terms of his schooling. In the early twentieth century, the average prairie farmer had only a grade five to eight education.[14] Walter Scott, Saskatchewan's first premier, had only elementary school, no high school at all.[15] In contrast, Jaxon was a man of letters, with (almost) a complete university education. He could speak not only English with great eloquence but also French and German, and he knew Latin and Greek. He could talk about Prince

Kropotkin's anarchist writings, discuss Karl Marx's *Das Kapital*,[16] or explore the religions of the Middle East.

Second, Honoré was a "celebrity," the recipient of a personal letter from President Theodore Roosevelt himself. Thanks to the recent biographical article in the popular American magazine *The Saturday Evening Post*, Honoré returned to western Canada in the fall of 1907 fully introduced. On June 1, the *Evening Post* recounted his life story, beginning with his birth as "a Buffalo Indian." The magazine gave full biographical details: "Jaxon's father was a Metis Indian, and Jaxon was born in a buffalo camp so near to the forty-ninth parallel, in sight of Woods Mountain, and between Montana and the Northwest Territory, that Jaxon has never been able to figure out whether he was born a British subject or an American citizen."[17] The wide-circulation magazine added that he had joined Louis Riel on the Canadian side of the border and become his secretary. After the failure of the Riel resistance in 1885, he had fled to the United States and become a high-profile labour leader in Chicago.[18]

The Trades and Labour Congress of Canada welcomed Honoré to its annual convention in Winnipeg. He attended as a representative of the radical miners' union, the Western Federation of Miners. Winnipeg remained the great metropolis of the Canadian prairies. In 1907, a recent immigrant named Jacob Penner wrote back to his family in Russia: "Our city of Winnipeg is rising with American speed. Ten years ago Winnipeg had 30,000 residents and now there are 120,000. Every year buildings worth more than twelve million dollars are built here, and the city administration spends huge amounts every year for improvements and beautification of the city. So now most of its streets are paved with asphalt."[19]

On Honoré's first visit to Winnipeg on his way to Prince Albert, way back in 1882, Winnipeg still had a Native face, a sizable Metis population. Not so now: the Aboriginal presence had almost vanished. In the 1901 census, individuals who identified themselves as Metis constituted only .03 percent, that is one-third of one percent, of Winnipeg's total population.[20] This statistic indicates that a large number of Metis had left. Even so, the rate at which the Metis had "disappeared" was too rapid. The statistic suggests that a number of

Main Street, Winnipeg, about 1904. Archives of Manitoba/ N7968

Winnipeg respondents of Native ancestry self-identified as "white" in the 1901 census.

Honoré went to the convention from a city much larger than Manitoba's capital. Chicago, the second largest city in the United States, now had a population of two million, greater than the entire population of Canada's three prairie provinces.[21] From Upton Sinclair's *The Jungle,* a bestseller the year before, the delegates knew of the horrors of working-class life in Chicago, the use of child labour in the meat-packing industry, the unsafe working conditions, the sexual harassment in the workplace. The book had been the sensation of the year. Novelist Jack London compared it to Harriet Beecher Stowe's *Uncle Tom's Cabin,* the pre–Civil War abolitionist novel, terming it "the 'Uncle Tom's Cabin' of wage-slavery."[22]

The delegates to the convention already knew of the Western Federation of Miners' heroic efforts to secure the release of their imprisoned officers: Moyer, Haywood, and friend Pettibone. The invited guest wisely kept his remarks brief. In the words of *The Voice,* Jaxon "made a short but effective speech and left an impression with his earnestness and ability."[23] In distant Toronto, the *Star* called it "a remarkable speech."[24]

At the Winnipeg convention, one of the real joys for Honoré was meeting again with R.C. Owens, an old comrade in the struggle in

Chicago for the eight-hour day two decades earlier. Now living in Edmonton, his good friend sported a long white beard, which gave him the appearance of an Old Testament prophet. Owens attended the convention as a fraternal delegate from the Canadian Branch of the American Society of Equity. A photographer from the Winnipeg labour paper *The Voice* photographed the two old veterans of the labour struggle standing side by side.

While in Manitoba, Jaxon visited the sons of two men who had been very important to him in 1884–85. His experiences in the troubles of that time remained the defining moment of his life. In Winnipeg, he saw Hugh John Macdonald, who had briefly served as premier of Manitoba in 1900.[25] His father, Sir John A. Macdonald, had sent Riel to the gallows in 1885. Jaxon also visited Jean, the twenty-five-year-old son of the executed Metis leader.[26] Jean then lived in the old Riel family home (built in 1880–81). There his father's body had lain in state for two days after his execution by the Canadian government.[27]

After Winnipeg, Honoré and Aimée travelled by rail to Duck Lake and then by wagon north to Mistawasis, where Eastwood worked as the agency clerk.[28] Once again, throughout the southern Canadian prairies, in the areas of settlement at least, the Native population had become vastly outnumbered. Prince Kropotkin himself referred after his 1897 western Canadian visit to "the boundless prairies, with their Indian population slowly dying out as a mute reproach to our present civilization."[29] But on the northern fringes of the prairies, the First Nations and Metis still constituted a sizable percentage of the total population.

Honoré Jaxon on the right, and R.C. Owens. Photo from *The Voice*, September 27, 1907. Archives of Manitoba

That summer at Mistawasis Eastwood Jackson had served as

the acting Indian agent.[30] Thomas Borthwick, the regular Indian agent, had just returned from his summer-long assignment as the treaty commissioner for Treaty Number Ten, which extended the treaty process to the First Nations in Saskatchewan north of the Treaty Number Six area. The creation of the province of Saskatchewan had made Treaty Ten possible. The federal government now wanted the treaty concluded to permit it to claim title to the land and to begin the exploitation of natural resources for its benefit.[31] Borthwick travelled more than two thousand miles that summer.[32]

Did Honoré get a chance to speak to the former Treaty Ten commissioner, now Mistawasis Indian agent once again, about the new treaty? Undoubtedly, in a tiny community such as Mistawasis, their paths must have crossed daily. Honoré had his own original opinions on treaties, one informed by meetings in the summer of 1884 with Plains leaders such as Big Bear. To Honoré, Treaty Six was not a land surrender agreement. By a strange coincidence, an opinion that he had expressed on treaties back in 1884 had just appeared in print. E.J. Chambers' *The Royal North-West Mounted Police: A Corps History* (1906) included on page 83 a mountie's report on "Will Jackson's" remarks at a meeting on the South Branch in September 1884. Although Treaty Six had been signed in 1876, Sergeant Keenan of the NWMP reported to his superiors that "Mr. Jackson stated that the country belonged to the Indians and not to the Dominion of Canada."[33]

Mistawasis was a small reserve of about 125 people. It was named after the first signatory of Treaty Six at Fort Carlton in 1876. Mistawasis' branch of the Plains Cree was known as the House People. They had acquired their name from their residency near the houses of the Hudson's Bay Company posts. They had moved out of the forested area entirely and lived exclusively in the mid-nineteenth century on the plains, hunting buffalo along the South Saskatchewan to support the HBC at Fort Carlton.[34]

The Dreavers were one of the leading families at Mistawasis. James Dreaver, an employee of the Hudson's Bay Company from the island of Westray in the Orkney Islands, had married one of Mistawasis' daughters. On account of his Orcadian son-in-law's adherence to the Presbyterian faith, Mistawasis welcomed that church to establish a mission on his reserve.[35] At the time that Honoré and Aimée visited, George Dreaver, Mistawasis' grandson, was chief and served as an elder in the Presbyterian Church.[36] The Cree Dreaver descendants spoke English with an Orcadian accent.[37] As a young man of about twenty, Chief George Dreaver had attended Treaty Six.[38] Old Mistawasis himself, who had died in 1896, had trained his grandson to become a leader.[39] George had guided his people through the difficult transition from buffalo hunting to farming and stock raising. Nearly thirty years after the Jaxons' visit, Chief Dreaver, who served as chief until his death in 1938, won a major treaty rights case in the Exchequer Court of Canada, a case that reaffirmed the right of Treaty Six First Nations to what is today called medicare.[40]

Individuals such as the Dreavers, bilingual and bicultural, made a successful adjustment to the larger society. Others had not. A large number of children in the Carlton Agency spent most of their time at residential schools. There they learned skills and trades in preparation for their adult lives. But to reach this goal, the Department of Indian Affairs took the boys and girls away from their parents at an ever-decreasing age. The policy separated many of the children from their families and their culture.[41] Ten years earlier Honoré had urged his mother to "Study the Indian and his ways if you would find the light which alone can save the white man's civilization."[42] Now he witnessed first-hand how government officials and Christian missionaries worked together to destroy the Aboriginal cultures that he so valued. The Indian Act of 1876, the collection of federal statutes that applied to legal Indians in Canada, regulated all aspects of the treaty Indians' lives, including the dispatch of children to residential schools.

Even in this relatively isolated area, the pressures on the First Nations to surrender reserve land, on what was the northern limit of good agricultural land, proved intense. A million people came and settled on the Canadian prairies between the late 1890s and the outbreak of World War I.[43] Edmonton's Frank Oliver, minister of the interior and superintendent general of Indian affairs, led the assault on the reserves. Fearing the pending shortage of homestead land, Oliver, as the head of the Department of Indian Affairs, favoured the wholesale alienation of reserve land. The push for surrenders now gained momentum. The defenders of the policy argued that the steady decline in First Nations numbers, due to chronic health problems and disease, meant that Indians had more land than they possibly needed. The non-Native settlers were Oliver's favoured people.[44] Oliver built his power base in western Canada on agriculture.

In early December, Jaxon travelled to Regina, now a town of 8,000,[45] at least eight times larger than it had been at the time of the rebellion trials in 1885. As an ugly reminder of his enforced stay there, the name of the major east-west avenue remained Dewdney. Thanks to a well-developed local economy, Regina no longer depended so heavily on the NWMP barracks and the government offices for its existence. To the small but growing labour force, Honoré introduced many of the ideas of radical Chicago. He addressed the local trade unionists as "comrades" and continually referred to the working-class struggle. Throughout western Canada, he urged wage earners to fight bosses' attempts to reduce them to "one level mass of broken wretches past salvation."[46]

At a Regina branch meeting of the Labour Party on December 8, the visitor from America's second-largest city went to the heart of the matter. Society, Honoré stated, divided into two classes, "the people who ate and those who were eaten."[47] He shared with his audience his belief that "he found that the North-west had developed to about the same-point in the industrial struggle in which he found the United States in '85."[48] So many injustices cried out for correction. Workers needed living wages. "A thousand babes go supperless to bed that one monster's brat may spew on silk."[49] Resource-rich Crown land should belong to all and not be divided up by an eastern government for sale to speculators. Above all, the farmers and labourers should strive for "fair play" for the First Nations and Metis, whose economic state remained inferior to even that of the hard-pressed workers. At the end, Honoré proposed the establishment in western Canada of Producers' Social and Economic Discussion Circles for workers and farmers in which they could explore the cause of their inferior economic status.[50]

A slender man in his late twenties, seated in the audience, had helped to arrange the Labour Party talk. Tom Molloy had been a dedicated socialist for some time. After several years as a typesetter and reporter for Regina newspapers, he became president of the local Typographical Union, which in 1906 had won for its members the right to an eight-hour working day. The newly organized Regina Trades and Labour Council had recently elected the young trade unionist as its first president. He also served in 1907 as the vice-president of the Regina Branch of the Labour Party.[51]

Tom Molloy, photo taken around 1910. Photo courtesy of Reverend Jack Molloy.

Tom's father, Richard Molloy, the telegraph operator at Clarke's Crossing southwest of Prince Albert, had relayed east the news of Riel's capture on May 15, 1885. Although Tom had been only two at the time of the Battle of Batoche, he had grown up with tales of 1885. Throughout the troubles, his father had kept the central repeating station for the North-West Territories on the South Saskatchewan, just fifteen or so miles from the centre of the troubles, operating. During the Battle of Batoche in early May, the Molloy children had hid in the vacant Caswell home, while their father had kept his "ear to the sounder."[52]

"Riel's secretary" struck Tom as quite a strange individual. He talked of "harmony" and "vibrations." He believed in the power of thought projection. These peculiarities aside, Tom respected this unique individual. He admired his commitment to social and economic justice. The president of Regina's Trades and Labour Council never forgot their talks. Many years later he recalled his visits to Jaxon's room at the Alexandra Hotel on Hamilton Street. Often he found his friend scribbling away on a small table. All around him lay pieces of paper covered with handwriting and rough sketches of the battlefields of 1885.[53]

Poor Honoré, once again he missed the crest of the wave and instead surfaced in a trough. Few people understood what he was saying. He had tried to make the economic analysis sound easy. As the *Moose Jaw Times* reported on his remarks in Regina to the Labour Party, "It was necessary that all should take an intelligent interest in public affairs. Economics was not as so many people supposed a dismal science, but on the contrary a joyous one."[54] Had this been a dozen years later in the Winnipeg or the Regina of 1919, his words would have found a ready audience. But at this time, the public, apart from a small number of adherents, ignored the invitation to establish Producers' Social and Economic Discussion Circles to explore the causes of their economic subordination.

Honoré returned to Mistawasis after attending a two-day farmers' convention in Regina.[55] He proved to be one of the most vocal delegates at the farmers' gathering; in fact, on the afternoon of the second day, he made no fewer than four motions. After his vigorous interventions, he ended the day with a plea for greater farmer-labour cooperation.[56]

Back on the reserve, life came to a complete halt. Once again Honoré familiarized himself with the Yorkshire accent of his beloved mother, so delighted to have him back with her after over twenty years. He loved her dearly but, unlike Eastwood, had great difficulty submitting to her micromanagement. He frequently left the reserve. Fortunately, since he was not a status Indian, he did not have to approach Agent Borthwick for a pass to leave the reserve, a necessary requirement under the Indian Act.[57]

Aimée provided a vivid description of the effect on Honoré of living with his mother. Her total control, well meaning though it might be, upset him greatly. He loathed "being followed up like a two year old." On account of the atmosphere in Mistawasis, he had involuntary physical responses in the night, in Aimée's words, "twitchings of the legs, spasmodic arm movements, jumpings, etc. all during sleep & so strong as to shake the bed to awaken me." Unable to cope with the atmosphere, Honoré had to escape, absenting himself for five to six weeks to undertake his historical and political work. On his return, he stayed only about one or two weeks at a time.[58] During his two winters at Mistawasis, Honoré discovered that he had lost his gift of winter travelling. On two occasions, he was almost overcome by subarctic cold on the trail.[59]

The stay at Mistawasis also proved very tough on Aimée. She liked Elizabeth, now almost eighty years old, but she found the atmosphere of living in the same house for such a long period repressive. Her staunchly Methodist mother-in-law showed absolutely no warmth whatsoever toward the Baha'i faith. Toward the end of their second winter together, Aimée described her mother-in-law as having a "domineering mind & habits." In despair, she wrote to her sister-in-law Cicely, then on the Plaxton farm at Colleston, east of Prince Albert, where she was raising, with her husband Amos, their six daughters. Aimée shared her unhappiness, the "mental oppression." Eastwood took "most of his dinners at Dreavers," so he was not available to lighten up the atmosphere.[60] Aimée nearly reached the end of her tether at one point. From Mistawasis, she wrote to an American playwright, an entire stranger to her. She asked him about her creative writing. The individual replied and encouraged her to continue. With envy, she later wrote, "This playwright travels and lives in the places where his dramas are laid."[61]

In the summer of 1908, Aimée and Honoré travelled across prairie trails as part of the research for his book. They visited 1885 battle sites "in a prairie schooner, with a teepee of his own design for shelter."[62] Honoré was overjoyed at Aimée's response to their camping out. As he wrote to his mother and Eastwood on July 12, 1908, "Aimée is enjoying herself immensely. She has now slept for two nights on the ground in the tepee and admits that she has slept soundly notwithstanding the hardness of the ground."[63] Honoré's comments inflated the situation somewhat; years later she wrote that "H[onoré] has always had a passion for igloos and tepees which I have never shared."[64]

Throughout their two years on the Canadian prairies, Honoré worked away with a passion on his book on the troubles of 1885. He had planned for over twenty years to write it.[65] In a note dated June 8, 1908, Jean Riel, whom he had last seen as a tiny boy of two at the Ouellettes at St. Laurent, encouraged him to write it, "Because you were an eye witness and know the truth."[66] In early spring 1908, Honoré visited

In the summer of 1908, the Jaxons travelled to historic sites and along historic trails in a prairie schooner. This image shows prairie schooners near Wainwright, Alberta, in March 1906. Glenbow Archives/NA-3205–10.

the South Branch. He scribbled down copious notes and took photos of Riel's surviving acquaintances, such as Louis Schmidt, Riel's boyhood friend and his secretary in Red River in 1869–70.[67] He called on Schmidt, a proud Metis patriot, on April 28, 1908.[68] Among those whom he photographed was old Jean-Baptiste Boucher, the father-in-law of La Rose Ouellette, who had married his son, Saloman Boucher.[69]

At Batoche, Honoré found many of the original families still in the district.[70] He looked up and met Moise Ouellette, the father of his Metis girlfriend Rose.[71] Moise, intensely proud of his Metis heritage, remained steadfast in his opposition to the Canadian government's land policies and refused to pay an entry fee on his land that, he claimed, remained his birthright.[72] In 1901, he had erected a funeral stone in the Batoche cemetery. It bore the names of the Metis and First Nations warriors from the Batoche area killed in the unrest of 1885. The monument included the name of his beloved father.[73] Never did Honoré permit himself to use the phrase the "Rebellion of 1885"; it always remained the "Metis War of 1885."[74]

Did he see Rose? On this important point, both the documentary and the oral history sources are unfortunately silent. A niece of hers recalls her as a happy and positive woman who never complained about hardships. A grandson remembered her as an attractive woman with "Métis features."[75] But neither recalls her mentioning the name of an *anglais,* Henri Jackson or Honoré Jaxon, who returned to visit nearly a quarter of a century after they had known each other at Batoche.

Sensitive and compassionate toward the Metis people, Honoré despaired at the injustice against them. The new immigrants knew nothing about the history of their new home and the Native peoples. They had no idea of the Metis side to the troubles of 1885. Even at the South Branch, some Metis, on account of the intense prejudice and discrimination against them, camouflaged their Aboriginal identity. They tried to fit into the new system. Later, in the 1911 federal census, for instance, a number of Metis in the South Branch self-identified as French or English "depending on their family names and cultural aspirations."[76]

In the fall of 1908, the lure of politics attracted Honoré again. He attended the first Liberal Party convention of the new federal electoral district of Battleford in early 1908, serving on both the resolution and the nomination committees.[77] Having never taken out American citizenship, he could run in the federal election. He decided to run as an independent candidate in the electoral district of Prince Albert. He brought forward for his deposit $200 from the money he had saved "for the writing of North Western History."[78]

Laurier again won the country, and the Liberals took the Prince Albert district. Jaxon suffered a crushing defeat, obtaining only 87 votes to the Liberals' 2,398 and the Conservatives' 2,209.[79] But for Honoré the precious $200 had been well spent. He had entered the contest to spread his ideas against tyranny. As he described himself on the front page of his election news sheet, *Fair Play and Free Play,* he was "a producer of Plans to Make Men think." *Fair Play and Free Play* contained the essence of his social philosophy, that "men are the creatures of their environment and of their heredity (which latter is in substance the environment of their ancestors)." The news sheet also contained some of his poetry. The third stanza of his "A Song of the Citizen" summarized his message to the electorate:

Thus, in human affairs
More than half of our cares

Come from men who in greed are enwrapped.
They're too lazy to work
And all effort they shirk,
Save to get honest people entrapped!
So, while others produce
All real wealth that we use,
They produce only schemes to possess!
And they chuckle in glee
Like a blood-sucking flea
While the real working man they assess.[80]

In early March 1909, Honoré again left Aimée at Mistawasis and appears to have made a short trip to the east, visiting Chicago, Toronto, and Ottawa. Only one of his letters mentions this trip, a short note dated March 4, 1909.[81] No further information is available. A better correspondence trail exists for the later part of March. At that time, he set off, via Calgary, for the coal mines of the Crowsnest Pass in the Rockies to help the workers fight for union recognition and greater pay. Frank Sherman, president of United Mine Workers of America, District 18, whose jurisdiction included southeastern British Columbia and southern Alberta, hired Jaxon as his assistant that spring to help in the union's struggle with the coal mine owners. Sherman, now in charge of the 6,000–member district, had worked in the coal mines of the Rhondda Valley of Wales before emigrating to work in Canadian coalfields in the late 1890s.[82]

En route to the Crowsnest Pass, Honoré spent a few days in Calgary. As he did in other western cities, he quickly made contact with the community's left-wing element to help educate the working class about their true condition. Riel's former secretary also looked up old participants in the troubles of 1885. But Honoré made no attempt to seek out William Pearce at Bow Bend Shack, his fine sandstone house on the south bank of the Bow River, just east of the city. As the federal government's superintendent of mines, or chief adviser on the development of the North-West Territories, Pearce had prepared the official report on the causes of the "Riel Rebellion." His summary, requested by Prime Minister John A. Macdonald, had exonerated the Canadian government from all responsibility. In a document that the former federal government official had written immediately after the rebellion, he had described Jackson's assistance to Riel in this way: "Such men as Jackson – and fortunately they are very few – joined this agitation to advance their own ends and if nothing else is accomplished, their vanity is flattered by being brought into prominence."[83]

In Calgary, Honoré might have stopped at Fort Calgary and called at the commanding officer's home.[84] In his mind's eye, he remembered Richard Burton Deane well: tall, soldierly carriage, with a drooping moustache and unsmiling eyes.[85] Deane had known well both Riel and Honoré himself. During Commissioner A.G. Irvine's absence in the fight against Riel, Deane had run the NWMP barracks in Regina. He'd known Honoré Jaxon as Will Jackson, one of the prisoners under his supervision in the early summer of 1885. Perhaps, too, the man from Mistawasis visited the convent in the city, run by the sisters, the Faithful Companions of Jesus. They had moved to Calgary from St. Laurent, next to Batoche, after the troubles of 1885.[86]

One residence would not have been opened to Riel's secretary in Calgary, the sandstone mansion of James and Belle Lougheed, Lougheed House, today a National Historic Site. Belle Lougheed had lost her beloved brother Richard, a Canadian soldier in the Battle of Batoche.[87] Yet Honoré did meet R.B. Bennett, the junior partner of Lougheed and Bennett, confident, polished, immaculately dressed in a Prince Albert coat and top hat.[88] Years later Jaxon recalled his encounter with Bennett, who later served as prime minister of Canada from 1930 to 1935: "He accosted me one day in 1909 on the streets of Calgary where I had received considerable publicity for my editing of the miners daily newspaper (the Fernie Ledger) and for my handling of their strike against the CPR coal mines." He found Bennett "very pleasant and interesting – not at all bigoted or over bearing – so that I really took a great liking for him and have kept track of him ever since."[89]

Honoré called in Calgary on W.M. Davidson, the founder and influential publisher of the *Albertan*, who had the reputation of being "a little left of centre."[90] The Ontario-born Davidson, a graduate of the

University of Toronto, came to the city in 1902 after working for Toronto newspapers and editing the *London News.* In 1905, *The Voice,* the Winnipeg labour newspaper, had referred to him as "belonging to what is becoming known as the Canadian radical school."[91] With letterhead generously supplied by the *Albertan*'s editor, Honoré wrote a number of letters to his wife and family back at Mistawasis.[92] The *Albertan* later described the newspaper's visitor "as a rebel in the Riel rebellion," a man "in full sympathy with what he describes as the downtrodden half breeds. After the rebellion, he drifted into the US, where he advocated the cause of the people against oppressive combinations."[93]

Either through Davidson or through his old Chicago friend now living in Alberta, R.C. Owens, Honoré also met farm leader William Tregillus. The wealthy English dairy farmer lived at his home, Roscarrock, just west of the city, south of the Bow River. Only two months earlier Tregillus and Owens had worked hard to unite the two rival Alberta farm organizations, the Society of Equity and the Alberta Farmers' Union, into a strong new union, the United Farmers of Alberta (UFA). Over half a century later, Tregillus' son Cyril still remembered the visit to their home, and he described Jaxon as an "interesting personality."[94]

Jaxon made few inroads with his ideas about the working class in Calgary in 1909, even though great social inequalities existed. In *The Limits of Labour: Class Formation and the Labour Movement in Calgary, 1883–1929* (1998), Canadian historian David Bright states that, "Just as in other Canadian cities undergoing industrialization, a single wage was inadequate to support the average working-class family."[95] Driven by the necessity to augment family incomes, second and third incomes, the taking in of boarders, and the keeping of pigs and cows became necessities for many. Every able-bodied individual over the age of fourteen was expected to work. Hours of employment extended from eight in the morning to six at night. The working week extended either five and a half or six days. At the job, few government regulations existed to protect the workers' health and safety.[96] Yet most working-class Calgarians in this period of incredible economic boom still believed that they could indeed improve their economic condition through application and hard work.

Jaxon travelled next to Bankhead and Banff at the "northern end of the disturbed area,"[97] then went south to the Crowsnest Pass, the big mining field shared by Alberta and British Columbia. On Sunday, May 9, he addressed hundreds of striking coal miners at Frank, Alberta. This multicultural mining camp included individuals from all parts of Europe as well as Canada and the United States. Only six years earlier, the coal town was the site of one of the greatest natural disasters in western Canadian history. At 4:10 a.m., on April 29, 1903, a huge mass of limestone broke loose from the top of Turtle Mountain overlooking the village. The slide, consisting of tiny chips to chunks the size of a house, crossed the valley, burying everything in its path, all within a hundred seconds. Fortunately the slide missed the central part of town, where most of the people lived, but still over seventy lives were lost. News of the tragedy sped across North America. Anxious to resume production, the owners had the mine operating again in about a month. By the time of Honoré's visit, the mine was producing more coal than it had before the slide.[98]

The *Frank Paper* reported on May 13, 1909 that "The meeting was a big one. A special train was run from Lille on the Frank and Grassy Mountain line which brought two carloads of members and many were in attendance from every camp of The Pass."[99] Honoré J. Jackson "of Mis-Ta-Wa-Sis, Saskatchewan," and Robert "Buck" Evans, acting president of the United Mine Workers of America, District 18, spoke to the large audience in the big Frank Town Hall. Evans substituted for President Frank Sherman, confined by ill health to his home in Taber, Alberta.[100] From his childhood, Buck Evans had been a miner, beginning at age nine in Welsh colleries dragging coal cars with a strap around his waist and a chain between his legs, just like a hauling dog.[101] "Riel's secretary" and Acting President Evans encouraged the strikers to stand firm in their demands.[102] The *Coleman Miner* noted that, when Honoré was introduced, "the audience, knowing of his ability as a public speaker, greeted him with a long round of cheers."[103] The *Frank Paper* noted that "The meeting was attended by many foreigners of different nationalities and the proceedings were translated to them by persons speaking their various languages."[104]

Labour Day Parade in Regina, around 1913. Saskatchewan Archives Board/R-A197

It was in the Crowsnest Pass that Honoré learned from Eastwood of Aimée's unhappiness. Immediately he wrote to his brother: "I do not blame either mother or Aimee. The trouble as it seems to me is simply that they belong to two entirely different generations and sets of environment and ha[ve] no common ground on which to stand." On account of his "present trip in the interest of the future," Honoré stated that he could not return immediately.[105] Any response from Eastwood is unrecorded, and he had to continue as the peacemaker until his brother returned. Fortunately Cicely came out to Mistawasis for a visit, which improved the tense situation.[106]

From the Crowsnest Pass, Honoré travelled back to Calgary, stayed a few days, then proceeded eastward to Regina. Earnestly he told his audience at the opening meeting of the Regina Producers' Social and Economic Circle, "It was the duty of all men to live for others."[107] Honoré next travelled north to Saskatoon, then in the midst of a strike by the labourers building the city's first sewer system. His reputation from the Crowsnest Pass had preceded him. The strikers requested help. He accepted.

During the first decade of that century, Saskatoon was the fastest-growing town in western Canada. Its population had risen from 113 people in 1901 to nearly seven thousand by 1908.[108] Saskatoon was now in 1909 the major city of central Saskatchewan. It had just been announced in April that Saskatoon had been chosen as the site for the University of Saskatchewan, with classes to begin that September.[109] Walter Murray, a philosophy professor from Dalhousie University in Halifax, was already in place as the first president. That October Honoré attended a lecture given at St. George's Church in Saskatoon by Reverend George Lloyd, who was introduced by Murray.[110]

As a contractor himself, Jaxon knew how much the city's sewer workers were being exploited. The city paid neither an adequate wage nor took enough safety precautions. The workers called for an increase of five cents per hour (to twenty-five cents) and requested that all the contractors or corporations conducting public works furnish adequate cribbing, after a depth of six feet, to prevent cave-ins. When a board of conciliation was struck, the workers asked their friend from Chicago to act as one of their three representatives on the six-man board. He gladly accepted. Don Kerr and Stan Hanson wrote of his contribution in *Saskatoon: The First Half-Century* (1982), "The newspaper accounts of the proceedings make Jaxon sound a more reasonable and adept negotiator than the Saskatoon elite."[111]

In late September, Honoré finally reached Mistawasis from Saskatoon. Apparently Harry Dreaver, Chief George Dreaver's brother, picked him up at the railway station in Eastwood's rig.[112] Finally Honoré and Aimée were together. Over the spring and summer, she had not been well, but Honoré's return helped her to rally. They had a wonderful trip to Edmonton. At last, they had a vacation together, staying at one of the city's best hotels, the Alberta, on Jasper Avenue.

Building sewers in Edmonton, 1907. The construction work would have been similar. Provincial Archives of Alberta/B-1306.

Like other western Canadian cities, Edmonton and Strathcona, its sister city across the North Saskatchewan River, expanded phenomenally at this time. Just a day or so before the Jaxons arrived at their hotel, the first sod was turned on the new arts building for the University of Alberta in Strathcona.[113] New subdivisions proliferated in all directions. Edmonton was now building brick structures three and even four storeys high.[114] The big event of the year, the laying of the cornerstone of the new legislature building on October 1, brought thousands to the Alberta provincial capital, including the governor general of Canada, Earl Grey, federal cabinet ministers, senators, and dignitaries from across western Canada, including Honoré and Aimée Jaxon from Mistawasis, Saskatchewan.

The *Edmonton Journal* described Riel's former secretary as "a rotund little man, with a huge forehead that shone out from beneath a spacious Christie set far back on his head, and with features that radiated good nature." One of the reporter's questions annoyed Honoré. Pounding the palm of his left hand with his right fist, Jaxon thundered back,

> Louis Riel died a patriot. He was not a corrupt man. He could not be bought. He had his ideals, and they were high ideals. He believed he was right in attempting to put them into effect. I believe he was right. Fresh from Toronto University, an idealist myself, I joined him and his party, and did my best to back him up in his fight. We did not want the rebellion. It was not our intention to rebel. The rebellion was forced upon us. What we wanted was justice for the half-breeds and justice for the white settlers.[115]

No doubt through Honoré's long-time association with Frank Oliver, federal minister of the interior, and local political potentate, the Jaxons received an invitation to the prestigious Edmonton Hospital Ball at the Thistle Rink on Saturday evening, October 2. Aimée loved it. She sent a full account to her mother-in-law. Emily Murphy, whom Aimée described as "the city's social leader" and as a "splendid woman, warm and friendly," introduced them to other guests. Murphy, an Ontario transplant to the Prairies, was just completing her second book, entitled *Janey Canuck in the West,* with a fine chapter on Edmonton. "There seems to be no limit to the possibilities of this northernmost city on the banks of the Saskatchewan River."[116] There certainly were no limits that evening, with dinner, dancing, good conversation. In Aimée's words, "The Hon Frank told me it was as good in every way as the West could produce."[117]

The next day Aimée greatly enjoyed meeting the vivacious "Miss Katharine Hughes who has charge of the Provincial Archives." The two women had much in common. Aimée continued, "She is young & good looking, keen of intellect, speaks English well & is generally interesting."[118] Honoré shared with Hughes the important information that, when Gabriel Dumont and the three others had ridden down to Riel in Montana in the summer of 1884, they had "brought Riel letters from leading white men among the old-timers and business men of the Saskatchewan valley, urging him to come back to curb the ambitions of the newcomers and secure the rights of his own people." Later, he added, these letters had been burned after the outbreak of trouble "in order that the writers might not be compromised should an investigation be held."[119]

On Sunday, October 3,[120] the Jaxons met William Carter, whom Honoré had known years ago in Prince Albert. The fact that Will had changed his name to Honoré surprised the wealthy contractor. As a friend of the Jackson family in Prince Albert in the early 1880s, Carter had well known that both his parents had been English-born, but he accepted Honoré on his terms and recognized his ability. The west was a little more lenient on name changes than elsewhere in Canada; Frank Oliver, for example, was originally Frank Bowsfield (he shucked off his father's name in Ontario after his mother's second marriage) and took his mother's maiden name as his own last name.[121]

The Edmonton festivities over, the Jaxons took the train to Saskatoon for Honoré to conclude his work for the sewer workers. Once the hearings ended, the Jaxons left Saskatoon for the Prince Albert area. In early October, they departed from Mistawasis to Duck Lake to take the train via Winnipeg to Ottawa.[122] Honoré wanted to gain the federal government's support for the preservation of Western Canada's heritage.[123]

The *Manitoba Free Press* interviewed him in Winnipeg. With Aimée at his side, Honoré told the journalist of his "mission" to preserve the old trails of the west and the spots of historic interest. "I found to my regret that many of those fine historic old trails had been fenced off, or plowed up, and that places of historic interest throughout the west had been desecrated or torn down altogether."[124] To the reporter from the *Winnipeg Telegram*, he termed this behaviour "ungodly vandalism."[125] Honoré had done his best to record all that he had seen. "I have been taking many photographs of the old places and old-timers, and am just like a man who has been up in the north for two years and has returned with his pelts. I have procured many photographs of value and have compiled many things of historical interest during my trip."[126] The Ottawa trip was not forthcoming, though. On the way home, Aimée's health failed, which necessitated heavy medical expenses that ruled out the Ottawa trip.[127] On the positive side, Honoré returned to Chicago with luggage full of information collected for his manuscript on the events of 1885.

CHAPTER 9

CRESCENDO

1910–18

UPON HIS RETURN TO CHICAGO FROM WESTERN CANADA, Honoré quickly resumed his frantic pace: meetings, work, and political action. Many years later Lloyd Lewis, a distinguished Chicago journalist and historian, quoted what Otto McFeeley, labour editor of the *Chicago Evening Post* at the turn of the century,[1] recalled about this extraordinary individual. McFeeley spoke of him as "very learned and very cultured." Although the police and middle-class Chicagoans might dismiss him as a crank, "the intelligentsia, the bankers, the college professors and the labor union men they knew he was worth listening to, for he could not only talk classic English with an Indian eloquence but he had an immense amount of learning."[2] Honoré reached the high point of his public life in the 1910s.

Aimée recovered after her emergency surgery in early November, but overall her physical state remained poor. Despite her far-from-robust health,[3] her outgoing nature resisted any temptation to withdraw from an active life or to slip into self-pity. Aimée kept working in her field of business correspondence.[4] Regularly she attended events in the city, sometimes with Honoré and sometimes without him. From her letters, her varied interests emerge. Just before Christmas one year, she heard Handel's *Messiah.*[5] One evening she caught a "moving picture lecture" on the Panama Canal.[6] Before a presentation of Euripides' play

Hippolytus, she provided for a group of friends a historical sketch of Athens in the fifth century BC.[7] She had an inquiring mind and a lively interest in the world around her. Some years later, when the Chicago Aquarium opened, Aimée was one of the early visitors.[8]

After he arrived back from western Canada, Honoré settled into his rented quarters in the West Side, actually in the Near West Side, on West Lake Street (at number 667, which later became number 1751 with the new system of city street numbering in 1909). On account of his three or four tons of possessions,[9] it proved problematic to move, and for his last decade in the city he stayed at the same address. Aimée loved Honoré dearly, but his spartan accommodations, little heat, no hot water, meant that cohabitation was out of the question. She explained why in a letter to his mother and brother on December 2, 1910: "No, I could not live as Honoré does, even if I wanted to. Physically I am wholly unequal to the conditions & mentally I would, in spite of determined efforts, succumb to depression."[10]

The Saturday Evening Post, when it interviewed Jaxon in the spring of 1907, found him living in two cluttered rooms.[11] McFeeley also provided a few details about his lodgings in Chicago. The veteran journalist recalled that Honoré lived in rooms in an abandoned Masonic Temple. A pickle factory was on the first floor. McFeeley gave a good description of the place and its atmosphere, for he had been to several of Honoré's pie and honey dinners, attended by banker friends, college professors, and big thinkers: "Jaxon's furniture was moth-eaten and all he ever served at his dinner was pie and honey but nobody noticed for Jaxon talked and made everybody else think they talked good, too – talked about ethics, progress, debentures, the disappearance of the buffalo, theoretical anarchy and bi-metallism."[12]

Aimée resided with her mother (until her death in 1917)[13] and her two sisters.[14] They lived in a comfortable West Side apartment. Aimée worked a great deal to beautify the interior.[15] Honoré joked about how women worked hard to improve their lodgings, only to see the landlord subsequently raise the rent: "It is astonishing to what extent an American girl's happiness depends upon the affixing to the walls of her abode of a few strips of polished mahogany for which the landlord exacts three times their value *every* year in increased rent."[16]

Although they lived separately, and often did things independently, the Jaxons still did a good deal together. Aimée and her husband went to public lectures and visited friends. In early 1911, for instance, they attended a series of medical lectures and some in law. They also took a course sponsored by the Alliance Française, in cooperation with the University of Chicago, on French literature. Aimée commented how delighted she was that Chicago could "support a French theatre where one may hear the French master-pieces unmarred by translation."[17]

She had an extensive social network. On one occasion, she helped, in Honoré's words, "a millionaire lady friend of ours in North Side Society" to put on a "benefit" for a maternity hospital for unmarried young women. Honoré continued, approvingly, "It is a sadly needed institution, and a fitting climax to Aimée's many good works in this wicked city."[18] As well as her involvement in Baha'i organizations as a devoted believer in the faith,[19] Aimée joined the Women's Civic Club, a statewide organization that fought for the vote for women.[20]

She thought the world of her husband: "He is not only abreast of most modern thought but in the front rank with the most radical. He is just the most splendid chap & I am very proud of him."[21] Yet, she admitted, he did have what she saw as a very serious personal shortcoming: he refused to try to make money for himself. As she wrote to her mother-in-law and brother-in-law in late 1911, "To me, monetary reward for legitimate effort, is both interesting & attractive; to him it seems to be the repellant element."[22]

At some point before their departure for western Canada in 1907, an architect and his wife in neighbouring Oak Park had befriended the Jaxons. Frank Lloyd Wright and his wife Catherine enjoyed their company. Already the Oak Park architect had evolved his own style of residential construction, developing what became known as his prairie style. Basically the approach led to an opening up of interior space, the fitting of the building to the site, and the elimination of extraneous detail. It was a revolutionary breakthrough and first brought the Oak Park architect to prominence.

Catherine got on well with Aimée, and, in fact, when Aimée was hospitalized for three weeks immediately after her return to Chicago from western Canada, Catherine sent her an inspirational book, Annie

Fellows Johnston's *In the Desert of Waiting: The Legend of Camel Back Mountain.*[23] The short volume emphasized the value of disappointment in preparing one for eventual happiness. In Aimée's words, the gesture and the gift itself showed "in every respect the elegant simplicity & culture of the sender."[24] Poor Catherine, at that point chaos reigned in her own life. Some months earlier, Frank had abandoned her and their six children, suddenly closed his practice, and left debts and unfinished projects behind. He departed for a year abroad with his mistress Mamah (pronounced Maymah) Cheney, who had once been a close friend of hers in Oak Park.[25] Later, in his autobiography, Wright rationalized his abrupt withdrawal from his wife and family responsibilities in this way: "When family-life in Oak Park that spring of 1909 conspired against the freedom to which I had come to feel every soul was entitled, I had no choice, would I keep my self-respect, but go out a voluntary exile into the uncharted and unknown."[26]

Things appeared to be on the mend in December 1910, shortly after his return from Europe. Frank came back (momentarily) to Catherine, his children, and their home in Oak Park. The Wrights invited the Jaxons to dinner, *en famille,* in mid-December. Honoré's impressions of the visit do not survive, but Aimée's do. Aimée so enjoyed their hospitality. She found the six children "handsome, intelligent."[27] In her words, they "spent a charming evening." She found particularly interesting Frank's comment about her husband. As she later recalled, "He was much interested in Honoré's recital of events & said he wished he had the money to back Honoré, to give him complete freedom to follow any trail he chose & sit back & watch Honoré play the game. He says he can't imagine a livelier, more interesting play. And he's right."[28]

Aimée had a real point of comparison to the Wrights' Oak Park home since she had recently attended a dinner party at the mansion of Charles McConnell, the president of the Economical Drug Company, the largest drugstore in Chicago. As the founder of the first cut-rate drugstore in the city, McConnell had made a huge fortune.[29] Aimée described where he lived: "Their house is in those choice & almost priceless blocks occupied by the Swift's, Armours, & a few other 'robber barons'. Rather than a 'house' it is a Venetian Palace, being patterned thereafter." How did the Wrights' home compare to the McConnells' Venetian mansion? In Aimée's opinion, it was far more impressive: "Mr. Frank Lloyd Wright's at doubtless less than half the cost is far more & artistic & beautiful. His whole place is in such perfect taste that we may go there time after time & come away without being able to recall any particular point about any part of it. It is all so delightfully restful. Its spaciousness seems to be limitless, owing to arrangement lighting." She also liked very much his exquisite and unique collection of Japanese prints.[30]

What a delightful evening it was, but Wright's return to his wife and family was only a ruse. Frank had not come home to his wife and family at all. It was just a short intermission before he set out again with his lover to build their country retreat on ancestral lands in Wisconsin. Honoré and Aimée met him next at Taliesin, their new home and studio. Honoré had just returned from the great adventure of his life, his extraordinary journey to England, where he had spent half a year, both feted and acclaimed.

With Honoré, new interests followed old ones, like a new coat of fresh paint over the same old, well-recognized piece of homemade furniture. In the spring of 1911, his passion swelled for the Mexican Revolution, for the anarchist leader in the struggle, Ricardo Magón, the son of a Zapotec Indian and his wife, a woman of mixed Spanish and Indian ancestry.

Francisco Madero, an idealistic revolutionary leader, had deposed the ruthless dictator Porfirio Diaz, who had sold the country to foreign interests. Originally Madero supported Magón, the Native leader of the extreme left Partido Liberal Mexicano, or Mexican Liberal Party (PLM), but later broke off with the anarchist leader and his followers. Under Magón's influence, peasants expropriated large areas of land in Mexicali and Tijuana in Baja, California, under the banner of "Land and Liberty," the motto of the PLM. The party platform called, among other things, for complete secular education for children up to the age of fourteen, a minimum working day of eight hours, the restitution of communal lands to villages, and the protection of all indigenous races.[31]

In late spring 1911, Madero launched a campaign of suppression against the PLM, jailing its members. His soldiers captured and shot PLM

Voltairine de Cleyre, Chicago, 1910. Labadie Collection, University of Michigan.

partisans in Sonora and then sent a federal force to put down the revolutionary movement in that state.[32] Magón in mid-June made clear the goal of the PLM: "our objective is that the land and the machinery of production will become the communal possession of all and every inhabitant of Mexico, with no distinction of sex."[33]

Magón fired the imaginations of American anarchists. In Chicago, Voltairine de Cleyre, a major figure in the American anarchist movement, became an impassioned defender of his movement. The renowned Emma Goldman, who published the anarchist paper *Mother Earth*, judged her the "most gifted and brilliant Anarchist woman America ever produced ... a forceful personality, a brilliant mind, a fervent idealist, an unflinching fighter, a devoted and loyal comrade."[34] De Cleyre devoted herself entirely to Magón's cause, writing, lecturing, and collecting funds for the PLM. She idealized the Mexican peons who seized the land, destroying the concept of private property.

A true believer in anarchist principles, Voltairine lived in total poverty. Her free-spirited French father, who had immigrated to the United States and married her American mother, gave his daughter her unique name in honour of Voltaire.[35] An attractive woman with a slender figure, soft brown hair, and piercing blue eyes,[36] Voltairine lived in great physical discomfort. In 1902, when she was thirty-six, an assassin's bullets nearly killed her, aggravating her already weak physical condition, leaving her in constant pain.[37] True to her anarchist principles, she refused to press charges against her assailant. In her words, "The boy who, they say, shot me is crazy. Lack of proper food and healthy labor made him so do. He ought to be put into an asylum. It would be an outrage against civilization if he were sent to jail for an act which was the product of a diseased brain."[38]

On July 2, 1911, Voltairine founded the Mexican Liberal Defense Conference with the help of her friend Honoré. De Cleyre became the treasurer and Jaxon the secretary.[39] They had first met in September 1893 at the World Conference of Anarchists in Chicago, organized and held in Honoré's office. Voltairine had then lived in Philadelphia, but they had remained in touch with each other, and now they lived in the same city. She had moved to Chicago in October 1910.[40] In a postcard written to her in French in May 1910, grammatically correct but with English structure, Honoré complained that his current job, ten hours a day, did not allow him to write to her as frequently as he wished.[41]

Outspokenly anti-racist herself, Voltairine was no doubt attracted to Honoré's supposed Native American ancestry, as well as his anarchist politics. She had a genuine appreciation of non-European cultures. As Franklin Rosemont writes, for her "Civilization" was "a term of utter contempt. She was not only an enemy of the State, but of all forms of domestication."[42] In her writings, de Cleyre accused the American government of having "murdered the aboriginal people, that you might seize the land in the name of the white race."[43]

Jaxon sailed in mid-July 1911 to England as a delegate to the Universal Races Congress in London,[44] organized to promote interracial harmony. Frank Lloyd Wright and Aimée helped to pay for his passage to Britain. Wright had loaned him fifty dollars.[45] Held at the University of London, July 26 to 29, the international gathering attracted more than two thousand participants from Europe, the Americas, Africa, and Asia.[46] The executive council of the congress had stated its broad aims in a preliminary circular: "The object of the Congress will be to discuss, in the light of science, and the modern conscience, the general relations subsisting between the peoples of the West and those of the East, between so-called white and so-called coloured peoples, with a view to encouraging between them a fuller understanding, the most friendly feelings, and a heartier co-operation."[47] Charles Eastman, a First Nations doctor and writer from the United States, attended the congress. In his autobiography *From the Deep Woods to Civilization,* he later recalled the gathering: "What impressed me most was the perfect equality of the races, which informed the background of all the discussions. It was declared at the outset that there is no superior race, and no inferior."[48]

After the London meetings of the Universal Races Congress, Honoré attended the Forty-Fourth Trade Union Congress in Newcastle as a "Special Envoy to Europe on behalf of the Insurrectos of Mexico."[49] He came with a document "prepared in the interest of united inter-racial working class action, and particularly for the giving of information and encouragement to the working class of Great Britain, in their similar struggle against evils caused by the privileged seizing of land and of the tools of production and exchange."[50] From England, Jaxon wrote to "Comrade Joseph Riel," Louis Riel's brother in Manitoba, explaining that he "had been presenting the case of the Spanish-Indian Metis of Mexico." Carried away with the moment, he included this additional reference to "their noble struggle for land and liberty against the financiering scoundrels whom we French-Indian Metis of the Red River and Saskatchewan have been trying to foil." Directly he informed Joseph that he too was "French-Indian Metis."[51]

These were intoxicating moments for Honoré. He wrote in one letter home to his mother and Eastwood about his incredible experiences: "Well, here I am as a guest in a fancy establishment at Bristol but somewhat in the predicament of the fellow who complained that if it should rain soup he would be caught with a fork in his pocket. In other words it has been raining so much that so far I have not seen all that I would like to."[52] His first cousin, Theo Barber, who met him in England, noted that "He seems to be at once in touch with all sorts of revolutionary people, and is reveling in new contacts."[53]

Several highlights stood out, and Honoré shared them in letters home. In London, for instance, he met George Davison, the managing director and second largest shareholder in Kodak after George Eastman, the firm's founder himself. Davison drove Honoré in his car to the Trades and Labour Congress in Newcastle and then took him to visit his castle at Harlech in northern Wales. The two men had a great deal in common as Davison, a millionaire, was also an anarchist-socialist. This capitalist financially supported many outreach programs to help the working class. Honoré called him "a great lover of freedom."[54]

Also in London, Lady Blomfield, a prominent member of the Baha'i community in Britain, invited Honoré with others to a special private supper. She was the widow of Arthur William Blomfield, a prominent English architect, one of the last great gothic revivalists, whose father had been bishop of London. As a young man, her husband had employed as a draftsperson in his office Thomas Hardy, later to become one of Britain's greatest novelists.[55] Lady Blomfield and others in the Baha'i community in England urged Honoré to make London his permanent home.[56]

Honoré had relatives in Britain: Reverend William Barber, the husband of his late aunt, Ann Jackson Barber, and their three sons, Theo, Edward, and Charles. Actually the Barbers' youngest son, Charles, was abroad at the moment of Honoré's visit. The Cambridge-trained botanist, with his doctorate in science, had first served as the superintendent of agriculture in the Leeward Islands, British West Indies, then taught for several years at the Royal Engineering College, Cooper's Hill, in England. Appointed in 1898 as government botanist in Madras, he had later become director of the Botanical Survey of Southern India. Recently he had joined the staff of the newly established agricultural college at Coimbatore.[57] While all the brothers had married, only Charles and his wife had a family. The brief family history notes written by Charles' son, Dr. Geoffrey Barber, add valued detail to the story of Honoré's English cousins.[58]

Several times in London Honoré got together with Edward, the middle Barber son, a prosperous merchant and Methodist lay preacher.[59] Edward liked him, as he wrote to Eastwood: "Your brother's irregular views are refreshing to us even if we cannot agree with his ideas. His principles are fine at any rate."[60] With more time, the English first cousin might have been able to teach his Canadian counterpart how to run a successful business, given him some pointers on how to collect his debts. Poor Honoré still could not collect on money owed to him. As he complained in a letter to his mother four years later, "If some one should some day do the square thing by me and pay up without trying to dodge I might die of the sudden shock!"[61] Edward had succeeded handsomely in the export business. He traded silver and electroplated goods in the Near East, in the old

Will's cousin Reverend Theo Barber. Reproduced courtesy of the University Librarian and Director, John Rylands University Library, University of Manchester.

Ottoman Empire, items such as knives, forks, teapots, jugs, and clocks. In his sketch of his uncle, Geoffrey Barber added this humorous detail: "He was a devout nonconformist and lay preacher with a life full of religious restrictions and missionary zeal, but he did a thriving business in supplying the harems and probably the brothels of Constantinople with large ornate brass bedsteads."[62]

Later, at Cambridge, Honoré met Edward's father, Reverend William Barber, his uncle by marriage, now in his eighties. His wife, Ann Jackson Barber, Honoré's aunt, had died several years earlier. Currently William lived with his oldest son, Theo, headmaster of The Leys School, a well-respected Methodist boarding school. *Good-Bye, Mr. Chips,* James Hilton's semi-autobiographical novel, is based on the school and in particular on one of the schoolmasters, W.H. Balgarnie, who began teaching when Theo was headmaster.[63] William had spent several decades in the Methodist mission fields of Ceylon and South Africa, and his health had been seriously weakened by his years in the tropics.[64]

Honoré's mother had found her son and daughter-in-law's discussions of the Baha'i faith a trial. They had taken a box of Baha'i publications to Mistawasis.[65] Honoré in a letter later implied what his mother thought of the faith: "My impression is that you look upon the Bahai Revelation as a 'new religion' – one more oriental cult or fad let loose upon an already crazy world of faddists."[66] Whatever his English relatives thought of the Baha'i faith, or of his anarchism, they said nothing to him. He found them "very cordial."[67] Theo wrote to his aunt at Mistawasis after he met Honoré that he was "an exceedingly

Headmasters and masters, The Leys School, 1902. Seated in the centre W.T.A. (Theo) Barber, and on the ground at the extreme left, W.H. Balgarnie. James Hilton's "Mr. Chips" is partially based on the teaching career of W. H. Balgarnie. The Leys School Archives, Cambridge.

interesting man."[68] And, as for his anarchism, "He is really a very lovable fellow with all sorts of good ideas and good intentions, a Methodist Christian in all essentials, thinking himself a formidable revolutionary and in reality one of the most harmless of men."[69]

Theo, who had a brilliant record at Caius College, Cambridge, entered the Methodist ministry, joining the Chinese mission, where he became headmaster of the missionary school at Wuchang. There he learned Chinese and published a biography of David Hill, a dedicated English Methodist Church worker who died in China. The book went through five editions from 1898 to 1909. Theo revealed his own attitude toward non-Christian lands clearly when he wrote, "Every missionary who has spent years amidst the mental and spiritual torpor of a heathen land feels most keenly the profit of a visit to his own Christian country. The whole atmosphere of life is different. The air of heathenism lacks oxygen, at best it is nitrogen which is in excess, – too often poisonous gases abound."[70]

Theo's first wife died shortly after their return to England in the mid-1890s. For three years in the late 1890s, Theo served as the missionary secretary of the Methodist Church. He was named headmaster of The Leys School in 1899.[71] Shortly after his appointment, he married Emma Clapham, the sister of Sir John Clapham, a distinguished English economic historian at Cambridge University. Thanks

Emma Clapham Barber (Mrs. W.T.A. Barber). The Leys School Archives, Cambridge.

to Emma Barber, we have a fine impression of her husband's North American cousin. After Honoré stayed with them at the school in September, Emma wrote to her husband's aunt Elizabeth, Honoré's mother: "How kind he is – how genial – how appreciative." She mentioned perceptively that she found "his Nature had a great many strata superimposed upon the original bed rock – but that the bed-rock was still there and it was old-fashioned Methodism!"[72] Two decades later Theo, retired, still vividly recalled his colourful North American cousin. In a note to Eastwood and Cicely, he asked, "What is the said Don Quixote doing now? Is he still Nihilist or Communist? He professed to be that, when he was in England twenty years ago – and I found him a chivalrous gentleman who wouldn't have hurt a fly! Is he still a Bahaist?"[73]

Upon his return to North America from Britain in early February 1912, Honoré spoke in Montreal to a meeting of the local Trades and Labour Council, where he was warmly received.[74] He also introduced others in Montreal to the Baha'i faith. In London, he had worked with members of the local Baha'i community to bring the two thousand Indian students from India into closer social contact with their English hosts.[75]

In Montreal, Honoré apparently stayed with the distinguished Canadian architect William Sutherland Maxwell or at least used his residence as his Montreal mailing address.[76] Maxwell had almost completed, with his brother Edward, one of their major commissions, the new Saskatchewan legislative building in Regina. The link here was through Maxwell's wife May with Honoré, one of the earliest adherents to the Baha'i faith. Honoré had recently served in

Chicago, the heart of the American Baha'i community, as the negotiator for land at Wilmette, north of the city, needed for the projected Baha'i house of worship.[77]

"Riel's secretary," while in Quebec, also visited Louis Riel's daughter-in-law, Madame Jean Riel (her husband had died in July 1908), in Quebec City.[78] In Montreal on February 17, 1912, the Montreal daily *La Patrie* ran a front-page article on Jaxon, with the caption "La Cause de Louis Riel triomphera. Les Métis ont uni leur cause à celle des classes labourieuses. L'Avenir est à eux" ("Riel's Cause Will Triumph. The Metis Have United Their Struggle with That of the Working Classes. The Future Is Theirs"), words taken directly from Jaxon.

As always, Honoré loved being in the limelight, as if it fulfilled some strange inner need. Although only in Toronto for two or three days,[79] he managed to contact the dailies and became the subject of articles in several of them. The *World* reported who he was: "Mr. Jaxon was secretary to Louis Riel during the rebellion, and was in full sympathy with the movement."[80] The *Telegram* included a reference to the troubles of 1885 in the caption to its story, "Riel's Secretary Here. Mexican Insurrecto Now."[81]

Did any of his former classmates or teachers in Toronto realize that Honoré Jaxon was really Will Jackson? If anyone could have successfully identified him, it would have been William Hanna, then living in the city. Hanna had attended Clinton High School, and then the University of Toronto at the same time as Will, later becoming a Presbyterian minister after graduating from classics. After several ministerial appointments in Ontario, he served in 1912 as the associate secretary for eastern Canada of the Lord's Day Alliance, an organization of Presbyterians, Methodists, and Congregationalists whose mandate was to protect the sacredness of Sunday in Canada. In his work, he followed the newspapers closely to monitor business openings, sporting events, and entertainments held on the Sabbath.[82] The statement that Jaxon had been Riel's secretary could have provided the clue, Jaxon being so close to Jackson.

Ontario had changed so much since Honoré's university days; in 1881, its population was two-thirds rural, while now it was less than half, with Toronto far and away the province's largest urban centre.[83]

The population of the city had grown from 85,000 in 1881 to 375,000 in 1911, four times what it had been in his university days.[84] On its central business streets, a number of tall buildings shot up. A distinct Chicago-like office canyon was beginning to take shape at King and Yonge Steets.[85] But some old visual landmarks remained. If Jaxon wandered up to University College, he would have seen some familiar sights: the two Russian cannons now in front of the new Ontario provincial legislature and the monument to the three undergraduates killed in the Fenian Raids. Very close to the Russian cannons, on the east side of the legislature, arose a new monument by the young Canadian sculptor Walter S. Allward.[86] At the time of its unveiling in 1896, the Toronto *Globe* explained that it "tells of the gallantry of the forty-one Canadians who laid down their lives in the task of restoring order to the Northwest." On the northern and southern faces appeared the names of those who had been killed and those who had later died from wounds received in action.[87]

Did Honoré take time to walk over to University College? The documentary record is silent. The university's enrolment had risen from several hundred in his day to over four thousand.[88] Three other denominational colleges, Victoria (Methodist), St. Michael's (Roman Catholic), and Trinity (Anglican) had federated with the University of Toronto to make it the largest university in Canada. If Honoré did visit his old college, he could have met someone from his class. Will Milner still remained. The top student in his class, the winner of the gold medal in classics in 1881, had taught high school for some years before gaining an appointment in 1891 as an associate professor at University College. He had become a full professor of classics in 1907.[89] The year of his appointment he had married Margaret, the sister of Joseph Flavelle, Toronto's millionaire meat packer.[90] Just northeast of University College stood her brother's mansion, Holwood, a magnificent Beaux-Arts house, seventeen rooms and servants' quarters.[91]

Alas, if he did make a short visit to the old campus, again no mention remains. That being said, one thing is certain: his radicalism came too soon for Toronto and his old alma mater. If he returned a little over half a century later, the student body and some of the faculty at the University of Toronto would have been ready for his assaults on the conventional wisdom of twentieth-century capitalist society. In 1969, one student activist wrote in the Toronto *Globe and Mail* this comment, Jaxonian in tone: "The Department of Political Economy at the University of Toronto does not offer a single undergraduate course in socialist economics. The History Department offers no history of the Canadian Indian. Medicine builds in profit motivation; English becomes picayune; sociology concentrates on problem-solving within the status quo; law doesn't question the assumptions of our legal system – it memorizes them."[92]

But, back to 1912, what had happened to his old University College classmates, now men in their fifties? Will Milner had been the secretary of the University College class of 1881. He later helped to write the history of the honours classics program at the University of Toronto in 1929, which included current locations for living graduates.[93] As he maintained close ties to Ontario high schools,[94] Milner certainly had news about former classmate Sam Passmore, who taught classics at Brantford High School. Honoré would have been interested to learn that he had married Minnehaha (Minnie) Copway, the daughter of Kahgegabowh, or George Copway, the celebrated Ojibwa author.[95] In 1921, Milner, Passmore, and Hanna were present for the fortieth class reunion of the University College class of 1881.[96]

We do know with certainty that Honoré met one individual from his past. On February 24, 1912, an extraordinary meeting occurred in City Hall, at Teraulay (now Bay) and Queen, in the heart of British Canada's largest metropolitan centre. The magnificent sandstone building had opened thirteen years earlier, in 1899. Its clock tower, 260 feet high, slender and Romanesque, dominated the city skyline. Its bronze bells had struck the hour and the half and quarter-hour for over a decade.[97] The west half of the massive square structure held the county offices and the east the municipal departments.

Through a large oak doorway on the Queen Street side, Honoré stepped into the cavernous two-storey main entrance hall. Here the visitor faced the large stained glass window by Robert McCausland, a well-known Toronto stained glass artist, depicting *The Union of Commerce and Industry*.[98] On either side of and between the main entrance doors, murals painted by George A. Reid commemorated pioneer life.

Only one First Nations person had obtained a spot in the mural, Tecumseh, the famous pan-Indian leader who formed a confederacy that fought for Britain in the War of 1812. Few Native people lived in Toronto in the 1910s. This was ironic since the city owed its name and its origin to the First Nations who had used the "Toronto Portage" as a shortcut for the trail and canoe routes between Lake Ontario and Lake Huron. But, by the early twentieth century, Aboriginals had become a distant people to Torontonians. Unlike Montreal, Vancouver, Calgary, and even Hamilton, close to the Six Nations territory on the Grand River, Toronto had no neighbouring First Nations reserve. In 1891, the late Goldwin Smith (1823–1910), a former professor of history at Oxford University and one of the Queen City's leading intellectuals, had dismissed the North American Indian in two sentences: "The race, everyone says, is doomed." He went on to add, "Little will be lost by humanity."[99]

The visitor ascended the stairs. Honoré directed himself to an office upstairs on the fourth floor, east side.[100] Two surviving letters of his mention the meeting. From Liverpool, England, on February 1, he had written to his mother and brother in Saskatchewan: "At Toronto I shall call on our old friend James Laughlin Hughes at Board of Education."[101] Back home in Chicago on March 17, Jaxon reported on their meeting: "In Toronto our old friend Jas L. Hughes entertained me finely."[102] Hughes had been his principal at the Toronto Model School forty years earlier. Unfortunately Honoré does not mention what they talked about, but one can always safely predict one topic that he loved to discuss, social justice for the working class. In April 1907, Henry Barrett Chamberlin had described him in these terms in the *Chicago Record-Herald:* "Weighing 150 pounds, eyes gray, piercing and steady, height 5 feet 8 inches, complexion dark, rather bald and wearing a small black mustache, Jaxon is alert, active and obsessed with the notion that he is the disinterested helper of the downtrodden."[103]

Like Chicago, Toronto was a city of obvious economic injustice. St. John's Ward, the centre of the city, reaching from the railway station to north of City Hall,[104] had the second-highest density of any other part of Toronto, except in Cabbagetown or East Toronto.[105] Throughout the city, health inspectors found "houses unfit for habitation, inadequate water supply, unpaved and filthy yards and lanes, sanitary conveniences so-called ... which have become a public nuisance, a menace to public health, a danger to public morals and in fact an offence against public decency."[106] Labour unrest had erupted in the district. Earlier that month more than one thousand garment workers in St. John's Ward's huge T. Eaton Company manufacturing complex had walked off their jobs in a dispute in one of the women's clothing departments. Issues included extremely low wages, harsh working conditions, and the exploitation of child labour. The strikers now faced one of Canada's most powerful employers.[107]

James L. Hughes. From Lorne Pierce, *Fifty Years of Public Service. A Life of James L. Hughes* (Toronto: S.B. Gundy; Oxford University Press, 1924), frontispiece.

Back at Mistawasis, both Elizabeth and Eastwood were most impressed by Honoré's letters and Aimée's summaries of his letters to her. His mother, and later her daughter Cicely, and then her daughter Cicely Jr. saved each one. But soon Eastwood and his mother would leave Mistawasis. With the Conservative victory in the federal election of September 1911, the Liberal Party went into opposition, which meant that Eastwood was out of a job. By the summer of 1913, he was back in Prince Albert, where he built a home for his mother and sister to allow Cicely's six daughters the best schooling possible.

Once back in Chicago from Britain, Honoré busily gave reports to different local groups and individuals. Aimée patiently waited for her turn to see him. During his absence abroad, she had collected newly released books, important ones that she thought he would like to read.

But when they met, she discovered that her wise husband had already read all of them. He brought her from England new titles to enjoy.[108]

One of the most enjoyable moments of their marriage came a few months after Honoré's return. In the summer and early winter of 1912, Frank Lloyd Wright invited Honoré and Aimée to Taliesin to meet his companion. Surprisingly they all got along very well. As Aimée wrote to Eastwood and her mother-in-law in mid-December 1912, "Honoré and I spent last June here and are back again before I had written our note of thanks." Mamah had an excellent education, with an MA from the University of Michigan. Aimée recalled how Mamah and Honoré recounted "their experiences in mastering Greek and Latin classics and quoting therefrom, while their ignorant mates sit aside wide-eyed and silent from astonishment."[109] In the summer of 1913, Honoré helped Frank to put in a vineyard and orchard at Taliesin. Frank and Mamah also invited Aimée to join them.[110] This horticultural assignment might have served as work in kind since the engaging champion of the underdog had little money and possibly could not repay his loan two years earlier for his journey to England.

Unfortunately a horrific event occurred at Taliesin but one year later. As Honoré reported to his family in Saskatchewan on August 16, 1914, "My friend Frank Lloyd Wright the architect received a terrible blow yesterday." In Chicago, he had learned by telephone that a crazed servant at Taliesin had taken a hatchet and killed Mamah, her two children, and four others and set fire to the house. All of this reinforced for Honoré the importance of simplicity: "The moral is get along simply, without servants and grandeur."[111]

In Chicago, as well as renewing his friendship with Wright, Honoré quickly resumed his participation in the Baha'i community. Two years earlier he had served as the executive board's negotiator responsible for purchasing land around the site of the United States' first Baha'i house of worship.[112] Ironically the location of the temple was once Metis land. The site was chosen in Wilmette, or Ouilmette, a Chicago suburb that bears the married name of Archange Chevalier Ouilmette, a Metis woman, the Ouilmette being spelled Wilmette. She had obtained this land grant in 1829. When the local Native Americans, the Potawatomis, had signed the 1833 Treaty of Chicago

Abdul Baha, Lincoln Park, Chicago. Honoré appears third from the end at the far right, Abdul Baha is in the centre left of the photo. National Baha'i Archives, United States National Baha'i Center, Evanston, Illinois.

and left the area, the Ouilmettes had relocated themselves to the new Potawatomi lands in the west.[113]

In Chicago in the spring of 1912, Abdu'l-Baha laid the cornerstone of the building that was to become the "Mother Temple of the West." Honoré wrote two articles in the Baha'i publication *Star of the West* about the visit to Chicago of Abdu'l-Baha, the world leader of the Baha'i community, the first about the cornerstone.[114] The title of the second article conveys its spirit, "A Stroll with Abdul-Baha Culminating in a Typical Baha'i Meeting under the Trees of Lincoln Park, Chicago." The article shows the restless warrior Honoré finally at rest in perfect harmony with his universe. Photos were taken, in one of which Honoré appears. In his article, he describes how Abdu'l-Baha used the occasion to give some timely advice to his Chicago followers:

> And now came the most striking feature of the morning's experience and the subject of the closing photographic illustration. ... Abdul Baha led the friends toward the lake, and taking one

> of a number of seats conveniently disposed under a group of trees, invited the friends to likewise be seated. They found themselves arranged in a circle, and, after dictating an answer to a letter which had been read to him that morning as he had walked along, Abdul Baha suddenly commenced talking to them in a strain of intimate and friendly counsel which exalted the hearts of all present and warmed the determination of each one to be doubly on guard against any future possibility of becoming a cause of disunion or discord. ... "I want you to be organized like a flock of the doves of Heaven, whose attitude and conduct toward each other is a symbol of that which will take place among human beings when human beings shall become willing to accept the guidance of the Holy Spirit."[115]

Honoré genuinely believed in the Baha'i faith. The initial open and non-restrictive approach to membership appealed to him. But, when he perceived this openness changing, his enthusiasm declined. In the mid-1910s, the Chicago and national Baha'i community, from his perspective, introduced too much organization and hierarchy, and he left.[116] Whenever walls and rules got too close, Honoré became uneasy.

His participation in the labour movement resumed as well upon his return to Chicago. At some point, he seems to have learned to speak some Yiddish, a language descended from the German of the Middle Ages, with many Hebrew and Aramaic words, and additions from Russian, Polish and various Romance languages. In one letter, he used the Yiddish phrase "Ish ka bibble (which being interpreted from the Yiddish, meaneth 'I should worry')."[117] He represented Local 504, the Jewish carpenters in the West Side, at the Chicago Federation of Labor[118] and in the Chicago District of Carpenters Council.[119] On February 20, 1916, he and J.J. Walt introduced a resolution, which the federation's executive recommended on March 5. It had all of Honoré's usual polemical style. The text reads,

> After a century and a quarter of legislative piracy, which has placed in their private control the forests and coal deposits and oil fields and a large part of the arable lands which by nature

are intended to be the common heritage of the people, the predatory interests of the United States are now reaching out (through the cunningly worded clauses of the so-called Shield's Bill, now pending in the United States Senate) to acquire private control of the immensely valuable water powers of the United States, with all their illimitable possibilities for providing the people at cost with heat and light and mechanical energy for vast co-operative enterprises.[120]

With the outbreak of World War I in Europe, Honoré immediately saw Germany as the aggressor state. "It seems to me," he wrote on September 27, 1914, "to be a crisis of the centuries and that personal liberty will disappear from the world of settled civilization for a long time if the unspeakable militarism of Germany should triumph. For once England seems to have entered upon a perfectly just war, and in spite of my being past 50 I have strong impulses to volunteer. Aimée of course objects!"[121] The United States remained out of the war until April 1917, but Honoré began to work right away for America's readiness for participation in the Great War. On account of his military appearance, others began to call him "Major."[122] He put this on the letterhead for his new organization, "League of Defensive Preparedness," with the motto "A Porcupine Bites No One. No One Wants to Bite a Porcupine."[123]

With America's entry into the war on April 6, 1917, the war became real for Honoré. He was given the assignment of speaking to a group of Russian anarchists in the city to win their support for the war effort.[124] Moral support was given for his work but "no financial backing."[125] After the war's end in November 1918, Jaxon wanted a change. He had lost many cherished acquaintances in Chicago and lamented "the decreasing number of my contemporary friends, while my enemies seemed to live forever!"[126] Aimée, too, began to pressure him to devote some time to financial security for their future. On May 3, 1919, he turned fifty-eight; how long could he continue devoting his life to others?

CHAPTER 10

TRYING TO BECOME A CAPITALIST

1919–36

SOME TOUGH YEARS IN THE MID-1910S ALLOWED AIMÉE TO win Honoré over to her point of view that they needed to make and to put away money for their old age.[1] In the summer of 1919, her beloved champion of the underdog attended the Atlantic City convention of the American Federation of Labor, his trip facilitated by a grant of $100 from the Chicago District of Carpenters.[2] He then went on to New York City for the Pan American Labor Convention.[3] In a letter to his mother, brother, and sister in Prince Albert, Honoré shared his first impressions: "The city is very fascinating but the congestion is terrible and the competition heartless."[4] But he saw in the New York area great economic opportunity. That winter he studied two new technological innovations, the "wireless," or radio, and tractors.[5]

With Aimée's approval, Honoré decided to stay there. In her own words to her sister-in-law, "I have always left him entirely free to follow his own guidance."[6] For several months or so, he lived on Staten Island,[7] just off Manhattan, and then in Atlantic Highlands, New Jersey, just an hour's ferry ride from New York.[8] There he wrote for the weekly paper, the *Atlantic Highlands Journal*.[9] According to Honoré, his articles were popular: "the people here think I am a vigorous and picturesque writer." Those who came out from New York for the summer, he added, appreciated "a little metropolitan pep in the local paper."[10] He later claimed that his investigatory articles on the bootlegging activities along that section of the New Jersey coast doubled the circulation of the paper.[11]

Aimée really liked the idea of Honoré remaining in newspaper work: "He is so eminently fitted for it and it gives a chance for expression which is absolutely necessary for a person who thinks originally on subjects. I also would like it and could help him considerably – take care of the society end, do an occasional short story, and fix up paragraphs of special interest to women, etc." But the editor and publisher died in August 1920, and the new owners did not, in the end, require his services.[12] He now moved to New York.

Honoré loved the opportunities that the huge metropolis offered, with its "facilities for culture and research."[13] Also, the real estate field beckoned him northward, a strange development, as he explained to his family back in Prince Albert: "It is very funny that I should have drifted into this real estate and insurance game considering my views about land title. Perhaps it will be another case of 'young radical-old conservative.'"[14] Over thirty years earlier, he had explained to his father his aversion to real estate speculation: "The light has been too strong for me and I shall probably die in the harness, fighting the evils of landlordism how could I become a land monopolist without searing my conscience."[15] Now, entering his sixties, he tried to change his direction.

Although no letters survive from the winter of 1921–22, a difficult moment for Honoré came in late 1921 when news reached him of his mother's death, at the age of ninety-three. Her obituary in the *Prince Albert Herald* on October 28, 1921 noted that unfortunately her last years had been marked by "senile decay." The paper noted this well-respected woman's "very large circle of friends" and added, "She is survived by two sons, Thomas Eastwood Jackson, of this city, and Honore Jackson, who resides in New York, and one daughter, Mrs. Amos Plaxton, with whom she had been residing on Twelfth street east." His mother had always offered him unconditional love, and while he had trouble with her attempts to mould him in her own way he had loved her dearly.

With Aimée's financial assistance,[16] Honoré purchased a number of properties in the Bronx, the only one of New York City's five boroughs

A photo of the house built by Eastwood for his sister and her family in Prince Albert. Mrs. Elizabeth Jackson, Honoré's mother appears in the centre of the group on the steps. Probably taken in the late 1910s. Courtesy of Joyce Arnold.

on the mainland. By 1924, he had assembled a chain of waterfront properties extending northeastward from the Bronx River along the Bronx shoreline.[17] Honoré reported that his wife was delighted "in my having taken to business at last instead of agitation."[18] Aimée proudly told her brother-in-law in a letter in 1925 that her husband's lots "have quadrupled in value in the last three years." She added that his "selections were strokes of genius."[19]

As late as 1890, the Bronx had a population of only one hundred thousand, at a time when Manhattan was home to one-and-a-half million. The Irish and Germans had long supplanted the original Dutch settlers. At the turn of the century came a third wave of migrants from the crowded tenements of lower Manhattan to the wide open borough. The newcomers filled up whole new neighbourhoods, built on former farms and estates. The competition of newly built subway lines in the first decade of the twentieth century increased the pace of development. Many New Yorkers realized that for only a nickel they could commute by rapid transit to Manhattan and live in the Bronx. Hundreds of thousands came north: Irish, Italians, and by far the largest contingent of all, Jews, transforming Bronx County into a metropolis in its own right. In 1923, the New

York Yankees themselves moved from the Polo Grounds in Manhattan to the new Yankee Stadium across the Harlem River. In a promotional pamphlet issued that year, the Bronx Board of Trade dubbed the borough "The Nation's Sixth City," with almost one million people, larger than major cities such as Baltimore, Saint Louis, and Boston.[20]

Honoré chose as the focal point of his real estate empire a strip of vacant land on the southwest bank of the Bronx River, just north of Hunt's Point. In 1923, he began building a "fort" out of 700 heavily constructed wooden ammunition boxes obtained, with permission, from an army base.[21] During the day, he worked on its construction. From the main tower on the top of his fort, Honoré told his sister and brother, he had a wonderful view, "extending for miles over the waters and islands and woods of East River and Long Island sound (Consult your maps) and yet backing up toward a subway station only 3 or 4 minutes walk away and then 25 minutes to B[road]way and 42nd the best of this world's amusement facilities."[22] He called his fort the Box Castle Garden.[23] It was quite an ingenious design. *The Home News, Bronx and Manhattan* later commented that his original structure was "visited by engineers and architects interested in the framing of the interior timbers of the main tower, which were specially arranged to resist the wind torsion incidental to the heavy northeast gales to which the site was exposed during the winter."[24]

Honoré still had the knack of getting good publicity; the *New York Times,* in fact, ran a story, "'Versatile' Jaxon Builds in Bronx," on November 29, 1925 on his fort. The paper provided an excellent physical description. "Single-handed he has erected this novel structure which towers above the Bronx River. It is in the midst of lumber yards, ice plants, stone works and a tin garage colony."

The "Major" gained the esteem of his community. In the words of *The Home News,* on March 23, 1927, "His learning is prodigious. Latin and Greek run through his mind as easily as do the charts of North wood trails."[25] The paper added, in a second article on April 3, 1927, that this descendant of the Metis Indians of Canada and Montana "was liked and respected by his neighbors and loved by the children."[26] For the benefit of the youngsters in the area, Honoré built a tower on his property for them to use as a clubhouse. The Major then organized them into Indian bands, with names such as Silver Foxes, Hawks, Gray Squirrels (for the younger children), Falcons, Eagles, Panthers, Black Beavers. "The condition of membership was to pledge themselves against playing hookey during school hours, against picking on smaller boys, against using obscene language and against thieving and malicious mischief." In addition, *The Home News* continued, this kind-hearted man "always placed the grounds at the disposal of the neighbors who wished to escape from their apartments during the hot, summer days and enjoy the view toward the shores and islands of the East River and the breezes that always pervaded the site even on the warmest days."[27]

Throughout the mid-1920s, Honoré tried to keep his mind focused on property values, mortgages and loans, but his interest occasionally strayed. In a letter to his sister Cicely on February 21, 1923, he wrote, "I am writing some lyrics and a comic song for a play expected to appear on B'way."[28] And despite the demands of his real estate work, he found time in May 1923 to give two talks, both for the Forum and Vocal Press, 279 Madison Avenue, with no titles specified. It billed him as "Major Honore J. Jaxon, foreign representative of the Metis Indians of Northwest Canada."[29]

Aimée, his best critic, identified the reoccurring problem that her husband faced in business: "Honore is a genius and practical to the extreme and unpractical to another extreme. In years gone by he would turn white and advance yards of reasons why it was wrong to even own any property or have any of the modern conveniences belonging to this age. I think he has left most of those ideas behind, but some are still present."[30] In the 1920s, he still refused to give capitalism the undivided attention that it required.

Under continual pressure to make mortgage payments and to pay the annual taxes on his lots, Honoré took a job as a night watch at a neighbouring lumberyard. For this work, he earned a welcome twenty dollars a week and was able to get some sleep, "having some good watchdogs to arouse me in case of invasion by thieves."[31] On his watch, he told Cicely, "I find myself often humming over the old hymns of our youth days." Although by now he had forgotten the words, the melodies and spirit of old Methodist gospel hymns remained. He loved the hymn that began "Some day the silver cord will break."[32]

Repeatedly in his correspondence in the mid-1920s, Honoré mentioned his memoirs. He told Eastwood that they would be "widely quoted, to match the wide range of experiences that they cover."[33] In another note, he stated that his recollections were "being called for from all sides."[34] Even Lyman Gage, his powerful banker friend from old Chicago days, wrote to him, he claimed, "urging me to write my memoirs and subscribing in advance for a copy of the book."[35] Why did he make no progress?

W.J. Carter, an old family friend of the Jacksons from early Prince Albert days, but now of Edmonton, contacted Eastwood in 1923 about the book that Honoré had planned to write on the early North-West Territories.[36] In a frank assessment in 1923, Eastwood informed him that his brother had forgotten a great deal. He added that, at the time of Honoré's visit in 1907, "I found that his recollection[s] of matters preceding the rebellion were generally very poor, especially during the period of his illness."[37] Maybe Honoré himself realized this. In any event, he made little progress in the mid-1920s on his memoirs. After the disaster that occurred in early 1927, the task became infinitely more difficult.

On March 22, *The Home News* reported on a fire that had led to the total destruction of Box Castle Garden. It began, "Now the pride of the Major's heart, his two-story home on the south bank of the Bronx River at Edgewater Rd. and Ludlow Ave., lies in ruins." The ammunition-box home, built without a heating plant, standing about twenty-five feet high, topped off by a tin cupola, with iron grilles in place of windows and a ladder in place of stairs, was no more.[38] The losses included "the unique historical and scientific collection stored in the castle." The fire had consumed "a highly decorated and very valuable Indian council tepee – together with books, private records and valuables assembled from various lands."[39] Honoré had lost the notes collected in western Canada from 1907 to 1909 for his memoirs.

He suspected arson, but the local police never found the culprits. Undeterred, he moved to another property of his, one located just a block or so to the south, still on the west bank of the Bronx River. There "Buffalo Heart" – this was the name he told *The Home News* that the Indians had bestowed on him[40] – established "Camp Contentment." As Honoré wrote back to his sister and brother in Prince Albert, it was the "first home S.W. of Bronx River."[41] But within three years he returned to his favourite property, the site of his Box Castle Garden, and began to build a new fort there.[42]

Originally Honoré hoped that Aimée would join him in the Bronx in late 1928, but limited finances prevented this move.[43] She had lent out so much of her capital. As she wrote to Cicely on July 4, 1930, "If I could collect the money I have loaned hereabouts to help others in stressful times I would have more than enough, but there is little hope of even eventually collecting."[44] Now in poor health, she simply wanted "a place to stay, very simple, plain, clean, with essential conveniences."[45] Her support for her husband had one condition. She refused to join him in the Bronx until she had proper assurances that he had installed running water and steam heat.

Her husband's choice of accommodations had distressed Aimée for years. As she wrote to Cicely, "He has roughed it so many years that he has little idea of what physical comfort means and basic necessities to me are luxuries to him. We just never could meet on these points. For years his ideal of living was the 'igloo' or tent."[46] Always the dreamer, Honoré wrote to her regularly about how close he was to securing enough income to have her come and join him and live in proper comfort. He needed only another six months. At long last, she refused to believe him any longer. In one of her last letters to Cicely, written on March 30, 1931, she lamented, "Do you know that for 30 years I have lived on that same idea of 'another six months would find us on easy street'? Do you wonder that it has ceased to mean anything beyond a sort of nightmare?"[47]

Aimée greatly admired Nathan Straus, the co-owner of Macy's, the world's largest store, in New York City. When the philanthropist died in early January 1931,[48] she commented in a letter to Cicely, "He had the right ideal. He had tremendous ability to make money in business, merchandising, and made fortunes over and over again and then used them to bring about better and healthier and happier conditions for people who for some reason cannot do things for themselves. His personal joy was in the using of them, the giving of them away to better the mass."[49] If only Honoré had first acquired a fortune and then concentrated on helping the underprivileged.

Desperately Aimée wanted her husband to sell one of his properties. "If he just let one go," she wrote to Cicely on May 15, 1930, "it will provide money enough to finance all the others and never miss what I want personally. Sometimes I feel that if things do not break now, it will be too late for me."[50] With incredible frankness, Aimée shared with Cicely, in whom she had complete trust, her frustration with her marriage to Honoré. She wrote on October 16, 1930, "Marriage with him has meant the privilege of supporting myself, being deprived of all other men's company while having very little of his, and feeling a great responsibility for his happiness and welfare. I have accepted the situation only because I know how sincere he is and how life has disappointed him and how he has struggled and that he could not do other than he has, nor did I expect it."[51]

Overnight the Great Depression, which began in late December 1929, changed all the old economic realities. Honoré became land poor. Although now willing to unload some of his lots, he could not, on account of the depressed economy, sell any of them. Countless numbers of businesses in the Bronx, Manhattan, and throughout North America shut their doors, causing widespread unemployment. National income fell from $81 billion the year of the crash to just $68 billion in 1930. By 1932, national income had plunged to $41 billion. All over New York City, shantytowns arose. Each day a ragged army of people looked for work or scrounged through garbage cans.[52]

Aimée died in Chicago on February 6, 1932.[53] What guilt her husband carried for his failure to meet her minimal demand, the installation of plumbing and heating in a proper house, remains unrecorded. Instead he had chosen to invest their hard-earned money in his New York property investments.[54] The unrealistic Honoré had believed that his land investments would result in a pot of gold, but they never did.

Honoré once described his opinion of marriage to one of his nieces in Saskatchewan. As far as the woman's interest was concerned, he saw the institution "as a man-made scheme for the annexing of female slaves."[55] Perhaps Honoré did put the needs of others before those of himself, but his blind spot remained the wishes of his wife. In his own way, he had truly loved Aimée; in fact, over the roughly ten-year period of their separation in the 1920s, he sent to her, by her count, five hundred letters.[56] With her death, he lost one of his few remaining links with reality. He had lost his wife, who had supported him loyally for a third of a century.

A natural disaster also struck later that year. The harsh weather in December 1932 led to a rat infestation. As Honoré wrote to his brother and sister on December 31, "The hard winter has set in motion against me a horde of waterside rats who gnaw through the boards of my shanty in search of food. One big fellow bit me on the nose while I was asleep the other night so I am now wearing a rat proof helmet over my head when I lie down."[57]

Honoré looked for audiences in the 1930s as his escape from reality became a full-time endeavour. He could still make important points. On December 8, 1933, the Major appeared before Mayor John P. O'Brien of New York and the city's Board of Estimate. The seventy-two-year-old protested against the city's expropriation of land for street purposes in the vicinity of McDowell Place, Schurr Avenue, and East Tremont Avenue in the Bronx. He argued that the Indians had not surrendered the district and then challenged the Board of Estimate to prove that any Natives had. Honoré told those assembled,

> The Corporation Counsel gave it as his opinion that Queen Anne gave the grant to the waterfront areas of this territory now under discussion to the town of Chester. But who granted the land to Queen Anne, gentlemen? There is no proof that the Indians ever gave up the grant to that land to anybody. What does the Corporation Counsel mean by denying these poor aborigines their rights? What would the early settlers have done if the Indians had not been so hospitable to them?[58]

Mayor O'Brien had no idea what he was talking about.[59]

The following year, while thumping a two hundred-year-old Bible, Honoré, in his loud, booming voice, told Mayor Fiorello La Guardia at

Honoré speaking in favour of the Lottery Bill, at hearing before Mayor La Guardia, at City Hall. *New York Daily News*/N1421876.

a public hearing on a proposed city lottery that no biblical injunction existed against one.[60] The two men crossed swords over this question, but Honoré bore no grievances and supported the "Little Flower" in subsequent elections. The *New York Daily News* on September 28, 1934 ran a magnificent photo of Honoré addressing the City Hall hearing. But, apart from these cameo appearances, he was absent from the public spotlight in the mid-1930s. Eastwood's death in 1935[61] came as another serious blow, just three years after he had lost Aimée. His sister Cicely, and her six daughters, were now his only immediate family members, as Eastwood was unmarried.

In Chicago, veteran journalist Charles H. Dennis, a former editor of the *Chicago Daily News* and the *Chicago Record,* began in the summer of 1936 a special historical series in the *Chicago Daily News* (Monday to Saturday, July 27 to September 5) entitled "Whitechapel Nights." It recalled Honoré in his glory days. In a letter on October 6, he commented to Cicely, "I am told that considerable newspaper mention of my activities of 30 years & 40 years ago has recently appeared in the

Chicago press – the writers being probably of the opinion that I have long since passed over the divide and can therefore be commended without danger to the established order of special privilege."[62] He would have loved the eighth article, that of August 4, 1936, with its full reference to Riel's secretary, "half French and half Blackfoot Indian." It was Riel's "final desperate experiment with armed rebellion," Dennis added, that sent his secretary into exile in Chicago, thus furnishing "the young geniuses of Chicago's Whitechapel Club with their most picturesque associate." Warmly in his article run on August 28, Dennis remembered Jaxon "with his coppery visage, his solemn demeanor, his high silk hat and his long black hair cut straight across his shoulders."

Dennis believed that the club owed Honoré Jaxon its best-remembered event, the cremation of Morris Collins. In article thirty, run on August 29, Dennis described how the "writings of the ancients from the Iliad down, were ransacked for light on approved procedure for reducing corpses to their simplest elements." Again Honoré's thought had preceded conventional wisdom. In 1892, there had been an uproar raised against the cremation of the dead. Twenty years later, by 1911, it had become almost commonplace. For over a quarter of a century, Chicago had its own properly equipped crematory.[63]

Aimée once wrote that "It's contact with other minds, and a variety of them, that stimulates thought and quickens all the mental processes." Honoré had lost his mother in 1921,[64] then his wife in 1932, then his brother in 1935. The deaths of many of his Chicago contemporaries, and his relocation to a new city, isolated the septuagenarian. As Honoré became more and more isolated, fixated on holding together his property, more and more he saw the forces of evil around him. His universe shrank to his nine properties in the Bronx.[65] So many were out to get him. As he wrote to Eastwood on December 3, 1930, "My income here is precarious for a Jew an Italian and an Irish Catholic – all Tammany men [the ruling Democratic Party machine] – are crazy to get someone else in my place."[66]

His interest in the Native peoples, with whom he had self-identified, declined. The political activist Rudolf Rocker, whom Honoré had met in England, visited Chicago in 1913. Rocker remembered many years later

Honoré's enthusiastic tour of "the big Ethnological Museum, which has a wonderful collection illustrating the life of the Red Indians."[67] But in New York, Honoré made no references in his correspondence to ethnology museums or Aboriginal gatherings. Apart from the 1933 hearing with the mayor about Aboriginal land rights in the Bronx, he seemed to have been totally disengaged from Native issues. His correspondence contains no references to New York's Museum of the American Indian – Heye Foundation or to the renowned American Museum of Natural History.[68]

Honoré, probably in his seventies, New York. Courtesy of Miss Cicely Plaxton

No references appear to lectures, such as that by the visiting Grey Owl, author, filmmaker, and popular lecturer from northern Canada, who visited New York in early 1938. What fun if the Major and the man whom the Toronto *Globe and Mail* in 1938 termed the "most famous of Canadian Indians"[69] had met. Both were gifted performers, shared a rich sense of humour, and had strong connections with Saskatchewan and Canada. They both regarded the Canadian government's attempt to assimilate the First Nations as despicable. In his first book, *The Men of the Last Frontier* (1931), Grey Owl wrote, "Under the white man's scheme of existence the Indian is asked to forget his language, his simple conception of the Great Spirit, and his few remaining customs, which if it were demanded of the Hindus, the Boers, the Irish, or the French-Canadians, would without doubt cause a rebellion."[70] Both men had something else in common: Grey Owl had the same Native ancestry as Honoré Joseph Jaxon – absolutely none. After Grey Owl's death on April 13, 1938, it was revealed within a week that he was not the North American Indian that he had claimed to be but the English-born Archibald Belaney, who had come to Canada in his late teens and lived with Ojibwa people in northern Ontario.[71]

But there is no record of Honoré attending. In his seventies, obsessed with his lots in the Bronx of now greatly diminished value, eating poorly, and living in a reconstructed fort without heat and running water, he began to lose his old equilibrium. About this time, Frank Lloyd Wright somehow located him in the Bronx and visited him. Otto McFeely, a newspaper friend of Wright's from his years in Oak Park, outside Chicago, later recalled his comments. The world-famous architect found Jaxon "living in New York in a big barn amid vast piles of stacked newspapers, dreaming of world reform while rats raced past him."[72]

CHAPTER 11

LIGHT, STORM, AND SHADOW
1937–45

IN TERMS OF BOTH THEIR APPEARANCE AND BACKGROUND, Lewis Stuyvesant Chanler and Honoré Joseph Jaxon differed substantially. Chanler, tall with greying hair, had the air of true patrician. In contrast, Jaxon, of medium height and balding, looked rather like an elderly professor. Chanler had enjoyed great professional success, Jaxon little. One lived in a four-storey house in the Upper East Side and had a country estate up the Hudson. The other resided in the Bronx, by the Bronx River, in a hut or what he called a fort. It had a foundation of granite paving blocks and walls of orange crates, filled with earth. One frequently dined at the finest restaurants and clubs. He and his wife had several servants: a butler, a parlourmaid, a lady's maid, and a family cook.[1] The other lived on a special cereal that he prepared himself in a great cauldron once a week.[2]

Chanler belonged to a wealthy and influential New York family with a family tree that included Peter Stuyvesant, the last Dutch governor of New Amsterdam (1647–64). His family also claimed among their ancestors John Winthrop, a Puritan governor of the Massachusetts Bay Colony. The family's wealth dated back to John Jacob Astor,[3] who had died in 1848 the richest man in the United States. Part of his fortune funded the Astor Library, a reference collection, later to form part of the New York Public Library. The Waldorf-Astoria was one of the Astor family's hotel properties at the turn of the century.[4]

Lewis Stuyvesant Chanler. Courtesy of Bronson W. Chanler.

Brought up like a young squire at Rokeby, the Chanler family's estate at Barrytown in Dutchess County, young Lewis lived a life of privilege. Educated by private tutors at home, he went on to Columbia University, then studied international law and jurisprudence at Cambridge University. In England, the articulate and engaging American law student became president of the Cambridge Union, the famous private debating society. Almost three centuries earlier, his ancestor, John Winthrop, had preceded him at Cambridge. Upon his return to New York, Lewis became an outstanding criminal lawyer. He took on more than one hundred murder cases with but one client paying the death penalty.[5] He later became a successful politician, serving as lieutenant governor of New York from 1906 to 1908.

Despite his privileged upbringing, this American patrician had a strong sense of social justice. Lewis gladly helped others in need. Despite his ability to charge the highest legal fees for his services, the distinguished criminal lawyer often defended clients who could not pay. In the words of his friend New York lawyer John Goodrum Miller, he was the "Knight Errant of the New York bar."[6]

Politically Jaxon and Chanler shared a common high regard for the incumbent Democratic president Franklin Delano Roosevelt. His administration, in the president's own words, fought "to find practical controls over blind economic forces and blindly selfish men." In his inaugural address on 20 January 1937, Roosevelt recognized the challenge of his second administration: "I see one-third of a nation ill-housed, ill-clad, ill-nourished." Then he added, "The test of our progress is not whether we add more to the abundance of those who have much, it is whether we provide enough for those who have too little."[7]

Lewis belonged to one of New York's most prestigious private men's clubs, the Knickerbocker, founded in 1871. Within the attractive red brick Georgian-style building, just off Central Park at Fifth Avenue and East Sixty-second Street, conservative attitudes dominated. The club took its name from the term that Washington Irving had popularized in his *A History of New York* (1809) to describe the "Dutch" families and customs in the Dutch region of early New York State.[8] The Knickerbocker's inaugural president had been Alexander Hamilton, namesake and grandson of George Washington's chief aide during the American Revolution and the first secretary of the Treasury. The New York lawyer's portrait in the club reading room reminded Knickerbocker members of their first president.[9] Egerton L. Winthrop, a relative of Lewis' and club president from 1911 to 1916, also had his portrait in the clubhouse. John Singer Sargent, one of America's foremost artists, was the artist.[10] Lewis enjoyed his lunches at the very comfortable club, only half a dozen blocks from his home, but held to his liberal ideas. As his second wife, Julie Olin Chanler, later recalled, "A Roosevelt man, he went daily to his fortress of reaction, the Knickerbocker Club, where the name Roosevelt was anathema, and extolled the exploits of our President in the gloomy circle of his friends."[11]

F.D.R. and teachings of the Baha'i faith constituted the bridges between Lewis Stuyvesant Chanler and "Major" Honoré Joseph Jaxon. They both belonged to the New History Society in New York City, led by the Persian Mizra Ahmad Sohrab. For over a decade, Julie Olin Chanler had acted as Sohrab's assistant and his associate editor on their monthly magazine, *New History.* At their request, Lewis had become chair of the New History Society in 1930. As he told an audience at Carnegie Hall in early February 1932, their group worked "to abolish all narrow expressions of patriotism, and to help establish a new form of World Patriotism, where the weakest will be as much considered as the strongest, where our neighbor of whatsoever race, color or creed will be thought of as our brother, and where the Golden Rule will be practiced by every nation on the earth."[12] Regularly he brought copies of *New History* to the Knickerbocker and left them on the club table.[13]

Julie had brought Lewis into the movement. The attractive, well-dressed woman[14] also had a privileged background: on her father's side, she was the granddaughter of the second president of Wesleyan University in Connecticut. Her father, a highly successful New York lawyer, a trustee of the New York Public Library, later became acting president of Wesleyan.[15] In her autobiography *From Gaslight to Dawn,* she wrote, "I also was born in the last century during which poverty and under-privilege were acceptable as in feudal times and when colonization was a God-given right. According to my upbringing, the Anglo-Saxon alone was civilized; even the European was suspect, while the natives of Asia and Africa were not to be considered. The Protestant religion was the sole respectable faith; Catholicism was endured; the rest were heathenism rampant."[16]

Only in her forties did Julie Chanler discover the Baha'i faith. As she wrote in her autobiography, "It was the modern revelation of the Ancient Truth that had been given humanity from time to time, its last expression being Islam, and its first that we know of being Hinduism at the beginnings of recorded history."[17] Through Baha'i teachings, she learned that "racial superiorities were a pitiful illusion." Everyone has "the same origin and destiny. Differences exist, but they are differences of climate and opportunity."[18]

Mizra Ahmad Sohrab became her great mentor in the faith. Born and raised in Persia, he had come to the United States as a young man in 1903. He translated from Persian to English, and from English to Persian, for the Baha'i community in Washington, DC, and worked for the Persian Legation.[19] He had served Abdul Baha as an interpreter on his North American tour in 1912. Honoré had met him at that time. After the tour, he had returned with Abdul Baha to Haifa, where he worked as a translator during the World War I years. After the end of the war, he had come again to the United States and lived for several years in California.[20] In 1927, on a visit to New York, Sohrab met Julie Chanler, who insisted that he come to New York and introduce others to Baha'i teachings. Quite early she learned that he was a controversial character in the Baha'i community since he opposed the formal organization of the Baha'i cause. "Some loved him; many mistrusted him; others were definitely opposed to him, and all were very conscious of him." Yet "Lewis and I saw nothing but good in Ahmad, so we went ahead, trusting to our own judgement."[21] Two years later they formed the New History Society but, as Sohrab insisted, without consulting the local Baha'i organization in New York or the National Spiritual Assembly.

In 1930, the National Spiritual Assembly responded. It informed "its friends that the activities conducted by Ahmad Sohrab through the New History Society are to be considered as entirely independent of the Cause, as outside the jurisdiction of the Local and National Assembly" and hence not entitled to the cooperation of the Baha'i community. Shoghi Effendi, the guardian of the faith, in Haifa, endorsed the excommunication.[22]

The New History Society reacted by expanding its activities. Its outreach in the early 1930s included the sponsorship of a series of talks at the Ritz-Carlton Hotel, and later the Park Lane Hotel, initially with very distinguished speakers such as Albert Einstein, already a renowned scientist; Rabindranath Tagore, the great Bengali poet and philosopher; Helen Keller, blind and deaf but one of the leading intellectuals of the twentieth century; the well-known John Dewey, American educationist; and Margaret Sanger, an early American champion of birth control.[23]

At the Chanlers' home, 132 East Sixty-fifth Street, the New History Society sponsored evenings with speakers such as Mizra Ahmad Sohrab discussing the Baha'i faith.[24] The house could accommodate a large crowd, and on at least one occasion nearly two hundred members and friends thronged the rooms on the first two floors and sat on the connecting stairs.[25] But subsequent consultation with the city buildings department led to a ruling regarding the exact number that the second floor could support, 140 only. When that number was reached, the Chanlers' butler hung a sign on the outside of the front door, and no more gained admittance.[26]

The New History Society tumbled greatly in the 1930s and could no longer hold public meetings in places like the Ritz-Carlton and the Park Lane. The Depression took its toll on the amount of money that Julie and Lewis Chanler could provide to support the activities of the society. By the estimate of Mirza Ahmad Sohrab, they covered more than ninety-nine percent of all expenses of the New History Society in its first eleven years of operation, from 1929 to 1940.[27]

But still, as late as April 1941, they organized a fine slate of Sunday-evening talks. Max Hudicourt, a political leader from Haiti, spoke on April 6, through a French interpreter, on "The Democratic Traditions of Haiti." The following week Dr. Haridas Muzumdar, a Gandhi scholar, reviewed *Toward Freedom,* Jawaharlal Nehru's recently released autobiography. The next week Frances Grant, the founder and president of the Pan-American Women's Association in New York, organized to work for greater unity among women of the Americas, gave a guest lecture on "Fundamentals for a New Pan-American." Then the evening of April 27 "Major Honore Jaxon," "one of the earliest Bahais in the United States," spoke on "Pathways toward God."[28] (In 1917 Honoré had awarded himself the title of Major,[29] which he now used constantly.)

The inclusion of Honoré in their program that spring indicates the Chanlers' respect for him. Interestingly Julie Chanler chose the same phrase that John Goodrum Miller used to describe her husband. She regarded Honoré as a "knight-errant." He was "a knight-errant through and through" whose "mind was fixed on causes preferably unpopular ones, and especially that of the American Indian for whose rights he fought unremittingly."[30] Later Mrs. Chanler summarized what their "part Indian" friend from western Canada had told the New History Society about himself, a wonderful concoction of fact and fiction:

> A graduate of the University of Canada where he took honors in the classics, he in 1885 figured as Major in the cavalry of the Metis tribesmen in an insurrection against the Canadian government. The leader and he were captured and charged with treason, the former being hanged while he escaped to the United States where, for the next thirty years, he roamed the Mid-West speaking of his experience. He came to New York about 1920 and established himself in the Bronx in a succession of make-shift cabins and shacks partly built of orange crates which he called "forts". There he spent most of his time

> poring over the books of his "library", a mass of material on the American Indian, weighing several tons.[31]

Both Lewis and Julie Chanler had an emotional tie with Native Americans. Lewis's family tree included the cleric and founder of the colony of Rhode Island, Roger Williams, educated at Cambridge University, from which he graduated in 1627. A trusted friend of the Narragansett First Nation, Williams wrote the *Key into the Language of America* in 1643 and tried to maintain good relations with the Native peoples.[32] Julie also sympathized with the North American Indians, "that race, whose rightful claims for a freer, richer life have unaccountably been ignored by the United States government."[33] Honoré's strong sense of social justice for the North American Indian drew the Chanlers to him. They also knew that Jaxon was one of the earliest American adherents of the Baha'i faith.

At the same time, the Chanlers retained some objectivity. They did not necessarily accept Honoré's racial claims. Julie later wrote, "Major Jaxon was part Indian, a fact of which he was very proud, although his delicately modeled Anglo Saxon features seemed to belie his claim."[34] Only a decade earlier, an experience with a "Blackfoot Indian," Chief Buffalo Child Long Lance, had sensitized Lewis to self-declarations of ethnic identity. William Chamberlain Chanler, Lewis's youngest son by his first marriage, had unmasked Long Lance.

Buffalo Child Long Lance had published his "autobiography" in 1928. His book about his Blackfoot youth in the days of the last buffalo hunts and skirmishes on the plains had gone through several printings and translations. Paul Radin, the distinguished American anthropologist, had praised it to the skies in the *New York Herald Tribune,* giving it his academic stamp of approval.

But William Chanler had harboured doubts. After studying law at Harvard, William joined the New York firm of Winthrop, Stimson, Putnam, and Roberts. In 1938, Mayor Fiorello La Guardia named him corporation counsel for the City of New York. A little over a decade before Honoré's lecture at his father's house on "Pathways toward God," William was legal counsel for the film *The Silent Enemy,* in which Buffalo Child co-starred. In the course of an investigation in early 1930 into

Honoré Jaxon. Photo taken from Mirza Ahmad Sohrab, *Broken Silence* (New York: Universal Publishing, 1942): 118. Glenbow Archives/NA-789--66.

Long Lance's alleged Plains Indian ancestry, William discovered that Long Lance was really one Sylvester Long, a man of some North American Indian ancestry but born and raised in the African American community of Winston-Salem, North Carolina.[35]

Yet, regardless of any doubts that they might have had about Honoré's racial claims, the Chanlers welcomed Jaxon into their movement. The fact that the local and national Baha'i organizations had ostracized the New History Society provided them with an added incentive to embrace "one of the earliest pioneers of the Bahai Cause in America."[36] For a decade, the national and local Baha'i leadership had opposed their teaching of the Baha'i faith and even disputed their right to make any use of the word *Baha'i*.[37]

In her reminiscences of Honoré, Julie recalled him as "Handsome in spite of his years, always well-dressed, speaking perfect English, never asking for anything and always afire with his thoughts and plans, he found a niche among us and was well-liked by all."[38] But he did have some failings, one being "overfluency of speech. Actually he could talk around the clock, and talk well, and he never saw reason for stopping." A photo of the New History Society six months later, on October 14, 1941, indicates individuals who might have been in attendance for his talk, a varied group from across the globe. Honoré appears as well, of course, as do the Chanlers and Mirza Ahmad Sohrab.[39]

Unfortunately no text of the talk survives. It undoubtedly was a long address. Honoré seemed to be unable or unwilling to limit his remarks, a problem that extended back to his nearly six hours speech in the Chicago Music Hall over half a century earlier. Lewis was not well in the late 1930s and early 1940s, so that left Julie as the time-keeper. At regular meetings, she constantly had to rein in the Major, who had no switch-off button. When told to limit his interventions, "He would say that at Indian meetings, all had a right to address the people, and if several attempted it simultaneously, that was acceptable too for the weaker vessels would fall out one by one, leaving the hardiest orator in full control."[40]

After an illness of several years,[41] Lewis died in late February 1942. The funeral was held on March 3 at St. Mark's-in-the-Bouwerie, the venerable Episcopal church in the Lower East Side, located on the site of Peter Stuyvesant's farm, precisely where his chapel once stood, where the last Dutch governor himself was buried. The farewell to Lewis, his friend John Goodrum Miller wrote, brought together "cavalier and yeoman, Jew and Gentile, Hindu and Mohammedan, Catholic and Protestant, all listening wistfully and willingly while an Episcopal clergyman and a Bahai representative read from the teachings of their two masters, finding no conflict of creed or practice."[42] By request, the church organist played music by Bach.[43]

Honoré's loquaciousness became too much for Julie after Lewiss' death. She had to let the servants go after he passed away, enter the kitchen, do the housework, as well as keep the organization alive. "Light, storm, shadow"[44] was how she later described this difficult period. Minor irritations had to go. Enough was enough. One day Julie bluntly told Honoré that he must limit his remarks: ten minutes maximum. The Major took this badly. In her words, "On account of this ten minutes limitation, he stopped coming to the meetings, but we heard from him occasionally when he was in trouble with the law, which was quite often, and our friendship continued to the end."[45]

Why this inflexibility on Honoré's part? Most likely the major reason for the break was the personal disaster that occurred in April 1942. This event apparently plunged Jaxon much further into the condition that his mother's obituary had termed, in her final years, "senile decay."

In mid-February 1942, the Health Department's inspector had charged in the Bronx Magistrate's Court that Jaxon's "Bronx Castle" was unsafe to live in, a fire hazard, and that it violated the city's sanitation laws. The eighty-one-year-old Jaxon shot back, "That's a misstatement of fact. For 20 years, I have lived there and there was nothing wrong with it. Why this proceeding?"[46] The *New York Times* quoted him as stating that the fence he had built of boards and corrugated tin around his home "is just the right kind of one to protect the Bronx against enemy submarines that might travel up the Bronx River."[47] But the city proceeded with the eviction. In late April it demolished his "palace," which contained almost all the personal papers he had saved since the fire of 1927 to write his memoirs. As he wrote to his sister Cicely in Saskatchewan, "In a way I am now free for new and joyous adventures, all my records having been scattered and destroyed."[48] His personal disaster left him more unhinged than before, and in a cantankerous mood he cut his link with Mrs. Chanler and her group.

Honoré's break with the New History Society left him, in his own words, with "no reliable friends around."[49] In the mid-1940s, he had really just one known acquaintance in New York, a German American, Kurt Mertig, who spoke with a strong Hamburg waterfront accent.[50] Julie Chanler knew of him as a "close friend" of Honoré's, an individual who often "took charge of the Major's affairs." She might have exaggerated the warmth of his relationship with Mertig, as Honoré distrusted Germans. Immediately after World War I, he had termed Germany "a murderer nation." He had argued that "Germany should be disintegrated and her entire able bodied manhood made prisoners of war and put to work under their own scientific 'regimentation' until an approximate national reparation is made."[51]

Mertig and Jaxon definitely knew each other by 1937, since in that year Honoré addressed two organizations connected to the forty-nine-year-old.[52] He spoke on April 5 at a meeting of the Citizens Committee of 500, at the New York Turnhall on East Eighty-fifth Street and Lexington, in the heart of Yorkville, known as the German quarter of Manhattan.[53] Although other people from Middle Europe lived there, in the vicinity of the Turnhall Germans and Austrians predominated. East Eighty-sixth Street, one block to the north, was known as "Yorkville's Broadway," lined with restaurants, cabarets, theatres, and meeting, and dance halls, as well as delicatessen and pastry shops.[54] Mertig chaired the Citizens Committee of 500.[55] His day job was working as a lower-echelon employee of the German American shipping line, but the busybody also headed the Citizens Protective League[56] and the German American Republican League. Both groups also met at the Turnhall.[57]

Major Honoré Jaxon spoke at a meeting of the German American Republican League at the Turnhall on June 14, 1937.[58] He claimed in a letter back to his sister on July 24, 1937, "Strange to say I myself seem to be getting stronger than ever as I become older. I am credited with being one of the most forcible and effective public speakers in the city and my verses on current events take the audiences in the solar plexus."[59]

Mertig's friendship with Jaxon represents the maximum possible misunderstanding. Mertig, described in the pages of the *New York Times* on March 16, 1937 as "an active organizer of pro-Nazi forces in this city,"[60] knew Jaxon as the Major,[61] a larger-than-life character, born in a buffalo camp, child of the endless prairies, with a Metis mother and a conscientious fur trader father. The American Nazi found it appealing that his friend was part Indian. In Germany, the author Karl May (1842–1912), who wrote books about American Indians set in the American west, enjoyed great popularity. Adolph Hitler, in fact, was a fanatical devotee of May's romantic novels.[62] Hitler himself declared that the American Indians were true Aryans.[63] To Mertig, Honoré represented an oppressed person. The Nazi propaganda machine portrayed the treatment of American Indians as horrific. The *Voelkischer Beobachter,* the Nazi Party's daily in Berlin, in mid-November 1938 attacked Canadian Indian policy as "inhuman"; the Native population, it claimed, had been "destroyed by starvation and liquor."[64]

According to Mertig, he and Jaxon had met around 1935. As he wrote in early 1952, "The old Major has come to my house practically every Saturday for supper during the last seventeen years, and sometimes two or three times weekly."[65] Whatever common issues they shared, they also had great differences. Honoré loathed regimentation and any kind of control over the individual. He loathed the tyranny of both communism and fascism. In terms of American and New

York politics, Mertig opposed Mayor La Guardia[66] and Franklin Roosevelt,[67] two politicians whom Honoré fully endorsed. As he wrote to his sister Cicely on July 24, 1937, "I am backing La Guardia for re-election as Mayor and Franklin Roosevelt for a third term."[68]

Honoré was not in any way a Nazi sympathizer. In the 1940 presidential election campaign, he served on the executive committee of the Bronx County Committee of Independent Voters for Roosevelt and Wallace.[69] He felt that Roosevelt, who fought for the common man,[70] was "our greatest President since Lincoln's death – with his wife even surpassing him!"[71] Jaxon supported the war, noting in a letter to his sister on July 22, 1944, "It seems to me that we have won through in Europe. The crack up is evidently commencing."[72] But Honoré, alienated and alone, was vulnerable. This fringe character Kurt Mertig took him seriously, made him feel important, and gave him a meal at least once a week.

In his old age, Honoré's obsession with conspiracies reached new levels. Although Jaxon tried to practise his belief that it was one's duty to love "one's neighbor as oneself,"[73] his letters in the 1930s and early 1940s betray an intense mistrust of his Bronx neighbours, who were, he felt, determined to steal his properties. The fact that his neighbours were Jewish led to a surfacing of anti-Semitic attitudes. Canadian historian Gerald Tulchinsky has noted that, in the late nineteenth century and early twentieth century, anti-Semitism "was part of Canada's general culture."[74] Why did these attitudes arise when Honoré reached his midseventies? He knew that his hero Riel had thought highly of the Jews and believed, in fact, that the American Indians were descendants of the Hebrews. Just after the fall of Batoche, Honoré had told Dr. George Orton that Riel had informed him that the Indians were "a portion of the lost tribe of Israel."[75] Moreover, in Chicago in the late 1910s, he had served as the Jewish carpenters' delegate to the Chicago Federation of Labor as well as to the Chicago Carpenters District Council.[76] Now Honoré lived in the South Bronx, one of the few areas of North America where the Jewish community constituted the overwhelming majority of the population.

By 1930, the population of the Bronx as a whole was forty-nine percent Jewish, and in the South Bronx, south of Tremont Avenue where Jaxon lived, over eighty percent were Jewish.[77] Honoré believed that the infamous Jewish mobster Dutch Schultz, or to use his real name, Arthur Flegenheimer (1902–35), who controlled the bootleg liquor business in the Bronx during Prohibition (1919–33), had burned down his original "castle" in 1927. Shortly after that disaster, he claimed, a "spiteful Jewish chief whom I had foiled" had torched the one-storey bungalow that he had put in its place.

It was not just the Jews; Honoré in his early eighties also lashed out at the "Irish Catholic functionaries who were in power politically for the benefit of Irish Catholic thieves."[78] The Democratic political clique led by the Irish and working-class Jews maintained its grip on the governmental and business life of the Bronx,[79] and to them he attached the blame for the loss of his properties. (Honoré, in reality, lost most of his real estate in the 1930s and early 1940s not on account of his neighbours but because of his failure to pay his taxes.)

Julie Chanler, even before America entered the war against the Nazis in late 1941, realized the extent of the "horror emanating from Germany." She knew of the concentration camps and the Nazi "determination to wipe a race from the surface of the earth." Originally a pacifist, she "wanted Hitler to be opposed, come what might."[80] Honoré opposed Germany as well, yet the confused individual kept up his ties with Mertig, who apparently became Jaxon's only human link in the city after his break with the New History Society.

Mertig claimed that Major Jaxon stayed with him for several weeks after the destruction of his Bronx fort and again for several weeks in early 1943.[81] Then there came a break. Late in 1943, the Army Exclusion Board ordered Kurt removed three hundred miles inland from the Atlantic coast as a security measure.[82] In 1945, Honoré left the South Bronx and relocated to Manhattan, to "a modest three room apartment – three feet below sidewalk level – in a location handy to street car, subway, bus, and elevated lines of transportation, and only five minutes walk from splendid facilities for study in the Arts and Sciences."[83]

CHAPTER 12
THE DESCENT, NEW YORK CITY
1945–52

In his eighties, Honoré Jaxon, once known as Will Jackson, was no longer a psychologically coherent personality. His descent downward had few landings or level places. Alone in New York City, he had but one known "friend" in the late 1940s, the strange, twisted individual named Kurt Mertig. Honoré's break with the New History Society in the 1940s had separated him from Julie Chanler, his only other known human connection in the city.

Mertig spent the spring and early summer of 1946 serving a six-month jail term in the psychopathic cellblock of the New York City Penitentiary and Workhouse,[1] Rikers Island, East River. He and two others had been arrested for distributing anti-Semitic literature at a Christian Front gathering in early October in the New York borough of Queens. Mertig had begun his talk at the Christian Front meeting with "I am speaking as an American, a Christian and a white man."[2] The released inmate returned to Manhattan in June 1946 to find even fewer adherents to his fascist cause than before the war. The horror of Nazi Germany had put anti-Semitism to shame in the United States. Publicly hardly anyone would have had the bad taste to be openly anti-Semitic after World War II,[3] yet Mertig did.

In March 1947, Victor Bernstein, a journalist for the New York daily *PM*,[4] attended a meeting of Mertig's Citizens Protective League held in a meeting hall above a Third Avenue saloon in Yorkville. Hardly anyone appeared. To the dozen assembled, eight men and four women, plus the one journalist in attendance, the meeting's sponsor declared, "I am not an anti-Semite. I am only against international bankers and against the people who have made poor Germany so unhappy." He proceeded to defend Hitler: "The only reason Germany turned to HITLER, was because the HARD PEACE after the first war threatened GERMANY with STARVATION." Throughout he apologized for the small attendance; "many of his brave followers, especially women, were afraid to come downtown into this rough neighborhood." Yet, as Bernstein noted in his article, this was a ludicrous suggestion, as just across the floor from Mertig's tiny gathering two hundred men and women listened in an adjacent room to a German-language lecture on theosophy.[5]

No evidence exists that Honoré attended Mertig's meetings. He abhorred regimentation of any sort, fascist or communist. He loved the poetry of Scottish national poet Robbie Burns, the champion of "freedom," poetry that provided "the necessary atmosphere for the developing of the human soul." As he wrote to his niece Mary Plaxton on 21 January 1949, "Bobby Burns is my favorite poet; and the world has not yet caught up with his profound humanitarianism and independence of thought."[6]

Yet, paradoxically, despite his love of the poetry of Burns and of liberty, Honoré in his eighties remained close with Mertig, a supporter of totalitarianism, the complete antithesis of freedom. In a typed letter to his sister and her daughter, Cicely Jr., written on March 28, 1949, Honoré wrote, "In case of anything happening to me, you must at once get in touch with my friend Kurt Mertig who has access to my affairs and can be depended upon to do the right and capable thing. You should, of course, compensate him according to your ability."[7] As previously mentioned, in her late eighties, Honoré's mother had suffered from "senile decay."[8] Apparently so did her second son in the same period of his life. This dementia helps to explain why Jaxon remained in close touch with Mertig after the war.

Beginning in the summer of 1945, Honoré lived in Manhattan, having finally moved from his apartment in the South Bronx.[9] The South Bronx in the early 1940s was becoming a dangerous neighbourhood. A member of a family who moved into Hunt's Point in 1943 later

Cicely Jackson Plaxton. Courtesy of Joyce Arnold

Cicely Plaxton, Jr. Courtesy of Joyce Arnold

recalled the safety precautions that they took at their four-bedroom apartment on the third floor of a four-storey brick tenement. "We kept our doors and windows locked. I remember a steel rod running from the back of our front door to a brace on the floor, so that no one could push open the door. Burglaries were common. Drug use was on the rise. Street fights and knifings occurred. Gangs armed with clubs, bottles, bricks and homemade .22 caliber zip guns waged turf wars."[10] Colin Powell, the future chair of the Joint Chiefs of Staff, and American secretary of state, was six in 1943 when his family relocated to the South Bronx from Harlem.

In mid-Manhattan, Honoré took a job as the janitor of a fourteen-suite apartment building on East Thirty-fourth Street. He lived in the basement unit that could be reached by a sidewalk trap door and a twenty-foot ladder.[11] There he stored his growing "library." This became his new obsession. Every morning he rose at 5 a.m. to feed the furnace with coal. Proudly Honoré told his sister Cicely in a letter postmarked May 17, 1947, "I can make out as a janitor filling furnaces, hoisting ashes, bringing down garbage and cleaning floors, if I get dead broke, although now 86 years old. Also I can tend a newsstand for a few hours each day at 50 cents per hour – enough to pay the $10 rent and a bread and milk diet."[12] At 6 a.m. all year long, he opened the newsstand at the northwest corner of Third Avenue and East Eighty-fourth Street in Yorkville.[13] For food, he relied mainly on milk and raw eggs for sustenance,[14] supplemented by a special cereal that he cooked in a great cauldron once a week.[15] During his afternoons, he went to auction sales looking for second-hand books.[16] In May 1947, he estimated that he had five tons of books in his library.[17]

In the summer of 1947, Cicely Plaxton, now eighty-four, and her eldest daughter, Cicely Jr., fifty-two, visited Honoré for two weeks in New York. His sister recognized his face, but he now looked so much older. They had not seen each other for nearly four decades. Cicely and her daughter stayed the first two nights at a YWCA and then moved to the suite in Yorkville that Honoré had charge of in the owner's absence, an apartment on the first floor of an old five-storey building.[18]

Perceptively Cicely wrote of her brother in her diary, "H[onoré] was well and can read without glasses but I think he has had some difficult times during the last forty years." He was delighted to see them and to show them the city." As she noted, "As Honoré says, there are wonderful facilities for acquiring knowledge in New York – Museums of all kinds[,] libraries with every facility to help gain knowledge on every subject in the universe, Zoological Gardens, parks galore, just to go thro' these and see everything would take months, and most of these are free [...] What we saw was infinitesimal when you think of the numbers of these institutions."[19]

In the company of his sister and niece, Honoré seemed intelligent enough, his critical outlook as sharp as ever. No, New York's museums were not the liberating forces that they might have appeared to be. "On the surface it looks as if the poor had so great a chance as the rich to acquire knowledge, but in reality since the hours these are open are from about 9 or 10 a.m. to 4 or 5 p.m. only the leisured class can take advantage of them."[20]

Yet a disturbing aspect of her brother surfaced at times. His memories had become hazy and confused, even about his family background, basic information to say the least. He held, for example, the bizarre idea that he had been adopted. This idea had already surfaced in his letters. It could be traced back almost two decades, to a note written about 1930 to Eastwood. Like a stone falling out of heaven, he asked, "I wonder if there is not something in what Riel's half breeds claimed that I was really the son of an English trader and a French half breed girl and taken down to Ontario to be adopted by the pater [Thomas Jackson] in place of a baby deceased."[21] His hypothesis had gathered momentum over the years, with the substitution of a Virginian father for the original English one. In a letter written on April 22, 1932, Jaxon had mentioned to Cicely, "I am very glad of my Virginia ancestry as declared to me by R. [Riel?] and others."[22] His overheated imagination had developed this further; in a letter dated June 9, 1946, Honoré had referred to Cicely as his "foster sister." In the next note, in late September, he had spoken about "your father," not "our father,"[23] and had introduced his "Virginia relatives."[24] These kinfolk had "advanced me the money" to assemble his library. *The Home News,* the Bronx newspaper, had reported on February 20, 1942, "He said he is a member of the Metis Indian Tribe of the Canadian Northwest. His mother was born in the tribe and his father was a Virginian who lived with the tribe."[25]

Cicely had the family archives. She might easily have shown Honoré two emotional letters sent back to grandmother Eastwood in England, later returned to them for their family's records. The first, written by their father, and the other by their mother, announced the birth of a treasured second son, "Wm Henry May 3rd 1861."[26] But she left it alone. Honoré had lost the ability, or perhaps the desire, to distinguish between fact and fantasy. In the late years of his life, he expanded in the same way upon his military title. He now replied to those who asked that he had "attained the rank of major while fighting in the Spanish-American War and World War I."[27]

Quickly Cicely sized up the situation: "As far as the city goes I cannot imagine a lonelier life than one lived there."[28] Elsewhere she wrote in her diary, "I don't think friends amount to much in that great city. It is a great city – crowds, crowds – people rushing here, rushing there, paying no attention to anyone else, catching buses – taxis, rushing down the subway, climbing to the overhead. The streets are like canyons between the skyscrapers."[29]

Honoré wanted the two Cicelys to stay in New York. Cicely Jr., he thought, could get a job teaching. But the low salaries for teachers and the high cost of living in New York City ruled that out.[30] When they left, his sister recorded in her diary, "I wanted him to come home with us but he would not. He came to the station with us and stood outside the window till the train left (the windows could not be opened) and walked alongside the train as it slowly started till it got too fast for him. My heart aches when I think of him there. (We were such dear playmates in our childhood)."[31]

Cicely and her daughter met Kurt Mertig. At the newsstand in Yorkville where Honoré worked, he introduced his friend to them.[32] They left no description of him, but the investigative reporter Avedis Derounian has. He described the German American as "a rolly-polly sort of man, wears glasses, double chin, red-cheeked, beer-guzzling sort." He spoke broken English with a thick accent,[33] stuttering when he could not find the right English word.[34]

Did Cicely know about his neo-Nazi links, his articles for the anti-Semitic San Diego weekly newspaper *The Broom*?[35] When they met in July, her brother's friend perhaps mentioned *The Broom* to her since he was the subscription agent.[36] Since 1943, Mertig had been a devoted reader and then contributor.[37] What did he say to her? Did he share his viewpoint that "the future of America, Christianity, the white race and the civilized world is inseparably linked with that of Germany"?[38] Cicely made no comment on the man in her diary.

From his articles in *The Broom,* Mertig presented himself as the voice of German Americans, yet even within the tiny New York neo-Nazi movement he had little support.[39] In a letter published in *The Broom* on December 1, 1947, a New York City reader described him "as a rather pathetic figure of a little man who means well but lacks the necessary zing and approach to put it over."[40] Leon de Aryan (he had changed his name from Constantin Lagenopol to Leon de Aryan to advertise the cause),[41] the editor of *The Broom,* had little respect for his contributor. Regularly in his paper he criticized his columnist.[42] In one issue, he even called him an "imbecile."[43]

Evidence exists that Cicely Plaxton mistrusted Mertig. Honoré's mailing address was care of Paladino's, a barbershop near his basement apartment on East Thirty-fourth Street. Although Cicely knew from Honoré where Mertig lived, 317 East Fifty-fourth Street, she chose to use the Paladino address in her correspondence with her brother. In the typed letter of June 19, 1948, Honoré noticed this: "I have received the red card signed by Cicily [corrected by hand to Cicely] Jr., but no other communication addressed to Mr. Mertig's care, as I suggested in my note of enclosure."[44] Cicely continued to send mail to "Major Jaxon c[are] of Paladino 161 E. 34th St."[45]

Honoré's situation in New York greatly troubled Cicely. A year after her return to Prince Albert, she asked the Salvation Army in Manhattan to visit him at his newsstand. On September 9, 1948, Captain Van Pelt reported back that one of their workers had called on him and "found him to be in excellent health, and seemed quite capable of handling the work of the newsstand. He was well groomed."[46] A few months later Honoré explained to Cicely's daughter, Mary Plaxton Grant, about his two jobs in a letter sent on 21 January 1949: "Before 5 A M I arise and attend to the furnace and other work of a fourteen apartment house. To give you an idea of my strength I may say that I use a coal shovel of the largest size, such as is usually selected by a man of 200 lbs. free from fat." Then he was off to the newsstand in Yorkville.[47]

Cicely wrote to the Salvation Army again in mid-February 1949. She explained her dilemma: "He writes me from time to time but I do not know where he lives or whether he had any real means of subsistence. I cannot tell from his letters what his health is." She knew, as he had written this to her daughter Mary, that he worked as a furnace man to earn his apartment and that he had two paid jobs: "One was gathering up garbage at an apartment house: 225 E. 83rd St., the other attending a news stand at 3rd Ave. and E. 84th St from 10 a.m. to 4 p.m." Cicely added, "It is terrible to think of him gathering garbage at any age but at 88!!! He used to be a fair French and German scholar and I think he learned Spanish at one time also the dead languages. I don't think he ever worked in any office, but I rather suspect that some people use his knowledge – getting it for nothing."[48] Her death on July 27, 1949[49] removed the closest person to Honoré left in the world.

After Honoré's death in early 1952, Mertig claimed in a note to his nieces that he had written many letters on Jaxon's behalf. Apparently the Major had claimed exemption from taxation for lots he had purchased over the years in the Bronx. "I wrote many letters of protest for him, but only last May or June [1951] the City claimed against foreclosure on account of unpaid taxes." Mertig suspected that the back taxes had exceeded the value of the property. "Major Jaxon was always secretive about these things and I did not inquire further, as he always launched into interminable discussions and asked me to write lengthy letters and poems to the tax people which I was afraid [would] take too much of my time – and would not be read anyway, as irrelevant."[50]

Cicely had doubts about Mertig, and evidence exists that her brother did too. Honoré withheld information, for instance, that he had a will. Feeling that something should be done, Mertig, "not knowing whether a last will existed,"[51] prepared one for him. On July 26, 1951, he had a notary sign it. Only after Honoré's death did he discover that Jaxon had already made one, prepared shortly after his sister's death. Mertig also learned that Jaxon had retained his own lawyers. On August 12, 1949, Manhattan lawyers Leo Kaplan and Hyman Diamond had prepared his will.[52] They were Jewish. Honoré had trusted Kaplan and Diamond, not Mertig, to execute this important document.

In April 1951, Jaxon left the Yorkville newsstand since he did not get along with the new young owner.[53] To help Honoré out, Mertig later claimed, "I paid the old Major from [two dollars to four dollars] a week for looking over some articles I wrote. I arranged with some friends to also pay him for his correcting their occasional articles." With the spare time Jaxon had after completing his janitorial duties, he bought books at auctions. "He was known there as a bargain-hunter, taking everything left over at 10 cents a book which accounts for the enormous stack of books, all piled in empty cartons at his two rented basements, which are all without light."[54]

Misfortune arrived twofold several months after Honoré left his newsstand job. First, in the early summer of 1951, a car knocked him down near the building at which he worked as a janitor. He let it drive on since he was at fault, crossing the street on a red light and did not think that he had been hurt. Second, the same summer, he became ill and was hospitalized for a week at the Bellevue.[55]

His hospitalization in early July 1951 set Honoré back a great deal financially. In his hour of need, he got in touch with an old acquaintance. As he wrote to his niece Cicely, "a lady of one of the Knickerbocker families came to my room with 25.00 so the 25.00 rent for August was taken care of." Later in his note to his niece, he identified his angel of mercy who had called on him at the Bellevue. "Julie Stuyvesant Chanler at 132 E. 65th St. is the one who paid my rent and told the old age Dept to look after me and is the one person both reliable and rich and influential."[56]

After their mother's death in 1949, Honoré's nieces Cicely and Mary tried to convince their uncle to come back home with them to Saskatchewan. Mary confided in a note to her sister on July 10, 1951 that "His position is so pitiful."[57] In September 1951, his obsession with being adopted reached a new level of intensity. In a letter to Mary, he told her that "in reality I am the son of a Virginia father and French Indian mother born in Montana but taken, by an English buffalo hunting relative of your grandfather, down to Canada and placed with your grandfather for custody but not adopted, thus not invalidating my American citizenship. Cicely Sr. confirmed this from remarks made by a hired domestic when we were both children."[58]

Mary and her husband wanted to bring Honoré up to their farm, where he could spend his last years "in comfort and write his memoirs." They offered to pay freight on a small number of the books as well as his fare. He could store the rest of his library and send for additional books left behind as he was able.[59] But Honoré replied that, if he put all the items in his apartment and two storage apartments together, he would have a stack of books "about 10 feet square and 7 feet high, and possibly weigh fifteen tons!"[60] He could not leave New York, he wrote on September 14, 1951, until he had sorted his books out "into at least three groups according to importance."[61] He believed that "among the thousands of volumes are books which would enable the Indians to recover the lost arts of their fathers."[62]

Isolated and alone in Manhattan, Honoré did make one attempt in the last year or so of his life to make human contacts beyond Kurt Mertig. Wanting to communicate with others, he regularly visited the *Bowery News* at 204 East Thirty-sixth Street, a three-room office in a shabby tenement, just two blocks away from his basement apartment on Thirty-fourth. Editor Harry Baronian later recalled that first meeting:

> He was first introduced to me by a good, if amusing character called "Wall Street Abie," a character who talked so much about knowing J.P. Morgan and all those Wall Street "wheels" that the 'boes finally monickered him "Wall Street Abie" and the name stuck. Abie knew the Old Majah who often stood him to a cuppa Java when [...] Abie was near to "carryin' the banner," (that is sleeping in the Park or a subway platform).[63]

Honoré would stay for two or three hours at the *Bowery News,* talking away in his powerful, booming voice. From his years among the disadvantaged of New York, Baronian knew many of its characters, including the Skid Row intellectuals. He included among his *Bowery News* distributors, for instance, the "Professor," or Walter Edwin Peck, who could discuss mathematics, physics, art, or literature. The tall, gaunt-looking man had grey flowing hair cut in the fashion of Lord Byron, his literary hero.[64] Peck had a Columbia MA and an Oxford PhD and was a former professor at Hunter College in New York, where initially he showed promise of a brilliant academic career.

In 1927, he published his two-volume study *Shelley: His Life and Work,* which earned the praise of English novelist and essayist Virginia Woolf:

> Molding the enormous mass of the Shelley papers with dexterous fingers, he contrives tactfully to embed dates and facts in feelings, in comments, in what Shelley wrote, in what Mary wrote, in what other people wrote about them, so that we seem to be breasting the full current of Shelley's life, and get the illusion that we are, this time, seeing Shelley, not through the rosy glasses or the livid glasses which sentiment and prudery have fixed on our forerunners' noses, but plainly, as he was.[65]

Peck's book was considered the standard biography of the English poet and essayist in the 1930s.[66]

A romantic scandal ended Peck's academic career. As the *New York Times* later recalled, "In 1929 his career was ruined by a sensational court action in which his wife won legal separation, charging Professor Peck with frequent misconduct with students, secretaries, and colleagues' wives."[67] He ended up in the Bowery washing dishes in cheap restaurants and peddling the *Bowery News.*[68] The once distinguished scholar of English literature and his cronies met at their favourite hangout, a bar called Mike's near Houston and Broome Streets, a sort of lower-depths version of the famous Round Table that formerly met at the Algonquin Hotel. They referred to their meeting place as "The Pitcher Joint," for there they could order a pitcher of wine for only fifty cents.[69]

Baronian knew Peck, but he respected Honoré. "He'd talk you blue in the face – and it was the talk of an intelligent man, too." He seemed to come from a larger universe. "You felt always he was a considerable man and had seen much of cities and people like Ulysses."[70] The old man took great pride in pulling out old letters "to prove to me he'd known some pretty big and some pretty tough people in Chi[cago], round about from 1900 to 1910."[71]

Just two and a half months away from his ninetieth birthday, Honoré wrote to nieces Cicely and Mary, on February 22, 1951, outlining the philosophy that had guided him for the past half century. With his mental decline from his sixties on, much had been lost, but still some fragments of his admirable early world view survived: his freedom from the constraints of conventional society. He still had insights worthy of imitation:

> First, I want to do everything that is humanly possible as my contribution to the peace of mind of the descendants of Cicely senior. Secondly, I want to do everything that I humanly can to promote the happiness and peace of mind of the French-Indian people with whose affairs I was so closely associated in the eighties of the last century – a people whose fine qualities were revealed to me during their struggle against great hardship, and connection with whom was accentuated by evidence brought through Louis Riel which I have never been able to dismiss as

irrelevant or incompetent. Thirdly, I want to do all that is humanly possible in the way of contributing to the solving of the difficulties and hardships of the many fine honest hard-working people with whom I have become associated in the United States during the last seventy years of my life, and fourthly, I want to do all this in submission to the will of God, and without foolishly interfering with the designs of God himself to bring about the elevating of the entire human race from its initial attribute of cannibalism – each person and each nation seeking only to grab for oneself – to that ultimate state of Grace in which each person and each nation will seek and find happiness only in promoting the general welfare – all in accordance with Christ's wonderful definition of pure religion; to "Love God with all one's heart and one's neighbor as oneself."[72]

Honoré's eviction occurred on December 12, 1951. Harry Baronian contacted the papers and supplied them with background information on Jaxon's life. The *New York Times* learned that Jaxon had been "a major in the cavalry of the Metis tribesmen, who fought the Canadian government." The *Herald-Tribune* reported that he had been "an aide to Louis Riehl [sic], leader of a half-breed rebellion in the Saskatchewan Valley." As the *World-Telegram* tersely summarized, "Honore J. Jaxon, for most of his 90 years a colorful fighter for lost causes, has lost his last fight."[73]

In New York, no one cared to chase down the pack rat's origins, the story being of purely entertainment value. In Canada, the association of the man with Riel made it of greater interest. The Metis leader's name remained alive north of the border; in fact, a rediscovery of Riel had just begun.[74] Only two years earlier, Canadian playwright John Coulter had written *Riel,* a powerful epic drama emphasizing his role as hero, prophet, and martyr.[75] The play portrayed him as the champion of a small oppressed nation.[76] The New Play Society had performed it at the Royal Ontario Museum Theatre in Toronto from 17 to February 25, 1950. Mavor Moore had played Riel, while Don Harron had played Thomas Scott. CBC Radio had adapted and broadcast the play in its *Wednesday Night* series in April and May 1951.[77] The message delivered in Part 1, Scene 2, restated a truth of universal significance: "The people of a country [His voice rises towards a passionate climax] can not be taken over and incorporated into some other country without their own consent. To try to do that to a people is an outrage. A violation of the rights and dignities of free men. We will fight against it. God has directed me. ..."[78] Moore later wrote that it was the New Play Society production "that sparked the revival in Rieliana that swept across the country" and inspired among other works the opera *Louis Riel* (1967).[79]

That August Louis St. Laurent had spoken up for Riel in a speech at Battleford, Saskatchewan. The French Canadian prime minister from Quebec had urged that the term "uprising" rather than "rebellion" be used to describe the troubles of 1885.[80] He added that the Metis at Batoche "wanted to be treated like British subjects and not bartered away like common cattle."[81] W.O. Mitchell, a writer for *Maclean's* magazine in Toronto, summarized the controversy that had followed: "Instantly, so powerful are the feelings engendered by his name, a storm of hot discussion spread through the west. Newspapers broke out in a rash of letters to the editor as church dignities, service clubs, Mounted Police veterans and plain citizens placed indignant or approving pen to paper."[82]

Realizing the potential Canadian interest, the New York City bureau of the Canadian Press wired the story of Jaxon's death northward on 14 January 1952. The report began, "Honore Joseph Jaxon, 90–year-old veteran of the Riel Rebellion, died last Thursday in Bellevue Hospital. Jaxon, a militant friend of the Indian and the underdog, had been a patient since last Dec. 27, two weeks after the latest in a series of evictions that had darkened his declining days."[83]

Bruce Peel, the newly appointed chief cataloguer for the Rutherford Library at the University of Alberta, read the Canadian Press despatch in the Edmonton *Journal.* At the time, Peel was working on a book, *The Saskatoon Story,* with Eric Knowles of the Saskatoon *Star-Phoenix.* Immediately he knew that Major Honoré Jaxon had really been Will Jackson, Riel's secretary in the Rebellion of 1885, as nearly a quarter of a century later he had appeared again in Saskatchewan.

In the summer of 1909, Saskatoon began a major public works project, the digging of sewers. In those days, workers dug sewers by hand. The workers objected to the low wages offered by the city as well as to the inadequate safety provisions to prevent the sewers from caving in. In August, the workers went out on strike. At that juncture, one Honoré Jaxon appeared. He introduced all the tactics of big-city labour against the City of Saskatoon.[84] On 17 January 1952, Peel wrote to his co-author about the Canadian Press story.

> Dear Eric, RE: Honoré Joseph Jaxon
>
> I presume that you saw and used the CP despatch from New York telling of the death on January 10 of a Bowery derelict named Honoré Joseph Jaxon, who was described as a 90–year-old veteran of the Riel Rebellion of 1885. The account was rather garbled and in places inaccurate. For that reason I am sending you the following information as I thought you might be interested in printing it as a postscript to the despatch. You will remember that Jaxon or Jackson was connected with Saskatoon's first labor strike.[85]

The librarian added that Jaxon had created a new identity for himself. He was not the son of a Virginian and a Metis mother but an English Canadian from Ontario. In Saskatchewan, the young political radical became the secretary of Louis Riel after the Metis leader arrived at Batoche, south of Prince Albert, in 1884. But the armed insurrection in March 1885 proved too much for the young man. Riel put him under guard. After the Canadians captured Batoche on May 12, they took Will prisoner, as Riel's secretary. At his trial two months later at Regina, the court judged Jackson not guilty of treason owing to insanity. It dispatched him to a mental institution in Manitoba. But weeks later he escaped to the United States, where he adopted the name of Honoré Joseph Jaxon. He was active in labour circles there. In 1909, he returned to Saskatchewan and participated, under his new name, in the labour dispute between the sewer workers and their employer, the City of Saskatoon.[86]

Honoré with his precious library and archives, December 12, 1951. *New York Mirror* December 13, 1951. Photo by Barney Coons.

The Saskatoon *Star-Phoenix* on January 21, 1952 carried Peel's account. Two days later, on January 23, the Regina *Leader-Post* picked up the story, titling it "New York Derelict Was Riel's Secretary." As columnist Kathleen Kritzwiser noted in the *Leader-Post* the next day, "The pieces of the story of the old Riel Rebellion veteran, Honore Joseph Jaxon are beginning to fall into place now." The columnist located Regina old-timer Tom Molloy, who remembered Jaxon nearly half a century earlier during his return to Saskatchewan: "He recalled that Jaxon came back to Regina to write a book on the rebellion from the Indian point of view." Tom booked a room for him in the old Alexandra Hotel, where many of the town's bachelors used to live. In his room Molloy remembered the small table covered with pages upon pages of notes on the troubles with rough sketches of the battlefields.

Thanks to Peel and Molloy, Honoré Jaxon's true identity as Will Jackson now became known. But it was too late to save his archives and library. Shortly after his eviction on December 12, 1951, his newspapers, magazines, and (probably bundled up within) scattered notes had been sold as waste paper, two tons of material. True, sixty boxes of books had been moved to the offices of the *Bowery News.* Honoré had also kept two Manhattan basement apartments as storerooms for his additional books. But it was too late to save them. After his death, all his books were sold. (They realized just $2,000, one-fiftieth of the value that he had placed on them.)[87] It has been argued that the loss of the huge pile of paper on a busy New York street meant that another cache of immense historical material was lost to Canadian history,[88] but this is most unlikely. Jaxon had lost his valuable materials in two earlier destructions of his personal archives, first in 1927 and then in 1942.

Honoré Joseph Jaxon was buried in the Salvation Army section of a cemetery in Flushing, New York.[89]

CONCLUSION

THE SUMMING UP

William Henry Jackson had one of the strangest trajectories of any Anglo-Canadian in the history of post-Confederation Canada. Born and raised in a good Methodist home in Ontario, he travelled west in 1882 to the Saskatchewan District of the North-West Territories. In the Prince Albert area, he helped to organize discontented western farmers, worked to link their protest to that of the Metis, and assisted Louis Riel in preparing a petition that argued for Aboriginal rights and settler self-government. He sought to achieve a new northwest, creating a new relationship between Native and non-Native. As he wrote to a correspondent on February 2, 1885,

> Let this be our aim. Let us sink all distinction of race and religion. Let the white man delight in seeing the Indian helped forward to fill his place as a producer of wealth, and let the Indian and Halfbreed scorn to charge a rent for the soil which God has given to man, upon the settler who comes in to help to build up the country and increase its public funds by his arts and machinery, and let us both unite in seeing that the fur country be managed for the benefit of the Indians who live by hunting not for the good of a grasping company.[1]

This young man of goodwill, just twenty-three years old, remained with the Metis in early 1885. He worked for peace and the avoidance of bloodshed.

"Riel's secretary" paid a high price for his noble sentiments to bring social and racial justice to the Valley of the Saskatchewan. At Batoche in February and early March, the stress of a disagreement with Louis Riel over land rights led to great inner turmoil for Jackson. Cyril Greenland, professor in the School of Social Work, Department of Psychiatry, McMaster University, and Dr. John Griffin, formerly general director of the Canadian Mental Health Association, believe that "he probably suffered from some transient form of hysteria precipitated by physical exhaustion and intense religious and political excitement."[2] Riel had him watched at Batoche, then kept as a prisoner in April and early May.

Jackson was captured at Batoche on May 12, and his Canadian captors branded him a "rebel." At his trial, he wanted to put those whom he held responsible for the troubles of 1885 under cross-examination. Before and at his short trial, Will held that Riel's resistance was justified. In his booming, powerful voice, he declared, "As far as responsibility of mine about what you call rebellion, I have always declared myself perfectly responsible, that is, to say, as Riel's secretary, and I wish to share his fate whatever that may be."[3] But the consensus reached by his family, his lawyer, and the prosecution, that he was insane, prevented a state trial. The non-Native closest to the Metis side at Batoche thus did not have a chance to reveal what he saw as the gross incompetence of Lieutenant Governor Edgar Dewdney and ultimately of Prime Minister John A. Macdonald, as federal administrators of the North-West Territories. His escape several months later led to a reinvention of himself in the United States. One month after Riel's execution, Prime Minister Macdonald wrote, "The Riel fever will I think die out. If not it will be the worse for those who keep the fever alive."[4] Will tried in exile in Chicago to keep "the fever alive."

The pivotal period of his life began in the late spring of 1885 during his incarceration with Metis prisoners in Prince Albert after Batoche fell. In his cell, Jackson began to wear a Metis headband. Those few weeks in that wretched jail became the focal point of his entire life. In the face of oppression, he now identified fully with the Aboriginal peoples. In exile in Chicago, he presented himself as Honoré Jaxon, a Metis. Outspoken, independent, and free of conventional society's constraints, he challenged the status quo. He opposed all forms of authority. He was obsessed with liberty. For over three decades in Chicago, he used his invented identity to champion the underprivileged.

Frank Lloyd Wright, a friend in Chicago, an individual who, like Honoré, had exaggerated his life story and invented all kinds of details about himself, provided one of the best assessments of this extraordinary individual. During a visit of the Jaxons to his home in Oak Park in late 1910, the man now regarded as America's greatest architect[5] made a very interesting comment. As reported by Aimée Jaxon, Wright "was much interested in Honoré's recital of events & said he wished he had the money to back Honoré, to give him complete freedom to follow any trail he chose & sit back & watch Honoré play the game. He says he can't imagine a livelier, more interesting play."[6]

Unfortunately Honoré's departure from Chicago for New York in 1919 and physical separation from Aimée cost this imaginative and compassionate individual his grasp on reality. Jaxon tried to be what he was not, a capitalist. In New York, in his advanced age, he became a prisoner of his own fantasies. Aimée's death in 1932 removed the only individual, outside his family in Saskatchewan, who loved and cared for him unconditionally. Embittered, with imagined enemies all around him, Honoré became increasingly confused and unbalanced. In his eighties, he was poorly fed, housed, and cut off from all meaningful human contact. His nieces' urgent pleas for him to return and live with them in Saskatchewan went unheeded.

Sixty-seven years after the troubles of 1885, Jaxon died on 10 January 1952. From a Canadian Press story from New York about the death of this human pack rat, University of Alberta librarian Bruce Peel made the vital identification: Honoré Jaxon was really William Jackson, Riel's secretary in 1884–85.

What is his place in history? He led a fascinating life, one truly stranger than fiction. His story includes two of the largest themes in the history of late-nineteenth-century and early-twentieth-century

North America, the rights of the Aboriginal peoples and those of the working class. Few other Canadians can rival in interest his unconventional life in Chicago, from the mid-1880s to the late 1910s, followed by his final, if less elevated, three decades in New York. But does his story merit higher rank than that of an extraordinary footnote? A plaque at l Campus Drive at the University of Saskatchewan in Saskatoon contains the answer.

The Students Union built the Place Riel Student Centre in three phases from 1976 to 1980. By 1980, the growing Aboriginal rights movement was well under way. It achieved a great victory two years later with the constitutional recognition of the Metis, for the first time in Canadian history, as an Aboriginal people, with the First Nations and the Inuit. Place Riel officially opened in September 1980. In the main hall of the complex, on the upper level, appears a plaque with a photo, with this inscription: "Louis Riel 1844–1885." The text reads,

> In 1869–1870, Metis leader Louis Riel led a successful Resistance at the Red River Settlement to force the Canadian Government to acknowledge Metis rights and bring Manitoba into Confederation as a province.
>
> Fifteen years later, Riel employed similar tactics on behalf of the Metis of the South Saskatchewan Valley in the Northwest Territories by declaring a provisional government at Batoche.
>
> The Canadian government quickly put down the insurrection by military force, and Riel was executed in Regina on November 16, 1885 for his part in the struggle. Today, his name is synonymous for leadership in the fight for Aboriginal, western and minority rights.

Jaxon provided the same assessment of the Metis leader in a Regina courtroom in 1885, in an interview at Edmonton's Alberta Hotel in 1909, and again in Manhattan after his eviction from his basement apartment in 1951. His insight into Riel is his lasting gift. He was prescient, a visionary, in 1885, 1909, and 1951; he expressed what has become the dominant interpretation of Louis Riel in Canada today. As he wrote of Riel in 1885 from the Lower Fort Garry lunatic asylum, "The oppression of the aboriginals has been the crying sin of the white race in America and they have at last found a voice."[7] Today the entry for the troubles of 1885 in *The Encyclopedia of Saskatchewan* (2005) is under the "North-West Resistance" and not the "North-West Rebellion."[8] For his contribution to our understanding of Louis Riel alone, Honoré Jaxon, once known as Will Jackson, deserves a prominent place in Canada's historical memory.

ACKNOWLEDGEMENTS

Honoré completes my trilogy on three fascinating individuals who reinvented themselves as North American Indians in the late nineteenth century and early twentieth century. Spread out over nearly four decades, the trilogy has had a long gestation period.

Grey Owl and Long Lance came first. Throughout the early 1970s, I collected information about Archie Belaney (1888–1938), an Englishman who immigrated to Canada as a young man of seventeen and who later became Grey Owl, the well-known "Indian" writer and lecturer, one of the country's first environmental defenders. In my first year teaching Canadian history at the University of Calgary in 1974–75, I discovered Chief Buffalo Child Long Lance, another reinvented personality. He presented himself in his "autobiography" as a Blackfoot from the northwestern plains but was actually Sylvester Long (1890–1932) from the American South. Although of partial North American Indian ancestry, he was born and raised not on the Great Plains but in the African American community of Winston-Salem, North Carolina. In the 1920s, he contributed in his writings to a positive image of the First Nations among Canadians and Americans. With future books about Long Lance and Grey Owl already planned, I opened files in the mid-1970s on a third individual, Honoré Jaxon, or William Henry Jackson (1861–1952), an English Canadian who served as Louis Riel's secretary in 1884–85 and who later recreated himself as a Metis in the United States. Geography gave unity to the trilogy since all three individuals had a close identification with western Canada.

My acknowledgements for *Honoré*, first and foremost, begin with the warmest thank you to my wife, Nancy Townshend, for putting up with my obsession with Long Lance, Grey Owl, and Honoré Jaxon for the quarter-century of our marriage. Without her incredible support, not one of the three books in this trilogy would have seen the light of day. At the outset, I also acknowledge the assistance of all those who helped with the preparation of *Honoré* for publication. I am most grateful to Dallas Harrison, my editor, for his excellent editorial work on my manuscript. He made an invaluable contribution to the final product. Nik Burton of Coteau Books spent an enormous amount of time encouraging me to complete this project within an acceptable time frame, encouraging me on at all times. I thank Geoffrey Ursell, publisher of Coteau Books, for the invitation to write this book, and for the suggestion of the subtitle, *Prairie Visionary*. I am most grateful to Duncan Campbell of Coteau Books for the page design, and I warmly thank Deborah Rush for all her marketing work. Shawn England in Calgary standardized and formatted my references. I am most grateful to my sister, Barbara Nair, for the index.

To any individuals whose names do not appear here, I offer my most sincere apologies. Three decades is a long time, and even with the best of intentions some omissions will undoubtedly have occurred.

I first learned of "Louis Riel's secretary" and his last days in New York City in the early 1970s while preparing for my comprehensive PhD examinations in Canadian history at the University of Toronto.[1] In George Stanley's biography *Louis Riel,* the standard work on Riel, I read a footnote about Will Jackson. It provided this intriguing detail about his final days and death in New York City in early 1952: "In later years he called himself Honoré Joseph Jaxon. He worked as a labour organizer in the US and died in poverty in New York."[2]

In the early 1970s, little existed in print on Will Jackson, or Honoré Jaxon, really just five items: Donatien Frémont's article "Henry Jackson et l'insurrection du Nord-Ouest," *Mémoires de la Société Royale du Canada,* troisiéme série, 46 (1952): premiére section, 19–48; Frémont's longer discussion in *Les Secrétaires de Riel: Louis Schmidt. Henry Jackson. Philippe Garnot* (Montréal: Les éditions Chantecler, 1953); Louis Blake

Duff's monograph *Amazing Story of the Winghamite Secretary of Louis Riel,* Western Ontario History Nuggets 22 (London: Lawson Memorial Library, University of Western Ontario, 1955); W.J.C. Cherwinski, "Honoré Joseph Jaxon, Agitator, Disturber, Producer of Plans to Make Men Think, and Chronic Objector ... ," *Canadian Historical Review* 46 (1965): 122–33; and Sandra Estlin Bingaman, "The Trials of the 'White Rebels,' 1885," *Saskatchewan History* 25 (1972): 41–54.

Will, or Honoré, as I prefer to call him, immediately captured my interest. As did Grey Owl with the environment, Honoré's lifelong struggle for equality and justice for working-class and Aboriginal peoples made an important point, simply this: that *occasionally those on the fringe may see things more clearly than those in the mainstream.* Jaxon made an important contribution to the political development of western Canada. What was his reward for arguing in 1884–85 for self-government and racial equality on the Canadian prairies? Dispatch to a lunatic asylum.

Many individuals helped me with my research in the late 1970s. In Calgary, I had arrived at the right spot for "Jaxonian" research. The first cache of information came from Tom Flanagan, a colleague in the Department of Political Science, who edited *The Diaries of Louis Riel* (Edmonton: Hurtig Publishers, 1976), then completed *Louis "David" Riel: "Prophet of the New World"* (Toronto: University of Toronto Press, 1978). Tom then helped to launch the Riel Project to collect and publish Riel's papers. Although we agreed to disagree on our interpretation of the Metis leader, in the spirit of true academic research he opened up his files and shared his contacts. His honours student Miriam Carey, now Dr. Miriam Carey, wrote her honours essay on "The Role of W.H. Jackson in the North West Agitation of 1884–85," which she defended in April 1980. It helped with my understanding of Jackson's concept of Aboriginal land rights. I am also grateful to my colleague Glen Campbell in the University of Calgary's Department of French for his insights into Louis Riel's poetry. Also on our campus, graduate students Keith Phillips and later Shawn England helped me to understand the Mexican anarchist movement of Ricardo Flores Magón, embraced by Honoré Jaxon in 1911.

Tom Flanagan put me in touch with two individuals of extraordinary generosity, Dr. Cyril Greenland, a professor in McMaster

University's School of Social Work, and Dr. J.D.M. (Jack) Griffin, a former director general of the Canadian Mental Health Association. They allowed me to examine their research notes for their important article "William Henry Jackson (1861–1952): Riel's Secretary. Another Case of Involuntary Commitment," *Canadian Psychiatry Association Journal* 23 (1978): 469–78. Subsequently they generously donated their research files to the Special Collections of the University of Saskatchewan Library, which already had items on Jaxon collected by Arthur Silver Morton in the 1930s. The wonderful Morton collection on Will Jackson includes the notes of his interview with Jackson's sister, Cicely Jackson Plaxton, on June 25, 1932 and his interview with their brother Eastwood Jackson the following day.

In my early research, I was extremely fortunate, on June 7, 1979, to be exact, to meet Honoré's niece Cicely Plaxton at her home in Prince Albert, Saskatchewan. Then in her early eighties, the retired schoolteacher had a great deal of information about her colourful uncle. She had met him as a young girl on his return to western Canada, between 1907 and 1909, and then again with her mother, Cicely Jackson Plaxton, on a visit to New York City in the summer of 1947. Her mother, her uncle Eastwood, and her grandmother Elizabeth Jackson had saved many of his letters over the years. The devotion of a mother, a sister, and a niece made my research possible. Miss Plaxton also had many photos that she shared with me. On February 16, 1980, she wrote, "I think it is wonderful that you have done all this research work about my uncle. Thanks for letting me know about it."[3] She died on March 26, 1981 at the age of eighty-five. Her obituary in the *Prince Albert Herald* on March 30 conveyed her deep love of history: "A staunch member of Calvary United Church, she was one of the founding members of the Historical Society when it was revived in the 1960s. She supported retaining historical buildings such as the old city hall and Central School." I dedicate this book to her.

My first article on Will reviewed his first years in the North-West Territories, leading up to and including the troubles of 1885, "William Henry Jackson: Riel's Secretary," *The Beaver* 311, 4 (1981): 10–19; a footnoted copy of this article was published in *Pelletier-Lathlin Memorial Lecture Series: Brandon University, 1979–1980*, ed. A.S. Lussier (Brandon:

Department of Native Studies, Brandon University, 1980), 47–81. My full account of his life, "Honoré Joseph Jaxon: A Man Who Lived for Others," appeared in *Saskatchewan History* 34, 3 (1981): 81–101. My thanks to Antoine Lussier, then chair of the Department of Native Studies at Brandon University, and later chair of the Department of Native Studies at the University of Saskatchewan, for his encouragement of my research. Miss Plaxton's nephew, Lorne Grant, generously allowed me to examine the materials that he had acquired. Other family members also provided invaluable assistance. My friends Judy Abel and Audrey Swaffield commented on an early draft of my essay, as did Tom Flanagan, who, while not necessarily sharing my interpretation of the events of 1885, provided a helpful critique.

Many assisted with my early research in the late 1970s and early 1980s, setting me on my way. These individuals included archivists Edwin Morgan of the Saskatchewan Archives Board, Regina, and Doug Bocking of the Saskatchewan Archives Board, Saskatoon. Lionel Dorge of La Société historique de Saint-Boniface in Winnipeg assisted me with information about Will Jackson in the papers of Bishop Taché. I am grateful to George F.G. Stanley, Riel's biographer, of Sackville, New Brunswick; and to Rossel Vien of Saint-Boniface, Manitoba, for their encouragement of my research on Honoré. Kay Kritzwiser and Reverend Jack Molloy helped me with memories of Tom Molloy, who knew Will Jackson as Honoré Jaxon in Regina between 1907 and 1909. It was my good friend George Molloy, grandson of Tom Molloy, who put me in touch with his uncle Jack. Clarence Kipling of Calgary and Father Denis Dubuc of Guy, Alberta, provided me with valuable Metis genealogical information. Ray Huel of the Department of History, University of Lethbridge, assisted me with background information on Louis Schmidt, Riel's secretary in 1869–70, and later an acquaintance of Will Jackson. For background on the University of Toronto in the late 1870s, I thank David Keane, who completed his PhD on the university's history in the late nineteenth century, and Harold Averill of the University of Toronto Archives, who continued to assist me for a quarter of a century with this project. Marion Wyse and Jeffrey Kastner of the archives helped me in the mid-1980s with further in-depth research on

Will Jackson at the university. At the United Church Archives in Toronto, Ernie Nix assisted with details on Methodism in Ontario in the mid-nineteenth century. Pat Hay of the Wingham Public Library provided background on Wingham and Huron County, where the Jackson family lived in the late 1860s and 1870s. On my behalf, Donna Bloomfield of Calgary read several Toronto newspapers in 1885 for items on the Jackson family, Riel, and 1885. Mary Wilson, of the *Chicago Tribune* Editorial Library, forwarded several items on Honoré from its news morgue. My good friend Fernand Harvey assisted with locating press clippings on Honoré's visit to Montreal and Quebec City in early 1912. An anonymous librarian at the *Chicago Sun-Times* sent me a copy of a column by Lloyd Lewis, "It Takes All Kinds. Honoré Jaxon, Forgotten Crusader," from the "Book Week" section of the paper, Saturday March 2, 1947. It was an invaluable addition to my research.

After completion of my *Saskatchewan History* article, other projects intervened. My biography *Long Lance: The True Story of an Impostor,* the first volume in the trilogy, appeared in 1982. Two collections of readings for university students in Canadian history, edited by my colleague Doug Francis of the Department of History and me, followed. The readers led to our Canadian history textbooks *Origins* and *Destinies* with a third colleague, Richard Jones of l'Université Laval, both books appearing in 1988. Then too I prepared two other biographies. The first was *Sacred Feathers: The Reverend Peter Jones (Kahkewaquonaby) and the Mississauga Indians* (which appeared in 1987) on Peter Jones, the central character in my PhD dissertation on the nineteenth-century Mississauga in Ontario. The second was book two in my trilogy, *From the Land of Shadows: The Making of Grey Owl,* which came out in 1990.[4]

In the mid-1980s, my summary of Will Jackson's years at the University of Toronto appeared in a short article, "Ordered to Winnipeg: Varsity Men Fought Louis Riel, but One Served as His Secretary," for the *Graduate: The University of Toronto Alumni Magazine* (November–December 1984): 5–9. I thank John Aitken, then editor of the *Graduate,* for accepting this unsolicited contribution. The *Toronto Star* on March 30, 1985 ran a story – "Riel's Right-Hand Man: Lunatic or Visionary?" – based on this article. Then a third "spin": CBC Radio's Ann Medina interviewed me on May 13, 1985, "Riel Archives Goes to New York City Landfill." (My thanks to Val Jobson for reminding me of this interview, now available on the CBC Archives website.)

I participated in 1985 in two important conferences organized to commemorate the one hundredth anniversary of the events of 1885, the first at the University of Saskatchewan in May and the second at the University of Alberta in November. My paper at Saskatoon, "Rip Van Jaxon: The Return of Riel's Secretary in 1884–1885 to the Canadian West, 1907–1909," later appeared in the proceedings, *1885 and After,* ed. F. Laurie Barron and James B. Waldram (Regina: Canadian Plains Research Center, 1986), 211–23, and was later summarized in "Return of the 'Native,'" *Horizon Canada* 4, 45 (1986): 1070–75. I also attended the Edmonton conference. Under the editorship of George F.G. Stanley, the University of Alberta Press brought out in 1985 *The Collected Writings of Louis Riel,* a major event in Canadian scholarly publishing. The Riel Project based at the University of Alberta produced four volumes of texts as well as a reference volume.

The University of Alberta's 1885 Conference and the Riel Project both received financial support from several sources, including the office of Gordin Kaplan, vice president of research, a position that the distinguished biochemist held from 1981 to 1987. The late Dr. Kaplan enjoyed such wide respect that today the University of Alberta's most prestigious research award bears his name, the Jacob Gordin Kaplan Award for Excellence in Research. The small building on campus that Dr. Kaplan's office provided for the editorial work of the Riel Project is still known as "Riel House."

I did not meet Dr. Kaplan at the Edmonton conference or at the banquet, at which one delegate wore a black arm band to mark Riel's execution one hundred years earlier. Would he have known about the connection of Leo Kaplan, his father's youngest brother, with Riel's secretary? Dr. Kaplan's famous ancestor was not his Uncle Leo but his grandfather on his mother's side, Jacob Gordin, who had once been the best-known Yiddish playwright in the world, the "Jewish Shakespeare."[5] Dr. Jacob Gordin Kaplan could never forget that since he bore his grandfather's last name as his second.

Not until twenty-one years after the University of Alberta's 1885 Conference did I learn Kaplan's connection to the Jaxon story, admittedly remote but nonetheless interesting. In April 2006, I saw the original of Honoré's will at the New York County Surrogate's Court in New York City. Lawyer Leo Kaplan had prepared it. The World Wide Web makes research so much easier. Through the Web, I discovered that Leo Kaplan's two sons, Ted and Robert, practised law in New York City. On October 6, 2006, I was able to meet Ted at his office on Third Avenue.

Ted did not recall his father talking about Honoré, but he did remember that his father as a young lawyer had been involved in a Native land title case in New York City, a Court of Appeals case concerning Native American rights to waterways in the New York area. Perhaps this was the link between the two men. We will never know.

If I had met Gordin Kaplan in Edmonton in 1985, I might have obtained his uncle's address and phone number and asked about his acquaintance with Honoré Jaxon. Leo Kaplan remained at work in 1985. Although eighty years old, the lawyer for the American Society of Composers, Authors, and Publishers (ASCAP), still oversaw the distribution of royalties paid out to songwriters and publishers, as he had for the past twenty years.[6] Gordin's daughter, Beth Kaplan, remembers her dad's uncle as "a marvelous man, energetic and sharp right up to the end."[7] Before he joined ASCAP, Leo Kaplan was in private practice and as Honoré's lawyer[8] prepared his will on August 12, 1949.[9]

Over fifteen years passed from the one hundredth anniversary of the troubles of 1885, to 2001, the fiftieth anniversary of Jaxon's eviction onto a New York City sidewalk. I continued collecting in the 1980s and 1990s, but big gaps remained. Perhaps, with so many chapters in the Jaxon story still not bridged, there would be no trilogy, just two single volumes on Long Lance and Grey Owl. In any event, my major project from the late 1990s to 2005 became the publication of a history of Calgary through the eyes of two buildings, the Grand Theatre and the Lougheed Building (1911–12), *Calgary's Grand Story* (2005).[10] Honoré did make an appearance in the book since, during his visit to Calgary in 1909, he had lived opposite the future Lougheed Building.

A number of American scholars assisted with additional Jaxon work. Roy Reynolds of Grossmont College, El Cajon, California, helped with research on Honoré's connection to the Chicago committee of the Topolobampo Bay settlement colony in Mexico. In the field of Chicago labour history, Steven Sapolsky and Richard Schneirov helped me generously. Robert St. John provided information on Otto McFeeley, who knew Honoré in Chicago at the turn of the century. I obtained important references from Paul Avrich on Honoré's friendship with the American anarchist Voltairine de Cleyre. Ronald Ramsay of North Dakota State University at Fargo shared information that he had collected on Honoré's association with Frank Lloyd Wright. Roger Grant of the University of Akron, and James Murphy of Ohio State University, helped with the history of the Spirit Fruit Society, a utopian sect in the Chicago area, to which Honoré belonged for several years.

For over two decades, Roger Dahl, archivist of the National Baha'i Archives in Wilmette, Illinois, provided invaluable information on Honoré's and his wife Aimée's work in the Baha'i community. At the beginning of my research, Janet Rubenstein, Office of the Secretary, National Spiritual Assembly of the Baha'is of the United States, assisted me. Robert Stockman provided information on the history of Baha'is in North America. Sophie Loeding of Wilmette, at the age of ninety-five, shared her memories with me of the Jaxons in the early Chicago Baha'i community.

In Canada, Bill Smiley of the Prince Albert Historical Society sent me interesting items. I thank Archdeacon W.F. Payton and David Smyth for information on the country-born, or English-speaking, Metis leader James Isbister. In preparing *Prairie Fire: The 1885 North-West Rebellion* (Edmonton: Hurtig, 1984) with Rod Macleod of the University of Alberta, Bob Beal shared with me thoughts about Will Jackson in 1885. Bruce Peel of the University of Alberta Library helped me with recollections of his identification of Honoré Jaxon of New York City in 1951–52 and Will Jackson. For a quarter of a century, my good friend Sid Holt encouraged me to hold the course and finish a full biography of Honoré. Hugh MacMillan provided a useful reference to Honoré in Washington, DC, in 1894. David Bright assisted me with a number of references to Honoré in southern Alberta in 1909. Julie Green provided several items on his appearances in Crowsnest Pass that year. I thank Merrily Aubrey, then with the Provincial Archives of Alberta, for biographical information on Archibald Young Blain, with the Alberta attorney general's office in 1908.

The fiftieth anniversary of Jaxon's eviction arrived in December 2001. Seizing the opportunity to write a commemorative piece, I scribbled away, and on December 15 "Right Dream, Wrong Time" appeared in the *Globe and Mail* with the striking photo from the New York *Daily News* showing Riel's former secretary on the streets of New York at ninety, with the three tons of paper that he had collected for his Saskatchewan library. This image appears on the cover of this biography. Joseph McCarthy, librarian of the New York *Daily News,* originally brought this image to my attention in a letter of February 13, 1980. The *Globe and Mail* article led to an invitation several months later to contribute to a collection of essays edited by Celia Haig-Brown and David Nock, "Honoré Joseph Jaxon: A Lifelong Friend of Aboriginal Canada." The essay appeared in *With Good Intentions: Euro-Canadian and Aboriginal Relations in Colonial Canada,* ed. Celia Haig-Brown and David A. Nock (Vancouver: UBC Press, 2006), 229–57. I am most grateful to Lisa D'Aiuto of the Faculty of Education, York University, for retyping the original text onto a computer disk, making my changes and additions possible. By going through my file boxes, I added new material to my essay in *Saskatchewan History* published in 1981.

The preparation of the revised paper led to a talk on Honoré Jaxon at the Native-Newcomer Relations Conference at the University of Saskatchewan in May 2003. Then, out of the blue in March 2004, came an invitation from Coteau Books in Regina to write a full-length biography of Jaxon. Could it be ready for 2007 "on the hundredth anniversary of his return to Regina following the events of 1885"?[11] Ironically Coteau's office at the time was on Dewdney Avenue, named after Edgar Dewdney, the lieutenant governor of the North-West Territories who, just prior to Riel's secretary's trial, described him to Prime Minister John A. Macdonald as "crazy."[12] I accepted.

Thanks to a six-month sabbatical leave from the University of Calgary from July to December 2005, I got back into my Jaxon research. One of the highlights was my visit to the battlefield at Batoche with my older son David, who had helped me search the Web for all available information about Honoré. Heather Maki of the University of Calgary Library informed me of new available databases, which vastly expanded my research. Dani Pahulje, of the University of Calgary Library, helped me with a search for a US congressional document. Many thanks are due to the Documentary Delivery Services of the University of Calgary Library, which obtained many valuable items for me from other university libraries and research centres. Many conversations over coffee with my good friend Dennis Burton helped to sustain my interest.

Maurey Loeffler, a great-great-nephew of Honoré's, put me in touch with several family members, as did Agnes Grant. Elizabeth MacLeod Simpson, who is writing a novel about her great-grandmother Elizabeth Eastwood Jackson, helped me enormously with information and moral support. Thanks to the kindness of Trish Gladdish, I was able to photocopy several items that Elizabeth had shown me. I am also very grateful to all Jackson family descendants who helped in some way.

In 2005–06, I made many research trips in Canada, one of the first to Regina. Carmen Harry, curator of the RCMP Centennial Museum, helped me with the events of 1885. I greatly appreciated as well the assistance extended by labour historians Garnet Dishaw and Jim Warren. Ken Aitken, prairie history librarian, Regina Public Library, aided me over a number of years. Bill Brennan helped me with images of Regina in 1885. The Saskatchewan Legislative Library provided several useful references. Kim and Luisa Graybiel of Regina, good friends of long standing, provided welcome hospitality. Tim Novak of the Saskatchewan Archives Board in Regina assisted with several enquiries.

Nadine Charabin, Ken Dahl, and Christie (Wood) Teterenko at the Saskatchewan Archives Board in Saskatoon assisted me on several occasions. Jamie Benson and Ron Smith of the Prince Albert Historical Society also helped me in my Saskatchewan research, as did the Saskatoon Public Library. Joan Weldon of Prince Albert's John

M. Cuelenaere Public Library helped me to locate Pauline Ford's excellent 1972 series of articles in the *Prince Albert Herald,* based on the recollections of Miss Cicely Plaxton. I obtained information from two graduate students in the Department of History, University of Saskatchewan: Paget Code and Selina Crosson. Peter Purdue of the Department of Art and Art History, University of Saskatchewan, showed me contemporary images of the Rebellion of 1885. Bill Waiser helped me with a question about Saskatchewan provincial government records. To both Lyle Jones and his son Terry, direct descendants of Thomas Scott and James Isbister, Will Jackson's allies in the struggle for responsible government in the North-West Territories, I owe a warm thank-you for information on their ancestors. They also took me in late May 2007 on a day trip to the "Ridge," where their ancestors had lived, south of Prince Albert. I thank Val Jobson for information on the Mistawasis Reserve in Saskatchewan. Soloman Asfada, at Special Collections at the University of Saskatchewan Library, helped me enormously on several visits to Saskatoon to examine the William Henry Jackson Collection, which now included Drs. Griffin and Greenland's substantial research files on Honoré, including material originally collected by the late Louis Blake Duff. As a token of my appreciation for their help, I am depositing all my research notes for *Honoré* in Special Collections, University of Saskatchewan Library.

Other Canadian archives and libraries proved very helpful. The Provincial Archives of Alberta and the City of Edmonton Archives assisted me during research visits. Library and Archives Canada in Ottawa holds important papers on 1885, collected by the Department of Justice, in particular microfilm reels C-1228 to C-1231. The Archives of Manitoba in Winnipeg has important Jackson and Riel items. Elizabeth Blight of the archives assisted me in the late 1980s. Diane Payment, formerly a historian with Parks Canada in Winnipeg, helped me over a twenty-five-year period. At the Société historique de St-Boniface in Winnipeg, Gilles Lesage, on several visits, introduced me to his archive's rich holdings on Riel and 1885. Ken Normand and Monique Gravel also assisted me. My good friend Jim Morrison provided welcome hospitality on several visits to Winnipeg. The Oblate Archives in the Provincial Archives of Alberta in Edmonton contained important Roman Catholic missionary records. I thank Diane Lamoureux for her invaluable help at the Provincial Archives of Alberta. Eloi DeGrâce of Edmonton assisted me with a number of references in late-nineteenth-century and early-twentieth-century western Canadian newspapers. Charmaine Sommerfeldt of the Archives of Ontario provided assistance in obtaining access to Ontario school records for Clinton High School in the 1870s.

Elysia DeLaurentis, Wellington County Museum and Archives, furnished information on Dr. George Orton, who did a mental assessment of Will Jackson after he was taken into custody at Batoche. Steve Thorning of Elora, Ontario, also provided background on Dr. Orton. Dr. Allan Sherwin of Montreal kindly helped me with the medical assessments of Will in 1885. I am greatly indebted to him for his comments. I thank Canadian historian, and now Aboriginal rights lawyer, Ken Tyler for information on late-nineteenth-century and early-twentieth-century Canadian Indian policy in the Canadian prairies. Julian Benson kindly shared information about his father, Nathaniel Benson, who interviewed Harry Baronian in New York City about his memories of Honoré Jaxon shortly before Jaxon's death.

Two trips to Wingham, Huron County, Ontario, led to new insights into Honoré's upbringing in that small Ontario town. Jim Currie recalled for me his memories of the town and country and drove me to the Huron County Museum in Goderich. Jodi Jerome of the North Huron Museum provided me with the local context of Honoré's upbringing. In neighbouring Clinton, both Kelvin Jervis and Reg Thompson contributed to my knowledge of the town in which Will attended high school. For an understanding of his years in Toronto and neighbouring Stanley Mills, I thank the Brampton Public Library, the Peel Regional Archives, the City of Toronto Archives, the United Church Archives, and Dorothy Kew of the Mississauga library system. I thank once again at the University of Toronto Archives Harold Averill, who assisted me over a quarter of a century, and Lagring Ulanday. Jim Lawson, University College's Senior Development Officer, helped with an enquiry about the college's archives.

In Calgary, Bob Stamp provided me with information about James L. Hughes, chief inspector of Toronto public schools and previously

Will Jackson's principal at the Toronto Model School. I thank Jack Dunn for comments by Louis Schmidt, Riel's first secretary, about Will Jackson. Haijo Westra helped me with a question about the teaching of the classics in the late nineteenth century. I thank Jon Swainger in Fort George, British Columbia, and my colleague in the Department of History, Lou Knafla, for advice about the interpretation of insanity in the Canadian courts in the late nineteenth century. My cousin, Catherine McLay, assisted me with information about W.O. Mitchell and his two articles on Louis Riel in 1952.

A research trip to England in late May 2005 led to important background information on the Jackson family. Particularly helpful was the assistance of Dr. Peter Nockles of the Methodist Archives and Research Centre, John Rylands University Library, University of Manchester. The British Library in London was wonderful. In London as well, Rob Weinberg provided information about the Baha'i faith in England in the early twentieth century. I thank Susanne Raum and Fariborz Tanhai of the Baha'i Information Office in London for their help. John Harding, honorary secretary of the Old Leysian Society, assisted me greatly with information about W.T.A. Barber, Honoré's first cousin, and headmaster of The Leys School, Cambridge. I have a warm memory of my visit to the school. I am indebted to Joyce Arnold, granddaughter of Cicely Jackson Plaxton, Honoré's beloved sister, for putting me in touch with her distant English cousins. I warmly thank the Barber family descendants in England, Philippa Lane, and Charles and Richard Barber, for their cooperation with my research on the Jackson and Barber families. Henry Srebrnik assisted me with information about the anarchist movement in England in the early twentieth century. I thank Paul Burrows for allowing me to read his paper "Anarchism, Colonialism, and Aboriginal Dispossession in the Canadian West," presented at the Canadian Historical Association Annual Meetings in Saskatoon on May 28, 2007.

I later made four research visits to Chicago and two to New York City. Previously, around 1980, I had visited both cities in an attempt to obtain additional information, but now with the benefit of the ProQuest Historical Newspaper search engines for both the *Chicago Tribune* and the *New York Times,* I entered a new era. A quarter of a century earlier I had to check the entire newspaper for a reference; now with the click of a button I could call up all articles in which "Honore Jaxon" appeared. At the University of Calgary Library, Heather Maki introduced me to the extremely helpful ProQuest search engine for the *New York Times,* which I used for the period from 1920 to 1952. At the Newberry Library, I consulted the ProQuest search engine for the *Chicago Tribune* from 1886 to 1952. Harold Hanen assisted me some years ago with background information on Frank Lloyd Wright and his contribution to architecture. Brian Sinclair provided background material on the Banff Park Pavilion, a building that Wright had designed in Banff, Alberta, about the time that he knew Honoré in Chicago.

The New York Public Library proved a treasure trove of information. I thank Art Einhorn for his help with the twentieth-century history of the Native Americans in New York City. Susan Tell of the New York County Surrogate's Court assisted me in locating Honoré's will. In Chicago, I benefited greatly from the kindness of the Chicago History Museum, Newberry Library, and the Chicago Public Library Harold Washington Library Center. I thank among others Katie McMahon and Grace Dumelle for their assistance at the Newberry Library. Dan Kane of Chicago helped me trace the family history of Aimée Montfort Jaxon, Honoré's wife, and assisted me with many other important items, including Honoré's participation in the Chicago Federation of Labor in the 1910s. I greatly appreciate the assistance in Chicago over a number of years of LaVonne Brown Ruoff. My friend Alice Kehoe of Milwaukee helped me with several research questions. In mid-March 2007, my last research trip to Chicago allowed me to thank in person three individuals who have assisted me for over a quarter of a century: Roger Dahl, Rich Schneirov, and Robert Stockman. I thank Amanda Seligman for references to the history of Chicago's West End.

Other archives assisted me with my final round of research. The Harvard University Archives in Cambridge helped with several items on Jaxon in the papers of Frederic Ward Putnam, the director of the anthropological department of the 1893 World's Columbian Exposition in Chicago. Paige Raibmon of Simon Fraser University told me about these references in the Harvard Archives. I thank Chris Bell-Puckett of the Cincinnati Historical Society Library for his assistance with the history of the Montfort family in the Cincinnati area. I used to great advantage the resources of the New York Public Library. Peter Derrick, chief archivist of the Bronx County Historical Society, aided me in finding the site of Honoré's "forts" on the Bronx River. Sidney Harring, City University of New York, School of Law at Queens College, Flushing, New York, assisted me with my questions about Native land claims in the New York City area. John Bradley allowed me to borrow a copy of his history of the Knickerbocker Club and gave me a wonderful tour of the club. Bronson W. Chanler shared with me memories of his grandfather, Lewis Stuyvesant Chanler, and provided a portrait photo.

Many individuals in a number of archives and museums helped me with illustrative material for my book. My thanks to all, particularly to Dave Brown of the University of Calgary's Image Centre, Information Resources, who copied many of the illustrations that I obtained from private individuals. I am most grateful to Bill Finley, Special Collections librarian, University of North Carolina at Greensboro, for the copy of the image of Honoré in the 1890s looking like a Wild West desperado, my favourite image of him as a young man in Chicago. Many thanks as well for the images dispatched in the final weeks of my research by Julie Herrada, curator of the Labadie Collection at the University of Michigan. Michael Massman and Phyllis Collazo assisted me with my inquiries about an image from the *New York Times* of Honoré, taken the day after his eviction on December 12, 1951 from his Manhattan basement apartment. Jeff Roth, archivist of the *New York Times*, found the image. He and Phyllis Collazo also kindly forwarded me copies of several valuable clippings from the paper's news morgue. I am grateful too for assistance with images of the Glenbow Archives, National Library and Archives of Canada, the Saskatchewan Archives Board (Regina), the Archives of Manitoba, and the Chicago History Museum.

Two appreciative audiences helped me to sustain my interest in the vital last lap of my research and writing. A real highlight was my talk in the Saskatchewan Centennial History Conference at the Hotel

Saskatchewan in Regina in mid-September 2005 on "Perceptions of 'Aboriginal People' in Early Twentieth Century Regina." I included Honoré of course. "Riel's secretary" was tried in the 1885 Regina courthouse, now long gone, but once located by the square directly opposite the present-day hotel. In late May 2006, I spoke at the annual meeting of the Canadian Historical Association at York University, on Honoré's visit to Toronto in February 1912.

Near the end of my research in 2006, I altered my central argument about Honoré. I had no choice. To the statement that *occasionally those on the fringe can see things more clearly than those in the mainstream,* I now added, *but later in life they can acquire impaired vision.* On March 18, 2006, a random search for "Kurt Mertig and New York" on the Web led to one of the greatest revelations of thirty years of Jaxon research.

On my first New York City trip on Jaxon research in early May 1979, I tried to locate Kurt Mertig in the city directories since I knew from several references that he had known Honoré toward the end of his life – no success, even though I had his address in the late 1940s and early 1950s: 317 East Fifty-fourth Street. I decided on March 18, 2006 to try the Web, and amazingly from my Google entry "Kurt Mertig and New York City" up popped several entries, including a Wikipedia article on the National Renaissance Party. What a surprise; it turned out to be a now-defunct neo-fascist group, "founded in 1949 by Kurt Mertig with its headquarters in Yorkville" (http://en.wikipedia.org/wiki/National_Renaissance_Party). Surely, I thought, this could not be the same individual.

But it was. On the *New York Times* search engine, up came several hits for Kurt Mertig. From the article "3 Agitators Convicted: Accused of Offering Anti-Semitic Pamphlets at Queen's Meeting," January 11, 1946, I saw in clear print, "Kurt Mertig of 317 East Fifty-fourth Street."

Through the Internet, I was able to contact two organizations that provided invaluable assistance on Mertig: first, the National Association for Armenian Studies and Research, in Belmont, Massachusetts, which holds the Avedis Derounian (a.k.a. John Roy Carlson) Collection on American fascist groups in the 1940s (I thank Marc Mamigonian, director of Programs and Publications, National

Association for Armenian Studies and Research, for his timely assistance); second, Alan Schwartz, research director of the Anti-Defamation League in New York City, who sent copies of some old clippings from the 1940s on Mertig. The Archives and Rare Books Division, Schomburg Center for Research in Black Culture, New York, had a valuable file on Mertig in its Stetson Kennedy Collection, box 4, folder l – reel 2 (Kurt Mertig 1947).

In his seventies and eighties, Honoré became entrapped in a fictional universe of his own creation, divorced from reality, alone in a city of eight million. Apart from letters with his sister and then, after her death in 1949, his nieces in Saskatchewan, his only known human links during his last years in New York City consisted of: the editor of the *Bowery News* and a group of hobos, occasional contact with a kind-hearted woman in the New History Society (to which he no longer belonged), and weekly contact with a neo-Nazi. What a bizarre and tragic end for a noble visionary who spent his early twenties fighting for self-government for the North-West Territories, today's provinces of Saskatchewan and Alberta, and who later struggled so hard to obtain racial and economic equality in Chicago from the late 1880s to the late 1910s.

My over thirty years with my Honoré Jaxon project ended on June 7, 2007 when I took my images for the book from my home in Calgary to the Coteau office, now relocated on Victoria Avenue, not far from the Hotel Saskatchewan, near the site of where both the Riel and Jaxon trials were held. At my request the Regina taxi driver drove me from the airport, along the route Honoré would have followed the day of his trial on July 24, 1885. We passed the RCMP barracks, the splendid new RCMP Heritage Centre, Government House on the site of Lieutenant-Governor Dewdney's residence in 1885, and then the North-West Territorial Building that is still standing. We stopped when I saw outside, at the back, a Historic Sites and Monuments Board of Canada marker. I read the plaque in memory of Edgar Dewdney, 1835–1916. What a surprise to read this line: "He was instrumental in establishing Regina as territorial capital, and after the North-West Rebellion his humane and sensible policies helped defuse a potentially dangerous situation." How true it is that history must be rewritten every generation.

ENDNOTES

ABBREVIATIONS

AO – Archives of Ontario

GGC – The documentary collection gathered by Cyril Greenland and John Griffin, Documentary History of Canadian Psychiatry Project, Canadian Mental Health Association, 2160 Yonge Street, Toronto, Ontario, has been donated to Special Collections, University of Saskatchewan Library, University of Saskatchewan, Saskatoon, where it is now known as the Griffin-Greenland Collection.

HUA – Harvard University Archives

LAC – Library and Archives Canada

PAA – Provincial Archives of Alberta

PAM – (Public) Archives of Manitoba

PLAX/PLAX-G/PLAX-T – In the endnotes, letters saved by Cicely Plaxton are identified as PLAX. A large portion of the family correspondence has been transcribed, and I refer to these letters as PLAX-T. Cicely's nephew Lorne Grant received some of this material, which he kindly allowed me to photocopy. These items are referred to as PLAX-G.

SHS – Société historique de Saint-Boniface Fonds corporation catholique romaine de Archiépiscopale Saint-Boniface, série Alexandre Taché.

WHJP – William Henry Jackson Papers, Special Collections, University of Saskatchewan Library, University of Saskatchewan.

PROLOGUE: NEW YORK CITY, WINTER 1951–52

1 Jaxon was popularly known by this name. Harry Baronian, quoted by Nathaniel A. Benson, in Louis Blake Duff, "Amazing Story of the Winghamite Secretary of Louis Riel," *Western Ontario History Nuggets* 22 (1955): 25.

2 For a lively impression of New York in this time period, see Jan Morris, *Manhattan '45* (1987; reprint, Baltimore: Johns Hopkins University Press, 1998).

3 Honoré Jaxon, New York City, January 21, 1949, to Mary Plaxton Grant, GGC.

4 "Warned of a Plot," *Washington Post*, June 18, 1894.

5 An earlier article, "Hut-Dweller, 80, Clashes with Law," *New York Times*, February 20, 1942, described "the major" as "a tall, somber person with thinning hair and a military bearing."

6 "Major Jaxon, Who's Used to It by Now, Finds Himself, at 90, Thrown out Again," *New York Times*, December 13, 1951.

7 Honoré Jaxon, quoted in "Evicted Indian Righter Rescued by Indian," New York *World-Telegram and Sun*, December 13, 1951.

8 For information on the colourful Baronian, see "Harry Baronian of Bowery News: Editor of Hoboes' Chronicle Is Dead Here at 54," *New York Times*, August 4, 1965. He called his twelve-page tabloid "The Voice of Society's Basement." The *Times* described it as "an occasional publication that celebrated the pleasures of unemployment."

9 "Champion of Indians Dispossessed Here," *New York Times*, December 14, 1951.

10 Harry Baronian, quoted in "Harry Baronian of Bowery News," *New York Times*, August 4, 1965.

11 Baronian, quoted by Benson, in Duff, "Amazing Story," 27.

12 "Bowery Planners Aiming at Culture," *New York Times*, June 11, 1946; see also *Time* [magazine], December 26, 1949, 24.

13 Baronian, quoted by Benson, in Duff, "Amazing Story," 29.

14 Ibid., 30. See also Benson's original notes of his interview with Baronian in New York, July 14, 1954, in the documents collected from Mrs. Benson by Greenland, GGC.

15 Baronian, quoted by Benson, in Duff, "Amazing Story," 29, 31.

16 Ibid., 30.

17 William A. Nolen, "Bellevue: No One Was Ever Turned Away," *American Heritage* 38, 2 (1987): 39–40, 43.

18 Dr. Joseph Zinkin, City of New York, Department of Hospitals, Bellevue Hospital Center, May 20, 1970, to Cyril Greenland, Ms. 52.12, GGC.

19 Bedside card, Bellevue Hospital, 45114–51, Ms. 52.10, GGC.

CHAPTER 1: YOUNG WILL, 1861–77

1 Robert H. Hare, "Memoir of the Rev. Richard Jackson," *Wesleyan-Methodist Magazine* 23, 3rd ser. (1844): 881–85.

2 Boys entered the school at age eight and left at age fourteen. F.C. Pritchard, *The Story of Woodhouse Grove School* (Bradford, UK: Woodhouse Grove School, 1978), 95.

3 T. Gething Jackson, "Correspondence: James Evans," *Christian Guardian*, April 15, 1891. I thank Reverend Ernie Nix for this reference.

4 Pritchard, *The Story of Woodhouse Grove School*, 58, 66.

5 "Obituary," *Prince Albert Advocate*, November 6, 1899. His birthdate is given as June 21, 1835.

6 "Deaths: Mrs. Elizabeth Eastwood Jackson," *Prince Albert Herald*, October 28, 1921. The obituary gives her birthdate as September 26, 1828.

7 "Copy of an Entry of Marriage," General Registry Office, London, England. Interestingly, his age appears as twenty-three, which it was, but her age is given as twenty-five when she was actually twenty-nine; in a couple of weeks, she turned thirty. His second name appears as "Gething." It seems that Thomas alternated between the two variants of his mother's maiden name: "Gethyn" and "Gething."

8 "Thomas Eastwood," in *Minutes of the Methodist Conferences* (London: Wesleyan Conference Office, 1859), 13: 193–94.

9 Copy, "Probate of the Will of the Rev. Thomas Eastwood, Deceased," September 12, 1855, extracted by Brown and Hotham Proctors, York, PLAX-G.

10 Cicely Plaxton, interview with the author, Prince Albert, June 7, 1979.

11 "Lizzie" [Elizabeth Jackson], Stanley Mills, ON, August 12, 1863, to "My very dear Mother & Sisters," PLAX.

12 Cicely E. Plaxton Prince Albert, February 16, 1980, to the author.

13 Elizabeth Jackson, October 9, 1865, to Hannah and Edward Calder, PLAX. She mentions that they left on October 8, 1858.

14 "Lizzie," Liverpool, September 1858, to "My very dear mother," and Elizabeth Jackson, 1860, letter fragment, to her mother, PLAX-T.

15 As early as November 8, 1858, Elizabeth was obliged to ask her sister Jennie to lend them 500 pounds; see "Lizzie," Wardlaw Farm, 5th Concession, York Township, near Weston, November 8, 1858, to Jane Eastwood [her sister], PLAX-T.

16 Ibid.

17 Ibid. Elizabeth wrote subsequently that one English pound equalled five Canadian dollars. See letter fragment, probably written the winter of 1859–60, PLAX-T.

18 Geo. S. Tavender, "Stanley Mills," in *From This Year Hence: A History of the Township of Toronto Gore 1818–1967* (Malton, ON: Geo. S. Tavender, 1967), 88. Nothing remains of the original Stanley Mills today. It was located just north of Castlemore Road on the Airport Road, just south of Humberwest Parkway.

19 "E.J." [Elizabeth Jackson], Stanley Mills, October 24, 1859, to "My own darling sister Jeannie," PLAX.

20 T.G. Jackson, Stanley Mills, June 8, 1859, to "My Dear Mrs. Eastwood," PLAX.

21 "Lizzie," Stanley Mills, February 16, 1859, to "My very dear good Mother," PLAX.

22 "Enumeration District No. 1.," *The Gore of Toronto Peel Co.*, 4, 1861 Census, Canada West, microfilm reel C-1064, AO.

23 On one side of the store to the west was a baker and on the other a cabinetmaker. His occupation is listed as "grocer and dry-goods dealer." Their store/home was

on the south side of Queen Street West, between John Street and Peter Street. See *Brown's Toronto General Street Directory for 1861,* 81, 201. For confirmation that they rented the spot, see the entry for "Thos. E. Jackson," 1861 Assessment Roll for the Ward of St. Andrews, 58, City of Toronto Archives.

24 T.G. Jackson, Toronto, May 5, 1861, to "My dear Mother & Sister," PLAX.

25 "Lizzie," 279 Queen Street West, Toronto, May 15, 1861, to "My very dear Mother," PLAX.

26 Thomas Jackson, Toronto, April 26, 1861, to "My dear sister Jane" [Jane Eastwood], PLAX. Thomas used the word drapery or cloth textile fabrics.

27 Cicely Plaxton, cited in Pauline Ford, "Pioneer Move to Western Canada Filled with Problems and Adventure," *Prince Albert Herald,* June 17, 1972. This is the first article of a four-part series compiled from the recollections of Cicely Plaxton.

28 Plaxton interview, June 7, 1979.

29 "Lizzie" to mother, February 16, 1859.

30 Brian Clarke, "English-Speaking Canada from 1854," in *A Concise History of Christianity in Canada,* ed. Terrence Murphy and Roberto Perin (Don Mills, ON: Oxford University Press, 1996), 296–97.

31 *Thirty-Sixth Annual Report of the Missionary Society of the Wesleyan Methodist Church in Canada, from June 1860 to June 1861,* xxv.

32 E. Jackson, Stanley Mills, October 23, 1861, to "My dear sister" [Hannah Calder], PLAX.

33 Ibid.

34 "Lizzie," Stanley Mills, February 10, 1863, to "My very dear Mother," PLAX.

35 "P.A. Pioneer Teacher Dies at Age of 86," Prince Albert Herald, July 29, 1949. See also "Lizzie," Stanley Mills, July 7, 1863, to "my very dear Mother & Sister," PLAX. Elizabeth lost a girl (1865) and a boy (1868) afterward. Cicely was her last surviving child.

36 "Lizzie" to mother, February 10, 1863.

37 "Lizzie," Stanley Mills, February 25, 1863, to "My own dear Jean," PLAX.

38 "Lizzie," Stanley Mills, April 22, 1863, to "My very dear Jane," PLAX.

39 "Lizzie" to mother and sisters, August 12, 1863.

40 Honoré Jaxon, New York City, May 17, 1947, to Cicely Plaxton, PLAX. In the letter, he refers to "foolish men like your father who refused your mother's advice to stay in a city and grow up with it."

41 Cicely Jackson Plaxton, "Reminiscences of an Old Timer," *Wingham Advance-Times,* November 9, 1933.

42 James Evans, "St. Clair, March 24, 1838," *Christian Guardian,* April 11, 1838.

43 Fred Lamorandiere, chief interpreter at Cape Croker in 1906, described the Saugeen and Cape Croker people's former hunting grounds as extending "from Meaford to the Maitland River, and included all the watershed to the Caledon Mountains as well as the Indian Peninsula." See Norman Robertson, *The History of the County of Bruce* (Toronto: William Briggs, 1906), 5.

44 M. Alice Aitken, *The Book of Turnberry, 1857–1957* (Wingham: *Wingham Advance-Times* Printers, 1957), 52.

45 Cicely Jackson Plaxton, "From Wingham, Ontario to Prince Albert," 1938, 20, PLAX.

46 *A Brief Historical Sketch of Wingham Methodist Church 1863–1924*, Diamond Jubilee Services October 26, November 2 and 9, 1924, 2.

47 Ibid., 4.

48 Thomas Hanna, "Blythe, March 24, 1868: 'Church Opening,'" *Christian Guardian*, April 1, 1868.

49 *A Brief Historical Sketch of Wingham Methodist Church*, 2, 7.

50 Ibid., 2.

51 Elizabeth Jackson, Wingham, February 7, 1865, to Mary Jackson Coates, PLAX-T.

52 Elizabeth Jackson, Stanley Mills, October 30, 1861, to Jane Eastwood, PLAX-T.

53 I am extremely grateful to Wingham historian Jim Currie and Jodi Jerome of the North Huron Museum in Wingham for all the background they provided on the history of the town.

54 *Illustrated Historical Atlas of the County of Huron* (Toronto: H. Belden, 1879), ix.

55 Elizabeth Jackson, Wingham, September 3, 1866, to her mother, PLAX-T. See also Elizabeth Jackson, Wingham, October 15, 1867, to "My very dear sister," PLAX-T.

56 Elizabeth Jackson, Wingham, January 25, 1864, to "My very dear Mother & Sisters," PLAX-T.

57 Elizabeth Jackson, Wingham, September 3, 1866, to "My very dear Mother," PLAX-T.

58 T. Gething [Gethyn] Jackson, "Jackson's Case," *Manitoba Free Press*, August 29, 1885.

59 H.D., "'A Question of Fact,' Letter to the Editor of the *Mail*, Wingham, July 3," Toronto *Daily Mail*, July 6, 1885.

60 Aitken, *The Book of Turnberry*, 20.

61 Elizabeth Jackson, Wingham, February 7, 1865, to Mary Jackson Coates, PLAX-T.

62 Honoré Jaxon, Christmas Day 1950, to Mary Plaxton Grant, PLAX-T.

63 Elizabeth Jackson, Wingham, February 10, 1868, to Jane [Jennie] Eastwood, PLAX-T.

64 T.G. Jackson, Prince Albert, August 5, 1885, to Dr. David Young, MG 3, C 20–1, PAM.

65 W.H. Jackson, Wingham, December 28, 1869, to "My dear Aunt," PLAX.

66 Elizabeth Jackson, c. 1865, letter fragment, to Jennie Eastwood, PLAX-T.

67 Elizabeth Jackson, probably 1866, letter fragment, to her mother, PLAX.

68 Plaxton interview, June 7, 1979. See also Cicely Plaxton, "Diary of New York Trip, 1947," PLAX-G. She wrote in her journal of her brother Will (now Honoré) that "We were such dear playmates in our childhood."

69 A note in "Correspondence of Cicely Jackson re: W.H.J. [William Henry Jackson] in fall of 1885," 5, PLAX.

70 "Your loving son and brother," Chicago, September 29, 1889, to "Dear Father and Mother Eastwood and Cicely," PLAX.

71 Pauline Ford, "Local Family Made Desperate Attempt to Free Relative from Riel's Prison," *Prince Albert Daily Herald*, June 20, 1972. In a subsequent article (Pauline Ford, "William Jackson Fled from Hospital and Journeyed to United States," *Prince Albert Daily Herald*, July 8, 1972), Cicely Plaxton is quoted as saying that her mother "probably would have been in favour of Women's Lib today."

72 Plaxton interview, June 7, 1979.

73 Plaxton, "Reminiscences."

74 Ibid.

75 In 1871, there were only fifteen Catholic families among over five hundred families in Turnberry Township, where Wingham was located. See 1871 Census, Province of Ontario, Sub-District K, Division No. 1 and 2, microfilm reel C-9933, AO.

76 Plaxton, "Reminiscences."

77 The poster survives in "Newspaper Scrapbook 1870," MG 12 E3, John Christian Schultz Papers, PAM.

78 Speech by Will Jackson, probably made on welcoming Louis Riel to the Prince Albert area, July 11, 1884, WHJP.

79 Elizabeth Jackson, Wingham, August 15, 1872, to Eastwood Jackson, PLAX.

80 Arthur Silver Morton, notes on interview with Mrs. Amos [Cicely Jackson] Plaxton, Prince Albert, June 25, 1932, Ms. C555/2/13.5, WHJP. This is the exact phrasing: "Mrs. Jackson Sr. when living in Ontario had written friend in England saying father had taken young Willy to his first political meeting and though boy was only eleven years old he became greatly excited."

81 Carlie Oreskovich, *Sir Henry Pellatt: The King of Casa Loma* (Toronto: McGraw-Hill Ryerson, 1982), 15.

82 Elizabeth Jackson, Wingham, October 29, 1872, to "My own very dear boys," PLAX.

83 Ibid.

84 Elizabeth Jackson, Wingham, November 21, 1872, to "My very dear boy students," PLAX.

85 Elizabeth Jackson, Wingham, October 6, 1872, to "My very dear Eastie & Willie," PLAX. See also Jackson to sons, October 29, 1872.

86 Elizabeth Jackson, Wingham, April 7, 1873, to "My very, very, very dear, dear boys," PLAX.

87 James Hughes, Toronto, December 6, 1872, to Thomas Jackson, PLAX.

88 James L. Hughes, quoted in Lorne Pierce, *Fifty Years of Public Service: A Life of James L. Hughes* (Toronto: S.B. Gundy; Oxford University Press, 1924), 169. The quotation is taken from his book *Adult and Child* (Syracuse: C.W. Bardeen, 1917).

89 Donald Goertz, *Walmer Road Baptist Church: A Century for the City, 1889–1989* (Toronto: Walmer Road Baptist Church, 1989), 7.

90 Nathaniel Burwash, "Typescript Autobiography," 5, United Church Archives, Toronto.

91 T.E. Jackson, in Manon Lamontagne et al., comps. and eds., *The Voice of the People* (Prince Albert: Prince Albert Historical Society, 1985), 144.

92 James Hughes, Toronto, December 6, 1872, to Thomas Jackson, PLAX.

93 Doug Weston, "Thomas Eastwood Jackson: Pharmacist Helps Shape Canadian History," *Canadian Pharmaceutical Journal* (February 1985): 70. See also Jackson in *The Voice of the People*, 144.

94 Elizabeth Jackson, March 17, 1874, to Jane [Jennie] Eastwood, PLAX. See also Plaxton, "Reminiscences."

95 Malcolm Lamont, *Bush Days* (n.p.: privately printed, 1933), 16–17.

96 R.D. Gidney and W.P.J. Millar, *Inventing Secondary Education: The Rise of the High School in Nineteenth-Century Ontario* (Montreal: McGill-Queen's University Press, 1990), 241.

97 Elizabeth Jackson, March 17, 1874, to Jennie Eastwood, PLAX.
98 Honoré Jaxon, Chicago, November 21, 1906, to his mother and Jennie Eastwood, PLAX-G.
99 J. Donald Wilson, "The Ryerson Years in Canada West," in *Canadian Education: A History*, ed. J. Donald Wilson, Robert M. Stamp, and Louis-Philippe Audet (Scarborough: Prentice-Hall, 1970), 226.
100 George E. Flower, "Education," in *The Canadians 1867–1967*, ed. J.M.S. Careless and R. Craig Brown (Toronto: Macmillan, 1967), 569. See also Gidney and Millar, *Inventing Secondary Education*, 260.
101 Gidney and Millar, *Inventing Secondary Education*, 267.
102 Arthur Lower, quoted in Paul T. Phillips, *Britain's Past in Canada: The Teaching and Writing of British History* (Vancouver: UBC Press, 1989), 4.
103 "Horatio Hale," in *A Cyclopedia of Canadian Biography Being Chiefly Men of the Time*, ed. Geo. Maclean Rose (Toronto: Rose Publishing Company, 1886), 375. For contemporary biographical information, see also "Sketch of Horatio Hale," *Appleton's Popular Science Monthly* 51 (May-October 1897): 409.
104 "Horatio Hale," A Cyclopedia, 375.
105 "Clinton High School," *Clinton New Era*, May 2, 1878.
106 J.M. Buchan, "Inspector's Detailed Report of the High School of Clinton for the Half-Year Ending June 30, 1873," Department of Education, RG 2–105–0–6, AO.
107 J.M. Buchan, "Inspector's Detailed Report of the High School of Clinton for the Half-Year Ending June 1875," Department of Education, RG 2–105–0–2, AO.
108 J.M. Buchan, "Inspector's Detailed Report of the High School of Clinton for the Half-Year Ending 31 Dec. 1878," Department of Education, RG 2–105–0–6, AO.
109 Horatio Hale, ed., *The Iroquois Book of Rites* (Toronto: University of Toronto Press, 1963), 83–84.
110 Jackson to Eastwood, March 17, 1874.
111 Enoch Wood, Toronto, February 25, 1875, to T.G. Jackson, PLAX.
112 Elizabeth Jackson, c. 1873–74, letter fragment, to unknown correspondent, PLAX-T. In 1871, Thomas owned fifteen town building lots; he obviously had accepted land instead of cash payments. 1871 Census, Province of Ontario, District No. 26, North Huron, Sub-District K, Division No. 2, Township of Turnberry, 62, no. 20, microfilm reel C-9933, AO.
113 Thomas Jackson, Wingham, September 6, 1877, to Eastwood Jackson, PLAX.

CHAPTER 2: CALL TO GREATNESS, 1878–84

1 Thomas Eastwood Jackson, in Manon Lamontagne et al., comps. and eds., *The Voice of the People* (Prince Albert: Prince Albert Historical Society, 1985), 144.
2 Thomas Eastwood, Wingham, September 6, 1878, to Eastwood Jackson, PLAX.
3 "Your Most Affectionate Brother Eastwood" [Eastwood Jackson], Toronto, February 28, 1878, to "My dearest Willie," PLAX.
4 "Riel's Youthful Secretary," *Toronto World*, May 19, 1885.

5 William H. Jackson, c. winter 1878–79, letter fragment, to his parents, PLAX.

6 W.H. Jackson, Toronto, October 18, 1878, to "Pa, Ma, Eastie, and Cicely," PLAX.

7 In December 1875, they were students at Clinton High School; see "High School Examination," *Clinton New Era*, December 23, 1875, and "Mr. W.G. Hanna," Clinton New Era, April 12, 1877. See also *Honours Classics in the University of Toronto by a Group of Classical Graduates* (Toronto: University of Toronto Press, 1929), 77.

8 William James Loudon, "Tempora Mutantur: Sidelights on the Early Days," *University of Toronto Monthly* 28, 4 (January 1928): 411. He writes, "At meals and lectures the students wore gowns. This was compulsory."

9 Jackson to family, October 18, 1878.

10 William Dean Howells in the *Cincinnati Gazette*, July 27, 1860, cited in Greg Gatenby, *Toronto: A Literary Guide* (Toronto: McArthur and Company, 1999), 210.

11 Donald Jones, "Two Bronze Cannon in Queen's Park Recall Canada's Greatest Military Heroes," in *Fifty Tales of Toronto* (Toronto: University of Toronto Press, 1992), 12–13. See also "Top Honour Now Cast in Canada," *Globe and Mail*, March 3, 2007.

12 Martin L. Friedland, *The University of Toronto: A History* (Toronto: University of Toronto Press, 2002), 74.

13 W. Stewart Wallace, *A History of the University of Toronto, 1827–1927* (Toronto: University of Toronto Press, 1927), 101–03. Also consult the *Calendar of University College, Toronto, for 1877–1878*, 21; 1878–1879, 25; and 1879–1880, 25.

14 Sir Robert Falconer, "The Tradition of Liberal Education in Canada," *Canadian Historical Review* 8 (1927): 108.

15 Malcolm Wallace, "Staff, 1853–1890," in *University College: A Portrait, 1853–1953*, ed. Claude T. Bissell (Toronto: University of Toronto Press, 1953), 39; see also Friedland, *The University of Toronto*, 85.

16 Carl Berger, "Sir Daniel Wilson," in *Dictionary of Canadian Biography*, vol. 12: 1891–1900 (Toronto: University of Toronto Press, 1990), 1113.

17 Bruce G. Trigger, "Sir Daniel Wilson: Canada's First Anthropologist," *Anthropologica*, n.s., 8 (1966): 3–28.

18 Daniel Wilson, "The Present State and Future Prospects of the Indians of British North America," in *Proceedings, Royal Colonial Institute* 5 (1874): 242.

19 J.M.S. Careless, *Toronto to 1918: An Illustrated History* (Toronto: James Lorimer, 1984), 202, table 8.

20 Paul Kane, *Wanderings of an Artist* (1859), reprinted in *Paul Kane's Frontier*, ed. J. Russell Harper (Austin: University of Texas Press, 1971), 51.

21 Daniel Wilson, quoted in Friedland, *The University of Toronto*, 86.

22 W.J. Loudon, *Studies of Student Life* (Toronto: University of Toronto Press, 1927), 218.

23 Jackson to family, October 18, 1878.

24 "Willie" [W.H. Jackson], Wingham, October 19, 1878, to his family, PLAX.

25 University of Toronto, *Class and Prize Lists 1878* (Toronto: Henry Rowsell, 1878), 10; University of Toronto, *Class and Prize Lists, 1879* (Toronto: Henry Rowsell, 1879), 17.

26 Honoré J. Jaxon, Advocate, Suite 10, 122 LaSalle St., Chicago, June 24, 1896, to Wilfrid Laurier, Laurier Papers, MG 26 G, vol. 11, 4409–10, microfilm C-740, LAC.

27 "William Stafford Milner," in *A Standard Dictionary of Canadian Biography: Canadian Who Was Who*, ed. Charles G.G. Roberts and Arthur L. Tunnel (Toronto: Trans-Canada Press, 1934), 1: 363. See also the *Class and Prize Lists* for 1878, 1879, 1880, and 1881. Milner came first in classics every year except the second, when he came second. He won the gold medal in classics in his final year. University of Toronto, *Commencement, Wednesday, June 8th, 1881* (Toronto: Rowsell and Hutchinson, 1881), 11.

28 University of Toronto, *Class and Prize Lists, 1879*, 18.

29 Jackson to family, October 18, 1878; T.A. Reed, comp., *The Blue and White: A Record of Fifty Years of Athletic Endeavour at the University of Toronto* (Toronto: University of Toronto Press, 1944), 80–81.

30 Personal communication, Harold Averill, May 12, 2007.

31 Jackson to family, October 18, 1878.

32 W.H. Joseph Jaxon, Chicago, April 4, 1888, to A.R. Owen, WHJP.

33 Honoré Jaxon, New York, January 21, 1949, to Mary Plaxton Grant, GGC.

34 "Your loving mother," Winnipeg, March 8, 1880, to "My very dear children," PLAX.

35 "Your loving mother," Portage la Prairie, April 5, 1880, to "My very dear Willie," PLAX; "Your very loving Mamma," Portage la Prairie, June 21, 1880, to "My very dear Willie," PLAX.

36 Ibid.

37 Jackson, *The Voice of the People*, 147.

38 In late November 1885, he told the *Fargo Argus* that he "was a student at Toronto University for four years." See "Riel's Secretary," *Fargo Argus*, November 28, 1885.

39 William Jackson, age twenty, indicated as "going to school," is listed in the 1881 Census, District No. 175, N. Huron, No. 2b, Turnberry Township, 68.

40 Cicely Jackson Plaxton, "From Wingham, Ontario, to Prince Albert," 1938, 10, 23, PLAX.

41 Ibid., 13.

42 Alexander Morris, *The Treaties of Canada* (Toronto: Bedfords, Clarke, 1880), 354.

43 Mistawasis, quoted in Peter Erasmus, *Buffalo Days and Nights: As Told to Henry Thompson* (Calgary: Fifth House, 1999), 247.

44 Gary William David Abrams, *Prince Albert: The First Century 1866–1966* (Saskatoon: Modern Press, 1966), 37.

45 "The Old Indian Graveyard," *Prince Albert Times*, November 1, 1882.

46 Plaxton, "From Wingham," 19; Alice Beck Kehoe, *The Ghost Dance: Ethnohistory and Revitalization*, 2nd ed. (Long Grove, IL: Waveland Press, 2006), 45.

47 Morris Zaslow, *The Opening of the Canadian North 1870–1914* (Toronto: McClelland and Stewart, 1971), 28–29.

48 See the ads for "Jackson and Jackson" in the *Prince Albert Times* January 10, 1883 and May 9, 1883; see also F.B.M., "A Nest of Traitors," Toronto *Mail*, July 6, 1885.

49 See "T. Getting Jackson," in Homestead Files, 148–448, Department of the Interior, Saskatchewan Archives Board, Saskatoon. See also William Pearce, Prince Albert, August 14, 1884, to the Agent of Dominion Lands, Land Claims, vol. 1, 1884 (Prince Albert), 9/2/4–3, William Pearce Papers, University of Alberta Archives, Edmonton.

50 Honoré Jaxon, Port Savanne on CPR, seventy-two miles west of Port Arthur, February 1891, to "Dear Family," PLAX. Later in the winter, he stated that one day he walked forty-eight miles on snowshoes. See Honoré Jaxon, Port Savanne, April 13, 1891, to Eastwood Jackson, PLAX.

51 William Francis Butler, *The Wild North Land* (1873; reprinted Edmonton: Hurtig, 1968), 43.

52 Plaxton, "From Wingham," 25.

53 Ibid.

54 Ibid., 26. He never forgot the claim and referred to it in two letters in 1926; see Honoré Jaxon, "Box Castle Garden," The Bronx, February 19, 1926, to Cicely Plaxton and Eastwood Jackson, PLAX; and Honoré Jaxon, "Box Castle Garden," March 18, 1926, to Eastwood Jackson, PLAX.

55 William Henry Jackson, "The Election for Lorne," *The Voice of the People,* April 11, 1883.

56 Photostat copies of the two issues are in PLAX.

57 Elizabeth Jackson, c. March 1883, letter fragment, to Cicely Jackson, WHJP.

58 Abrams, *Prince Albert,* 49.

59 Plaxton, "From Wingham," 6.

60 Ibid.

61 Abrams, *Prince Albert,* 53.

62 W.L. Morton, *Manitoba: A History* (Toronto: University of Toronto Press, 1957), 211.

63 Plaxton, "From Wingham," 23.

64 Ibid., 16.

65 See the obituary for Thomas in the *Prince Albert Advocate,* November 6, 1899.

66 Plaxton, "From Wingham," 25.

67 Ibid., 23.

68 Brian Titley, *The Frontier World of Edgar Dewdney* (Vancouver: UBC Press, 1999), 86, 90.

69 Ibid., 82, 86.

70 Abrams, *Prince Albert,* 64.

71 June Kelly, "Thomas Scott, Sr.," in *Echoes of Our Heritage* (Prince Albert: Clouston History Book, 1985), 357–58.

72 David Smyth, "James Isbister," in Historic Sites and Monuments Board of Canada, Agenda Paper 1996–52, 649.

73 James Isbister, "Letter, Prince Albert, Saskatchewan, St. Catherine's Parish, June 10," *Winnipeg Sun,* June 19, 1885.

74 See *Prince Albert Times,* April 18, 1884.

75 W.J. Carter, "Forty Years in the North-West," Ms. C550/1/24, 1, 141, W.J. Carter Papers, Special Collections, University of Saskatchewan Library.

CHAPTER 3: "RIEL'S SECRETARY," 1884–85

1 Jules Le Chevallier, *Batoche: Les missionaries du Nord-Ouest pendant les troubles de 1885* (Montréal: L'Oeuvre de Presse Dominicaine, 1941), 41.

2 James Isbister stated that there "arose a subscription from the English speaking people for my delegation." James Isbister to Colonel Irvine, Commander, NWMP Prince Albert, St. Catherine's Parish, April 15, 1885, RG 13, F 2, vol. 806, microfilm C-1228, Louis Riel Papers, Department of Justice, LAC.

3 The English version of the text appears in Thomas Flanagan, *Riel and the Rebellion: 1885 Reconsidered* (Saskatoon: Western Producer Prairie Books, 1983), 4–5, 153.

4 Ibid., 6–7.

5 Statement by Charles Nolin and Maxime Lépine, in "Rapport de M. Cloutier," 1886, D-IV-116, Oblate Archives, PAA. Bishop Taché commissioned l'Abbé Gabriel Cloutier to gather accounts among the Metis about the troubles of 1885. He visited the South Branch and interviewed many witnesses, mainly men. In a two-volume handwritten journal, he recorded their accounts. His journal, containing Metis accounts of the resistance, is now in the archives of the Société Historique de St. Boniface, with transcriptions in the Oblate Archives, PAA.

6 Vital Fourmond, Directeur de la Mission de Saint-Laurent, 27 décembre 1884, *Missions de la Congregation des Oblats de Marie Immaculée* 91 (septembre 1885): 277.

7 Louis Riel, July 31, 1885 statement to the jury, in *The Queen v Louis Riel*, ed. Desmond Morton (Toronto: University of Toronto Press, 1974), 312.

8 George F.G. Stanley, *Louis Riel* (Toronto: Ryerson, 1963), 276.

9 T. Getting [Gethyn] Jackson, "Riel at Prince Albert, Prince Albert, Aug. 19," *Toronto Globe,* September 4, 1884.

10 Located about 149 River Street West in Prince Albert. Thomas Eastwood Jackson, in Manon Lamontagne et al., comps. and eds., *The Voice of the People* (Prince Albert: Prince Albert Historical Society, 1985), 151.

11 "Public Meeting," *Prince Albert Times,* July 25, 1884.

12 Cicely Jackson Plaxton, "From Wingham, Ontario, to Prince Albert," 1938, 28, PLAX. Cicely was an excellent recorder of detail. Her physical description of Riel conforms well to the description of his schoolmate, J.O. Mousseau at the Collège de Montréal, who stated that Riel was a "fine looking man," almost six feet in height, strong curly hair, high forehead, and broad shoulders. See Stanley, *Louis Riel,* 27–28.

13 Stanley, *Louis Riel,* 277.

14 Will Jackson, July 28, 1884, to the Citizens of Prince Albert, reprinted in George F.G. Stanley, *The Birth of Western Canada* (1936; reprinted Toronto: University of Toronto Press, 1961), 300–01. Also included in the article "No Word," Toronto *Daily Mail* May 8, 1885.

15 "The Rebellion," Toronto *Daily Mail,* July 17, 1885.

16 Hugh A. Dempsey, *Big Bear: The End of Freedom* (Vancouver: Douglas and McIntyre, 1984), 135–36.

17 "Statement about Treaties by an Indian," RG 13, B 2, microfilm C-1228, 144–45, Louis Riel Papers, Department of Justice, LAC. I thank Miriam Carey, author of "The Role of W.H. Jackson in the North West Agitation of 1884–1885" (honours essay, Department of Political Science, University of Calgary, April 7, 1980), for this reference.

18 William H. Jackson, Lower Fort Garry, 19 September 1885, to "My dear Family," MG 3, C 20, PAM.

19 For Cicely Jackson Plaxton's recollection of the meeting, consult "Notes of an Interview by Arthur S. Morton with Mrs. Amos [Cicely Jackson] Plaxton at Prince Albert," June 25, 1932, WHJP. See also Plaxton, "From Wingham," 29–30, and Sergeant W.A. Brooks, August 21, 1884, to Officer Commanding, NWMP Battleford, RG 13, B 2, microfilm C-1228, 522, Louis Riel Papers, Department of Justice, LAC. Eastwood also recalled the meeting with Big Bear in his testimony, RG 13, F 2, vol. 823, 3661, microfilm C-1231, Louis Riel Papers, Department of Justice, LAC.

20 Plaxton, "From Wingham," 29.

21 Ibid.

22 Thomas Eastwood, "Testimony," RG 13, F 2, vol. 823, microfilm C-1231, Louis Riel Papers, Department of Justice, LAC.

23 George Woodcock, *Gabriel Dumont* (Edmonton: Hurtig, 1975), 47, 45.

24 Gabriel Dumont, "Gabriel Dumont's Account of the North West Rebellion, 1885," trans. and ed. George F.G. Stanley, *Canadian Historical Review* 30 (1949): 261.

25 Constance Kerr Sissons, *John Kerr* (Toronto: Oxford University Press, 1946), 159–61. See also Dempsey, *Big Bear,* 53–55.

26 Stanley, *Louis Riel,* 283.

27 Lewis Herbert Thomas, *The Struggle for Responsible Government in the North-West Territories 1870–97,* 2nd ed. (1956; reprinted Toronto: University of Toronto Press, 1978), 127. See also Stanley, *The Birth of Western Canada,* 442n40.

28 Frank Oliver, quoted in Earl G. Drake, *Regina: The Queen City* (Toronto: McClelland and Stewart, 1955), 28.

29 Frank Oliver, quoted in the *Edmonton Bulletin,* February 22, 1884; see also Stanley, *Louis Riel,* 271, 410.

30 Frank Oliver, October 22, 1884, to William Henry Jackson, quoted in Stanley, *The Birth of Western Canada,* 308–09. See also the original letter in RG 13, F 2, vol. 805, microfilm C-1228, Louis Riel Papers, Department of Justice, LAC.

31 Sergeant Brooks, quoted in letter of L.N.F. Crozier, Battleford, August 14, 1884, RG 13, B 2, microfilm C-1228, 520, Louis Riel Papers, Department of Justice, LAC.

32 Will mentioned in a letter to Frank Oliver that "We are morally certain that our correspondence is tampered with." See William Jackson, January 21, 1885, to Frank Oliver, WHJP.

33 Louis Riel, St. Louis de Langevin, September 29, 1884, to T.E. Jackson, WHJP.

34 Diane Payment, "The Métis Homeland: Batoche in 1885," in *The 1885 Issue,* special issue of *NeWest Review* (May 1985): 11.

35 Diane Payment, *"The Free People-Otipemisiwak": Batoche, Saskatchewan, 1870–1930* (Ottawa: Minister of Supply and Services Canada, 1990), 311.

36 Bob Beal and Rod Macleod, *Prairie Fire: The 1885 North-West Rebellion* (Edmonton: Hurtig, 1984), 41, 151.

37 David Lee, "The Métis Militant Rebels of 1885," in *Readings in Canadian History: Post-Confederation, 7th ed.,* ed. R. Douglas Francis and Donald B. Smith (Scarborough: Thomson Nelson, 2006), 82–83.

38 Louis Schmidt, "Journal de Louis Schmidt, extraits, le 19 mars 1885," Accession 84.400, box 22, item 747, PAA. "Ce Jackson était un jeune Canadien-Anglais de Prince Albert, très exalté, mais possédant d'assez grandes connaissances. Il fut feu et flammes à l'arrivée de Riel, et il s'attacha tout de suites à ses pas, se rendent à toutes les assemblées où il faisant de longs discours. A la fin, il prit sa demeure parmi les Métis." The passage concludes, "et bientôt il eut l'idée d'adjurer le protestantisme pour se faire catholique" ("and very quickly he had the idea to leave Protestantism to become a Catholic").

39 N.C.W., "Letter to Louis Riel, St. Louis de Langevin, May 18, 1884," translation, in Canada, *Sessional Papers,* 1886, no. 48g, p. 2.

40 Payment, "The Métis Homeland," 12.

41 Philippe Garnot, "Garnot Mémoire," quoted in Beal and Macleod, *Prairie Fire,* 130.

42 Payment, *The Free People,* 204.

43 William H. Jackson, September 19, 1885, to "My dear Family," PAM.

44 Alexander Ross, *The Red River Settlement: Its Rise, Progress, and Present State with Some Account of the Native Races and Its General History to the Present Day* (1856; reprinted Edmonton: Hurtig Publishers, 1972), 252.

45 Ibid., 191.

46 Payment, *The Free People,* 63.

47 Canada, *Sessional Papers,* 1886, no. 52, p. 385.

48 For Rose Ouellette's baptism on April 20, 1868, see Fond Paroisse St. Norbert, 1866–68, *Baptêmes, Marriages, Sépultures,* SHS. Also, her marriage to Salomon Boucher on September 20, 1886 appears in Fond Paroisse St. Laurent, *Baptêmes, Marriages, Sépultures,* SHS.

49 Peter Erasmus, *Buffalo Days and Nights: As Told to Henry Thompson* (Calgary: Fifth House, 1999), 172.

50 It is possible that the Ouellettes had two homes on their family farm, or they might have intended to build a second one in 1884–85; see endnote 2 in Louis Riel, *The Collected Writings of Louis Riel,* ed. Thomas Flanagan (Edmonton: University of Alberta Press, 1985), 3: 506. Charles Nolin indicated at the trial that the Ouellettes had two homes; see Morton, *The Queen v Louis Riel,* 201.

51 A.H. De Trémaudan, interview with Moise Ouellette, MG 10, F 1, PAM, cited in endnote 2, Riel, *The Collected Writings,* 3: 89. See also 53.

52 Charles Nolin stated at the trial that Riel lived with him and his family for three months, then "went into his own house that he thinks was given to him by Mr. Ouellette." See Riel, *The Collected Writings,* 3: 201.

53 See Riel, *The Collected Writings,* 3: 45n1.

54 "Your loving son Willie," September 24, 1888, to "My dear, dear Mother," PLAX.

55 This register, "Batoche AF 0111," is not housed at the Société Historique de St. Boniface but is still at Batoche. Information received from Ken Normand, Assistant Genealogist, Société historique de St. Boniface.

56 John MacBeth, "The Social Customs and Amusements in the Early Days in the Red River Settlement and Rupert's Land," in *A Thousand Miles of Prairie: The Manitoba Historical Society and the History of Western Canada,* ed. Jim Blanchard (Winnipeg:

University of Manitoba Press, 2002), 101.

57 Testimony of Charles Nolin and Maxime Lépine, 1886, in "Rapport de M. Cloutier," 1886, D-IV-116, Oblate Archives, PAA.

58 Louis Riel, *The Diaries of Louis Riel*, ed. Thomas Flanagan (Edmonton: Hurtig, 1976), 38. For the French original, see Riel, *The Collected Writings*, 3: 364. The text is so important that it is reproduced here; apparently it was written around Riel's fortieth birthday, October 23, 1884; see Riel, *The Collected Writings*, 3: 383n1. The text reads, "Nous vous remercions par Jésus, Marie, Joseph, d'avoir eu soin à venir jusqu'aujourd'hui et nous vous supplions par Jésus, Marie Joseph, d'avoir soin toujours s'il vous plaît, de mon ami William Henry Jackson, du choix que j'ai fait de Lui comme ami particulier, et de tous ses partisans de bonne volonté."

59 Riel, "Les Métis du Nord-Ouest," in *The Collected Writings*, 3: 290.

60 Dumont, "Gabriel Dumont's Account," 266.

61 Diane P. Payment, "'La Vie en Rose'? Métis Women at Batoche, 1870 to 1920," in *Women of the First Nations: Power, Wisdom, and Strength*, ed. Christine Miller and Patricia Chuchryk (Winnipeg: University of Manitoba Press, 1996), 20.

62 Ibid., 24–25.

63 Honoré Jaxon, Chicago, November 1, 1891, to "Family," PLAX. "I am hungry for the bannock of the trail," he wrote.

64 Peter Bakker, "The Michif Language of the Metis," in *Métis Legacy: A Métis Historiography and Annotated Bibliography*, ed. Lawrence J. Barkwell, Leah Dorion, and Darren R. Préfontaine (Winnipeg: Pemmican Publications, 2001), 177.

65 Father Moulin, quoted in Payment, *The Free People*, 118.

66 In the 1890s, he presided over the citizens' committee that organized the festivities for St. Joseph's Day, the "national day" of the South Branch Metis, July 24; see Payment, *The Free People*, 56.

67 John Hawkes, *The Story of Saskatchewan* (Chicago: S.J. Clarke, 1924), 1: 333.

68 Reverend Father Jules Le Chevallier, OMI, *Saint-Laurent de Grandin* (Vannes, France: LaFolye and J. de Lamarzelle, 1930), 38.

69 D.F. Robertson, "Alexis André," in *Dictionary of Canadian Biography*, vol. 12: 1891–1900 (Toronto: University of Toronto Press, 1990), 22–23.

70 Jules Le Chevallier, "Aux Prises avec la Tourmente: Les missionaires de la colonie de Saint-Laurent-de-Grandin durant l'insurrection métisse de 1885," extrait de la *Revue de l'Université d'Ottawa* (livraisons d'octobre-décembre 1939, avril-juin et juillet-septembre 1940): 21. See also Le Chevallier, *Batoche*, 55–56.

71 William H. Jackson, Lower Fort Garry, September 19, 1885, to "My dear Family," MG 3, C 20–1, 4, PAM.

72 "Documents of Western History: Louis Riel's Petition of Rights, 1884," ed. Lewis H. Thomas, *Saskatchewan History* 23 (1970): 19–22.

73 Henry J. Morgan, Department of State, January 5, 1885, to W.H. Jackson, Secretary General Committee, District of Lorne, Grandin P.O., NWT, Ottawa, RG 15, B-1A, vol. 97, LAC.

74 T.E. Jackson, "Riel's Secretary," Toronto *Globe*, July 2, 1885.

75 Louis Riel, June 9, 1885, to Julie Riel, in *The Collected Writings*, 3: 98n6.

76 "Notes of an Interview by Arthur S. Morton with Mrs. Amos Plaxton," June 25, 1932, WHJP. Riel mentioned the "poisoning" to his mother as well; see Riel, *The Collected Writings*, 3: 97–98.

77 Louis Schmidt, "Notes, mouvement des Métis à St. Laurent, Sask. TNO en 1884," T29811, Archives of the Archdiocese of St. Boniface, SHS. I thank Tom Flanagan for this reference.

78 William Jackson, February 2, 1885, to Albert Monkman, cited in T.E. Jackson, Prince Albert, NWT, June 17, "Letter to the Editor," Toronto *Globe*, July 2, 1885.

79 Ibid.

80 William H. Jackson, September 19, 1885, to "My dear Family," MG 3, C 20–1 #4, PAM. Canaan refers to the Promised Land of the Israelites, or ancient Palestine, lying between the Jordan River, the Dead Sea, and the Mediterranean Sea.

81 Jackson, "Letter to the Editor," July 2, 1885.

82 "February 24, 1885," in *Extraits du journal du Pére Fourmond*, in *Journal de l'Abbé Gabriel Cloutier, 1886*, unpublished manuscript, transcription par Gilles Martel, 197, SHS.

83 P. Fourmond à Mgr Grandin, St. Laurent, le 17 mars 1885, Accession 71.220, box 165, file 6715, Oblate Archives, PAA.

84 T. Gething [Gethyn] Jackson, "Jackson's Case," *Manitoba Free Press*, August 29, 1885. See also affidavit of John Slater, July 28, 1885, WHJP.

85 Jackson, "Jackson's Case," August 29, 1885.

86 Reverend A. Sutherland, October 5, 1885, to T. Getting Jackson, "Sutherland Letter Books, June 1885–March 1886," United Church Archives, Toronto.

87 "March 17, 1885," in *Extraits du journal du Pére Fourmond*, in *Journal de l'Abbé Gabriel Cloutier, 1886*, 197, SHS.

88 T.E. Jackson, Prince Albert, March 5, 1885, to Louis Riel, Fonds Louis Riel, SHS.

89 "March 7, 1885," in *Extraits du journal du Pére Fourmond*, in *Journal de l'Abbé Gabriel Cloutier, 1886*, 207–08. See also "Notes of an Interview by Arthur S. Morton with Mrs. Amos Plaxton," June 25, 1932, WHJP.

90 For additional information on Riel's religion, see Thomas Flanagan, *Louis "David" Riel: "Prophet of the New World"* (Toronto: University of Toronto Press, 1979).

91 "Riel and His Secretary: Dr. Orton, MP, Gives an Interesting Account of Two Worthies," Toronto *Daily Mail*, June 9, 1885. Riel's suppression of papal infallibility and his advocacy of free access to scripture, both Protestant elements, might have appealed to Will. Ken Munro discusses Riel's religion in his review of Gilles Martel's *Le Messianisme de Louis Riel* in *Canadian Ethnic Studies* 17, 2 (1985): 151.

92 Le Rev. P. Moulin à R.P. Soulier, Batoche, 7 juillet 1885, transcription de correspondence provenant des archives de la maison générale (Rome), juillet 1862–décembre 1894, Accession 71.220, box 211, file 8426, Oblate Archives, PAA.

93 Jackson to family, September 19, 1885.

94 Jackson, "Letter to the Editor," July 2, 1885. See also Jackson, "Jackson's Case," August 29, 1885.

95 Cyril Greenland and John D. Griffin, "William Henry Jackson (1861–1952): Riel's Secretary: Another Case of Involuntary Commitment?" *Canadian Psychiatric Association Journal* 23 (1978): 471.

96 *Journeying through a Century: Sister Pioneers, 1883–1983* (Edmonton: Sisters, Faithful Companions of Jesus, 1983), 202.

97 Jackson, "Jackson's Case," August 29, 1885. See also H.S. Nelson, *Four Months under Arms* (New Denver: n.p., n.d.), 17–18; Hugh Nelson, New Denver, April 29, 1944, to Jack Smith, "Honoré" Jackson File 81, Saskatchewan (Regina) Archives Board (SAB); and "Career of Honoré Jaxon," *Washington Post*, April 30, 1907.

CHAPTER 4: THE TRIAL, THE LUNATIC ASYLUM, AND EXILE, 1885

1 Pierre Berton, *The Last Spike* (Toronto: McClelland and Stewart, 1971), 120.

2 Brian Titley, *The Frontier World of Edgar Dewdney* (Vancouver: UBC Press, 1999), 84.

3 B.B. Osler, Regina, July 12, 1885, to "Hon. [?] Foster, Toronto," F 1032, Mu 2303, B.B. Osler Papers, AO.

4 J. William Brennan, *Regina: An Illustrated History* (Toronto: Lorimer, 1989), 18.

5 William H. Jackson, "Synopsis of Address, Tuesday Evening, March 16 [1886] at the Central Music Hall [Chicago], Anniversary Celebration of the Recent Northwestern Declaration of Independence, *Why We Fought; How We Fought; Why We Shall Fight Again*, by William H. Jackson, Private Sec'y of Louis David Riel," enclosed with a letter from W.H. Riley, Chicago, March 30, 1886, to T.V. Powderly, Terence Vincent Powderly Papers, American Catholic History Research Center and University Archives, Catholic University of America, Washington, DC, microfilm reel 14, Microfilming Corporation of America, 1974.

6 William Jackson, Chicago (written on the stationery of Peck Bros. & Co.), January 24, 1886, to "My dear Family," PLAX.

7 Titley, *The Frontier World*, 42, 44.

8 Ibid., ix.

9 Blair Stonechild and Bill Waiser, *Loyal till Death: Indians and the North-West Rebellion* (Calgary: Fifth House, 1997), 195.

10 Titley, *The Frontier World*, 20.

11 Ibid., 28, 73, 112, 115.

12 Ibid., 49.

13 "Dewdney and the North-West," *Manitoba Free Press*, March 26, 1885.

14 Frank Oliver, "Telegraphic," *Edmonton Bulletin*, August 4, 1888; quoted in Titley, *The Frontier World*, 99.

15 Clifford Sifton, quoted in August 1897; see John W. Dafoe, *Clifford Sifton in Relation to His Times* (Toronto: Macmillan, 1931), 153.

16 Titley, *The Frontier World*, 81.

17 Edgar Dewdney, June 27, 1885, to Sir John A. Macdonald, MG 26 A, vol. 107, 43219, microfilm C-1524, Macdonald Papers, LAC.

18 William H. Jackson [probably written June 26, 1885] to Edgar Dewdney, Lieutenant Governor, NWT, MG 26 A, vol. 107, 43220, microfilm C-1524, Macdonald Papers, LAC. The copy of the letter in the Ministry of Justice Papers, RG 13, F 2, vol. 807, 1084–85, LAC, contains this annotation: "This letter bears no date but was delivered

to his Honor on the 26th June and was presumably written on that date."

19 Descriptions of the courtroom appear in George F.G. Stanley, *Louis Riel* (Toronto: Ryerson, 1963), 345; see also Desmond Morton, ed., *The Queen v Louis Riel* (Toronto: University of Toronto Press, 1974), xiv.

20 A. Jukes and R.B. Cotton, July 20, 1885, to Superintendent Deane, NWMP, Regina, in "Louis Riel-Proceedings of Trial and Correspondence on W.H. Jackson," RG 13, F 2, vol. 2132, part 21, LAC.

21 Pierre McLeod, "Lettre de Regina," *Le Monde* (Montréal), 3 août 1885.

22 A.E. Porter, "Dr. A.E. Porter," in *The Voice of the People*, comp. and ed. Manon Lamontagne et al. (Prince Albert: Prince Albert Historical Society, 1985), 198.

23 Pierre McLeod, "Lettre de Regina," *Le Monde* (Montréal), 3 août 1885.

24 "Riel's Private Secretary: W.H. Jackson Lecturing in Fargo, Dakota, St. Paul, Minn., Nov. 28–A Special to the *Pioneer Press* from Fargo, Dakota," *New York Times*, November 29, 1885.

25 Hugh Richardson, cited in "The Queen vs. William Henry Jackson," in Canada, *Sessional Papers*, 1886, no. 52, p. 340.

26 Thomas Flanagan, "Hugh Richardson," in *Dictionary of Canadian Biography*, Vol. 14: 1911–20 (Toronto: University of Toronto Press, 1990), 870.

27 "The Adjourned Courts: Sentence of Big Bear et al.," *Regina Leader*, October 1, 1885.

28 Will Jackson, cited in "The Queen vs. William Henry Jackson," in Canada, *Sessional Papers*, 1886, no. 52, p. 340.

29 These phrases are his own. He used them in his address in Crookston, Minnesota, on November 25, 1885; see "Lecture of W.H. Jackson," *Crookston Times*, November 28, 1885.

30 "Riel's Private Secretary," *New York Times*, November 29, 1885.

31 *Henderson's Winnipeg Directory* for 1885, 225. My thanks to Elizabeth Blight, Manitoba Archives, April 23, 1993, to the author for this information.

32 The eminent criminal lawyer had dined with Edgar Dewdney at Government House about ten days earlier; see Osler to Foster, July 16, 1885.

33 Transcript, "The Queen vs. William Henry Jackson: Louis Riel-Proceedings of Trial and Correspondence on W.H. Jackson," RG 13, F 2, vol. 2132, part 21, LAC.

34 George R.D. Goulet, *The Trial of Louis Riel, Justice and Mercy Denied: A Critical Legal and Political Analysis* (Calgary: Tellwell Publishing, 1999), 60.

35 Ibid.

36 Hugh Richardson, cited in "The Queen vs. William Henry Jackson," in Canada, *Sessional Papers*, 1886, no. 52, p. 344.

37 "Local News," *Regina Leader*, July 30, 1885.

38 Eastwood Jackson, Prince Albert [Regina], August 2, 1885, to "My dear parents & Cicely," PLAX. Eastwood himself was so upset when he scribbled out his letter that he wrote Prince Albert rather than Regina at the top. He wrote, "As you will have seen by the papers Riel's trial has ended with a verdict of guilty and he has been sentenced to be hanged on the 18 of September my evidence was very nearly the strongest against him and yet I feel a pity for the positions in which he has placed himself. ..."

39 Excerpts, "Dr. David Young's Daily Journal, 1885," in note from R.H. Young, Selkirk, Manitoba, September 9, 1964, Ms. 52.7, GGC. Will stated that he was brought to Lower Fort Garry in handcuffs; see William H. Jackson, Lower Fort Garry, September 19, 1885, to "My dear Family," MG 3, C 20–1, no. 4, PAM.

40 Edgar Dewdney, August 8, 1885, to Superintendent, Selkirk Asylum, MG 3, C 20–1, PAM.

41 For my description of the temporary lunatic asylum at Lower Fort Garry, and Will's several months there, I rely heavily on the very useful article by John D. Griffin and Cyril Greenland, "The Asylum at Lower Fort Garry 1874–1886," *The Beaver* (Spring 1980): 18–23.

42 Excerpts, "Dr. David Young's Daily Journal, 1885," contained in a note from R.H. Young, Selkirk, MB, September 9, 1964, Ms. 52.7, GGC.

43 "Dr. David Young's Daily Journal," cited in Griffin and Greenland, "Asylum," 22–23.

44 Jackson to family, September 19, 1885.

45 Ibid.

46 Ibid.

47 Cicely Jackson, Winnipeg, November 4, 1885, to Dr. David Young, MG 3, C 20–1, PAM.

48 Jackson to family, September 19, 1885.

49 David Young, January 6, 1886, to S.L. Bedson, Inspector of Asylums, in Canada, *Sessional Papers*, 1886, no. 2, p. 46.

50 See "Correspondence of Cicely Jackson re: W.H.J. [William Henry Jackson] in Fall of 1885," 12, PLAX. See also "Jackson's Case," Toronto *Daily Mail*, November 25, 1885.

51 A note in "Correspondence of Cicely Jackson re: W.H.J.," 6, 10.

52 Ibid., 10.

53 Will Jackson, Crookston, Minnesota, November 13, 1885, to "My dear Mr. MacArthur," PLAX. Excerpts from the letter also appear in "Jackson's Case," Toronto *Daily Mail*, November 25, 1885.

54 William H. Jackson, Crookston, November 13, 1885, to "The Rt. Hon. Sir John A. Macdonald," MG 26, A 1(a), vol. 108, 43641, John A. Macdonald Papers, LAC.

55 William Henry Jackson, Crookston, November 15, 1885, to Dr. Young, reprinted in "Jackson's Escape," *Manitoba Free Press*, November 24, 1885. See also W. Jackson, Crookston, November 15, 1885, telegram to Sir John A. Macdonald, MG 26, A l(a), vol. 108, 43644, John A. Macdonald Papers, LAC. The French message reads, "Si Riel sera pendu vous provoquerez une gurre [sic] plus atociuse [sic]." Unilingual English telegraph dispatchers and receivers best explain the two spelling errors.

56 Jackson, telegram to Macdonald, November 15, 1885. The telegraph operators made a mess of this telegram; it reads, in part, "Commuez [sic] tous les condamnes a deux ans prison et [je] servirai. Jackson."

57 Stonechild and Waiser, *Loyal till Death*, 223–26.

58 "Riel's Secretary," *Crookston Herald*, November 20, 1885.

59 "Crookston Brevities," *Crookston Herald*, November 24, 1885.

60 "An Interesting Lecture," *Crookston Herald*, November 28, 1885.

61 "Riel's Secretary Speaks," *Crookston Herald*, November 28, 1885.

62 "Sympathy for the Nor'Westers," *Crookston Herald*, November 28, 1885.

63 "Extrait d'une lettre de William H. Jackson à [unknown]," in Papiers de Riel, boîte 18, série Alexandre Taché, T-53004, Fonds corporation catholique romaine de Archiépiscopale Saint-Boniface, SHS.

64 "W.H. Jackson: How He Appeared on Arriving at Fargo," Toronto *Daily Mail*, December 3, 1885. I thank Miriam Carey for pointing out this clipping.

65 See *Fergus Falls Journal*, December 8, 1885.

66 See "Louis Riel and the Northwest: Lecture of W.H. Jackson," *Crookston Times*, November 28, 1885, and "Riel's Secretary," *The Daily Argus* (Fargo, ND), November 28, 1885. The *Argus* termed him a "very fluent speaker." See also "Riel's Private Secretary Says the Cause of the Late Chief Is Not Yet Dead," *St. Paul Globe*, January 2, 1886, and "Brief Items," *The Herald* (Chippewa Falls, WI), January 8, 1886. Here it was observed that "Jackson is an eloquent speaker." Finally, see "Minneapolis: A Benefit for Riel's Family," *Manitoba Free Press*, January 20, 1886: "The secretary gave a comprehensive and interesting statement of the circumstances which led to the insurrection."

67 "W.H. Jackson," *Chippewa Falls Times*, January 6, 1886.

68 Honoré J. Jaxon, "A Reminiscence of Charlie James," *Mother Earth* 6, 5 (July 1911): 146.

69 William Henry Jackson, quoted in "Riel's Private Secretary," *St. Paul Globe*, January 2, 1886.

70 "W.H. Jackson: How He Appeared on Arriving at Fargo," *Toronto Daily Mail*, December 3, 1885.

71 Ibid.

72 Jackson to family, January 24, 1886. See also note 5.

73 Oliver D. Peck, Chicago, April 5, 1886, to "Mrs. Jackson," PLAX.

74 Ibid.

75 Riley to Powderly, March 30, 1886.

76 Joseph Howard, *Strange Empire: Louis Riel and the Métis People* (1952; reprinted Toronto: James Lewis and Samuel, 1974), 544.

77 "Two Martyrs: Memorial Services Held by Working People over the Murder of Lieske and Riel," *The Alarm*, November 28, 1885.

78 J. Seymour Currey, *Chicago: Its History and Its Builders* (Chicago: S.J. Clarke, 1912), 3: 260. It would be replaced as Chicago's finest theatre with the completion in 1889 of the magnificent Auditorium Theater, now part of Roosevelt University.

79 The program is attached to the letter, Riley to Powderly, March 30, 1886.

80 Richard Schneirov, *Labor and Urban Politics: Class Conflict and the Origins of Modern Liberalism in Chicago, 1864–97* (Urbana: University of Illinois Press, 1998), 204.

81 "Riel's Secretary," *Chicago Inter-Ocean*, March 17, 1886.

82 Ibid.

83 "Riel's Private Secretary," *Chicago Tribune*, March 17, 1886.

CHAPTER 5: JACKSON BECOMES JAXON, 1886–89

1 James Green, *Death in the Haymarket: A Story of Chicago, the First Labor Movement, and the*

Bombing that Divided Gilded Age America (New York: Pantheon Books, 2006), 145.

2 Lady Duffus Hardy, "Through Cities and Prairie Lands" (1881), in *As Others See Chicago: Impressions of Visitors, 1673–1933*, comp. Bessie Louise Pierce (1933; reprinted Chicago: University of Chicago Press, 2004), 228–29.

3 "A Visit to the States" (1887), in Pierce, *As Others See Chicago*, 230.

4 Green, *Death in the Haymarket*, 93.

5 Ray Ginger, *Altgeld's America* (Chicago: Quadrangle Books, 1958), 5; Bessie Louise Pierce, *A History of Chicago* (New York: Alfred A. Knopf, 1957), 3: 22; Walter Nugent, "Demography," in *The Encyclopedia of Chicago*, ed. James R. Grossman, Ann Durkin Keating, and Janice L. Reiff (Chicago: Chicago Historical Society, 2004), 233, 235.

6 Green, *Death in the Haymarket*, 38.

7 William Adelman, *Haymarket Revisited* (Chicago: Illinois Labor History, 1976), 2; Ginger, *Altgeld's America*, 8; Henry Ferns and Bernard Ostry, *The Age of Mackenzie King* (Toronto: James Lorimer, 1976), 36–37.

8 William Jackson, Headquarters, Labor Political Party of Cook County, Room 17, Greenebann's Building, 76 and 78 Fifth Ave, Chicago, September 6, 1886, to Michel [Dumas], typed copy of original letter, Série Alexandre Taché, boîte 38, T53009, Fonds corporation catholique romaine de Archiépiscopale Saint-Boniface, SHS.

9 Richard Schneirov and Thomas J. Suhrbur, *Union Brotherhood, Union Town: The History of the Carpenters' Union of Chicago, 1863–1987* (Carbondale: Southern Illinois University Press, 1988), 28.

10 "Eight Hour Movement," *Chicago Inter-Ocean*, March 16, 1886.

11 Richard Schneirov, *Labor and Urban Politics: Class Conflict and the Origins of Modern Liberalism in Chicago, 1864–97* (Urbana: University of Illinois Press, 1998), 26.

12 Ibid., 76–86.

13 Ibid., 80.

14 Albert Parsons, quoted in Green, *Death in the Haymarket*, 100.

15 Schneirov and Suhrbur, *Union Brotherhood*, 173.

16 Green, *Death in the Haymarket*, 128–29.

17 Ibid., 141.

18 "Origin of Union 'Slugging' and Its Picturesque Progenitor," *Chicago Record-Herald*, November 5, 1905. This article was later reprinted under the heading "The Origin of Union Slugging" in the *Los Angeles Times*, November 12, 1905. A shorter mention later appeared in the *Chicago Tribune*, "Father of Labor Sluggers Joins US Army Camp," September 18, 1915. Interesting references to Jackson's first year or so in Chicago also appear in Steven Sapolsky, "The Making of Honoré Jaxon," in *Haymarket Scrapbook*, ed. Dave Roediger and Franklin Rosemont (Chicago: Charles H. Kerr Publishing Company, 1986), 103–05.

19 My thanks to Richard Schneirov, a PhD candidate at Northern Illinois University in the early 1980s, for the reference to this article.

20 Jackson to Dumas, September 6, 1886.

21 Green, *Death in the Haymarket*, 145–46.

22 Donald L. Miller, *City of the Century: The Epic of Chicago and the Making of America* (New York: Simon and Schuster, 1996), 473.

23 Adelman, *Haymarket Revisited,* 15–19; Miller, *City of the Century,* 473–76.

24 Schneirov and Suhrbur, *Union Brotherhood,* 311. See also Philip S. Foner, Introduction, in *The Autobiographies of the Haymarket Martyrs,* ed. Philip S. Foner (New York: Monad Press, 1969), 1–13.

25 Richard Schneirov, "The Knights of Labor in the Chicago Labor Movement and in Municipal Politics, 1877–1887" (PhD diss., Northern Illinois University, 1984).

26 "Origin of Union 'Slugging,'" *Chicago Record-Herald,* November 5, 1905.

27 Ibid.

28 Ibid.

29 Schneirov, *Labor and Urban Politics,* 203.

30 "Origin of Union 'Slugging,'" *Chicago Record-Herald,* November 5, 1905. Schneirov and Suhrbur point out that the larger "millmen-contractors" who employed a majority of Chicago's carpenters continued to defy the union; see *Union Brotherhood,* 33.

31 Honoré Jaxon, quoted in "Urges a Union of All Forces," *Chicago Tribune,* November 13, 1893.

32 Miller, *City of the Century,* 476–77.

33 Pierce, *A History of Chicago,* 3: 285.

34 Will Jackson, Chicago, November 14, 1887, to "Dear Father," PLAX.

35 "New Trial Fund," *The Labor Enquirer,* September 11, 1886; see also *Chicago Tribune,* December 22, 1886 (my thanks to Richard Schneirov for this reference).

36 "Anarchist Publishing Association Articles of Agreement, October 21, 1886," Haymarket Affair Digital Collection, Chicago History Museum, www.chicagohistory.org/hadc/manuscripts/m16/M160000.html (accessed March 21, 2007).

37 Green, *Death in the Haymarket,* 232–38.

38 Will Jackson, quoted in "Angry Anarchists," *Chicago Inter-Ocean,* December 31, 1888. See also Carolyn Ashbaugh, *Lucy Parsons: American Revolutionary* (Chicago: Charles H. Kerr Publishing Company, 1976).

39 Paul Avrich, *The Haymarket Tragedy* (Princeton: Princeton University Press, 1984), 37.

40 Green, *Death in the Haymarket,* 142.

41 Louis Lingg, quoted in Avrich, *Haymarket Tragedy,* 289.

42 Adelman, *Haymarket Revisited,* 15–19; James D. Forman, *Anarchism: Political Innocence or Social Violence?* (New York: Dell, 1975), 15.

43 David Miller includes a chapter on philosophical anarchism in his study *Anarchism* (London: J.M. Dent, 1984), 15. Honoré described himself as a "philosophical anarchist" in "Who's Who-And Why: Serious and Frivolous Facts about the Great and the Near Great," *The Saturday Evening Post,* June 1, 1907.

44 Louis Zelloy, Secretary, et al., "Authority Revoked," letter to the editor, *The Knights of Labor,* December 4, 1886.

45 Jackson to father, November 14, 1887.

46 Schneirov, *Labor and Urban Politics,* 227, 220.

47 "Labor's Broil," *Chicago Times,* January 9, 1887.

48 The Carpenters' Assembly of the Knights of Labor, quoted in "The Disunited Labor Party," *Chicago Tribune,* January 8, 1887.

49 Elizabeth Eastwood Jackson, Claim No. 34, S. Sask., April 13, 1886, to Cicely Jackson, PLAX.

50 "Your loving mother," The Claim, December 30, 1886, to "My very dear Cicely," PLAX.

51 Will Jackson, Chicago, May 25, 1887, to "Dear Mother & Family," PLAX.

52 Will Jackson, Chicago, December 18, 1887, to Cicely Jackson, PLAX-G.

53 Will Jackson, Chicago, December 18, 1887, to "Dear Father," PLAX.

54 Cicely Plaxton, quoted in Pauline Ford, "Pioneer Move to Western Canada Filled with Problems and Adventure," *Prince Albert Herald*, June 17, 1972.

55 The *Chicago Times* ("Labor's Broil," January 9, 1887) reported that some delegates to the United Labor Party meeting on January 8 accused Jackson of being "guilty of sharp practice with the Central Labor union when he was employed by them and paid to print the speeches of Spies et al. in pamphlet form."

56 Jackson to sister, December 18, 1887.

57 H. Joseph Jaxon, Chicago, March 18, 1890, to A.K. Owen, WHJP.

58 Jackson to Dumas, September 6, 1886.

59 August Spies, "Autobiography," in *The Autobiographies of the Haymarket Martyrs*, ed. Philip S. Foner (New York: Monad Press, 1969), 65.

60 Oliver D. Peck, Chicago, April 5, 1886, to "Mrs. Jackson," PLAX.

61 William H. Jackson, Secretary for the Metis Council of the North-West Territories, Chicago, December 8, 1888, to A.K. Owen, WHJP. For information about Owen, see David M. Pletcher, "Utopian Reformer: Albert Kimsey Owen," in *Rails, Mines, and Progress: Seven American Promoters in Mexico, 1867–1911* (Ithaca: Cornell University Press, 1958), 106–48.

62 William H. Jackson, Chicago, April 4, 1888, to A.R. Owen, WHJP.

63 Ibid.

64 Schneirov, *Labor and Urban Politics*, 147.

65 Ibid.

66 Jackson to Owen, April 4, 1888.

67 Ibid.

68 Ibid.

69 Online Archive of California, "Biography: Inventory of the Albert Kimsey Owen Papers, 1872–1909," http://content.cdlib.org/view?docId=tf0m3n97kf&chunk.id=bioghist-1.8.3&query=biography&brand=oac (accessed March 23, 2007). An entertaining account of Owen and the Topolobampo project is Ray Reynolds, *Cat's Paw Utopia* (El Cajon, CA: Communications Arts Department, Grossmount College, 1972).

70 Jackson to sister, December 18, 1887.

71 Ibid.

72 "Your loving son Willie," September 24, 1888, to "My dear, dear Mother," PLAX.

73 Ibid.

74 Eve Fine, "Medical Education," in *The Encyclopedia of Chicago*, 518.

75 "Your affectionate brother," Savanne, April 13, 1891, to Eastwood Jackson, PLAX.

76 "Willie" to mother, September 24, 1888.

77 "He Is Opposed to Work," *Chicago Tribune*, March 27, 1889.

78 "Not the Hon. William H. Joseph Jaxon," *Chicago Tribune*, April 10, 1889.
79 "Riel's Secretary," *The Daily Argus* (Fargo), November 28, 1885.
80 Jackson to Owen, April 4, 1888.
81 He used William H. Jackson in his letter to A.K. Owen on December 8, 1888, he used W.H. Joseph Jackson on March 4, 1889, and by May 30, 1889 he had dropped the William for H. Joseph Jaxon. These three letters are held in WHJP.
82 The earliest surviving letter in which he signed his name Honoré Joseph Jaxon was to Eastwood, dated Port Arthur, June 5, 1891. This was also the name that he used in his letter to George A. Davis, Director General, World's Columbian Exposition, December 24, 1891, box 32, correspondence A-Z, HUG 1712, 2, 12, Frederic Ward Putnam Papers, Harvard University Archives (HUA). All quotations from the Frederic Ward Putnam Papers are made with the permission of the Harvard University Archives.
83 D. Bruce Sealey and Antoine S. Lussier, *The Métis: Canada's Forgotten People* (Winnipeg: Manitoba Métis Federation Press, 1975), 148–49.
84 Olive Patricia Dickason, *Canada's First Nations*, 3rd ed. (Don Mills, ON: Oxford University Press, 2002), 293.
85 Vernon R. Wishart, *What Lies behind the Picture? A Personal Journey into Cree Ancestry* (Red Deer: Central Alberta Historical Society, 2006), 181.
86 Mary Plaxton Grant, Glenbush, Saskatchewan, April 7, 1970, to Cyril Greenland, GGC.
87 Ibid.
88 One can date his name change from his letters to A.K. Owen. See note 81.
89 P. Fourmond, le 18 mars 1885, Petite Chronique de St. Laurent, D-IV-125, PAA.
90 Louis Schmidt, "Extraits, Journal de Louis Schmidt," le 19 mars 1885, 71.220, D-IV-III, PAA.
91 Donatien Frémont, *Les secrétaires de Riel: Louis Schmidt. Henry Jackson. Philippe Garnot* (Montréal: Les éditions Chantecler, 1953).
92 Gabriel Dumont, quoted in Adolphe Ouimet, *La vérité sur la question métisse au Nord-Ouest* (Beauceville, QC: Les Presses de l'éclaireur, s.d.), 124–25; also see Gabriel Dumont, "Gabriel Dumont's Account of the North West Rebellion, 1885," trans. and ed. George F.G. Stanley, *Canadian Historical Review* 30 (1949): 267.

CHAPTER 6: "CHICAGO'S LONG-HAIRED CHILD OF DESTINY," 1889–96

1 "Does Jaxon Injustice," *Chicago Times*, June 19, 1894.
2 Willis J. Abbot, *Watching the World Go By* (Boston: Little, Brown, 1933), 82.
3 William H. Jackson, April 4, 1888, to A.K. Owen, WHJP. See also "Jaxon Will Bear Watching," *Washington Post*, June 19, 1894.
4 "Does Jaxon Injustice," *Chicago Times*, June 19, 1894. According to the paper, he charged "the minimum price of $2 for two hours' instruction."
5 Cicely Plaxton, interview with the author, Prince Albert, June 7, 1979. Possibly he also learned some Yiddish; see Honoré to "Dear Mother," dated [Chicago], May 24, 1914, PLAX.
6 "Does Jaxon Injustice," *Chicago Times*, June 19, 1894.

7 In 1910, the census reported that Chicago had an Indian population of 188. Anne Terry Straus and Debra Valentino, "Gender and Community Organization Leadership in the Chicago Indian Community," *American Indian Quarterly* 27, 3–4 (2003): 523.

8 Carter H. Harrison, *A Race with the Sun* (Chicago: Dibble Publishing, 1889), 4.

9 The American press apparently believed that he was of Indian ancestry. The *New York Times* wrote on November 28, 1885, "He looks as if he has some Indian blood in his veins." Seven years later, on July 3, 1892, the *Omaha World Herald* noted, "He is a man below medium in height with straight cut semi-aboriginal features and long black hair which protrudes in massive locks from a massive forehead." On June 18, 1894, the *Washington Post* reported that he had "the high cheek bones and coppery complexion of the red men. His hair is raven black and very straight."

10 "Does Jaxon Injustice," *Chicago Times,* June 19, 1894.

11 "Denounced the Anglo-Saxon Race: A.[H.] J. Jaxon's Lecture before the Chicago Secular Union," *Chicago Tribune,* October 19, 1891.

12 "From Gage to my old friend Jaxon-a (half-Indian)," message in pencil at the bottom of the letter, Lyman Gage, First National Bank of Chicago, August 14, 1893, to H.J. Jaxon, folder 1, James Franklin Aldrich Collection, Chicago History Museum.

13 Carleton Beals, *The Great Revolt and Its Leaders: The History of Popular American Uprisings in the 1890's* (London: Abelard-Schuman, 1968), 14.

14 "Have Begun: The People's Party National Convention Makes a Start in Its Work," *Omaha World-Herald,* July 3, 1892; see also "All at Sea Now," *Omaha Bee,* July 3, 1892, and "Jaxon Has a Record," *Washington Post,* June 18, 1894.

15 Carlos A. Schwantes, *Coxey's Army: An American Odyssey* (Lincoln: University of Nebraska Press, 1985), 47.

16 Beals, *The Great Revolt,* 277.

17 Ibid., 87.

18 Ibid., 16.

19 Mary Lease, cited in the *Pittsburgh Press,* March 22, 1894, referenced in Donald L. McMurry, *Coxey's Army: A Study of the Industrial Army Movement of 1894* (Seattle: University of Washington Press, 1929), 43.

20 Jean Larmour, "Edgar Dewdney and the Aftermath of the Rebellion," *Saskatchewan History* 23, 3 (1970): 114.

21 William Jackson, Headquarters, Labor Political Party of Cook County, Room 17, Greenebann's Building, 76 and 78 Fifth Avenue, Chicago, September 6, 1886, to Michel [Dumas], typed copy of original letter, série Alexandre Taché, boîte 38, T53009, Fonds corporation catholique romaine de Archiépiscopale Saint-Boniface, SHS.

22 Diane Paulette Payment, *"The Free People-Otipemisiwak"* (Ottawa: Minister of Supply and Services Canada, 1990), 153.

23 L.W. Herchmer, Commissioner, North West Mounted Police, Regina, April 19, 1892, to E.C. Sickels, Regina, RG 18, vol. 1254, no. 305, LAC.

24 "Your affectionate son and brother," Chicago, May 25, 1887, to "Mother & Family," PLAX. Here he writes, "Ask Louis Schmidt for the present address of Michel Dumas."

25 *Edmonton Bulletin,* April 27, 1889. My thanks to Eloi DeGrâce for this reference.

26 George Woodcock, *Gabriel Dumont* (Edmonton: Hurtig, 1975), 243. On his drinking, also see "Michel Dumas," *Manitoba Free Press*, February 16, 1886.

27 Honoré Jaxon, Savanne on CPR seventy-two miles west of Port Arthur, February 1891, to "Dear Family," PLAX. He mentions that he has "visited with some of our French Metis friends on Lake Manitoba."

28 H. Joseph Jaxon, Chicago, March 18, 1890, to A.K. Owen, WHJP.

29 "Plans of the States Association," *Chicago Tribune*, June 7, 1890.

30 Ibid.

31 "Promises Made Live Stock Men," *Chicago Tribune*, June 28, 1890.

32 "World's Columbian Exposition," in *The Encyclopedia of Chicago*, ed. James R. Grossman, Ann Durkin Keating, and Janice L. Reiff (Chicago: University of Chicago Press, 2004), 899.

33 Reginald C. McGrane, "Lyman Judson Gage," in *Dictionary of American Biography* (New York: Charles Scribner's Sons, 1931), 7: 85–86.

34 Robert W. Rydell, "World's Columbian Exposition," in *The Encyclopedia of Chicago*, 900.

35 Paige Raibmon, *Authentic Indians: Episodes of Encounter from the Late-Nineteenth-Century Northwest Coast* (Durham: Duke University Press, 2005), 34–37.

36 Abbot, *Watching the World Go By*, 83.

37 Their association went back to at least 1889, as Honoré mentions his name in a letter to Colonel Owen, Chicago, May 39, 1889, WHJP.

38 L.J. Gage, Chicago, November 21 [1891], to Colonel George R. Davis, box 32, Correspondence J, HUG 1712, 2, 12, Frederic Ward Putnam Papers, HUA.

39 "James W. Nye, Merchant and Politician, Dies," *Chicago Tribune*, February 5, 1925.

40 James Nye, Chicago, November 21, 1891, to George R. Davis, box 32, Correspondence J, HUG 1712, 2, 12, Frederic Ward Putnam Papers, HUA.

41 Lyman Gage, quoted in "Chairman Lyman Gage," *Chicago Inter-Ocean*, June 7, 1890.

42 Honoré Jaxon, Chicago, November 1, 1891, to family, PLAX.

43 Henry Standing Bear, from Pine Ridge Agency, South Dakota, addressed to 170, E. Washington St., Chicago, IL (Honoré's office address), January 15, 1891 [1892], box 32, Correspondence J, HUG 1712, 2, 12, Frederic Ward Putnam Papers, HUA. The letter was written on January 15, 1892, not 1891 as written; Henry was still at Carlisle Indian School until the summer of 1891.

44 Honoré J. Jaxon, Mato Najin Cinca (Henry Standing Bear), Manuel S. Molano, Chicago, February 15, 1892, to Professor F.W. Putnam, box 32, Correspondence J, HUG 1712, 2, 12, Frederic Ward Putnam Papers, HUA.

45 Richard N. Ellis, "Luther Standing Bear," in *Indian Lives: Essays on Nineteenth- and Twentieth-Century Native American Leaders*, ed. L.G. Moses and Raymond Wilson (Albuquerque: University of New Mexico Press, 1985), 141.

46 Luther Standing Bear, *Land of the Spotted Eagle* (Boston: Houghton Mifflin, 1933), 42.

47 Ibid., 14–15.

48 H. Jaxon to family, November 1, 1891.

49 Alice Beck Kehoe, *The Ghost Dance: Ethnohistory and Revitalization*, 2nd ed. (Long Grove, IL: Waveland Press, 2006), 26.

50 Henry Standing Bear, from Pine Ridge Agency, South Dakota, addressed to 170, E.

Washington St., Chicago, IL, box 34, Sickels Correspondence, HUG 1712, 2, 12, Frederic Ward Putnam Papers, HUA.

51 F.W. Putnam, Cambridge, MA, December 30, 1891, to Emma Sickels, box 34, Sickels Correspondence, HUG 1712, 2, 12, Frederic Ward Putnam Papers, HUA.

52 Herchmer to Sickels, April 19, 1892.

53 John A. Macdonald, July 7, 1888, to Edgar Dewdney, private, Dewdney Papers, Glenbow Archives, Calgary, quoted in Sue Baptie, "Edgar Dewdney," *Alberta Historical Review* 16, 4 (1968): 1.

54 Edgar Dewdney, cited in E.C. Sickels, Washington, May 26, 1892, to Professor F.W. Putnam, box 34, Sickels Correspondence, HUG 1712, 2, 12, Frederic Ward Putnam Papers, HUA.

55 "Hot Shot for Davis: Miss Sickels Strikes Back at the World's Fair Director General," *New York Recorder,* June 2, 1893, clipping, box 34, Sickels Correspondence, HUG 1712, 2, 12, Frederic Ward Putnam Papers, HUA.

56 F.W. Putnam, November 24, 1892, to George R. Davis, Director General, box 32, Correspondence J, HUG 1712, 2, 12, Frederic Ward Putnam Papers, HUA.

57 Carolyn Ashbaugh, *Lucy Parsons: American Revolutionary* (Chicago: Charles H. Kerr, 1976), 192. I thank Professor William J. Adelman of the University of Illinois, Chicago Circle Campus, for this reference.

58 Honoré Jaxon, Chicago, May 26, 1893, to "Dear Mother," PLAX.

59 "Mr. Gage Says 'No,'" *Chicago Tribune,* March 11, 1893; see also "Jaxon Will Bear Watching," *Washington Post,* June 19, 1894.

60 "Does Jaxon Injustice," *Chicago Times,* June 19, 1894.

61 Elmer Ellis, *Mr. Dooley's America: A Life of Finley Peter Dunne* (New York: Alfred A. Knopf, 1941), 48.

62 Opie Read, *I Remember* (New York: Richard R. Smith, 1930), 232.

63 Wonderful details of the club appear in Larry Lorenz, "The Whitechapel Club: Defining Chicago's Newspapermen in the 1890s," *American Journalism* 15, 1 (1998): 83–102. I have relied heavily on this article for this sketch of the club. Was Jaxon a member? Lorenz's article implies that Jaxon was included in only some of the festivities, but in an interview with the *Chicago Daily News,* April 24, 1907, Honoré claimed that he did belong.

64 Ellis, *Mr. Dooley's America,* 50.

65 "A Mysterious Vigil: Romantic Tale of the Sand Hills," *Chicago Tribune,* April 26, 1896.

66 Walter Edwin Peck, *Shelley: His Life and Work* (1927; reprinted New York: Burt Franklin, 1969), 2: 295.

67 Abbot, *Watching the World Go By,* 89.

68 "The Burning of Mr. Collins' Body," editorial, *Chicago Inter-Ocean,* July 24, 1892.

69 "Jaxon Will Bear Watching," *Washington Post,* June 19, 1894.

70 Lorne Pierce, *Fifty Years of Public Service: A Life of James L. Hughes* (Toronto: S.B. Gundy; Oxford University Press, 1924), 124. The educational meetings were held in the middle of July; see "World's Fair Conventions," *New York Times,* April 30, 1893.

71 Annual Report of the Toronto School Board, 1893, quoted in R.M. Stamp, "James L. Hughes Proponent of the New Education," in *Profiles of Canadian Educators,* ed.

Robert S. Patterson, John W. Chalmers, and John W. Friesen (n.p.: D.C. Heath, 1974), 201.

72 The Congress of Anthropology was held in late August; see "World's Fair Conventions," *New York Times,* April 30, 1893.

73 Horatio Hale, "The Fall of Hochelaga," *Journal of American Folk-Lore* 7, 24 (1894): 13.

74 Ibid., 14.

75 Horatio Hale, cited in "Introductory, First General Report on the Indians of British Columbia," in *Report of the 59th Meeting of the British Association for the Advancement of Science, 1889* (London: John Murray,1890), 801. I thank Barnett Richling for this reference.

76 Voltairine de Cleyre, "C.L. James," *Mother Earth* 6, 5 (1911): 142.

77 Abbot, *Watching the World Go By,* 82–83.

78 Ashbaugh, *Lucy Parsons,* 192.

79 On her life, see the excellent biography by Paul Alvich, *An American Anarchist: The Life of Voltairine de Cleyre* (Princeton: Princeton University Press, 1978).

80 Cleyre, "C.L. James," 142.

81 "'Anarchy's Head Again: Conference of the Leaders Recently Held in Chicago,' Special Telegram, New York, Oct. 20," *Chicago Inter-Ocean,* October 21, 1893.

82 The manifesto is quoted in "Anarchy's Ugly Hiss: It Is Heard at a Meeting at Jaxon's Office in Chicago," *Chicago Tribune,* November 2, 1893.

83 Abbot, *Watching the World Go By,* 84.

84 Schwantes, *Coxey's Army,* 49.

85 Ibid., 43.

86 "Again on the Road," *Pittsburgh Post,* March 31, 1894; Schwantes, *Coxey's Army,* 43.

87 "Again on the Road," *Pittsburgh Post,* March 31, 1894.

88 "Coxey's Indian Ally," *The Woman's Tribune,* May 12, 1894. My thanks to Hugh MacMillan for this reference.

89 Abbot, *Watching the World Go By,* 84.

90 "Warned of a Plot," *Washington Post,* June 18, 1894.

91 "Does Jaxon Injustice," *Chicago Times,* June 15, 1894.

92 Honoré Jaxon, Washington, July 9, 1894, to "Dear Folks," PLAX-G.

93 "Your son and brother," Chicago, October 15, 1894, to "Dear Folks," PLAX.

94 Lorenz, "The Whitechapel Club."

95 Honoré Jaxon, Chicago, August 12, 1895, to "Dear Father Mother Eastwood and Cicely and Niece," PLAX.

96 "Your affectionate son Honoré J. Jaxon," Chicago, January 10, 1895 [1896], to "Dear Mother," PLAX-G. The letter envelope is postmarked "10 Jan 96"; hence, Honoré wrote the note in 1896 and incorrectly wrote 1895.

97 Honoré Jaxon, Chicago, May 3, 1896, to "Dear Father," PLAX.

98 Honoré Jaxon, Chicago, November 7, 1895, to "Dear Father Mother Eastwood and Cicely," PLAX-G.

99 "A Mysterious Vigil," *Chicago Tribune,* April 26, 1896.

100 Jaxon to his mother, January 10, 1895 [1896]; see note 96.

CHAPTER 7: HONORÉ IN LOVE, 1897–1907

1 Doug Weston, "Thomas Eastwood Jackson: Pharmacist Helps Shape Canadian History," *Canadian Pharmaceutical Journal,* 118 (1985): 71.

2 Pauline Ford, "Pioneer Move to Western Canada Filled with Problems and Adventure," *Prince Albert Daily Herald,* June 17, 1972. This article was compiled from the recollections of Cicely Plaxton.

3 Honoré J. Jaxon, Advocate, Suite 10, 122 LaSalle St., Chicago, June 24, 1896, to Wilfrid Laurier, MG 26 G, vol. 11, 4409–10, microfilm C-740, Laurier Papers, LAC.

4 Wilfrid Laurier, quoted speaking in Montreal, November 22, 1885, in *War in the West: Voices of the 1885 Rebellion,* comp. and ed. Rudy Wiebe and Bob Beal (Toronto: McClelland and Stewart, 1985), 191.

5 Canada, *House of Commons Debates,* March 16, 1886, 182.

6 Jaxon to Laurier, June 24, 1896.

7 Canada, Department of Indian Affairs, *Annual Report for the Year Ended March 31, 1913,* 140. "The resignation of Mr. T. Eastwood Jackson, clerk, fourteen years in the service, took effect during the end of July." Hence, he began in 1898. The description of the Carlton Agency comes from Canada, Department of Indian Affairs, *Annual Report for the Year Ended 30th June 1898,* 130.

8 "Obituary," *Prince Albert Advocate,* November 6, 1899.

9 William S. Hatcher and J. Douglas Martin, *The Baha'i Faith: The Emerging Global Religion* (Wilmette, IL: Baha'i Publishing, 2002), 2. A useful short summary is J. Douglas Martin, "Baha'i Faith," in the *Canadian Encyclopedia* (Edmonton: Hurtig, 1985), 127–28. I have used both sources in the preparation of this sketch.

10 Mrs. Janet Rubenstein, for the Office of the Secretary, National Spiritual Assembly of the Baha'is of the United States, Wilmette, IL, June 26, 1979, to the author.

11 "Your ever loving son," Chicago, March 7, 1913, to "Dear Mother," PLAX.

12 Robert H. Stockman, *The Baha'i Faith in America: Origins 1892–1900* (Wilmette, IL: Baha'i Publishing Trust, 1985), 1: 92.

13 "List of American Baha'i, ca. 1897," Chicago House of Spirituality Records, Chicago.

14 "Aimee Jaxon," Standard Certificate of Death, February 6, 1932, State of Illinois.

15 Robert H. Stockman, *The Baha'i Faith in America: Early Expansion, 1900–1912* (Oxford: George Ronald, 1995), 2: 173–74. See also "A Brief History of the Assembly of Teaching from Its Inception, May 23, 1901, to May 23, 1909," M-955, box 13, 4, 8, 14, 17, Ahmad Sohrab Papers, National Spiritual Assembly of the Baha'is of the United States Archives.

16 Honoré Jaxon, Chicago, November 5, 1903, to "Dear Mother and Eastwood and Cicely," PLAX-G.

17 William Jackson, Headquarters, Labor Political Party of Cook County, Room 17, Greenebann's Building, 76 and 78 Fifth Avenue, Chicago, September 6, 1886, to Michel [Dumas], typed copy of original letter, série Alexandre Taché, boîte 38, T53009, Fonds corporation catholique romaine de Archiépiscopale Saint-Boniface, SHS.

18 Will Jackson, Chicago, May 25, 1887, to "Dear Mother & Family," PLAX.

19 Marriage of Rose Ouellette and Salomon Boucher, September 20, 1886, Fonds Paroisse St-Laurent, Baptêmes, Mariages, Sépultures, 1885–96, SHS.

20 Will Jackson, December 18, 1887, to "Dear Father," PLAX.

21 In the Chicago City Directory for 1897, on page 1458, the occupation of "Miss Aimee Montfort" appears as "teacher." In her letters in the late 1920s and 1930s, she comments on her office work. In the 1910 census for Chicago, she stated that her occupation was "story writer" for a "newspaper."

22 Aimée Jaxon, Chicago, April 11, 1930, to "Dearest Cicely and Family," PLAX-G.

23 Ibid.

24 Aimée Jaxon, Chicago, December 2, 1910, to "Dear Mother & Eastwood," PLAX-G.

25 Aimée Jaxon, Chicago, December 29, 1920, to "Dear Mother and Folks," PLAX-G.

26 Aimée Jaxon, Chicago, January 3, 1930, to "Dearest Cicely and Everybody," PLAX-G.

27 Aimée Jaxon, c. mid-January 1900, to "My dear Mrs. Jaxon and very dear mother," PLAX. Note that at this stage Aimée understandably assumed that Elizabeth Jackson's last name was Jaxon, like Honoré's.

28 Aimée Jaxon, Chicago, October 27, 1930, to "Dearest Cicely," PLAX.

29 H.J.J., Chicago, January 20, 1898, to "Dear Father and Mother and Eastwood and Cicely," PLAX.

30 Honoré J. Jaxon, Chicago, February 24, 1899, to "Dear Mother and family," PLAX.

31 Honoré Jaxon, Chicago, January 18, 1900, to "Dear Mother," PLAX.

32 Ibid.

33 Myriam Pauillac, "Near West Side," in *The Encyclopedia of Chicago*, ed. James R. Grossman, Ann Durkin Keating, and Janice L. Reiff (Chicago: University of Chicago Press, 2004), 563–64.

34 "Your very, very loving son," Chicago, October 7, 1900, to "Dear Mother," PLAX-G.

35 "Your affectionate son," Chicago, November 26, 1900, to Elizabeth Jackson, PLAX-G.

36 David M. Young, *Chicago Transit: An Illustrated History* (DeKalb: Northern Illinois University Press, 1998), 92.

37 Honoré Jaxon, Chicago, December 12, 1902, to "Dearest Mother," PLAX-G.

38 Ibid.

39 Honoré Jaxon, Chicago, July 25, 1897, to "Dear Father and Mother and Eastwood and Cicely," PLAX.

40 Honoré sent a prospectus of this venture, a single typed page, to his family on October 21, 1897. There is a reference to it in the article "E.C. Bice: Stockholders in Annual Session Re-Elect the 'Gold Maker' a Director," *Chicago Tribune*, September 13, 1898.

41 Jaxon to mother, January 18, 1900.

42 Dan Kane, who kindly undertook census research on my behalf, failed to find him in the federal censuses for Chicago, 1900–10. A fire destroyed almost all of the 1890 census returns.

43 "Jaxon May Aid Filipinos," *Chicago Tribune*, February 18, 1899. Nye had written a character reference for Honoré in connection with his proposal to have a Metis presence at the Columbian Exposition in 1892. Aimée comments on their strong friendship in later letters, all dated Chicago, in particular those to Eastwood on November 8, 1910, to her mother-in-law and Eastwood on December 2, 1910, and to "Dear Folks" on December 30, 1910, PLAX-G.

44 Charles Laurier, "Skyscrapers," in *The Encyclopedia of Chicago,* 756.

45 Blair Kamin, "The Home Insurance Building," in *Chicago Days: 150 Defining Moments in the Life of a Great City,* ed. Stevenson Swanson (New York: McGraw-Hill, 1997), 46–47.

46 Honoré Jaxon, Chicago, July 21, 1901, to "Dear Mother & Cicely & Eastwood," PLAX-G.

47 The publication was published by the Behais Supply and Publishing Board of Chicago. The Newberry Library in Chicago contains a copy.

48 Jessie W. Cook, "The Representative Indian," *The Outlook* 65, 1 (1900): 82–83.

49 "Society of Anthropology," *Lucifer: The Light-Bearer,* 3rd ser., 5, 2 (1901): 14.

50 Honoré J. Jaxon, Chicago, December 24, 1900, to Henry Standing Bear, PLAX-G.

51 Leon Speroff, *Carlos Montezuma, M.D., A Yavapai American Hero: The Life and Times of an American Indian, 1866–1923* (Portland: Arnica Publishing, 2003), 193–98.

52 "Aid Indians Hurt in Wreck," *Chicago Tribune,* May 29, 1904; "Citizens to Sue for Indians," *Chicago Tribune,* June 8, 1904.

53 Luther Standing Bear, *Land of the Spotted Eagle* (Boston: Houghton Mifflin, 1933), 73.

54 John Maclean, *Canadian Savage Folk: The Native Tribes of Canada* (Toronto: William Briggs, 1896), 286–303.

55 Principal Grant, quoted in ibid., 291.

56 "Miners' Friends Call Jaxon 'Undesirable,'" *Chicago Inter-Ocean,* May 15, 1907.

57 Cook, "The Representative Indian," 83.

58 I thank Dr. Allan Sherwin for this insight.

59 "Honoré J.J.," Chicago, November 5, 1903, to "Dear Mother and Eastwood and Cicely," PLAX-G.

60 "Quinn, Pioneer Labor Leader Dies at Meeting," *Chicago Tribune,* February 23, 1932.

61 "Bondage His Refuge," *Chicago Tribune,* April 15, 1904.

62 "Who's Who-And Why," *Saturday Evening Post,* June 1, 1907.

63 "Labor Union of 2 Quits," *Chicago Tribune,* April 19, 1907.

64 George Hodge, Publisher, *Union Labor Advocate,* Chicago, June 29, 1906, to Frank Oliver, Minister of the Interior for Dominion of Canada, copy of letter, PLAX-G.

65 "An Appeal to Chicagoans in Their Own Interest," undated circular containing the name "Honoré J. Jaxon, Sec'y Fellowcraft Ass'n, Room 614, 108 Dearborn St.," PLAX-G.

66 A drawing of the periscope, and a copy of the petition, are in PLAX-G. From the *Book of Chicagoans,* 1905 and 1911 editions, the occupations of the petition's co-sponsors with Honoré can be established: Granville W. Browning (lawyer), George Jenney (capitalist), Fernando Jones (title examiner), Frank Lydston (surgeon), Stuart Shepard (lawyer), and Robert J. Thompson (consul).

67 James L. Murphy explains the origin of the society's name in *The Reluctant Radicals: Jacob L. Beilhart and the Spirit Fruit Society* (Lanham, MD: University Press of America, 1989), 2. Apparently Beilhart, the society's founder, suggested this name on account of his belief that humans "remained in a spiritual state akin to the bud or blossom, that man's soul had not yet achieved the spiritual perfection analogous to full fruition."

68 H. Roger Grant, *Spirit Fruit: A Gentle Utopia* (DeKalb: Northern Illinois University Press, 1988), 104–05.

69 Elbert Hubbard, in *The Philistine,* February 1905, 86–88, quoted in Grant, *Spirit Fruit,* 114.

70 "Who's Who-And Why," *The Saturday Evening Post,* June 1, 1907. See also "Highbrows Told of Spirit Fruit," *Chicago Tribune,* June 17, 1907.

71 Honoré Jaxon, Chicago, May 22, 1905, to "Mother and Eastwood," PLAX-G.

72 Honoré Jaxon, Chicago, May 23, 1906, to "Mother and Eastwood," PLAX-G.

73 "Ever your loving son," Chicago, March 15, 1906, to "Mother," PLAX-G. Information on the section Art and Architecture of the National Cement Users Association appears on the letterhead.

74 Honoré Jaxon, Chicago, August 30, 1905, to "Dear Eastwood and Mother," PLAX.

75 Honoré Jaxon, Chicago, November 9, 1899, to Eastwood Jackson, PLAX-G.

76 Honoré Jaxon, Chicago, November 21, 1906, to "Dear Mother and Eastwood," PLAX-G.

77 Honoré Jaxon, Chicago, April 6, 1907, to "Dear Mother and Eastwood," PLAX-G.

78 Aimée Jaxon, Chicago, November 27, 1930, to Cicely Jackson Plaxton, PLAX-G.

79 Jaxon's letter has not survived; this phrase is that of Theodore Roosevelt, who paraphrased Jaxon's note. See T. Roosevelt, April 22, 1907, to Honoré Jaxon, microfilm 345 (vol. 72), 259, Theodore Roosevelt Papers, Library of Congress. For an account of Jaxon's role in the incident, see J. Anthony Lucas, *Big Trouble* (1997; reprinted New York: Touchstone, 1998), 462–63. The defence of the three by Clarence Darrow led to their eventual acquittal.

80 The letter heading is quoted by Roosevelt in his letter to Jaxon, April 22, 1907.

81 I thank Dan Kane for this detail. "Shaw's Pickles" appears in the Chicago directories where Honoré lived at the time, 681 W. Lake St. Formerly the building had been a Masonic Temple; see the Chicago directories for 1907–10 and 1879. This is also confirmed in Lloyd Lewis, "It Takes All Kinds: Honore Jaxon, Forgotten Crusader," *Chicago Sun,* March 2, 1947.

82 "Who's Who-And Why," *The Saturday Evening Post,* June 1, 1907.

83 Henry Barrett Chamberlin, "Honore Joseph Jaxon: Militant Non-Resistant," *Chicago Record-Journal,* April 28, 1907.

84 None of the biographical summaries came close to discovering that detail. See "President Chides Treason Fugitive," *Chicago Daily News,* April 24, 1907; "Feel the Halter," *Los Angeles Times,* April 25, 1907; "Chicago Men Angry," *New York Times,* April 25, 1907; "Honore Joseph Jaxon: Militant Non-Resistant," *Chicago Record-Herald,* April 28, 1907; "Career of Honore Jaxon" (Chicago dispatch to the *New York Herald*), *Washington Post,* April 30, 1907; "Who's Who-And Why," *The Saturday Evening Post,* June 1, 1907.

85 "Chicago Federation to Expel Jaxon for Stirring President," *Chicago Inter-Ocean,* April 26, 1907.

86 Thomas Gethyn Jackson died on October 31, 1899. Cicely Plaxton, interview with the author, Prince Albert, June 7, 1979.

87 "Your loving son," Chicago, July 19, 1906, to "Mother," PLAX-G.

88 Honoré Jaxon, Chicago, November 18, 1906, to "Dear Eastwood and Mother," PLAX-G.

89 I thank Dan Kane for his discovery in the Chicago directories for 1907 and 1908 of Honoré's name as the secretary of the mail-order house.

90 W.E.B. Du Bois, *Economic Co-Operation among Negro Americans* (Atlanta: Atlanta University Press, 1907), 166. (Electronic edition, Chapel Hill: University of North Carolina, 2000.)

91 C.E. Mahoney, Acting President of the Western Federation of Miners, Denver, June 5, 1907, letter to "Honore J. Jaxon," PLAX.

92 "Want President to Investigate," *St. Louis Times*, July 15, 1907.

93 "Honoré J.J.," Minneapolis, September 15, 1907, to "Dear Mother and Eastwood," PLAX-G.

CHAPTER 8: RETURN OF THE "NATIVE" SON, 1907–09

1 For an earlier account of Jaxon's return, see Donald B. Smith, "Rip Van Jaxon: The Return of Riel's Secretary in 1884–1885 to the Canadian West, 1907–1909," in *1885 and After*, ed. F. Laurie Barron and James B. Waldron (Regina: Canadian Plains Research Center, 1986), 211–23.

2 Oliver became minister of the interior on April 8, 1905; see *The Canadian Who's Who* (London, UK: *Times* Publishing, 1910), 176.

3 Honoré Jaxon, Chicago, May 22, 1905, to "Dear Mother and Eastwood," PLAX-G.

4 Grant MacEwan, *Frederick Haultain: Frontier Statesman of the Northwest* (Saskatoon: Western Producer Prairie Books, 1985), 69–70.

5 Edmund A. Aunger, "Justifying the End of Official Bilingualism: Canada's North-West Assembly and the Dual-Language Question, 1889–1892," *Canadian Journal of Political Science/Revue canadienne de science politique* 34 (2001): 451. Hugh St. Quentin Cayley (1857–1934) later moved to Vancouver in the 1890s. His name appears in *University of Toronto: Class and Prize Lists, 1878* (Toronto: Henry Rowsell, 1878), 10. He edged out Will Jackson for the fourth slot in the Class II standing in classics. For biographical details, see "Judge Hugh Cayley Dies at Vancouver," Toronto *Daily Mail*, April 14, 1934.

6 "Origins of the People," in *Census of the Three Provisional Districts of the North-West Territories, 1884–85; Recensement des trois districts provisoires des Territoires du Nord-Ouest* (Ottawa: Maclean, Roger, 1886), 10–11, table 3. In 1885, there was a majority of non-Natives in Assiniboia, the third district, located in what is now southern Saskatchewan, including the Regina Plains and Qu'Appelle Valley.

7 Sarah Carter, *Aboriginal People and Colonizers of Western Canada to 1900* (Toronto: University of Toronto Press, 1999), 161.

8 Constance Backhouse, *Colour-Coded: A Legal History of Racism in Canada, 1900–1950* (Toronto: University of Toronto Press, 1999), 3–4, 283–84.

9 Joseph F. Dion, *My Tribe the Crees* (Calgary: Glenbow Museum, 1979), 182. For references to discrimination in the mid-twentieth century, see Maria Campbell, *Halfbreed* (Toronto: McClelland and Stewart, 1973).

10 A.E. Smith, *All My Life: An Autobiography* (Toronto: Progress Books, 1949), 28.

11 John Blue, *Alberta, Past and Present* (Chicago: Pioneer Historical Publishing Company, 1924), 3: 88. I thank Merrily Aubrey, then with the Provincial Archives of Alberta, for biographical information on Archibald Young Blain. See Order in Council, 64/08, signed by the lieutenant governor, March 5, 1908, 90.427, PAA. This document signified that he would temporarily be the acting deputy attorney general.

12 Archibald Blain, Edmonton, March 27, 1908, to S.H. Blake, GS 75–103, series 2–14, box 14, MSCC Special Indian Committee, S.H. Blake Correspondence, Anglican Church of Canada General Synod Archives, Toronto.

13 Leonard Peterson, *Almighty Voice* (n.p.: Book Society of Canada, 1974), vi.

14 C.A. Dawson and Eva R. Younge, *Pioneering in the Prairie Provinces: The Social Side of the Settlement Process* (Toronto: Macmillan, 1940), 120–21, cited in Dick Harrison, *Unnamed Country: The Struggle for a Canadian Prairie Fiction* (Edmonton: University of Alberta Press, 1977), 38.

15 Gordon L. Barnhart, *"Peace, Progress, and Prosperity": A Biography of Saskatchewan's First Premier, T. Walter Scott* (Regina: Canadian Plains Research Center, 2000), 14.

16 A list of books recommended by Honoré Jaxon in his address to the working people of Regina in mid-July 1909 appears in *Saskatchewan Labor's Realm*, August 2, 1909.

17 "Who's Who–And Why," *The Saturday Evening Post*, June 1, 1907.

18 Ibid.

19 Jacob Penner's observations from a letter home to his family in Russia, February 23, 1907, quoted in Victor G. Doerksen, trans., "Letter from Winnipeg in 1907," *Journal of Mennonite Studies* 15 (1997): 192–96, and cited in Charlotte Gray, *Canada: A Portrait in Letters, 1800–2000* (n.p.: Anchor Canada, 2004), 266.

20 Nathaie J. Kermoal, "Le 'Temps de Cayoge': La vie quotidienne des femmes métisses au Manitoba de 1850 à 1900" (PhD diss., University of Ottawa, 1996), XLIII n23, 40, cited in Olive Patricia Dickason, *Canada's First Nations: A History of Founding Peoples from Earliest Times*, 3rd ed. (Don Mills: Oxford University Press, 2002), 242, 479.

21 In 1911, the growing population of the three Prairie provinces was almost two million. M.C. Urquhart and K.H.H. Buckley, "Series A2–14: Population of Canada, by Province, Census Dates, 1851 to 1961," in *Historical Statistics of Canada* (Toronto: Macmillan Company of Canada, 1965), 14.

22 Jack London, quoted in Jan Pinkerton and Randolph H. Hudson, *Encyclopedia of the Chicago Literary Renaissance* (New York: Facts on File, 2004), 187.

23 *The Voice* (Winnipeg), September 20, 1907.

24 "Labor Approved Lemieux Act," *Toronto Star*, September 20, 1907.

25 Honoré Jaxon, Winnipeg, September 17, 1907, to "Mother and Eastwood," PLAX-G. He met Hugh John Macdonald on September 16.

26 "Il a vu la veuve du fils Louis Riel," *La Presse* (Montréal), 22 février 1912. My thanks to Diane Payment, historienne, projet de Batoche et Maison Riel, Parcs Canada, for this reference.

27 Parks Canada, *Riel House, National Historic Site*, 1980 (pamphlet Q-5–R103–000–BB-A1).

28 Honoré's forwarding address in Mistawasis indicates that it was their next stop after Winnipeg that November. See the letter of James Kirwan, Acting Secretary-

Treasurer, Western Federation of Miners, Denver, November 6, 1907, to Honoré J. Jaxon, Mis-ta-wa-sis Indian Agency, Saskatchewan, NWT [sic], PLAX-G.

29 Peter Kropotkin, "Some of the Resources of Canada," *The Nineteenth Century* 43 (1898): 498; cited in Paul Burrows, "Anarchism, Colonialism, and Aboriginal Dispossession in the Canadian West," paper presented at the annual meeting of the Canadian Historical Association, Saskatoon, May 28, 2007, 5.

30 W.J. Chisholm, Inspector of Indian Agencies, Prince Albert, April 20, 1908, Department of Indian Affairs, *Annual Report,* 1907–8, 161.

31 Anthony G. Gulig, "Yesterday's Promises: The Negotiation of Treaty Ten," *Saskatchewan History* 50, 1 (1998): 26. The Prairie provinces obtained control over their natural resources only in 1930.

32 Ibid., 32–33.

33 Sergeant Kennan, quoted in Ernest J. Chambers, *The Royal North-West Mounted Police: A Corps History* (Montreal: Mortimer Press, 1906), 83.

34 Edward Ahenakew, *Voices of the Plains Cree,* ed. Ruth M. Buck (Toronto: McClelland and Stewart, 1973), 167. See also David G. Mandlebaum, *The Plains Cree: An Ethnographical, Historical, and Comparative Study,* rev. ed. (Regina: Canadian Plains Research Center, 1979), 10.

35 Edward Ahenakew, "Genealogical Sketch of My Family," B/W15P E, 27, Paul Wallace Papers, American Philosophical Society, Philadelphia.

36 "Mistawasis Indians Mourn Death of Chief," *Prince Albert Herald,* August 4, 1938.

37 "Looking Around," *The Orcadian* (Kirkwall, Orkneys), February 12, 1970. Here I am taking a slight liberty. If Joe Dreaver, as the article states, spoke with an Orcadian accent, then his father must have spoken with one as well.

38 George Dreaver, quoted in Canada, Exchequer Court, "In the Matter of the Petition of Right of George Dreaver, Chief [...], Angers, J. Judgment, April 10, 1935." Also printed in Dreaver v. R., April 10, 1935, unreported, Exchequer Court of Canada, in *Aboriginal Peoples and the Law: Indian, Metis, and Inuit Rights in Canada,* ed. Bradford W. Morse (Ottawa: Carleton University Press, 1985), 401.

39 E.W.M., "Looking Around," *The Orcadian,* October 17, 1974. See also "Mistawasis Indians Mourn Death of Chief," *Prince Albert Herald,* August 4, 1938.

40 Dreaver v. R., in *Aboriginal Peoples,* 399–401.

41 Deanna Christensen, *Ahtahkakoop: The Epic Account of a Plains Cree Head Chief, His People, and Their Struggle for Survival, 1816–1896* (Shell Lake, SK: Ahtahkakoop Publishing, 2000), 685. The Ahtahkakoop Reserve, located just north of Mistawasis, was in the Carlton Indian Agency.

42 Honoré Jaxon, Chicago, January 10, 1895 [1896], to "Dear Mother," PLAX-G. The letter envelope is franked "10 Jan 96," so Honoré wrote it in 1896 instead of 1895.

43 Pierre Berton, *The Promised Land: Settling the West, 1896–1914* (Toronto: McClelland and Stewart, 1984), 1.

44 Bill Waiser, *Saskatchewan: A New History* (Calgary: Fifth House, 2005), 77–78.

45 Earl G. Drake, *Regina: The Queen City* (Toronto: McClelland and Stewart, 1955), 131.

46 Honoré J. Jaxon, "The Struggle for Life under Western Conditions," *Saskatchewan Labor's Realm,* August 2, 1909.

47 "The Function of the Labor Party: Honore J. Jaxon Addresses Meeting of Canadian Labor Party," *Regina Morning Leader*, December 9, 1907.

48 "Canadian Labor Party: Address by Honore J. Jaxon-Denounces Special Privilege," *Saskatchewan Labor's Realm*, December 13, 1907.

49 Ibid. This is cited as a direct quotation by Jaxon.

50 "The Function of the Labor Party," *Regina Morning Leader*, December 9, 1907.

51 Muriel Clements, *By Their Bootstraps: A History of the Credit Union Movement in Saskatchewan* (Toronto: Clarke, Irwin, 1965), 152–54. He is mentioned as the vice-president of the Labour Party in *The Voice*, October 25, 1907.

52 The references to Tom Molloy's memories of Jaxon are taken from Kay Kritzwiser, "K.M.K.'s Column," *Regina Leader-Post*, January 24, 1952.

53 Ibid.

54 "Function of the Labor Party: Address by Honore J. Jaxon," *Moose Jaw Times*, December 17, 1907.

55 "Convention Opens at Regina Today," *Regina Morning Leader*, December 11, 1907. See also "Honoré J. Jaxon at Farmers' Convention," *Saskatchewan Labor's Realm*, January 3, 1908.

56 W.J.C. Cherwinski, "Honoré Joseph Jaxon, Agitator, Disturber, Producer of Plans to Make Men Think, and Chronic Objector. ..." *Canadian Historical Review* 46, 2 (1965): 129–30.

57 Sarah Carter, "Controlling Indian Movement: The Pass System," *NeWest Review* (May 1985): 8–9.

58 Aimée Jaxon, Mistawasis, April 16, 1909, to "Darling Cicely," PLAX.

59 Honoré Jaxon, The Bronx, November 19, 1925, to Cicely, PLAX.

60 Aimée Jaxon to "Cicely," April 16, 1909. It is hard to say which Dreaver family Eastwood had his dinner with since several Dreaver families lived on the reserve.

61 Aimée Jaxon, Chicago, April 11, 1930, to "Cicely and family," PLAX-G.

62 "Was Secretary of Louis Riel," *Manitoba Free Press*, October 14, 1909. I thank Clarence Kipling of Calgary for this reference.

63 Honoré Jaxon, Daunais' Ranch, July 12, 1908, to "Dear Eastwood and Mother," PLAX-G.

64 Aimée Jaxon, Chicago, October 6, 1931, to Eastwood Jackson, PLAX-G.

65 William H. Jackson, September 6, 1886, to Michel [Dumas], SHS. See also Kritzwiser, "K.M.K.'s Column," January 24, 1952.

66 Jean Louis Riel, Saint Vital (Manitoba), le 8 juin 1908, à Honoré Jaxon, cited in "Il a vu la veuve du fils de Louis Riel," *La Presse* (Montréal), 22 février 1912: "Je vous prie d'écrire l'histoire de la rébellion de 1885, au Nord Ouest, parce que vous avez été témoin oculaire et que vous pourrez dire la vérité." The translation into English is the author's.

67 Raymond Huel, "Louis Schmidt: A Forgotten Métis," in *Riel and the Métis*, ed. A.S. Lussier (Winnipeg: Manitoba Métis Federation Press, 1979), 103; see also Katherine Hughes, *Father Lacombe, the Black-Robe Voyageur* (Toronto: William Briggs, 1911), 294.

68 Huel, "Louis Schmidt," 103.

69 Gail Morin, *Métis Families: A Genealogical Compendium* (Pawtucket, RI: 1996), 107. Morin states that Jean-Baptiste Boucher lived to September 30, 1911. My genealogical information on the Bouchers comes from her entry on the family. Ray Huel kindly sent me a copy of the reference in Louis Schmidt's diary to Honoré Jaxon's visit, April 28, 1908. The entry ends, "Il a pris mon portrait en passant de même que celui du vieux Boucher."

70 Diane P. Payment, "'La Vie en Rose'? Métis Women at Batoche, 1870 to 1920," in *Women of the First Nations: Power, Wisdom, and Strength,* ed. Christine Miller and Patricia Chuchryk (Winnipeg: University of Manitoba Press, 1996), 31.

71 Honoré Jaxon, July 23, 1938, to "Cicely and folks," PLAX.

72 Diane Payment, email to the author, March 31, 2007.

73 Louis Schmidt, "Short Story of Batoche, Dated St. Louis, July 30, 1923," in John Hawkes, *The Story of Saskatchewan* (Chicago: S.J. Clarke, 1924), 1: 279.

74 Honoré Jaxon, The Bronx, April 29, 1931, to Eastwood Jackson, PLAX.

75 Payment to author, March 31, 2007.

76 Diane Payment, *"The Free People-Otipemisiwak: Batoche, Saskatchewan, 1870–1930* (Ottawa: Minister of Supply and Services Canada, 1990), 79.

77 Honoré Jaxon, Old Battleford, January 11, 1908, to "Dear Folks," PLAX-G.

78 See *Fair Play and Free Play* 1, 1 (October 29, 1908): 8.

79 Jaxon was a British subject; see "Rutan's Majority 189," *Prince Albert Times,* December 2, 1908, and "Conciliation Board Opens with a Spat," *Saskatoon Daily Phoenix,* August 13, 1909.

80 *Fair Play and Free Play* 1, 1 (October 29, 1908): 5.

81 Honoré Jaxon, March 4, 1909, to "Dear Mother and Eastwood," PLAX.

82 Bruce Ramsey, *The Noble Cause: The Story of the United Mine Workers of America in Western Canada* (Calgary: District 18, United Mine Workers of America, 1990), 61. I thank Doug Cass of the Glenbow Archives in Calgary for bringing this book to my attention. See also Allen Seager, "Frank Henry Sherman," *Dictionary of Canadian Biography,* vol. 13: 1901–10 (Toronto: University of Toronto Press, 1994), 951.

83 William Pearce, "Memorandum: Department of the Interior," *Saskatchewan History* 23, 1 (1970): 24.

84 The house that the NWMP built for Burton Deane at Fort Calgary was the best on any NWMP barracks at the time. Today it is known as the Deane House, a historic site and restaurant.

85 William M. Baker, "Superintendent Deane of the Mounted Police," *Alberta History* 41, 4 (1993): 20, 22.

86 Barbara Hoffman, "Women of God: The Faithful Companions of Jesus," *Alberta History* 43, 4 (1995): 2–6.

87 Belle told her grandson Don Lougheed about his great-uncle, who was killed at Batoche. As he added, "She would be terribly upset with all this talk of Riel today." Don Lougheed, quoted in David Bly, "A Daughter of the West Who Made a Difference," *Calgary Herald,* December 30, 2001.

88 Grant MacEwan, *Eye Opener Bob: The Story of Bob Edwards* (Edmonton: Institute of Applied Art, 1957), 87.

89 Honoré Jaxon, The Bronx, February 22, 1935, to Cicely Plaxton and Eastwood Jackson, PLAX.

90 Ethel (Mrs. W.M.) Davidson, "About the Author," in William McCartney Davidson, *Louis Riel 1844–1885* (Calgary: Albertan Publishing Company, 1955), i.

91 "J.M. Davison, Editor and Manager of *The Albertan*, Calgary," *The Voice*, July 14, 1905.

92 Honoré used the letterhead for his letters to his family near Prince Albert. See letters dated June 11, June 23 and June 29, 1909, PLAX-G.

93 "Honore Jaxon Out for Persians," *Albertan*, February 16, 1912.

94 Cyril Alwin Tregillus, "Reminiscences," 35, typed copy of original manuscript, private collection, Richard Tregillus.

95 David Bright, *The Limits of Labour: Class Formation and the Labour Movement in Calgary, 1883–1929* (Vancouver: UBC Press, 1998), 38.

96 Joe Cherwinski, *Early Working-Class Life on the Prairies, Canada's Visual History Series* 69 (Ottawa: National Museum of Man, n.d.), 5.

97 Honoré Jaxon, Fernie (BC), April 17, 1909, to Eastwood Jackson, PLAX-G.

98 J. William Kerr, *Frank Slide* (Calgary: Baker Publishing, 1990), 6, 20, 27, 36.

99 "Would Force Lewis' Hand: Mine Workers After International Help in Strike; Mass Meeting Held," *Frank Paper*, May 13, 1909.

100 Frank Sherman died later that year, on October 11, from Bright's disease. "A degeneration of the kidneys," his biographer writes, "often associated with exposure to toxic materials and a commonplace affliction among underground miners." Seager, "Sherman," *Dictionary of Canadian Biography*, 951.

101 Honoré J. Jaxon, "The Struggle for Life under Western Conditions," *Saskatchewan Labor's Realm*, November 20, 1909.

102 "Would Force Lewis' Hand," *Frank Paper*, May 13, 1909.

103 "Strong Resolutions Passed by Miners," *Coleman Miner*, May 14, 1909. I thank Julie Green for this reference and for another account of the gathering, "Monster Meetings Refute Falsehoods," *The District Ledger* (Fernie, BC), May 15, 1909.

104 "Would Force Lewis' Hand," *Frank Paper*, May 13, 1909.

105 Honoré Jaxon, [Crowsnest Pass], April 29, 1909, to Eastwood Jackson, PLAX.

106 Aimée Jaxon, Mistawasis, June 29, 1909, to "Dearest Honoré," PLAX-G.

107 "Economic Circle: Honore Jaxon Addresses Opening Meeting of New Society," *Regina Leader*, July 19, 1909.

108 James Oliver Curwood, "Saskatoon-The Wonderful," *Saskatoon Daily Phoenix*, September 11, 1909.

109 "The University of Saskatchewan Is Located at Saskatoon City," *Saskatoon Daily Phoenix*, April 8, 1909.

110 "Rebellion of 1885 Is Recalled," *Saskatoon Daily Phoenix*, October 9, 1909.

111 Don Kerr and Stan Hanson, *Saskatoon: The First Half-Century* (Edmonton: NeWest Press, 1982), 102.

112 Eastwood Jackson, Mistawasis, September 21, 1909, to Honoré Jaxon, PLAX-G.

113 "Work Begun on Arts Building," *Edmonton Bulletin*, September 29, 1909.

114 J.G. MacGregor, *Edmonton: A History* (Edmonton: Hurtig, 1967), 177.

115 "Riel a Martyr Says H. Jaxon," *Edmonton Journal*, October 4, 1909.

116 Emily Murphy, *Janey Canuck in the West* (1910; reprinted Toronto: McClelland and Stewart, 1975), 206.

117 Aimée Jaxon, Edmonton, October 2, 1909, to "Dear Folks," PLAX-G.

118 Ibid. For a good sketch of the life of Katherine Hughes, see Pádraig Ó Siadhail, "Katherine Hughes, Irish Political Activist," in *Edmonton: The Life of a City,* ed. Bob Hesketh and Frances Swyripa (Edmonton: NeWest Press, 1995), 78–87.

119 Hughes, *Father Lacombe,* 294.

120 Aimée Jaxon, Edmonton, October 2, 1909, to "Dear Folks," PLAX-G.

121 "Hon. Frank Oliver," in *The Canadian Men and Women of the Time,* 2nd ed., ed. Henry James Morgan (Toronto: William Briggs, 1912), 869; see also Berton, *The Promised Land,* 206.

122 "Witnesses Tell of Conditions of Work," *Saskatoon Daily Phoenix,* August 18, 1909; "Saskatoon Labour Dispute Findings," *Saskatoon Daily Phoenix,* September 14, 1909; "Official Report on the Dispute," *Saskatoon Daily Phoenix,* September 18, 1909; "Was Secretary of Riel," *Manitoba Free Press,* October 14, 1909.

123 "Jaxon Would Preserve Historic Landmarks," *Edmonton Journal,* October 14, 1909.

124 Honoré Jaxon, cited in "Was Secretary of Riel," *Manitoba Free Press,* October 14, 1909.

125 Honoré Jaxon, cited in "Wants to See Old Trails Preserved: Honore Jaxon Will Place Demand before Canadian House of Commons," *Winnipeg Telegram,* October 14, 1909.

126 Honoré Jaxon, cited in "Was Secretary of Riel," *Manitoba Free Press* October, 14, 1909.

127 Honoré Jaxon, Chicago, October 21, 1909, to "Dear Mother and Eastwood," PLAX-G.

CHAPTER 9: CRESCENDO, 1910–18

1 Richard H. Brown, "Lloyd Lewis: A Chicago Journalist," *The Encyclopedia of Chicago,* ed. James R. Grossman, Ann Durkin Keating, and Janice L. Reiff (Chicago: University of Chicago Press, 2004), 439. For information on Otto McFeeley, see Robert St. John, *This Was My World* (Garden City, NY: Doubleday, 1953), 111. St. John (1903–2003) was a celebrated American war correspondent and print and broadcast journalist. As a young man, he worked for Otto McFeeley after McFeeley had left the *Chicago Evening Post* to edit *Oak Leaves,* a weekly published in Oak Park, Illinois.

2 Lloyd Lewis, "It Takes All Kinds: Honore Jaxon, Forgotten Crusader," Book Week, *Chicago Sun,* March 2 1947, 4.

3 References appear in several of her letters in the 1910s to her less than robust health, but the specific physical condition or illness is not mentioned; see, for instance, Aimée Jaxon, Chicago, December 2, 1910, to "Dear Mother & Eastwood," PLAX-G. Later, in 1913, she suffered from serious eye problems. Aimée Jaxon, Chicago, November 7, 1913, to "Dear Eastwood & Mother," PLAX.

4 She described herself in the 1920 census as a "stenographer," but her letters in the late 1920s and early 1930s indicate that she composed letters on her own initiative.

5 Aimée Jaxon, Chicago, December 30, 1910, to "Dear Folks," PLAX-G.

6 Aimée Jaxon, Chicago, December 2, 1910, to "Dear Mother & Eastwood," PLAX-G.

7 Aimée Jaxon, Chicago, December 14, 1911, to "Dear Folks," PLAX-G.

8 Aimée Jaxon, Chicago, July 4, 1930, to "Dearest Cicely and Folks," PLAX-G. The Shedd Aquarium officially opened on May 30, 1930, and Aimée visited it about one month after its opening.

9 Honoré Jaxon, Chicago, November 18, 1906, to "Dear Eastwood and Mother," PLAX-G.

10 Aimée Jaxon, Chicago, December 2, 1910, to "Dear Mother & Eastwood," PLAX-G.

11 "Who's Who-And Why," *The Saturday Evening Post,* June 1, 1907.

12 Lewis, "It Takes All Kinds."

13 "Minerva J. Montfort," Certificate of Death, October 1, 1917, no. 29482, State of Illinois.

14 1910 United States Census, April 22, 1910. Aimée, her mother, her sister Blanche, and her half-sister Victoria McMillan all lived in an apartment at 4425 West End. I thank Dan Kane, my researcher in Chicago, for this information.

15 Aimée Jaxon, Chicago, April 18, 1910, to Eastwood Jackson, PLAX-G.

16 Honoré Jaxon, Chicago, May 10, 1910, to "Dear Mother and Eastwood," PLAX.

17 Aimée Jaxon, Chicago, March 7, 1911, to "Dear Eastwood & Mother," PLAX-G.

18 Honoré Jaxon, Chicago, October 28, 1906, to Eastwood Jackson, PLAX-G.

19 Sophie Loeding, Wilmette, IL, February 17, 1985, to the author.

20 Aimée Jaxon, Chicago, September 5, 1911, to Eastwood Jackson, PLAX-G.

21 Aimée Jaxon, Chicago, July 26, 1911, to "Dear folks," PLAX-G.

22 Aimée Jaxon, Chicago, October 4, 1911, to "Mother & Eastwood," PLAX-G.

23 Annie Fellows Johnston, *In the Desert of Waiting: The Legend of Camel Back Mountain* (Boston: Page Company, 1904), an inspirational account of the value of disappointment in preparing one for eventual success.

24 Aimée Jaxon, Chicago, December 22, 1909, to "My dear Eastwood & Mother," PLAX-G.

25 There are many biographies of Frank Lloyd Wright; for a satisfying quick overview, see Ada Louise Huxtable, *Frank Lloyd Wright* (New York: Viking, 2004). For the most precise details, see Meryle Secrest, *Frank Lloyd Wright* (New York: Alfred A. Knopf, 1992), a well-documented study. After looking at the Huxtable and Secrest biographies, Wright's own self-serving memoirs are most entertaining; see *An Autobiography* (1932; reprinted New York: Horizon Press, 1977).

26 Wright, *An Autobiography,* 192.

27 Aimée Jaxon, Chicago, December 30, 1910, to "Dear Folks," PLAX-G.

28 Ibid.

29 Louis E. Cooke, "Charles H. McConnell," *Newark Evening Star,* December 2, 1915. Cooke's series, "Reminiscences of a Showman," are available online at the Circus Historical Society site on the World Wide Web.

30 Aimée Jaxon, Chicago, December 30, 1910, to "Dear Folks," PLAX-G.

31 Ricardo Flores Magón, *Land and Liberty: Anarchist Influences in the Mexican Revolution,* comp. David Poole (Montreal: Black Rose Books, 1977), 21, 15.

32 Ibid., 21.

33 Ricardo Flores Magón, in *Regeneración* (Los Angeles), June 16, 1911, cited in Poole, *Land and Liberty,* 22.

34 Emma Goldman, quoted in Paul Alvich, *An American Anarchist: The Life of Voltairine de Cleyre* (Princeton: Princeton University Press, 1978), 93.

35 Alvich, *An American Anarchist*, 19.

36 Ibid., 90.

37 Ibid., 11, 171–77.

38 Voltairine de Cleyre, quoted in Alvich, *An American Anarchist*, 174.

39 "Chicago Comrades Display Great Activity," *Regeneración*, August 19, 1911.

40 Alvich, *An American Anarchist*, 216.

41 H. [Honoré Jaxon], 531 N. Marshall St., Philadelphia, PA, May 20, 1910, to Miss V. de Cleyre, Voltairine de Cleyre Papers, Labadie Collection, University of Michigan. Estelle Dansereau of the Department of French, University of Calgary, July 9, 1991, kindly gave me an assessment of his French: "Grammatically correct, literal English structures."

42 Franklin Rosemont, Introduction, in *Voltairine de Cleyre, Written in Red: Selected Poems*, ed. Franklin Rosemont (Chicago: Charles H. Kerr Publishing Company, 1990), 7.

43 Voltairine de Cleyre, quoted in Alvich, *An American Anarchist*, 166, see note 48.

44 See Aimée Jaxon, Chicago, July 26, 1911, to "Dear folks" [the Jackson family in Saskatchewan], and Honoré Jaxon, Newcastle-upon-Tyne, England, September 4, 1911, to "Mother and Eastwood," both in PLAX-G.

45 Aimée Jaxon, Chicago, July 21, 1911, to "Dear folks," and Honoré Jaxon, Chicago, May 31, 1913, to "Folks," both in PLAX-G.

46 A. Jaxon to family, July 26, 1911, and H. Jaxon to family, September 4, 1911; see also "World Congress on Races Assembles," *New York Times*, July 24, 1912.

47 Executive Council of the Universal Races Congress, cited in Michael D. Biddiss, "The Universal Races Congress of 1911," *Race* 13, 1 (1971): 37.

48 Charles A. Eastman, *From the Deep Woods to Civilization* (1916; reprinted Lincoln: University of Nebraska Press, 1977), 189.

49 Honoré J. Jaxon, Special Envoy to Europe on Behalf of the Insurrectos of Mexico, "A Statement from the Working Class of Mexico to the 44th Annual Congress of the Trades Unions of Great Britain," four-page circular, no. 475, Fonds Louis Riel, SHS.

50 Ibid.

51 Honoré Joseph Jaxon, London, England, October 11, 1911, to Joseph Riel, no. 475, Fonds Louis Riel, SHS.

52 Honoré Jaxon, Bristol, England, letter envelope postmarked December 27, 1911, to "Dear Mother and Eastwood," PLAX-G.

53 "Your affectionate Nephew William [Barber]," Holmrook, Cumberland, August 22, 1911, to "My dear Aunt," PLAX.

54 Colin Osman, "George Davison," *Oxford Dictionary of National Biography* (Oxford: Oxford University Press, 2004), 15: 482–83; Honoré Jaxon, Newcastle-upon-Tyne, September 4, 1911, to "Dear Mother and Eastwood," PLAX-G; Aimée Jaxon, Chicago, October 4, 1911, to "Dear mother & Eastwood," PLAX-G.

55 Philip Hainsworth, "Sara Louisa Blomfield," *Oxford Dictionary of National Biography* (Oxford: Oxford University Press, 2004), 6: 264–65; Paul Waterhouse and Reverend John Elliott, "Sir Arthur William Blomfield," *Oxford Dictionary of National*

Biography (Oxford: Oxford University Press, 2004), 6: 255–56.

56 Aimée Jaxon, Chicago, September 5, 1911, to "Dear Eastwood & Mother," PLAX-G; Aimée Jaxon, Chicago, November 7, 1911, to "Very Dear Folks," PLAX-G.

57 H.M.L., "Dr. C.A. Barber, C.I.E., Sc.D. A Memoir," *International Sugar Journal* (March 1933), 93–95. I thank Dr. Charles Barber, the grandson of Charles Alfred Barber, for sending me a copy of this article.

58 My thanks to Dr. Charles Barber, son of Geoffrey Barber, for showing me his father's manuscript introduction to a presentation of the diaries of his father, Charles Alfred Barber, kept while he was in India.

59 "Edward Gethyn Barber," *The Methodist Who's Who*, 1912 (London: Charles H. Kelly, n.d.), 19.

60 E.G. Barber, Hendon NW, London, August 15, 1911, to Eastwood Jackson, PLAX.

61 Honoré Jaxon, Chicago, January 1915, to "Dear Mother," PLAX.

62 Geoffrey Barber, "Introduction," 13.

63 Geoff Houghton and Pat Houghton, *Well-Regulated Minds and Improper Moments: A History of The Leys School* (Cambridge: Governors of The Leys School, 2000), 240–47.

64 Ann Jackson Barber, Trynmawrn [?], South Wales, March 8, 1872, to "My very dear Brother & Sister," PLAX.

65 Aimée Jaxon, Chicago, March 7, 1910, to Eastwood Jackson, PLAX-G.

66 Honoré Jaxon, Chicago, March 7, 1913, to "Dear Mother," PLAX.

67 A. Jaxon to family, September 5, 1911.

68 "William [Barber]," Holmrook, Cumberland, August 22, 1911, to "My dear Aunt," PLAX. Interestingly Theo was known to his North American relatives as William but to his family in England as Theo. He wrote under the name of W.T.A. Barber.

69 "Your Affectionate Nephew W.T.A. Barber," The Leys School, Cambridge, February 21, 1912, to "My dear Aunt," PLAX.

70 W.T.A. Barber, *David Hill: Missionary and Saint*, 5th ed. (London: Robert Culley, 1909), 240.

71 Frank Tice, "William Theodore Aquila Barber, M.A., D.D.," in T*he History of Methodism in Cambridge* (London: Epworth Press, 1966), 118–21.

72 Emmie C. Barber, The Leys, Cambridge, October 2, 1911, to "My dear Mrs. Jackson," PLAX.

73 W.T.A. Barber, Cambridge, probably the winter of 1931–32, to Eastwood Jackson and Cicely Jackson Plaxton, PLAX-G.

74 "Dans le monde ouvrier," *Le Devoir*, 16 février 1912.

75 Arthur Cuthbert, "London, Eng.," *Star of the West* 2, 16 (1911): 13.

76 This is the forwarding address that he gives in his letter to Joseph Riel; see H. Jaxon to J. Riel, October 11, 1911.

77 Bruce W. Whitmore, *The Dawning Place: The Building of a Temple, the Forging of the North American Baha'i Community* (Wilmette, IL: Baha'i Publishing Trust, 1984), 54.

78 "Il a vu la veuve du fils de Louis Riel," *La Presse*, le 22 février 1912.

79 "H.J. Jaxon Has Been in Europe to Confer with Trades Unionists," *Toronto Star*, February 26, 1912.

80 H.J. Jaxon, quoted in "Mexicans Dominated by Vested Interests," Toronto *World,* February 25, 1912.

81 "Riel's Secretary Here: Mexican Insurrecto Now," *Toronto Telegram,* February 26, 1912.

82 In December 1875, they were both students at the Clinton High School; see "High School Examination," *Clinton New Era,* December 23, 1875; see also "Rev. W.G. Hanna Leaves the Lord's Day Alliance," Toronto *Globe,* April 9, 1913, William Girdwood Hanna clipping file, United Church Archives, Toronto.

83 R.M. Stamp, "James L. Hughes Proponent of the New Education," in *Profiles of Canadian Educators,* ed. Robert S. Patterson, John W. Chalmers, and John W. Freisen (n.p.: D.C. Heath, 1974), 190, 197.

84 J.M.S. Careless, *Toronto to 1918: An Illustrated History* (Toronto: James Lorimer, 1984), 200.

85 Gunter Gad and Deryck W. Holdsworth, "Streetscape and Society: The Changing Built Environment of King Street, Toronto," in *Patterns of the Past: Interpreting Ontario's History,* ed. Roger Hall, William Westfall, and Laurel Sefton MacDowell (Toronto: Dundurn Press, 1988), 188.

86 Fern Bayer, *The Ontario Collection* (Markham, ON: Fitzhenry and Whiteside, 1984), 124. Allward later designed the Vimy Ridge Memorial in France, unveiled in 1936, commemorating Canadian World War I soldiers who had died overseas.

87 "The Noble Dead," Toronto *Globe,* June 29, 1896.

88 Martin L. Freidland, *The University of Toronto: A History* (Toronto: University of Toronto Press, 2002), 233.

89 "William Stafford Milner," in *The Canadian Men and Women of the Times,* 2nd ed., ed. Henry James Morgan (Toronto: William Briggs, 1912), 809.

90 Ibid.

91 Michael Bliss, *A Canadian Millionaire: The Life and Business Times of Sir Joseph Flavelle, Bart. 1858–1939* (1978; reprinted Toronto: University of Toronto Press, 1992), 97.

92 Stephen Langdon, "Why Student Activists Are Zeroing In on a New Target," Toronto *Globe and Mail,* March 1969; reprinted in *The Underside of Toronto,* ed. W.E. Mann (Toronto: McClelland and Stewart, 1970), 177.

93 Honours Classics in the *University of Toronto by a Group of Classical Graduates* (Toronto: University of Toronto Press, 1929), 11.

94 "William Stafford Milner," in *A Standard Dictionary of Canadian Biography: Canadian Who Was Who,* ed. Charles G.G. Roberts and Arthur L. Tunnel (Toronto: Trans-Canada Press, 1934), 1: 363.

95 "Passmore-Copway," *Brantford Courier,* December 16, 1905, and the *Courier's* subsequent article on the wedding, December 18, 1905. I thank Doug Leighton for these references. See also "S.F. Passmore Is Victim of Auto," *Brantford Expositor,* September 29, 1927, and Donald B. Smith, "Kahgegagahbowh: Canada's First Literary Celebrity in the United States," in *Life, Letters, and Speeches: George Copway (Kahgegagahbowh),* ed. Donald B. Smith and A. LaVonne Brown Ruoff (Lincoln: University of Nebraska Press, 1997), 23–60.

96 A fabulous resource at the University of Toronto Archives is the newspaper clipping files kept on University of Toronto graduates, which were maintained until the

early 1940s or so. For example, I know that Professor W.S. Milner was secretary of the University College class of 1881; I know this from a tiny item in the *University of Toronto Monthly,* April 1925. The archives also supplied the note about the University College class of 1881's fortieth class reunion.

97 Joseph Schull, *Ontario since 1867* (Toronto: McClelland and Stewart, 1978), 205.

98 For a good description of Toronto City Hall, see Marilyn M. Litvak, *Edward James Lennox: "Builder of Toronto"* (Toronto: Dundurn Press, 1995), 22–24.

99 Goldwin Smith, quoted in Carl Berger, Introduction, in *Canada and the Canadian Question,* by Goldwin Smith (Toronto: University of Toronto Press, 1971), xi.

100 Toronto City Clerk, *Municipal Hand-Book:* City of Toronto, 1912 (Toronto: Carswell, 1912), 92. My thanks to Steve MacKinnon, Archivist, City of Toronto Archives, for his help with this detail.

101 Honoré Jaxon, Liverpool, February 1, 1912, to "Mother and Eastwood," PLAX-G.

102 Honoré Jaxon, Chicago, March 17, 1912, to "Mother and Eastwood," PLAX-G.

103 Henry Barrett Chamberlin, "Jaxon," *Chicago Record-Journal,* April 28, 1907, part 2, 4.

104 Stephen A. Speisman, "St. John's Shtehl: The Ward in 1911," in *Gathering Place: Peoples and Neighbourhoods of Toronto, 1834–1945,* ed. Robert F. Harney (Toronto: Multicultural History Society of Ontario, 1985), 107–20.

105 Ibid., 110.

106 "Report of the Medical Health Officer Dealing with the Recent Investigation of Slum Conditions in Toronto 1911, 1104, Vol. 5," cited in Schull, *Ontario since 1867,* 195.

107 Stephen A. Speisman, *The Jews of Toronto: A History to 1937* (Toronto: McClelland and Stewart, 1979), 193. See also Ruth A. Frager, "Class, Ethnicity, and Gender in the Eaton Strikes of 1912 and 1934," in *Gender Conflicts: New Essays in Women's History,* ed. Franca Iacovetta and Mariana Valverde (Toronto: University of Toronto Press, 1992), 191–93.

108 Aimée Jaxon, Chicago, October 16, 1930, to Cicely, PLAX.

109 Honoré and Aimée Jaxon (a joint letter with separate sections written by both), Taliesin, December 17, 1912, to "Dear Mother and Eastwood," PLAX.

110 Honoré Jaxon, Spring Green, Wisconsin, May 31, 1913, to T. Eastwood Jackson, PLAX-G.

111 Honoré Jaxon, August 16, 1914, to "Dear Mother and Folks," PLAX-G.

112 Honoré Jaxon, "Brief Report to Date on Site Negotiations," *Bahai News* 1, 4 (1910): 19–20.

113 Terry Straus, "Founding Mothers: Indian Women in Early Chicago," in *Native Chicago,* ed. Terry Straus and Grant P. Arndt (Chicago: McNaughton and Gunn, 1998), 68–70.

114 Honoré J. Jaxon, "Dedication of the Mashrak-El-Azkar Site," *Star of the West* 3, 4 (1912): 5–7.

115 Honoré J. Jaxon, "A Stroll with Abdul-Baha, Culminating in a Typical Bahai Meeting under the Trees of Lincoln Park, Chicago," *Star of the West* 3, 4 (1912): 27–29. The article uses the form Abdul-Baha, not Abdu'l-Baha, which is now the usage in English.

116 Peter Smith, "The American Baha'i Community, 1894–1917: A Preliminary Study," in *Studies in Babi and Baha'i History*, ed. Moojan Momen (Los Angeles: Kalimat Press, 1982), 1: 192.

117 Honoré Jaxon, Chicago, May 24, 1914, to "Dear Mother," PLAX.

118 I am most grateful to Daniel Kane, who carefully read the minutes from 1911 to 1918 of the Chicago Federation of Labor at the Chicago History Museum on my behalf. For information on Local 504, see Richard Schneirov and Thomas J. Suhrbur, *Union Brotherhood, Union Town: The History of the Carpenters' Union of Chicago 1863–1987* (Carbondale: Southern Illinois University Press, 1988), 125–26, 179.

119 Chicago District of Carpenters Council, Minutes, August 3, 1918. I thank Richard Schneirov for this reference.

120 Minutes, Chicago Federation of Labor, meeting of March 5, 1916 held at the Chicago History Museum, passage transcribed by Daniel Kane.

121 Honoré Jaxon, Chicago, September 27, 1914, to "Dear Mother and family," PLAX-G.

122 Honoré Jaxon, Chicago, May 6, 1915, to "Dear Mother," PLAX-G.

123 He used this letterhead in his note to his mother, dated Chicago, September 24, 1916, PLAX.

124 Honoré Jaxon, Chicago, September 26, 1917, to "Dear Mother," PLAX.

125 Honoré Jaxon, Chicago, January 19, 1918, to "Dear Folks," PLAX-G.

126 Honoré Jaxon, April 16, 1920, to "Dear Mother and Folks," PLAX-G.

CHAPTER 10: TRYING TO BECOME A CAPITALIST, 1919–36

1 In Aimée's own words, "Am very anxious that he find something that will give us a living for the days to come." Aimée Jaxon, Chicago, December 29, 1920, to "Dear Mother and Folks," PLAX-G.

2 Chicago District of Carpenters Council, Minutes, June 7, 1919. Note provided by Richard Schneirov, October 14, 1981.

3 Honoré Jaxon, New York, December 12, 1919, to "Mother and folks," PLAX-G.

4 Honoré Jaxon, September 10, 1919, to "Dear Mother and Folks," PLAX-G.

5 Aimée Jaxon, Chicago, April 7, 1920, to Cicely Plaxton, PLAX.

6 Ibid.

7 "'Versatile' Jaxon Builds in Bronx," *New York Times*, November 29, 1925. As this article was killed after the first edition of the paper, it was not copied on microfilm or preserved by ProQuest. The only surviving copy is in the *New York Times'* news morgue in New York City. My warmest thanks to Jeff Roth, archivist of the *New York Times*, who located it, and to Michael Massman and Phyllis Collazo for their assistance in my obtaining copies of this very valuable article.

8 Honoré Jaxon, Atlantic Highlands, New Jersey, May 12, 1921, to "Dear Mother and folks," PLAX.

9 Honoré Jaxon, Atlantic Highlands, July 15, 1920, to "Dear Mother and Folks," PLAX-G.

10 Ibid.

11 "'Versatile' Jaxon Builds in Bronx," *New York Times*, November 29, 1925.

12 Aimée Jaxon, Chicago, September 14, 1920, to "Dear Mother, Eastwood, and all the other good folks," PLAX. The editor and publisher, B.F.S. Brown, died in August, and the paper for the rest of the year was run by J. Mabel Brown and Herbert F. Brown, administrators of the estate. Gregory J. Plunges, Librarian, Monmouth County Historical Association, Freehold, NJ, February 24, 1980, to author.

13 Honoré Jaxon, April 16, 1920, to "Dear Mother and Folks," PLAX-G.

14 Fragment of a letter by Jaxon, c. spring 1921, PLAX-G.

15 Will Jackson, Chicago, to "Dear Father," November 14, 1887, PLAX.

16 Honoré Jaxon, New York City, March 6, 1922, to Eastwood Jackson, PLAX-G; Honoré Jaxon, New York City, September 11, 1922, to Eastwood Jackson, PLAX; Honoré Jaxon, New York City, December 15, 1922, to Eastwood Jackson, PLAX-G; Honoré Jaxon, New York City, February 21, 1923, to Cicely Plaxton, PLAX-G.

17 Honoré Jaxon, New York City, April 22, 1924, to Cicely Plaxton Jr., PLAX.

18 H. Jaxon to E. Jackson, December 15, 1922.

19 Aimée Jaxon, Chicago, September 20, 1925, to Eastwood Jackson, PLAX-G.

20 Jill Jonnes, *South Bronx Rising: The Rise, Fall, and Resurrection of an American City* (New York: Fordham University Press, 2002), 4, 11, 33, 35, 39, 49. See also Lloyd Ultan and Barbara Unger, *Bronx Accent: A Literary and Pictorial History of the Borough* (New Brunswick, NJ: Rutgers University Press, 2000), 46.

21 "'Versatile' Jaxon Builds in Bronx," *New York Times*, November 29, 1925.

22 Honoré Jaxon, New York City, c. summer 1924, to "Eastwood and Cicely," PLAX; see also H. Jaxon to E. Jackson, February 15, 1924.

23 Honoré Jaxon, the Bronx, November 10, 1925, to "Cicely and Eastwood," PLAX.

24 "Builds 'Box Castle' along Bronx River Bank to Fight Crime, but Only Its Ashes Remain," *The Home News* (the Bronx and Manhattan), April 3, 1927.

25 "Weird Windowless House of Major Jaxon beside Bronx River, Now a Heap of Ruins," The Home News, March 23, 1927.

26 "Builds 'Box Castle' along Bronx River Bank," *The Home News,* April 3, 1927.

27 Ibid.

28 Honoré Jaxon, New York City, February 21, 1923, to Cicely Plaxton, PLAX-G.

29 "Current Events of the Week," *New York Times,* May 6, 1923, May 13, 1923.

30 Aimée Jaxon, Chicago, October 16, 1930, to "Dearest Cicely," PLAX.

31 Honoré Jaxon, the Bronx, November 19, 1925, to Cicely Plaxton, PLAX.

32 Honoré Jaxon, the Bronx, February 19, 1926, to Cicely Plaxton and Eastwood Jackson, PLAX.

33 Honoré Jaxon, the Bronx, November 10, 1925, to Cicely Plaxton and Eastwood Jackson, PLAX.

34 H. Jaxon to Cicely Plaxton and E. Jackson, February 19, 1926.

35 Honoré Jaxon, the Bronx, August 6, 1926, to Cicely Plaxton and Eastwood Jackson, PLAX. Lyman Gage died shortly after this, on January 26, 1927; see Leslie V. Tischauser, "Lyman Judson Gage," in *American National Biography* (New York: Oxford University Press, 1999), 8: 606.

36 William J. Carter, Edmonton, August 24, 1923, to Eastwood Jackson, PLAX.

37 Copy of letter, Eastwood Jackson, Prince Albert, September 6, 1923, to W.J. Carter, PLAX.

38 "Weird Windowless House," *The Home News*, March 23, 1927.
39 "Builds 'Box Castle' along Bronx River Bank," *The Home News*, April 3, 1927.
40 Ibid.
41 Honoré Jaxon, "Camp Contentment, N.W. side of Lafayette Ave First home S.W. of Bronx River, the Bronx," October 20, 1927, to Eastwood Jackson and Cicely Plaxton, PLAX.
42 Honoré Jaxon, Chicago, April 23, 1930, to Cicely Plaxton, PLAX.
43 Honoré Jaxon, the Bronx, October 16, 1928, to "Dear Folks," PLAX.
44 Aimée Jaxon, Chicago, July 4, 1930, to "Cicely and Folks," PLAX-G.
45 Aimée Jaxon, Chicago, August 28, 1931, to Cicely Plaxton, PLAX.
46 Aimée Jaxon, Chicago, February 4, 1931, to "Cicely and all," PLAX-G.
47 Aimée Jaxon, Chicago, March 30, 1931, to "Dearest Cicely and all," PLAX-G.
48 "Nathan Straus Dies: Nation Mourns Loss of Philanthropist," *New York Times*, January 12, 1931.
49 A. Jaxon to family, February 4, 1931.
50 Aimée Jaxon, Chicago, May 15, 1930, to "Dearest Cicely," PLAX-G.
51 Aimée Jaxon, Chicago, October 16, 1930, to "Dearest Cicely," PLAX.
52 Jonnes, *South Bronx Rising*, 65, 69.
53 "Aimee Jaxon," Standard Certificate of Death, no. 3636, February 6, 1932, Department of Public Health, Division of Vital Statistics, State of Illinois.
54 Honoré Jaxon, New York, February 21, 1923, to Cicely Plaxton, PLAX-G.
55 Photostat copy of a letter, Honoré Jaxon, "Bronx Castle Garden," the Bronx, February 25, 1931, to Mary Plaxton (his niece), GGC.
56 A. Jaxon to "Cicely and all," March 30, 1931.
57 Honoré Jaxon, the Bronx, December 21, 1932, to "Dear Folks," PLAX.
58 Honoré Jaxon, quoted in "Virginia Orator Baffles Mayor by Claiming Bronx for Indians," *New York Herald Tribune*, December 9, 1933. My thanks to Jeff Roth, Michael Massman, and Phyllis Collazo for forwarding me a copy of this article, which is in the *New York Times'* news morgue.
59 The mayor and the vast majority of New Yorkers had absolutely no idea of the Aboriginal history of New York City. Professors Diana diZerega Wall and Anne-Marie Cantwell do. In their recent book, *Touring Gotham's Archaeological Past* (New Haven: Yale University Press, 2004), 103–06, the two anthropologists establish the inhuman treatment meted out to the Aboriginal peoples of the Bronx and surrounding area during the Dutch regime. In 1644, according to a Dutch account, a Dutch force under the command of John Underhill, an English mercenary, killed somewhere between five hundred and seven hundred Munsee people, often called the Siwanoy. According to the account, the encircled Siwanoy villagers were burned alive in their bark houses.
60 Jaxon appears in a photo of the hearing in the *New York Daily News*, September 28, 1934. See also "Foes Assail City Lottery as Immoral," *New York Daily News*, September 28, 1934. The *New York Herald Tribune* also ran a story about the hearing, "Mayor Will Put Pay Roll Tax up to Aldermen," September 28, 1934, which also included a photo of "Major Honore J. Jaxon" speaking in favour of the proposed city lottery.

61 "T.E. Jackson Dies at Prince Albert," *Saskatoon Star-Phoenix,* December 11, 1935.

62 Honoré Jaxon, the Bronx, October 6, 1936, to "Dear Cicely," PLAX.

63 Charles H. Dennis, "Whitechapel Nights," *Chicago Daily News,* August 31, 1936.

64 "Deaths: Mrs. Elizabeth Eastwood Jackson," *Prince Albert Herald,* October 28, 1921.

65 Honoré Jaxon, Chicago, April 29, 1931, to Teddy Plaxton, PLAX-G.

66 Honoré Jaxon, the Bronx, December 3, 1930, to Eastwood Jackson, PLAX.

67 Rudolf Rocker, *The London Years,* trans. Joseph Leftwich (Nottingham, UK: Five Leaves Publications, 2005), 140.

68 Federal Writers' Project, *New York City Guide* (1939; reprinted New York: Random House, 1973), 364–66, 395–97.

69 "Grey Owl's Final Journey," Toronto *Globe and Mail,* April 14, 1938.

70 Grey Owl, *The Men of the Last Frontier* (London: Country Life, 1931), 212.

71 Donald B. Smith, *From the Land of Shadows: The Making of Grey Owl* (Saskatoon: Western Producer Prairie Books, 1990).

72 Otto McFeely, paraphrased in Lloyd Lewis, "It Takes All Kinds: Honore Jaxon, Forgotten Crusader," Book Week, *Chicago Sun,* March 2, 1947, 4. McFeely dated this story "around 1930." With Honoré's subsequent deterioration in the early 1930s, I would date the reference to after 1930 rather than before.

CHAPTER 11: LIGHT, STORM, AND SHADOW, 1937–45

1 Julie Chanler, *From Gaslight to Dawn: An Autobiography by Julie Chanler* (New York: New History Society, 1956), 271. This book, written by his wife, is a good source of information on Lewis Stuyvesant Chanler.

2 Julie Chanler, "A Scholarly Hobo," *The Caravan of East and West,* April 1952. For a description of Jaxon's fort, see "Soldier of Fortune, 80, Rails at City Charge His Shelter of Crates Violates Health Laws," *The Home News, Bronx and Manhattan,* February 20, 1942.

3 Chanler, *From Gaslight to Dawn,* 68.

4 Biographical information on Lewis Stuyvesant Chanler's ancestors is taken from *The Columbia Encyclopedia,* 3rd ed. (New York: Columbia University Press, 1963).

5 John Goodrum Miller, "A Knight Has Ridden Away," reprinted from *New History,* April 1942, 11. *New History* (during its first year, it appeared as *The New Historian*) was published monthly from the Chanlers' home, 132 East 65th Street, New York City, by the New History Foundation. The article originally appeared in the magazine under the same title. See "A Knight Has Ridden Away," *New History* 11, 7 (1942): 1–9. The pagination in these references comes from the offprint. The New York Public Library has back copies of the publication. My thanks to John Atwater Bradley, historian of the Knickerbocker Club, for kindly sending me a copy of the offprint.

6 Miller, "Knight," 10.

7 Franklin Delano Roosevelt, "The Inaugural Address," *New York Times,* January 21, 1937.

8 John Atwater Bradley, ed., *Knickerbocker Centennial: An Informal History of the Knickerbocker*

Club, by William J. Dunn (New York: Knickerbocker Club, 1971), 19.

9 Ibid., 29–30. A beautiful colour photo of the library on the second floor, with the portrait of the first president of the Knickerbocker Club, appears opposite the title page of *Knickerbocker Centennial*.

10 Ibid., 133. Chanler's son, also named Lewis Stuyvesant Chanler, served as club president from 1949 to 1960 (see 136–37). My warmest thanks to the Knickerbocker Club's historian John Atwater Bradley for a tour of the club, October 6, 2006.

11 Chanler, *From Gaslight to Dawn*, 265. Ironically Roosevelt had belonged to the Knickerbocker Club from 1905 to 1937; see his letter of resignation in Bradley, *Knickerbocker Centennial*, 157–58.

12 Lewis S. Chanler, quoted in "Debate Resolved: That Continuous Preparedness Is Necessary for the United States," *The New Historian* 1, 6 (1932): 3. This statement also appears in Chanler, *From Gaslight to Dawn*, 207.

13 Chanler, *From Gaslight to Dawn*, 265.

14 Numerous photos of Julie Chanler and her husband appear in her autobiography, *From Gaslight to Dawn*.

15 "S.H. Olin Dies at 78; 50 Years a Lawyer," *New York Times*, August 7, 1925.

16 Chanler, *From Gaslight to Dawn*, 391–92.

17 Ibid., 121.

18 Ibid., 122.

19 Robert H. Stockman, *The Baha'i Faith in America*, vol. 2, Early Expansion, 1900–1912 (Oxford: George Ronald, 1995), 220; see also "Mizra Ahmad Sohrab Dies Here at 65: Leader of the Reform Baha'i Movement," *New York Times*, April 22, 1958.

20 Vernon Elvin Johnson, "An Historical Analysis of Critical Transformations in the Evolution of the Baha'i World Faith" (PhD diss., Baylor University, 1974), 311–12.

21 Chanler, *From Gaslight to Dawn*, 161.

22 "The Case of Ahmad Sohrab and the New History Society," *Baha'i News* 43 (1930): 3; see also "Cablegram from the Guardian to the National Assembly," *Baha'i News* 46 (1930): 9.

23 Chanler, *From Gaslight to Dawn*, 179–82, 199.

24 Mirza Ahmad Sohrab, "Statement," *New History* 9, 7 (1940): 7.

25 See *New History* 2, 1 (1932): 10. The occasion was Mizra Ahmad Sohrab's account of his recent trip to Europe.

26 Chanler, *From Gaslight to Dawn*, 200.

27 Mirza Ahmad Sohrab, "Statement," 7.

28 "Events Today," *New York Times*, April 27, 1941. See also "Lectures for the Spring Session," *New History* 10, 7 (1941): back page.

29 He told his mother and sister and brother in a letter sent in early June 1917 that he could be reached in Washington, DC, at this address: "Major Honore J. Jaxon C[are] of Joseph Hannen, P.O. Box 1319, Washington, D.C." Honoré Jaxon, letter postmarked Philadelphia, June 2, 1917, to "Dear Mother and Folks," PLAX-G.

30 Chanler, "Scholarly Hobo."

31 Ibid.

32 Miller, "Knight," 7.

33 Chanler, "Scholarly Hobo."
34 Ibid.
35 Donald B. Smith, *Chief Buffalo Child Long Lance: The Glorious Impostor,* 2nd ed. (Red Deer, AB: Red Deer Press, 1999), 206, 228–49, 267–84.
36 Mirza Ahmad Sohrab, *Broken Silence: The Story of Today's Struggle for Religious Freedom* (New York: Universal Publishing Company, for the New History Foundation, 1942), 118.
37 Chanler, *From Gaslight to Dawn,* 259–64.
38 Chanler, "Scholarly Hobo."
39 The photo appears as an illustration in Sohrab, *Broken Silence.*
40 Chanler, "Scholarly Hobo."
41 Chanler, *From Gaslight to Dawn,* 268.
42 Miller, "Knight," 19.
43 "City Officials Attend Lewis Chanler Rites: Many Other Friends at Funeral of Ex-Lieutenant Governor," *New York Times,* March 4, 1942.
44 This is the title of Chapter 12 in her autobiography, *From Gaslight to Dawn,* 247–70.
45 Chanler, "Scholarly Hobo."
46 "Soldier of Fortune, 80, Rails at City," *The Home News,* February 20, 1942.
47 "Hut-Dweller, 80, Clashes with Law," *New York Times,* February 20, 1942.
48 Honoré Jaxon, New York, April 28, 1942, to Cicely Plaxton, PLAX-G.
49 Honoré Jaxon, letter postmarked September 28, 1946, to "Dear Folks," PLAX-G.
50 Victor H. Bernstein, "New York: Social Note: Kurt Mertig Entertains 12 Old Friends at Soiree," PM (New York City), March 30, 1947.
51 Honoré Jaxon, letter postmarked Chicago, November 20, 1918, to "Dear Mother and Folks," PLAX.
52 He was described as fifty-nine in "Christian Front Member Given Year Jail Term," *Chicago Daily Tribune,* March 1, 1946.
53 "Events Today," *New York Times,* April 5, 1937.
54 Federal Writers' Project, *New York City Guide* (1939; reprinted New York: Random House, 1976), 184, 243, 251.
55 "Aid to Hoffman Pledged," *New York Times,* January 30, 1936.
56 "Untermyer Explains Schmeling Boycott," *New York Times,* January 14, 1937.
57 "Events Today," *New York Times,* March 1, 1937.
58 "Events Today," *New York Times,* June 14, 1937.
59 Honoré Jaxon, July 24, 1937, to Cicely Plaxton, PLAX-G.
60 "Nazi Rally Draws 65 in Yorkville," *New York Times,* March 16, 1937.
61 Kurt Mertig, quoted as referring to Honoré as the "Major" in Chanler, "Scholarly Hobo."
62 W. Raymond Wood, "The Role of the Romantic West in Shaping the Third Reich," *Plains Anthropologist* 35, 132 (1990): 313.
63 "Indian a 'True Aryan': Race Is Acceptable in Hitler's View" (Associated Press, Washington), *Calgary Herald,* June 8, 1940.
64 "Canadian 'Atrocities,'" *Regina Leader-Post,* November 22, 1938; Chester Bloom, "Crerar Denies Indians Abused," *Regina Leader-Post,* November 22, 1938.
65 Kurt Mertig, New York, January 31, 1952, to Miss Cicily [Cicely] Plaxton, Ms. 52.17, GGC.

66 "Mayor Welcomes Protest," *New York Times,* March 5, 1937. Later Mertig described him as "half-Jew Fiorello La Guardia" in a vicious anti-Semitic article, "Racial Politics Undermine U.S.A.: The Loyalty of the Jew Is to the Jew Only!" *The Broom* (San Diego), October 1, 1945.

67 Kurt Mertig and his Citizens Protective League actually proposed Henry Ford for the American presidency in 1938; see "Ford for Presidency," *The Broom,* May 14, 1938. Ford's anti-Semitic views were well known; see Thomas F. Gossett, *Race: The History of an Idea in America* (Dallas: Southern Methodist University Press, 1963), 371–72. For Mertig's views on Roosevelt, see Kurt Mertig, "The Roosevelt Myth," *The Broom,* March 20, 1950.

68 Honoré Jaxon, the Bronx, July 24, 1937, to Cicely Plaxton, PLAX-G. The following year Honoré would rejoice to learn that F.D.R.'s Fair Labor Standards Act finally made the eight-hour day a legal day's work throughout the United States. Honoré had fought for this in Chicago half a century earlier. John B. Jentz, "Eight-Hour Movement," in *The Encyclopedia of Chicago,* ed. James R. Grossman, Ann Durkin Keating, and Janice L. Reiff (Chicago: University of Chicago Press, 2004), 265.

69 See the letterhead used for Honoré's letters to Miss Rae Plaxton, November 10, 1940, and Cicely Plaxton and Cicely Jr. Plaxton, November 13, 1940, PLAX.

70 Honoré Jaxon, October 2, 1942, to Cicely Plaxton, PLAX.

71 Honoré Jaxon, May 1, 1944, to Cicely Plaxton, PLAX-G.

72 Honoré Jaxon, July 22, 1944, to Cicely Plaxton, PLAX-G.

73 Photostat copy, Honoré Jaxon, New York, February 22, 1951, to Cicely Plaxton and Mary Grant, GGC.

74 Gerald Tulchinsky, *Taking Root: The Origins of the Canadian Jewish Community* (Toronto: Lester Publishing, 1992), 238.

75 Dr. George Orton, quoted in "Riel and His Secretary," Toronto *Daily Mail,* June 9, 1885.

76 Steven Sapolsky, August 26, 1987, to author, and Richard Schneirov, October 14, 1981, to author. The Chicago District Carpenters Council Minutes, August 3, 1918, state that "Honore Jaxon was ordered seated as a delegate to represent Local 504."

77 Lloyd Ultan and Barbara Unger, *Bronx Accent: A Literary and Pictorial History of the Borough* (New Brunswick, NJ: Rutgers University Press, 2000), 78.

78 Honoré Jaxon, the Bronx, July 11, 1942, to "Cicely and Folks," PLAX-G.

79 Ibid., 158.

80 Chanler, *From Gaslight to Dawn,* 247.

81 K. Mertig to C. Plaxton, January 31, 1952.

82 John Roy Carlson, *Under Cover* (New York: E.P. Dutton, 1943), 502.

83 Honoré Jaxon, letter postmarked September 28, 1946, to "Dear Folks," PLAX-G. In his letter to Cicely, dated June 17, 1945, he supplied a Manhattan address, PLAX-G.

CHAPTER 12: THE DESCENT, NEW YORK CITY, 1945–52

1 Kurt Mertig and Ernest Elmhurst, "You're Next, Writes Mertig," *The Broom,* May 6, 1946.

2 Kurt Mertig, "'Free Speech' and 'Free Assembly' for Christians?," *The Broom*, October 29, 1945.

3 Jan Morris, *Manhattan '45* (1987; reprinted Baltimore: Johns Hopkins University Press, 1998), 111–12.

4 Victor Bernstein had just published his account of the Nuremberg Trials, *Final Judgment: The Story of the Nuremberg.* See "Books Published Today," *New York Times*, March 3, 1947; see also Alfred Werner, "The Blight of Nazism," *New York Times*, April 27, 1947.

5 Victor H. Bernstein, "New York Social Note: Kurt Mertig Entertains 12 Old Friends at Soirée," *PM* (New York City), March 30, 1947.

6 Photostat copy, Honoré Jaxon, New York, January 21, 1949, to Mary [Plaxton Grant], GGC.

7 Honoré Jaxon, New York, March 28, 1949, to "Dear folks," PLAX. But did Honoré actually say this? His typed letters to his sister Cicely and his niece, while signed and annotated by him, suggest that they were dictated and typed by another hand. To whom did he dictate these letters? Why was their common name misspelled in the typed letter of June 19, 1948? This letter spells their names as Cicily, not Cicely, which is the form that they used. In this letter, Honoré corrected in pen most of the Cicily spellings to Cicely. See "Honoré Jaxon," June 19, 1948, to "Cicily" Plaxton, PLAX. (Mertig never did catch on to the correct spelling of Cicely. His two letters to Honoré's niece after her uncle's death, January16, and January 31, 1952, are addressed to "Miss Cicily Plaxton"; Ms. 52.17, GGC.) Even if Mertig typed the letter and embellished it, in a handwritten note to Cicely Jr. postmarked August 1, 1949 Honoré wrote, "Mertig is the only friend upon whom I could rely. [...]" See Honoré Jaxon, New York, August 1, 1949, letter fragment, to "Cicely," PLAX.

8 "Deaths: Mrs. Elizabeth Eastwood Jackson," *Prince Albert Herald*, October 28, 1921.

9 Honoré Jaxon, New York City, June 9, 1946, to "Cicely and Folks," PLAX.

10 Colin I. Powell, with Joseph Persico, *My American Journey* (New York: Random House, 1995), quoted in Lloyd Ultan and Barbara Unger, *Bronx Accent: A Literary and Pictorial History of the Borough* (New Brunswick, NJ: Rutgers University Press, 2000), 160.

11 "Fought All His Life for Others: At 91, He's Evicted from Cellar," *New York Herald-Tribune*, December 13, 1951.

12 Honoré Jaxon, New York City, postmarked May 17, 1947, to Cicely Plaxton, PLAX.

13 Photostat copy, Honoré Jaxon, New York City, January 21, 1949, to Mary [Plaxton Grant], GGC. The address of the newsstand appears in this letter.

14 Honoré Jaxon, the Bronx, March 16, 1945, to Cicely Plaxton, PLAX-G.

15 Julie Chanler, "A Scholarly Hobo," *The Caravan of East and West*, April 1952.

16 Photostat copy, Kurt Mertig, New York City, January 31, 1952, to Miss Cicily [Cicely] Plaxton, Ms. 52.17, GGC.

17 Honoré Jaxon, New York City, May 17, 1947, to Cicely Plaxton, PLAX.

18 Cicely Plaxton, "Diary of New York Trip," 1–4, PLAX-G.

19 Ibid., 3–4.

20 Ibid., 7.

21 See letter fragment in Honoré's hand, apparently a note to Eastwood Jackson, written in the early 1930s, only pages 5 and 6 survive, PLAX.

22 Honoré Jaxon, the Bronx, April 22, 1932, to Cicely Plaxton, PLAX.

23 Honoré Jaxon, New York City, June 9, 1946, to "Cicely and Folks," PLAX-G; Honoré Jaxon, September 28, 1946, to "Folks," PLAX-G.

24 Ibid.

25 See *The Home News* (the Bronx and Manhattan), February 20, 1942. He also advanced the Virginia link in his interview with the *New York Herald-Tribune,* "Virginia Orator Baffles Mayor by Claiming Bronx for Indians," December 9, 1933. I thank Jeff Roth, archivist of the *New York Times,* for a copy of this clipping from the *New York Times'* news morgue.

26 Thomas's letter is quoted in Chapter 1. See T.G. Jackson, Toronto, May 5, 1861, to "My dear Mother & Sister," PLAX. "We propose to call him William Henry in memory of my poor brother who was drowned." Elizabeth's letter announcing the birth was sent to "My very dear Mother," dated Toronto, May 15, 1861, PLAX.

27 Honoré Jaxon, quoted mentioning this in William D. Laffler, "Old Indian Fighter, 91, Put out into Street," *Long Island Press* (Jamaica, NY), December 13, 1951. The *New York Mirror* picked up this information as well. To its reporter, Jaxon "proudly" spoke of his participation in "the Indian and Spanish-American Wars"; see "Indian Crusader, 91, Evicted Here," December 13, 1951. The *New York Daily News,* December 13, 1951, "Old Soldier's Sidewalk Dunkirk," stated that he had served as a major in the resistance of 1885 as well: "In 1885 he said he fought as a major in the short-lived rebellion of the French-Indian halfbreeds of the Canadian Northwest against the Canadian Government. He was captured at the Battle of Batoche. He said he served in the Spanish-American War, also as a major, with what he called the Blue and Gray Legion."

28 Plaxton, "Diary of New York Trip," 11.

29 Ibid., 4.

30 Ibid., 3.

31 Ibid., 4.

32 Photostat copy, Kurt Mertig, New York City, January 16, 1952, to Miss Cicily [Cicely] Plaxton, Mss 52.17, GGC.

33 John Roy Carlson, *The Plotters* (New York: E.P. Dutton, 1943), 5. See also Avedis Derounian [John Roy Carlson], "April 24, 1939, Meeting of the Citizens Protective League," Avedis Derounian Papers (ADP), National Association for Armenian Studies and Research, Belmont, MA.

34 Avedis Derounian [John Roy Carlson], "March 9, 1942, Meeting of the Citizens Protective League," ADP.

35 This obscure publication was recently recalled in the *San Diego Jewish Journal* as "a crass anti-Semitic smear sheet"; see Sue Garson, "The End of Covenant," *San Diego Jewish Journal,* a 2003 article now available online at www.sdjewishjournal.com/stories/jewishnewstory.html.

36 The ads appeared in *The Broom*; see, for example, the issues for June 30, and July 14, 1947.

37 C. Leon de Aryan to Kurt Mertig, in "Kurt Mertig vs. Bernard Baruch," *The Broom,* May 3, 1948. "You have been reading and promoting the circulation of our paper for nigh five years now."

38 This line is the first in his petition to President Truman; reproduced in *The Broom,* September 6, 1948.

39 In 1949, Mertig passed the torch to someone younger, James Madole, just twenty-two years old but already a fanatic. Mertig, Madole, and their small group of followers founded the National Renaissance Party. Nicholas Goodrick-Clarke, *Black Sun: Aryan Cults, Esoteric Nazism, and the Politics of Identity* (New York: New York University Press, 2001), 72–74.

40 "De Casseres Describes the Jew," *The Broom,* December 1, 1947. For three months or so after the attack, Mertig stopped writing for the weekly. But he returned to its pages in the March 8, 1948 issue. Leon de Aryan, the editor of the *The Broom,* pointed out that Mertig had "no other outlet" for his views; see the editorial note at the end of Mertig's article, "Why German-Americans Have Become 'Under-Dogs' in America," *The Broom,* August 25, 1947.

41 "C. Leon de Aryan," *The Broom,* January 9, 1950. More biographical detail, all supplied by him, appears in his article "Kurt Mertig and '*The Broom*,'" *The Broom,* January 19, 1948. Lagenopol himself shared with his readers that as a young man he had been committed to an insane asylum from which he escaped, then to a psychiatric clinic in Vienna for another three months, until his release. He described himself as an American of Greek and Polish ancestry who had grown up in Romania and gone to school in Austria.

42 "'Unlawful' Assembly in Queens Village," *The Broom,* October 15, 1945; "Mertig Defends Gerald Smith," *The Broom,* September 15, 1947; "Kurt Mertig's Job," *The Broom,* November 16, 1947; "Kurt Mertig and '*The Broom*,'" *The Broom,* January 19, 1948; "Should de Aryan Finance Mertig's Propaganda among Unappreciative Germans?," *The Broom,* November 28, 1949.

43 "The Flying Saucers," *The Broom,* September 22, 1952.

44 Honoré Jaxon, June 19, 1948, to Cicely Plaxton, PLAX.

45 Mrs. C.J. Plaxton, New York, [February 21, 1949], to "The Officer in Charge," PLAX. The date of the letter appears in the letter from E. Van Pelt, Salvation Army, Territorial Headquarters, 120–130 W. 14th Street, New York 11, NY, August 4, 1949, to Mrs. Cicely Plaxton, PLAX.

46 Captain E. Van Pelt, New York, September 9, 1948, to Mrs. Cicely Plaxton, PLAX.

47 Honoré Jaxon, 161 East 34th Street, c/o Paladino, New York City, January 12, 1949, to Mary Plaxton Grant, GGC.

48 Plaxton to "The Officer in Charge," [February 21, 1949].

49 "P.A. Pioneer Teacher Dies at Age of 86," *Prince Albert Herald,* July 29, 1949.

50 Mertig to Plaxton, January 31, 1952. Honoré claimed to have "a dozen waterfront properties which are now in much demand." See Jaxon to Cicely Jr., August 1, 1949, letter fragment.

51 Mertig to Plaxton, January 31, 1952.

52 Will of Honoré Joseph Jaxon, prepared August 12, 1949, Surrogate's Court

New York County (Manhattan), Estate of Honoré Joseph Jaxon, file #1952–1604.

53 Honoré Jaxon, April 16, 1951, to Cicely Jr., PLAX-T, and Mertig to Plaxton, January 31, 1952.

54 Mertig to Plaxton, January 31, 1952.

55 Mertig to Plaxton, January 16, 1952.

56 Honoré Jaxon, July 10, 1951, to Cicely Plaxton, PLAX.

57 Mary Grant, July 10, 1951, with attached letter from Honoré Jaxon, to "Cis" [Cicely Plaxton], PLAX.

58 Honoré Jaxon, New York City, September 14, 1951, to Mary Grant, PLAX-T.

59 Grant to Plaxton, July 10, 1951.

60 Honoré Jaxon, New York City, August 27, 1951, to Mary Grant, GGC.

61 Jaxon to Grant, September 14, 1951.

62 Honoré Jaxon, Christmas Day 1950, to Mary Grant, PLAX-T.

63 Harry Baronian, quoted by Nathaniel A. Benson, in Louis Blake Duff, "Amazing Story of the Winghamite Secretary of Louis Riel," *Western Ontario History Nuggets* 22 (1955): 26.

64 "'Leading Citizen' of Bowery Dead," [Peck's obituary], *New York Times*, January 16, 1954.

65 Virginia Woolf, quoted in "Books and Authors," *New York Times*, January 1, 1928.

66 Desmond King-Hele, *Shelley: His Thought and Work*, 3rd ed. (Cranbury, NJ: Associated University Presses, 1984), 375.

67 "Funeral Tomorrow for Professor Peck," *New York Times*, January 17, 1954.

68 Ibid. Peck's papers are at Yale University; see Janet Elaine Gertz, comp., "Preliminary Guide to the Walter Edwin Peck Papers, Manuscript Group 390," April 1983.

69 "'Leading Citizen' of Bowery Dead," *New York Times*, January 16, 1954.

70 N.A. Benson to L.B.D. [Louis Blake Duff], July 14, 1954, Ms. 52.27(a), GGC.

71 Harry Baronian, quoted by Benson, in Duff, "Amazing Story," 27.

72 Ibid. Jaxon's sister had died two years earlier, in 1949.

73 "Honore Jaxon, 91, Friend of Indians, Major with Metis Tribesmen During Fight in Canada, Is Dead-Later Jersey Editor," *New York Times*, January 12, 1952. See also "Honore Joseph Jaxon, 90, Dies: Long a Fighter for Indian Rights," *New York Herald-Tribune*, January 12, 1952, and "H.J. Jaxon Dies: Defender of Lost Causes," *World-Telegram*, January 12, 1952.

74 For a summary of views of Riel, see Douglas Owram, "The Myth of Louis Riel," *Canadian Historical Review* 63, 3 (1982): 315–36.

75 Kathleen Garay, "John Coulter's Riel: The Shaping of 'A Myth for Canada,'" *Canadian Drama* 11, 2 (1985): 293–309. This is a marvellous summary.

76 Mavor Moore, *Reinventing Myself. Memoirs* (Toronto: Stoddart Publishing Company, 1994), 176.

77 Geraldine Anthony, "The Riel Trilogy," in *The Oxford Companion to Canadian Theatre*, ed. Eugene Benson and L.W. Conolly (Toronto: Oxford University Press, 1989), 466. In 1967, Coulter wrote *The Trial of Louis Riel*. It is a one-act documentary of the famous trial based on the trial transcripts. Highly successful as a tourist event, it has been performed annually in Regina for forty years.

78 Cited in Garay, "John Coulter's Riel," 307.

79 Moore, *Reinventing Myself*, 177.

80 "P.M.'s Remarks 'Shock' Former R.C.M.P. Official," *Calgary Herald*, August 8, 1951. I thank Jon Swainger for this reference. See also Alan McCullough, "Parks Canada and the 1885 Rebellion/Uprising/Resistance," *Prairie Forum*, 27, 2 (2002): 172–73.

81 Louis St. Laurent, quoted in McCullough, "Parks Canada," 172–73.

82 W.O. Mitchell, "The Riddle of Louis Riel," *Maclean's*, February 1, 1952, 7.

83 See "Indians' Friend, Jaxon Was Colorful Figure," *Edmonton Journal*, January 14, 1952; see also "Riel Veteran Dies in New York at 90," Toronto *Globe and Mail*, January 14, 1952.

84 Bruce Peel, Edmonton, March 9, 1970, to Cyril Greenland, GGC.

85 Bruce Peel, Edmonton, January 17, 1952 to Eric [Knowles], a copy of this letter was enclosed in Bruce Peel's letter to Donald Smith, June 13, 1985.

86 Ibid.

87 Mertig to Plaxton, January 16, and January 31, 1952; Harry Baronian, quoted by Benson, in Duff, "Amazing Story," 31.

88 David Orchard, "The Jackson Tragedy," letter to the editor, Toronto *Globe and Mail*, November 21, 1985. Maggie Siggins, *Riel: A Life of Revolution* (Toronto: HarperCollins, 1994). Mea culpa! I raised this possibility in several of my early articles.

89 Doris Decorato (case supervisor), Salvation Army, "Re: Funeral," Ms. 52.17, GGC.

CONCLUSION: THE SUMMING UP

1 William Jackson, February 2, 1885, to Albert Monkman, cited in T.E. Jackson, Prince Albert, NWT, June 17, "Letter to the Editor," Toronto *Globe*, July 2, 1885.

2 Cyril Greenland and John D. Griffin, "William Henry Jackson (1861–1952): Riel's Secretary: Another Case of Involuntary Commitment?" *Canadian Psychiatric Association Journal* 23 (1978): 471.

3 Will Jackson, cited in "The Queen vs. William Henry Jackson," in Canada, *Sessional Papers*, 1886, no. 52, p. 340.

4 John A. Macdonald, London, England, December 12, 1885, to J.R. Gowan, MG 27 IE17, J.R. Gowan Papers, LAC, cited in Ged Martin, "Archival Evidence and John A. Macdonald Biography," *Journal of Historical Biography* 1, 1 (2007): 104.

5 *Frank Lloyd Wright*, dir. Ken Burns and Lynn Novick, PBS DVD, c1998 American Film Project I, Warner Home Video. This is a fascinating presentation with clips of Wright himself being interviewed, rare archival footage, and interviews with members of Wright's family and his biographers.

6 Aimée Jaxon, Chicago, December 30, 1910, to "Dear Folks," PLAX-G.

7 William H. Jackson, Lower Fort Garry, September 19, 1885, to "My dear Family," MG3 C20, PAM.

8 Stewart Mein, "North-West Rebellion," in *The Encyclopedia of Saskatchewan* (Regina: Canadian Plains Research Center, 2005), 655–57.

ACKNOWLEDGEMENTS

1 The date is easy to recall since I recorded it, winter of 1971–72, in my copy of George F.G. Stanley, *Louis Riel* (Toronto: Ryerson Press, 1963), 414n66.

2 Ibid.

3 Cicely Plaxton, Jr., February 16, 1980, to the author.

4 Donald B. Smith, *Long Lance: The True Story of an Impostor* (Toronto: Macmillan, 1982); *Sacred Feathers: The Reverend Peter Jones (Kahkewaquonaby) and the Mississauga Indians* (Lincoln: University of Nebraska Press, 1987); *From the Land of Shadows: The Making of Grey Owl* (Saskatoon: Western Producer Prairie Books, 1990); Donald B. Smith and R. Douglas Francis, eds., *Readings in Canadian History: Pre-Confederation Canada* (1982), and *Readings in Canadian History: Post-Confederation Canada* (1982); Donald B. Smith, R. Douglas Francis, and Richard Jones, eds., *Origins: Canadian History to Confederation* (1988), and *Destinies: Canadian History since Confederation* (1988). Our books of *Readings* are now in their 7th edition. The 6th editions of *Origins* and *Destinies* will be published in 2008.

5 Beth Kaplan, "The Family Kaplan," *Pakn Treger: Magazine of the National Yiddish Book Center* 46 (2004), available at http://yiddishbookcenter.org/pdf/pt/46/PT46_kaplan.pdf.

6 "Leo Kaplan," *New York Times*, March 17, 1995.

7 Beth Kaplan, November 16, 2006, e-mail to the author.

8 Mary Elizabeth Dunn, January 31, 1952, to Cicely Plaxton, PLAX.

9 The will is included in the estate file of Honoré Joseph Jaxon, file #1952–1604, New York County Surrogate's Court, 31 Chambers Street, Room 402, New York, New York. I warmly thank Susan Tell for her assistance in locating the documentation.

10 It was published by the University of Calgary Press.

11 Geoffrey Ursell, Publisher, Coteau Books, #401, 2206 Dewdney Avenue, Regina, March 25, 2004, to the author.

12 Edgar Dewdney, June 27, 1885, to "My Dear Sir John" [Sir John A. Macdonald], MG 26, A1(a), vol. 107, Macdonald Papers, LAC.

A SHORT BIBLIOGRAPHY

UNPUBLISHED SOURCES

Archives of Ontario
B.B. Osler Papers (F1032 MU2302)

Chicago History Museum
Chicago Federation of Labor, Minutes, 1911–January 1918

Glenbow Archives
Edgar Dewdney Papers (M320)

Harvard University Archives
Frederic Ward Putnam Papers

Labadie Collection at the University of Michigan
Voltairine de Cleyre Papers

Library and Archives Canada
Wilfrid Laurier Papers, MG 26, g, vol. 11, microfilm reel C-740
John A. Macdonald Papers, MG 26, A1(a), vol. 108
Department of Justice, RG 13, Records relating to Louis Riel and the North-West Rebellion, 1873–86, in particular microfilm reels C-1228 to C-1231

Methodist Archives and Research Centre, John Rylands University Library, University of Manchester

National Association for Armenian Studies and Research, Belmont, Massachusetts
Avedis Derounian (a.k.a. John Roy Carlson) Papers

National Spiritual Assembly of the Baha'is of the United States Archives, Wilmette, Illinois

Provincial Archives of Alberta
Oblate Papers

Saskatchewan Archives Board
Hugh Nelson, "Four Months under Arms" (HS 159)

Schomburg Center for Research in Black Culture, Archives and Rare Books Collection, New York
Stetson Kennedy Collection, box 4, folder l, reel 2 (Kurt Mertig 1947)

Société historique de St-Boniface, Archives, Winnipeg

Fonds corporation catholique romaine de Archiépiscopale Saint-Boniface, série Alexandre Tache, boîte 38

Surrogate's Court, New York County (Manhattan)

Will of Honore Joseph Jaxon, file #1952–1604

University of Saskatchewan Library, Special Collections

W.J. Carter Papers

William Henry Jackson Papers, gathered by Cyril Greenland and John Griffin Documentary History of Canadian Psychiatry Project, Canadian Mental Health Association

A.S. Morton Manuscript Collection, William Henry Jackson Papers (C555/2/13.1–13.13g)

A.E. Porter Papers

UNPUBLISHED PRIMARY SOURCE

Plaxton, Cicely Jackson. "From Wingham to Prince Albert." 1938.

PUBLISHED PRIMARY SOURCES

Abbot, Willis J. *Watching the World Go By.* Boston: Little, Brown, and Company, 1933.

Chanler, Julie. *From Gaslight to Dawn: An Autobiography.* New York: New History Foundation, 1956.

Cleyre, Voltairine de. "C.L. James." *Mother Earth* 6, 5 (1911): 142–44.

Cook, Jessie W. "The Representative Indian." *The Outlook* 65, 1 (1900): 80–83.

Dumont, Gabriel. "Gabriel Dumont's Account of the North West Rebellion, 1885." Trans. and ed. George F.G. Stanley. *Canadian Historical Review* 30 (1949): 249–69.

Jackson, Thomas Eastwood. "'Riel's Secretary.'" Toronto *Globe,* July 2, 1885.

—. In *The Voice of the People.* Comp. and ed. Manon Lamontagne et al. Prince Albert: Prince Albert Historical Society, 1985. 144–55.

Jackson, T. Getting [Gethyn]. "Riel at Prince Albert, Prince Albert, Aug. 19." Toronto *Globe,* September 4, 1884.

_____. "Letters to the Editor. The North-West Territories, June 29." Toronto *Globe,* July 27, 1885.

_____. "Jackson's Case." *Manitoba Free Press,* August 29, 1885.

[Jackson, William H.] *The Voice of the People,* March 12, 1883, March 17, 1883.

_____. "The Election for Lorne." *Prince Albert Times* April, 11, 1883.

Jaxon, Honoré J. "A Talk about the Ward Clubs." *Union Labor Advocate* 4, 7 (1904): 18.

_____. *Fair Play and Free Play* (successor to *The Voice of the People,* established at Prince Albert, March 12, 1883), October 29, 1908.

_____. "The Struggle for Life under Western Conditions." *Labor's Realm,* August 2, 1909, 3–7; September 6, 1909, 2–3, 18–19; October 1, 1909, 12–14; November 20, 1909, 12–16; December 1, 1909, 12.

_____. "Brief Report to Date on Site Negotiations." *Bahai News* 1, 4 (1910): 25–26.

_____. "A Stroll with Adbul-Baha." *Star of the West* 3, 4 (1912): 27–29.

_____. "Dedication of the Mashrak-El-Azkar Site." *Star of the West* 3, 4 (1912): 5–7.

_____. "A Reminiscence of Charlie James." *Mother Earth* 6, 5 (1911): 144–46.

_____. *A Statement from the Working Class of Mexico to the 44th Annual Congress of the Trades' Unions of Great Britain. Distributed by Order of the Standing Orders Committee of the 44th Annual Congress.* Newcastle: J. Dowling and Sons, [1911].

_____. "Notes from Chicago." *Freedom: A Journal of Anarchist Communism* 29, 311 (1915): 23.

Lamont, Malcolm. *Bush Days.* N.p.: privately printed, 1933.

Lamontagne, Manon, et al., comps. and eds. *The Voice of the People.* Prince Albert: Prince Albert Historical Society, 1985.

Nelson, H.S. *Four Months under Arms.* New Denver, BC: n.p., n.d.

Pierce, Bessie Louise, comp. *As Others See Chicago: Impressions of Visitors, 1673–1933.* Chicago: University of Chicago Press, 2004 [1933].

Plaxton, Cicely Jackson. "Travelled First Trip Ever Made Port Arthur to Winnipeg along C.P.R. Rails on Day after Fatal Trestle Accident." *Prince Albert Daily Herald,* March 1, 1924.

_____. "Reminiscences of an Old Timer." *Wingham Advance-Times,* November 9, 16, 23, 30, 1933.

_____. A four-part series in the *Prince Albert Daily Herald,* compiled by Pauline Ford from the recollections of Cicely Plaxton, June 17, June 24, June 30 and July 8, 1972.

Riel, Louis. *The Collected Writings of Louis Riel.* Gen. ed. G.F.G. Stanley. 5 vols. Edmonton: University of Alberta Press, 1985.

_____. *The Diaries of Louis Riel.* Ed. Thomas Flanagan. Edmonton: Hurtig, 1976.

Rocker, Rudolf. *The London Years.* Trans. Joseph Leftwich. Nottingham, UK: Five Leaves Publications, 2005.

Ross, Alexander. *The Red River Settlement: Its Rise, Progress, and Present State with Some Account of the Native Races and Its General History to the Present Day.* Edmonton: Hurtig Publishers, 1972 [1856].

Wiebe, Rudy, and Bob Beal, comps. and eds. *War in the West: Voice of the 1885 Rebellion.* Toronto: McClelland and Stewart, 1985.

The Queen v. Louis Riel [trial transcript]. Introd. Desmond Morton. Toronto: University of Toronto Press, 1974.

NEWSPAPERS AND PERIODICALS CONSULTED

The Albertan (Calgary), March 31, to end of June 1909.

The Alarm (Chicago), April 1885 to April 1886.

Banff Cragg and Canyon, May 1, 1909 to September 4, 1909.

The Broom (San Diego), March 6, 1944 to December 21, 1953.

Canadian Illustrated War News, 1885.

Chicago Inter-Ocean, January 19, to May 2, 1886.

Chicago Record Herald, Index, 1904 to 1912.

Chicago Times, 1 to 5 and 10 to July 25, 1892, 1 to April 5, 1894.

Chicago Tribune, indexed articles from ProQuest Historical Newspapers, viewed online at the Newberry Library, Chicago, and the Chicago Historical Museum.

Clinton New Era (Clinton, ON), August 27, 1874 to October 10, 1878.

Common Sense (Union, NJ), May 19, 1946 to December 14, 1947.

The Home News (the Bronx and Manhattan), February 1, to April 27, 1927.

The Knights of Labor (Chicago), August 14, 1886 to February 20, 1887.

Labor Enquirer (Chicago), February 23, to April 6, 1887.

Manitoba Free Press, January to March 1886.

Moose Jaw Times, September 20 to December 31, 1907.

New York Times, indexed articles from ProQuest Historical Newspapers, viewed online at the University of Calgary.

Ottawa Journal, February 15, to March 15, 1885.

Prince Albert Times, November 1, 1882 to October 17, 1883, and March 1907 to February 1909.

Qu'Appelle Vidette (SK), April 2, to December 3, 1885.

Regeneracion (Los Angeles), 1909 to 1912.

St. Paul Dispatch, November and December 1885.

Saskatoon Daily Phoenix, August 15, to October 1, 1909.

Saskatchewan Legislative Library Newspaper Indexes

Saskatchewan Times (Prince Albert), November 1899.

Toronto *Globe,* selected issues from 1884 to 1912.

Toronto *Daily Mail,* April 22, to early September 1885.

Toronto *World,* April 1, to July 23, 1885.

Union Labor Advocate (Chicago), 1903 to 1907.

BOOKS

Abrams, Gary William David. *Prince Albert: The First Century 1866–1966.* Saskatoon: Modern Press, 1966.

Adelman, William. *Haymarket Revisited.* Chicago: Illinois Labor History, 1976.

Aitken, M. Alice. *The Book of Turnberry, 1857–1957.* Wingham, ON: *Wingham Advance-Times* Printers, 1957.

Alvich, Paul. *An American Anarchist: The Life of Voltairine de Cleyre.* Princeton: Princeton University Press, 1978.

______. *The Haymarket Tragedy.* Princeton: Princeton University Press, 1984.

Ashbaugh, Carolyn. *Lucy Parsons: American Revolutionary.* Chicago: Charles H. Kerr, 1976.

Baker, Derek. *Partnership in Excellence: A Late-Victorian Educational Venture: The Leys School,*

Cambridge 1875–1975. Cambridge, UK: Governors of The Leys School, 1975.

Beal, Bob, and Rod Macleod. *Prairie Fire: The 1885 North-West Rebellion.* Edmonton: Hurtig, 1984.

Beales, Carleton. *The Great Revolt and Its Leaders. The History of Popular American Uprisings in the 1890s.* London: Abelard-Schuman, 1968.

Brennan, J. William. *Regina: An Illustrated History.* Toronto: James Lorimer, 1989.

Careless, J.M.S. *Toronto to 1918: An Illustrated History.* Toronto: James Lorimer, 1984.

Dempsey, Hugh A. *Big Bear: The End of Freedom.* Vancouver: Douglas and McIntyre, 1984.

Erasmus, Peter. *Buffalo Days and Nights: As Told to Henry Thompson.* Calgary: Fifth House, 1999.

Flanagan, Thomas. *Louis "David" Riel: "Prophet of the New World."* Toronto: University of Toronto Press, 1979.

______. *Riel and the Rebellion: 1885 Reconsidered.* Saskatoon: Western Producer Prairie Books, 1983.

Frémont, Donatien. *Les Secrétaires de Riel: Louis Schmidt. Henry Jackson. Philippe Garnot.* Montréal: Les éditions Chantecler, 1953.

Friesen, Gerald. *The Canadian Prairies: A History.* Toronto: University of Toronto Press, 1984.

Ginger, Ray. *Altgeld's America: The Lincoln Ideal versus Changing Realities.* New York: Funk and Wagnalls, 1958.

Grant, H. Roger. *Spirit Fruit: A Gentle Utopia.* Dekalb: Northern Illinois University Press, 1988.

Green, James. *Death in the Haymarket: A Story of Chicago, the First Labor Movement, and the Bombing that Divided Gilded Age America.* New York: Pantheon Books, 2006.

Grossman, James R., Ann Durkin Keating, and Janice L. Reiff, eds. *The Encyclopedia of Chicago.* Chicago: University of Chicago Press, 2004.

Hale, Horatio, ed. *The Iroquois Book of Rites.* Introd. William N. Fenton. Toronto: University of Toronto Press, 1963.

Hatcher, William S., and J. Douglas Martin. *The Baha'i Faith: The Emerging Global Religion.* Wilmette, IL: Baha'i Publishing, 2002.

Houghton, Geoff, and Pat Houghton. *Well-Regulated Minds and Improper Moments: A History of The Leys School.* Cambridge, UK: Governors of The Leys School, 2000.

Hughes, Katherine. *Father Lacombe: The Black-Robe Voyageur.* Toronto: William Briggs, 1911.

Larson, Erik. *The Devil in the White City.* New York: Vintage Books, 2004.

Le Chevallier, Jules. *Saint-Laurent de Grandin.* Vannes, France: LaFolye and J. de Lamarzelle, 1930.

______. *Batoche: Les Missionaries du Nord-Ouest pendant les troubles de 1885.* Montréal: L'Oeuvre de Presse Domincaine, 1941.

Miller, Donald L. *City of the Century: The Epic of Chicago and the Making of America.* New York: Simon and Schuster, 1996.

Morris, Jan. *Manhattan '45.* Baltimore: Johns Hopkins University Press, 1998 [1986].

Murphy, James L. *The Reluctant Radicals: Jacob L. Beilhart and the Spirit Fruit Society.* Lanham, MD: University Press of America, 1989.

McNickle, Chris. *To Be Mayor of New York: Ethnic Politics in the City.* New York: Columbia University Press, 1993.

Payment, Diane. *"The Free People – Otipemisiwak": Batoche, Saskatchewan 1870–1930.* Ottawa: Minister of Supply and Services Canada, 1990.

_____. *Batoche (1870–1910).* St. Boniface: Les éditions du Blé, 1983.

Pierce, Lorne. *Fifty Years of Public Service: A Life of James L. Hughes.* Toronto: S.B. Gundy; Oxford University Press, 1924.

Ramsay, Bruce. *The Noble Cause: The Story of the United Mine Workers of America in Western Canada.* Calgary: District 18, United Mine Workers of America, 1990.

Reynolds, Ray. *Cat's Paw Utopia.* El Cajon, CA: Communications Arts Department, Grossmont College, 1972.

Schneirov, Richard. *Labor and Urban Politics: Class Conflict and the Origins of Modern Liberalism in Chicago, 1864–97.* Urbana: University of Illinois Press, 1998.

Schneirov, Richard, and Thomas J. Suhrbur. *Union Brotherhood, Union Town: The History of the Carpenters' Union of Chicago 1863–1987.* Carbondale: Southern Illinois University Press, 1988.

Schwantes, Carlos A. *Coxey's Army: An American Odyssey.* Lincoln: University of Nebraska Press, 1985.

Scott, James. *The Settlement of Huron County.* Toronto: Ryerson, 1966.

Sealey, D. Bruce, and Antoine S. Lussier. *The Métis: Canada's Forgotten People.* Winnipeg: Manitoba Métis Federation Press, 1975.

Stanley, George F.G. *The Birth of Western Canada.* Toronto: University of Toronto Press, 1961 [1936].

_____. *Louis Riel.* Toronto: Ryerson, 1963.

Stockman, Robert H. *The Baha'i Faith in America: Origins 1892–1900.* Vol. 1. Wilmette, IL: Baha'i Publishing Trust, 1985.

_____. *The Baha'i Faith in America: Early Expansion, 1900–1912.* Vol. 2. Oxford: George Ronald, 1995.

Stonechild, Blair, and Bill Waiser. *Loyal till Death: Indians and the North-West Rebellion.* Calgary: Fifth House, 1997.

Swanson, Stevenson, ed. *Chicago Days: 150 Defining Moments in the Life of a Great City.* New York: McGraw-Hill, 1997.

Tavender, George S. *From This Year Hence: A History of the Township of Toronto Gore 1818–1967.* Malton: George S. Tavender, 1967.

Wallace, W. Stewart. *A History of the University of Toronto, 1827–1927.* Toronto: University of Toronto Press, 1927.

Waiser, Bill. *Saskatchewan: A New History.* Calgary: Fifth House, 2005.

Warren, Jim, and Kathleen Carlisle. *On the Side of the People: A History of Labour in Saskatchewan.* Regina: Coteau Books, 2005.

White, E.B. *Here Is New York.* New York: Little Bookroom, 2005 [1949].

Whitehead, O.Z. *Some Early Baha'is of the West.* Oxford: George Ronald, 1976.

Whitemore, Bruce W. *The Dawning Place: The Building of a Temple, the Forging of the North American Baha'i Community.* Wilmette, IL: Baha'i Publishing Trust, 1984.

Woodcock, George. *Gabriel Dumont.* Edmonton: Hurtig, 1975.

ARTICLES AND PAMPHLETS

A Brief Historical Sketch of Wingham Methodist Church 1863–1924, Diamond Jubilee Services October 26th, November 2nd and 9th, 1924. N.p.: n.p., n.d.

Bingaman, Sandra Estlin. "The Trials of the 'White Rebels,' 1885." *Saskatchewan History* 25, 2 (1972): 41–54.

Cherwinski, W.J.C. "Honoré Joseph Jaxon, Agitator, Disturber, Producer of Plans to Make Men Think, and Chronic Objector. ..." *Canadian Historical Review* 46, 2 (1965): 122–33.

Clarke, Brian. "English-Speaking Canada from 1854." In *A Concise History of Christianity in Canada,* ed. Terrence Murphy and Roberto Perin. Don Mills, ON: Oxford University Press, 1996). 261–359.

Duff, Louis Blake. "Amazing Story of the Winghamite Secretary of Louis Riel." *Western Ontario History Nuggets* 22 (1955): 1–37.

Greenland, Cyril, and John D. Griffin. "William Henry Jackson (1861–1952): Riel's Secretary: Another Case of Involuntary Commitment?" *Canadian Psychiatric Association Journal* 23 (1978): 469–78.

Griffin, John D., and Cyril Greenland. "The Asylum at Lower Fort Garry 1874–1886." *The Beaver* 310, 1 (1980): 18–23.

Gulig, Anthony G. "Yesterday's Promises: The Negotiation of Treaty Ten." *Saskatchewan History* 50, 1 (1998): 25–39.

Le Chevallier, Jules. "Aux prises avec la Tourmente: Les Missionaires de la colonie de Saint-Laurent-de-Grandin durant l'insurrection métisse de 1885." *Extrait de la Revue de l'Université d'Ottawa, livraisons d'octobre-décembre 1939, avril-juin et juillet-septembre 1940.*

Lee, David. "The Métis Militant Rebels of 1885." In *Readings in Canadian History: Post-Confederation,* 7th ed., ed. R. Douglas Francis and Donald B. Smith. Scarborough: Thomson Nelson, 2006. 80–95.

McCullough, Alan. "Parks Canada and the 1885 Rebellion/Uprising/Resistance." *Prairie Forum* 27, 2 (2002): 161–98.

Owram, Douglas. "The Myth of Louis Riel." *Canadian Historical Review* 63, 3 (1982): 315–36.

Sapolsky, Steven. "The Making of Honore Jaxon." In *Haymarket Scrapbook,* ed. Dave Roediger and Franklin Rosemont. Chicago: Charles H. Kerr, 1986. 157–59.

Smith, Donald B. "William Henry Jackson: Riel's Secretary." *The Beaver* 311, 4 (1981): 10–19; a footnoted copy of this article appears in *Pelletier-Lathlin Memorial Lecture Series. Brandon University, 1979–1980,* ed. A.S. Lussier. Brandon: Department of Native Studies, 1980. 47–81.

_____. "Honoré Joseph Jaxon: A Man Who Lived for Others." *Saskatchewan History* 34, 3 (1981): 81–101.

_____. "Rip Van Jaxon: The Return of Riel's Secretary in 1884–1885 to the Canadian West, 1907–1909." In *1885 and After: Native Society in Transition,* ed. F. Laurie Barron and James B. Waldram. Regina: Canadian Plains Research Center, 1986. 211–23.

_____. "Honoré Joseph Jaxon: A Lifelong Friend of Aboriginal Canada." In *With Good Intentions: Euro-Canadian and Aboriginal Relations in Colonial Canada,* ed. Celia

Haig-Brown and David A. Nock. Vancouver: UBC Press, 2006. 229–57.

Smith, Peter. "The American Baha'i Community, 1894–1917: A Preliminary Study." In *Studies in Babi and Baha'i History,* Volume One, ed. Moojan Momen. Los Angeles: Kalimat Press, 1982. 85–223.

Van den Hoonaard, Will. "Social Activism among Some Early Twentieth-Century Baha'is." *Socialist Studies* 2, 1 (2006): 77–97.

Weston, Doug. "Thomas Eastwood Jackson: Pharmacist Helps Shape Canadian History." *Canadian Pharmacists Journal* (February 1985): 70–71.

THESES

Carey, Miriam. "The Role of W.H. Jackson in the North West Agitation of 1884–1885." Honours essay, Department of Political Science, University of Calgary, 1980.

Millions, Erin Jodi. "The Undone: A Gendered and Racial Analysis of the Impact of the 1885 Northwest Rebellion in the Saskatchewan District." MA thesis, University of Saskatchewan, 2004.

Schneirov, Richard. "The Knights of Labor in the Chicago Labor Movement and in Municipal Politics, 1877–1887." PhD diss., Northern Illinois University, 1984.

Index

PHOTO: DAVE BROWN

ABOUT THE AUTHOR

Honoré Jaxon: Priairie Visionary completes Donald Smith's "Prairie Imposters" popular history trilogy concerning three prominent figures who all pretended an ancestry they did not, in fact, possess – Honoré Jaxon, Grey Owl, and Long Lance.

In addition to his Native History biographies, Donald B. Smith has co-edited such books as *The New Provinces, Alberta and Saskatchewan, 1905–1980* (with the late Howard Palmer), and *Centennial City: Calgary 1894–1994.* His popular articles have appeared in a variety of local and national publications including *Alberta History, The Beaver,* the *Globe and Mail,* and the *Calgary Herald.* With Douglas Francis and Richard Jones, he published the popular two-volume history text, *Origins, and Destinies,* and the single-volume history of Canada, titled *Journeys.* He has also written *Calgary's Grand Story,* a history of twentieth-century Calgary from the vantage point of two heritage buildings in the city, the Lougheed Building and Grand Theatre, both constructed in 1911/1912.

Born in Toronto in 1946, Dr. Smith was raised in Oakville, Ontario. He obtained his BA and PHD at the University of Toronto, and his MA at the Université Laval. He has taught Canadian History at the University of Calgary since 1974, focusing on Canadian history in general, and on Native History, Quebec, and the Canadian North in particular. His research has primarily been in the field of Native History, combined with a strong interest in Alberta history.